W9-BTN-691

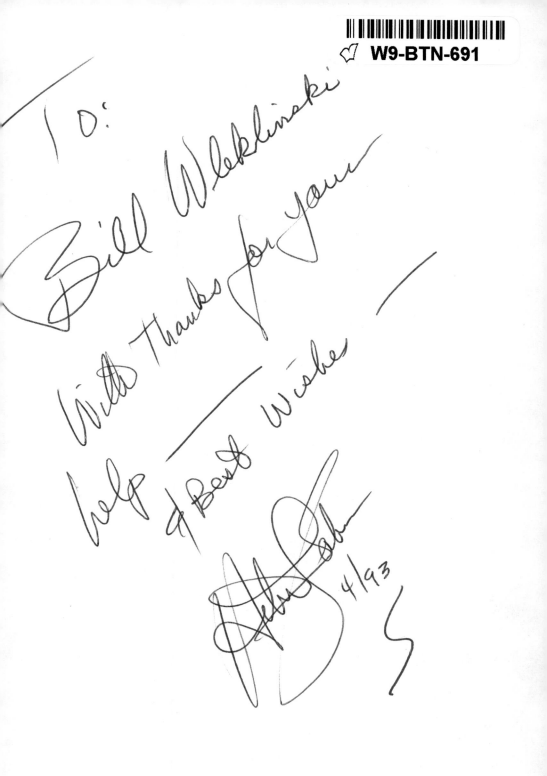

TO:

Bill Wleklinski

With Thanks for your

help & Best Wishes

4/93

Red Scare in Court

Red Scare in Court

New York versus the
International Workers Order

Arthur J. Sabin

FOREWORD BY HOWARD FAST

upp

UNIVERSITY OF PENNSYLVANIA PRESS   Philadelphia

Interviews conducted during this study are quoted with permission of the interviewees:

Mr. and Mrs. E. L. Greene, Arthur Kinoy, John Middleton, Marshall Perlin, the Hon. George Postel, Jerry Trauber, and Paul Williams

Cover: Rockwell Kent lithographs: IWO tenth anniversary commemorative logo, 1940; "The Smith Act," 1951. Courtesy of the Rockwell Kent Legacies

Copyright © 1993 by the University of Pennsylvania Press
All rights reserved
Printed in the United States of America

Library of Congress Cataloging-in-Publication Data

Sabin, Arthur J., 1930–
  Red scare in court : New York versus the International Workers Order / Arthur J. Sabin ; foreword by Howard Fast.
      p.   cm.
    ISBN 0-8122-3189-9
1. New York (State).   Insurance Dept.—Trials, litigation, etc.   2. International Workers Order—Trials, litigation, etc.   3. Insurance law—New York (State)
4. Insurance, Fraternal—New York (State)   5. Liquidation—New York (State)
6. Communist trials—New York (State)   7. United States—Politics and government—1945–1953.   I. Title.
KF228.N49S22   1993
346.73'086—dc20
[347.30686]   92-30645
                                                                            CIP

In memory of
Nattie and Martin Sabin,
who were "true believers"

Contents

Illustrations

Foreword

In 1946, with the dead of the great war against fascism and Nazism still warm in their graves, another kind of war was declared in the United States. It was a war against dissent, a war against ideas—particularly the ideas of socialism—and against the people who promulgated these ideas. The Soviet Union, which had seen 20 million of its citizens perish in the war against Hitler, was declared the enemy of mankind, and a kind of demented civil war was waged in the United States against anyone who defended any aspect of Communism, Socialism or the Soviet Union.

The beginning of this war was declared by the Truman White House, with an executive order requiring people working for the government to state under oath that they were not nor had ever been members of the Communist Party. From this beginning, it spread like a plague across the country, penetrating every level of society, industry, schools, film, literature, and, of course, government.

The chief instrument in spreading and enforcing this new terror was the House Committee on Un-American Activities. It conducted a series of star chamber hearings that led to the imprisonment of dozens of men and women—labor leaders, writers, actors, filmmakers, teachers—a list that included some of the best-known and most talented people of the time.

One of the organizations caught up and eventually destroyed by this network of terror that had spread across the country was an insurance company called the International Workers Order. In this book, Arthur J. Sabin tells the heartbreaking story of how this organization, and with it the hopes and dreams of thousands of American working people, was destroyed. It is a very important story, a grim and awful story. It must be read and understood so that nothing like it will ever happen again.

Howard Fast

Preface

Throughout the history of Western civilization, from Biblical times on, people have exhibited a fascination with trials. The human dramas involved, the clashing of wits, arguments, and personalities against the background of the legal system of the time, have fired the interest of entire nations as news of a trial's proceedings reach the populace. Though less a punctuation of the flow of human history than wars, famous trials have frequently resulted in developments far beyond the fate of the particular litigants.

In the United States, trials have historically been a valued form of public entertainment and education. Since colonial times, attending, reading, hearing about, and discussing trials have been, particularly before the advent of radio and television, major diversions in the lives of multitudes of citizens. With modern media, the ability to be part of a trial, albeit vicariously, has only expanded participation.

Movies and television have actually invaded the courtroom; a new cable television network has been developed that will place viewers in courtrooms throughout America around-the-clock. This has followed on the heels of successful TV presentations of small claims courts at work. Furthermore, not a year goes by in which a courtroom drama is not present in Hollywood movies and on the stage.

The popular mystique surrounding trials in England and the United States can be attributed to the wide use of juries, in criminal cases only in England and in both criminal and civil cases in the United States. The viewer, as a citizen who could be sitting in that jury box weighing the evidence and determining guilt or innocence, has no difficulty identifying with the cause of one side or the other as the trial unfolds.

This book focuses on one trial whose drama and historical relevance have generally been overlooked. While the verdict would have a significant impact on the lives of tens of thousands, there were reasons for its lack of notoriety. On the surface, it appeared to be missing certain elements of drama: it was a civil trial; no one was threatened with death or jail; it was tried by a judge, without a jury; and it involved an insurance company and insurance law. Furthermore, this case was tried during the Red Scare, a time when the nation had a surfeit of dramatic, high-visibility trials to digest.

The Red Scare, the domestic counterpart of the Cold War, had commenced in 1946. By the time this case began in the New York courts, in late 1950, the nation already had seen many quasi-trials in the form of Congressional hearings, had beheld Alger Hiss on trial, had witnessed the top leadership of the American Communist Party convicted of violating the Smith Act, and would soon read about the trial of the Rosenbergs as atom spies. In fact, within a few hundred yards of where the State of New York prosecuted its case against the International Workers Order (IWO), a fraternal benefit insurance company, because of its alleged relationship with the Communist Party, the Rosenberg case began and ended while the IWO case ground on.

With so many fascinating, highly dramatic cases to follow, frequently involving well-known political and even movie star personalities, the IWO trial was fairly well lost in the milieu. Besides, since the summer of 1950, the nation was at war in Korea. Thus, the fate of an insurance company and the issues and personalities involved could not realistically have generated a great deal of notice.

Yet the IWO trial was then and is still today worthy of attention. Never before or since has an insurance company in the United States been brought to court because of its politics, with the State calling for its destruction as part of a war against domestic Communism. The IWO was the most enduring, successful, and stable Communist-affiliated organization in American history. Born in the breakoff of a few thousand members of an existing fraternal benefit insurance company, the IWO went on to become the fastest growing organization of its kind during the 1930s. By 1948, it had almost 200,000 members. Over its life, some one million Americans joined the IWO.

The organization itself makes for an interesting study; to tens of thousands of its members, it was the centerpiece of their lives. The leaders, almost all dedicated Communists, ran a uniquely politicized insurance company in a highly successful capitalist fashion. Notably, the IWO was also the only multiracial, multiethnic fraternal benefit insurance company of its day.

Awakening to "an enemy within its gates," the Insurance Department of the State of New York contended that IWO activities were all on orders from Moscow. Using paid professional informer witnesses, all former Communists, the State exploited every Red Scare theme of the times in order to destroy the Order.

The IWO case involved plenty of courtroom drama, colorful characters and personalities, and, above all, the question of the law's ability to control unpopular political thought and action. The implications of the IWO case go to the heart of this question: would the law remain silent in the face of an attempt by government to liquidate a perceived political threat?

A unique opportunity was presented to the author in writing this story: the lawyers for the State and the IWO turned over the files they used in the case, allowing an inside view of the trial techniques and strategy employed as these two sides battled in a Manhattan courtroom for over four months.

The lessons to be learned from the IWO case are for the reader, the bench, and the bar to ponder.

Acknowledgments

Without the consistent support of the administration of The John Marshall Law School, this book could not have been written. Over a period of five years, the total commitment of the school was there. Funds for travel, research costs, and assistance in typing the manuscript were always available.

Special thanks are due Dean Peter J. McGovern and Dean Robert G. Johnston; the latter not only was avid in his support, but also read and critiqued the manuscript.

A unique opportunity was gained through the generosity of the firm of Cahill Gordon and Reindel of New York City. Paul W. Williams, the lead prosecuting attorney, was a partner in the firm when, in 1950, Governor Thomas E. Dewey appointed him as Special Assistant Attorney General and as Counsel to the New York State Insurance Department. The voluminous office files that he and his associates at the firm created were graciously lent to The John Marshall Law School for my use.

Similarly, Professor Arthur Kinoy, now of Rutgers University School of Law, one of the IWO defense attorneys, gave me his files on the case. These office files allowed me to compare, contrast, and follow the behind-the-scenes activities and trial strategy of the opposing sides in the case, as well as giving me access to court documents and records. Mr. Williams and Professor Kinoy were also most helpful in freely providing interviews, which yielded further insight into the case.

Jerry Trauber, who was an IWO officer, was extremely helpful in explaining the Order's position on issues, as well as the backgrounds and motivations of its leadership. He actively supported my work, made contacts for me, indicated specific sources for material, and arranged interviews that could not have happened without his enthusiastic assistance.

Other attorneys connected with the case also provided interviews;

these include Marshall Perlin, an IWO attorney, and Arthur D. Emil, who worked with Williams on the State's case. The families of the late Judge Henry Clay Greenberg and attorney Raphael H. Weissman were most helpful in providing material and interviews. Judge George Postel, one of Judge Greenberg's law clerks at the time of the IWO trial, also provided a valuable interview.

The archivists at the New York State School of Industrial and Labor Relations, Labor-Management Documentation Center, saved many IWO records from negligent destruction, creating an IWO archival collection. Richard Strassberg, Director and Archivist, was most helpful in providing access to these IWO archival materials, and in having photocopies made of needed material.

The personnel at The John Marshall Law School Law Library were of significant assistance in providing information and in arranging for interlibrary loans.

Duke Frederick, Professor Emeritus of History, Northeastern Illinois University, read and critiqued the entire manuscript. His expert advice and sharp eye for historical detail, as well as his command of English, were invaluable.

The typing of the book was performed with zeal and dedication by the secretarial pool of The John Marshall Law School. I am especially grateful to Joanne Sorce, who made this work her particular province and who provided most dedicated service on my behalf. She was unfailingly gracious in retyping the text countless times.

A rare benefit was bestowed upon me and this work by Sheila Mahoney, whose superb editorial skills were so important and so generously given.

Thanks are due Timothy R. Clancy and other members of the staff of the University of Pennsylvania Press for their expertise, guidance and encouragement throughout the publication process.

Many other people and institutions, too numerous to mention, provided materials, interviews, or expertise. To all, I am grateful. An involvement of over five years in research and writing this book makes one realize the interdependence of the broadest range of academicians and academic institutions in the production of any work. We all stand on the shoulders of those who have trod these paths.

A Note on Sources

The major sources for this work are as follows: The International Workers Order, Inc., archives located at the Documentation Center of the New York State School of Industrial Relations, Cornell University, Ithaca, New York; the Trial Record contained in *People of the State of New York by Alfred J. Bohlinger, Superintendent of Insurance v. The International Workers Order, Inc.*, 199 Misc. 941 (1950), Six Volumes, as well as the appellate record in the Appellate Division and Court of Appeals of New York and as appealed to the United States Supreme Court.

The office files of the prosecuting attorneys consisting of twelve transfer cases as maintained by the law firm of Cahill Gordon and Reindel, New York City, were made available. The contents of these files include court exhibits used by the State, all briefs used at the trial and on appeal, and all documents, including all pleadings filed by all parties in the trial and on appeal. Additionally, their files contained office memoranda, the results of legal research, correspondence and clippings from newspapers, including translations where the original was not in English. The files also contained extensive materials developed by the IWO (correspondence, news releases, bulletins) during the years of joint control by the IWO and Department of Insurance.

Arthur Kinoy, one of the IWO defense attorneys, provided those portions of his office files that are extant.

Reference is made to the *Daily Forward,* published in Yiddish by the Forward Publishing Company, Inc., in New York. The use of the word *Forward* in this work refers to the daily or Sunday editions of the paper.

Reference is made to the *Morning Freiheit,* which was published in Yiddish by the Freiheit Association in New York. The use of the word *Freiheit* in this work refers to the daily or Sunday editions of the paper.

Chapter I
Cold War-Red Scare in Perspective

"The Cold War. It gave you a reason to get up in the morning."
Harry "Rabbit" Angstrom, in John Updike, *Rabbit at Rest*

This book is about a case that was tried in 1951. The year 1951 places this trial in the midst of a storm of litigation over political beliefs and domestic security issues; the Alger Hiss case, the trial of the top leadership of the Communist Party, and the Rosenberg atom spy case were but a few of the trials taking center stage during that time. The United States was in the grip of a Red Scare, the domestic counterpart of the predominant Cold War scene. The powerful figure of Senator Joseph R. McCarthy loomed as a dark shadow across the nation. Furthermore, since mid-1950, a war had raged in Korea.

The legal action by the State of New York's Department of Insurance against an organization known as the International Workers Order on its surface appeared to be nothing more than a local matter: a battle between a Department of Insurance and a fraternal benefit insurance company (the IWO) over insurance law. The State's real purpose, however, was to destroy this organization because of its politics.[1]

This case was litigated against the background of the Cold War-Red Scare era in American history. Writing about this period changed dramatically in the summer of 1989. Until then, the accepted basics were these: following the breakup of the Second World War alliance between the Soviet Union and the West, a "Cold War" developed, geographically defined between Russian-dominated countries and those outside its orbit. The threat of war, the contest for control of countries and areas susceptible to favoring one side or the other, and the fighting of limited wars commanded the world scene from 1946 onward.

Winston Churchill's 1946 "Iron Curtain" speech represented a clear articulation of the view of most Americans that the world was truly divided; well into the 1980s, President Ronald Reagan's attribution of Russia as the Evil Empire continued the Cold War theme. Heating up and cooling off for over forty years, it was the preeminent international theme, explaining, justifying, and labeling world events as well as reflexive national postures. The Cold War carried with it the benefit of assured clarity of issues, of right and wrong, of good and evil—all without compromise or doubt. Dictionaries accepted and defined the term, and nations directed armed preparedness and global strategies in response to its existence.

A major Cold War component was fear of domestic subversion, or at least contamination of the population by the other side. With the United States playing the role of Superpower in the Cold War with Russia, there was a dread of Communist subversion, spying, and influence in this country; these fears gripped the nation with varying degrees of intensity throughout these decades and generated the era of the Red Scare. In the Soviet Union, parallel developments reflected fear of Western values and subversion. The Cold War for both sides was particularly "hot" from 1946 through the mid-1960s. But even in the "cooled-down" state of affairs in the 1980s, any reference to the Cold War still could be depended upon as meaningful and possibly determinative of attitudes and actions.

When Soviet President Mikhail Gorbachev announced on June 15, 1989 that the Cold War was over and predicted that the leading symbol of its existence, the Berlin Wall, would "one day" come down, the impact of his statement followed by the dramatic events of the ensuing six months changed the task of this and every writer dealing with the Cold War era.[2] A reader's basic intellectual understanding and gut emotional response, which could for over forty years be assumed, may now no longer be a working premise in light of recent events. Such emotionally charged words as "McCarthyism," "commie," "fellow traveler," "pinko," and "Fifth Amendment Communist" will now require definition and explanation. Even the very concept of "Cold War" may soon fail to generate that assumed generic understanding.

The events of 1989 and after were so dramatic, so disruptive of what was generally assumed and understood, that a real effort to resurrect and reassess the pre-1989 events is apropos, especially as the generation that experienced them recedes. History, plainly put, was simpler in post-World War II, pre-1989 times. Then, the Soviet Union had an empire that spread westward to Berlin and encompassed countries whose individuality was overwhelmed by Soviet control. Now, with the walls tumbling (including *the* Wall) and the fences and gates torn down, the picture has become much more complex. The monolithic Communist control that Russia had signified in the eyes of the West is now broken, not only in its empire but in the Soviet Union itself, which has ceased to exist, and has been replaced by a Confederation of Independent States.

In the United States, the President, Congress, and the press and other media are in the process of coping with these swift-moving events as the 1990s open. Astonishment reigns. Nascent nationalism in Communist-dominated countries presents prospects both exciting and confusing. German reunification is a fact, and the collapse of world Communism seems at hand.

U.S. media have been examining both the global and domestic implications of this new world situation. A question is raised: whom shall we hate? The answer for over forty years was Russian Communism and its tentacles of internal subversion. A recent article in *Newsweek* described how political psychologists have defined this persistent need for an enemy:

After 40 years the cold war finally appears to be crumbling, and all over the land can be heard the sounds of . . . dismay? Curiously, instead of rejoicing, many Americans seem unsettled, as if they had lost a central article of faith. "You have to worry: Has the world slipped off its hinges?" mused *New York Times* columnist Russell Baker, reflecting the general unease. "Where can we look for assurance that it's still the same reliably inevitable old world we loved to hate?"[3]

The comments, the analyses, the reactions continue to flow in an attempt to cope with the meaning of the end of the Cold War for U.S. domestic and foreign policy. Responses to the editorial announcement in the *New York Times* on April 2, 1989 that the Cold War had indeed ended have varied greatly, including self-styled conservative reactions of triumph and warning—questioning whether changes are but a ruse. As one professional anti-Communist has stated, "At the core of 75 percent of conservative thinking and action is anti-Communism. You take that away and you take away the glue that has held the movement together for a generation."[4] Reflective of that fact, one humorist has announced, "the good news is that international Communism now ranks as a threat to our national security somewhere below mildew."[5]

Even the question of what this new era will be called has been raised. William Safire, critical of "Post-Postwar Era," invited readers of his language column to submit suggestions that would more accurately and succinctly characterize the new times.[6]

The scramble to assess as well as cope with the breakup and demise of the Soviet empire in Europe in terms of its various implications (e.g., the "peace dividend") is just that: an attempt to keep up with shattering events (because events can shatter fears as well as create new ones) that only time will place into perspective. This will take another generation or more as historians, political scientists, and sociologists sift through the facts and artifacts of the events. In turn, another generation will rethink, reanalyze, and vent new and controverted perspectives on this time of Cold War dissolution. Clearly, human history leaves no vacuums, and what follows as a post-Cold War era will be replete with the continued dynamics of human, national, and world events which must be accurately and meaningfully characterized and labeled.

Another result of the end of the Cold War will be a continued opening up of the era itself. If the Cold War is now in the wastebin of the past, the freedom to rummage through and pick up what is no longer considered essential (i.e., worthy of protection or in some way sacrosanct) will yield vital records, remembrances, sources, and documents that will allow a new, dispassionate evaluation. What a storehouse must lie deep in the Kremlin walls: the Russian source materials on the Cold War era. Can it be that there will soon be access to that treasure trove? When the Bolsheviks gained power in 1917, they threw open Czarist records that were otherwise unavailable, for the purpose of discrediting that regime. Perhaps the post-Cold War Soviet government will do the same to prove some portion of its Cold War case to the world. In turn, the U.S. and other Western governments may do likewise in response to such a release.

With the lessening of Cold War tensions in the decade of the 1980s, a new openness toward that era had already become evident. Its manifestations in the United States have included greater access to government records and FBI and CIA documents, and the apparent willingness of individuals to talk openly about the Cold War-Red Scare era, what it meant to them, and what they did or failed to do during those years. Such openness reflects a diminution in the threatening nature of the domestic scene, a tolerance extant today that simply did not exist in the Red Scare-Cold War decades.

Thus, personal reminiscences and biographies have appeared that could not and would not have been written in prior decades. Roy Cohn, Joseph McCarthy, Carl Bernstein, Edward R. Murrow, Zero Mostel, J. Edgar Hoover, Alger Hiss, the Rosenbergs, Richard M. Nixon, and William L. Shirer are but a few persons who exemplify this process in autobiography and biography. With the danger of "admissions" past, descriptions of damaged and destroyed lives and organizations can now be "safely" accounted. To select but one example, William L. Shirer stated in an interview about his autobiographical volume covering those years:

I was never accused of being a Communist and I was never brought before any committee and that was the thing that puzzled me. . . . But it was a terrible era in American life and a lot of people suffered much more than I did. Their careers were ruined and they went to jail. I just couldn't make a living for a time.

He went on to state that in his view America had been turning toward Fascism during the McCarthy era.[7]

Beyond the leading players, what happened during this time to many quite ordinary and some quite extraordinary people has also been forthcoming. In part, this is the result of knowledge gained through requests or suits under the Freedom of Information Act that have revealed, for the first time, the behind-the-scenes acts of government, administrative agencies, and individuals. Such revelations include, for example, that Morris Ernst of the American Civil Liberties Union was working with J. Edgar Hoover[8] and that the FBI deliberately forged a letter to discredit Communist Party leader Bill Albertson to effect his expulsion from the Party.[9]

A distinction must be made. While the Cold War as an international phenomenon was inextricably interwoven with the anti-Communist crusade carried on in the United States, the Red Scare (as it is generally termed) had an active, virulent life that was shorter than that of the Cold War which had nurtured it. By 1957 the domestic scene had changed sufficiently that it reasonably may be argued that the worst of the domestic Red Scare had ended. Nikita Khrushchev's denunciation of Stalin in 1956, the admission that purge trials in Eastern Europe had involved innocent victims, and the brutal suppression of the Hungarian democratic rebellion devastated Communists in the West. These developments, in addition to the ravages of the McCarthy era, left the Party and its close sympathizers in disarray. By 1957 three-quarters of the members of the American Communist Party of just a year before had quit.[10]

At the same time as the Party was itself practically vanishing, the Red Scare had been fading away. The 1954 Army-McCarthy hearings, followed by U.S. Senate condemnation of McCarthy, marked a turning point. From 1956 to 1958, seven major decisions of the Warren-led Supreme Court dismantled major components of judicial acquiescence to the domestic Red Scare: dismissal from a job for claiming one's rights under the Fifth Amendment to the U.S. Constitution; the validity of state sedition laws; the right to investigate a person's beliefs, utterances, and affiliations; the power of Congressional investigations; the power of professional groups to bar admissions of radicals; and the FBI informer systems.[11] Together with other cases, the 1957 Supreme

Court's decision in *Yates v. U.S.* signaled the end of prosecutions of Communist Party members. This dampened the hopes and powers of many state and federal administrative "loyalty" boards and other agencies that had used the courts for prosecutions.[12]

The year before, Steve Nelson, a Communist Party leader who had been under a long sentence for violation of the Pennsylvania sedition law, had his conviction overturned.[13] In 1957, once again, a union leader challenged the House Un-American Activities Committee's power and won. Even the sacrosanct nature of FBI files was challenged in another decision that same year.[14] Then came the *Yates* decision, which reversed the conviction of fourteen "second string" Communist Party leaders. While the *Yates* defendants adopted different defense tactics that stressed their civil liberties, as opposed to the position taken in 1949 by the top eleven Communists in the *Dennis* case,[15] the decision reflected more than a matter of trial tactics: the times and the Court had changed. By negating the effectiveness of the Smith Act (under which the top Communist Party members in the *Dennis* case had been convicted) and by emphasizing the difference between "advocacy of abstract doctrine and advocacy of action," the Supreme Court sent a clear message that it was cooling down, if not halting, Red Scare prosecutions. Although attempts were made in Congress to legislate around these decisions, with Senator McCarthy's death in 1957 most of the storm of anti-Communism abated.[16]

Justice Black, dissenting in the *Dennis* case in 1951, had expressed the hope that in calmer times First Amendment liberties would be restored. That "calmer time" arrived in 1957, in part reflecting the growing influence of the liberals on the Court, particularly the authority of Earl Warren after he became Chief Justice in 1953. William Brennan, joining the Court in 1956, added to the majority voice in these 1957 cases.

By then, most contemporary leadership recognized that the U.S. Communist Party of the Depression days was dead, bereft of committed as well as fringe supporters. No internal subversive threat was left, if there had ever been one. The court system was itself ready to change—and did so under Supreme Court leadership. American courts, consistent with legal history, reflected the mood, temper, and priorities of the times. In the Red Scare years of 1946 to 1957, the Supreme Court had upheld Smith Act convictions, loyalty programs, and most state and local (e.g., school board) anti-subversive activities, had enforced the sanctions against Communists in labor unions, and had permitted draconian prosecutions of alien radicals by the Immigration and Naturalization Service (which also was permitted to deny passports to suspected radicals even though they were American citizens). The Supreme Court did this by affirming lower court convictions (e.g., the *Dennis* case) or by refusing to hear review appeals from lower courts (e.g., the Rosenberg case).

By 1957 McCarthy and the Rosenbergs were dead, the former from drink, the latter from execution. The Korean War, which had fueled so much of the domestic Red Scare, had been in a prolonged state of uneasy armistice since 1953. The Cold War was still the centerpiece of American foreign policy, but its "fellow traveler" the Red Scare was no longer frightening the courts, the majority in Congress, or the American public.

The new openness, availability of sources, and willingness to speak out in the 1980s have produced significant studies on major players and events, including the first two presidents of the post-World War II era, Harry S. Truman and Dwight D. Eisenhower. The origins of the Cold War; the trial of leading Communists; the role of Communist influence in Hollywood, in unions, with farmers, and among minorities and intellectuals; as well as the continuing battles over the guilt or innocence of Alger Hiss and the Rosenbergs have come under renewed scrutiny. In 1982, a group of historians founded an organization called Historians of American Communism. Their newsletters are replete with numerous publications, books, articles, and speeches about the history of Communism and left-wing politics in the United States, much of it devoted to the Cold War-Red Scare era. In 1987, one of its members published an annotated guide to Communism and anti-Communism in the United States listing over 2,000 items.[17]

Never without strong partisans, the interpretation of Cold War-Red Scare times, issues, and personalities continues to generate vociferous positions. Theodore Draper's defense of the validity of the Red Scare has, for example, prompted strong condemnation and challenge by a group of younger historians of American Communism.[18] While Communism and the Communist party in the United States have been of general and academic interest for decades, it was not until the 1980s that an appreciable outpouring of analytical material began to appear. Realistically, the American Communist Party has become an anachronism, and as such, the history of its work, leaders, and influence are now available for academic dissection. The historians' organization dedicated to the study of American Communism exemplifies the willingness of scholars to devote themselves to this study at a time when they can freely (and safely) challenge as some have, assumed interpretations about American Communism, the Party, and its role during the 1930s through the 1970s.

Historians, political scientists, and sociologists looking at political behavior have become roughly divided into two groups: those defending the older interpretations and those challenging these past views. Adherents to the older position maintain the following premises as given: that the Cold War was the result of Soviet expansion, deceit, paranoia, and the destructive influence of Joseph Stalin; that American Communism and the Communist Party of the United States was not a normal political party but was made up of a group whose loyalty was first, foremost, and last with Russia and was controlled from Moscow, obeying Cominform and Politboro dictates; that this Party sought the overthrow of the American government and its replacement with a Soviet-style state; and that the Party and its members were a subversive, dishonest, and destructive element in American life who manipulated otherwise worthy causes, groups, and individuals for their own interests. While these advocates do not necessarily make heroes of Senator McCarthy or J. Edgar Hoover, they do appreciate, for example, the work of Walter Reuther, leader of the United Auto Workers Union, who ultimately repudiated and defeated Communist support; they tend to believe Alger Hiss and the Rosenbergs guilty, and to support those who turned from Communist to become anti-Communists. These advocates have not ventured far from the bases laid in the 1950s by writers on domestic Communism.

Those who have raised voices in opposition instead postulate the following: that American Communists, left-wingers, and fellow travelers were those most genuinely concerned with and active in the areas of unemployment, Social Security, black and other minority rights, women's rights, union power, and civil liberties; that there was an authentically American and freethinking grass-roots American Communism; that the growth of industrial unions was, in substantial measure, the result of organizing efforts by American Communists; that the advent of the Cold War was, in important measure, the deliberate act of American leadership; and that domestic anti-Communism was an unmitigated disaster for the health of the nation, with its roots traceable to the desire to disparage the New Deal, Fair Deal, and the Democratic Party. They tend to believe that Hiss and the Rosenbergs were innocent, or at least that the latter should not have been executed, and that the legal pursuit of Communist Party leadership violated the Bill of Rights.

One group sees a justifiable Cold War reaction on the domestic front; the other, by contrast, sees a disastrous outbreak of manipulated hysteria and national paranoia that damaged the country and presaged a form of domestic Fascism.

This conflict is healthy. Out of continued research and writing, the availability of new material, and the resultant clash of positions, the truth about the Cold War and the Red Scare, so far as the truth can be stated, will advance.

Notes

1. *People of the State of New York by Alfred J. Bohlinger, Superintendent of Insurance v. The International Workers Order, Inc.,* 199 Misc. 941, 106 N.Y. S.2d 953 (N.Y. Sup., June 25, 1951).

2. *Chicago Tribune,* June 16, 1989.

3. "Why We All Love to Hate," *Newsweek,* August 28, 1989, p. 62.

4. Richard Viguerie, quoted in *Newsweek,* December 18, 1989, p. 25.

5. Dave Barry, "Communism Goes Bust, But Birds Go Boom!" *Chicago Tribune,* January 28, 1990, p. 27.

6. William Safire, "And After Post-Postwar?" *New York Times Magazine,* December 31, 1990.

7. Thomas Craughwell, "An Interview with William L. Shirer," *News from the History Book Club,* January 1990, p. 17.

8. See Samuel Walker, *In Defense of American Liberties: A History of the ACLU* (New York: Oxford University Press, 1989).

9. Reported in *Jewish Currents,* January 1990, p. 26.

10. Cited in Maurice Isserman, "The 1956 Generation," *Radical America* 14 (March–April 1980).

11. *Slochower v. Board of Higher Education of the City of New York,* 350 U.S. 551, 76 S. Ct. 637, 100 L. Ed. 692 (1956); *Sweezy v. State of New Hampshire,* 354 U.S. 234, 77 S. Ct. 1203, 1 L. Ed. 2d 1311 (1957); *Watkins v. U.S.,* 357 U.S. 936, 78 S. Ct. 1384, 2 L. Ed. 2d 1550 (1958); *Schware v. Board of Bar Examiners of the State of New Mexico,* 352 U.S. 959, 77 S. Ct. 350 (1957); *Jencks v. U.S.,* 423 U.S. 1078, 96 S. Ct. 865, 47 L. Ed. 289 (1957); *Yates v. U.S.,* 354 U.S. 298, 77 S. Ct. 1064, 1 L. Ed. 2d 1356 (1957).

12. *Yates v. U.S.,* 354 U.S. 298, 77 S. Ct. 1064, 1 L. Ed. 2d 1356 (1957).

13. *Pennsylvania v. Nelson,* 350 U.S. 497, 76 S. Ct. 477, 100 L. Ed. 640 (1956).

14. *Jencks v. U.S.,* 423 U.S. 1078, 96 S. Ct. 865, 47 L. Ed. 289 (1957).

15. *Dennis v. U.S.,* 341 U.S. 494, 71 S. Ct. 857, 95 L. Ed. 1137 (1951); Peter L. Steinberg, *The Great "Red Menace": United States Prosecution of American Communists, 1947–1952* (Westport, CT: Greenwood Press, 1984), pp. 279–80.

16. Smith Act, 18 USCA, §2385.

17. John Earl Haynes, *Communism and Anti-Communism in the United States: An Annotated Guide to Historical Writings* (New York: Garland Publishing Co., 1987).

18. See James R. Barrett, Paul Buhle, Maurice Isserman, Mark Naison, and Roy Rosenzweig letters, *New York Review of Books* (August 15 & September 26, 1985) in reply to Theodore Draper's review essays "American Communism Revisited" (May 9, 1985) and "The Popular Front Revisited" (May 30, 1985).

Chapter II
The First Twenty Years

The journey to Foley Square in New York City where the trial of the International Workers Order (IWO) would commence in December 1950 started with the organization's formation in 1930. Those twenty years were packed with a whirlwind of momentous events. This journey began in the depths of a domestic and later world depression and moved through Franklin D. Roosevelt's New Deal (1933–1942) into the Second World War and post-World War II age, dominated by the Cold War (1946–1989) and the Red Scare.

The IWO is often confused with a different organization, the Industrial Workers of the World (IWW). The two groups were not related, and there is no evidence that IWO leadership came from the IWW. Confusion has been heightened, however, by those who mistakenly refer to the IWW as the *International* Workers of the World, instead of *Industrial*. More popularly, the IWW people were called "Wobblies."

Linked in the public mind with wild-eyed anarchists, foreigners, and Bolsheviks, and perceived as un-American because of its opposition to U.S. participation in World War I, the IWW's meager power was broken by continual persecution that took various forms and left in its wake labor martyrs such as Joe Hill and William D. (Big Bill) Haywood. Never strong in numbers (its membership rarely exceeding 100,000), the IWW's legacy of attention to social injustice and the need for industrial (as against trade) unionization nevertheless was the precursor of the Congress of Industrial Organizations' (CIO) militant-type unions of the 1930s. By 1924, six years before the formation of the IWO, the IWW's organizational effectiveness was over.[1]

Because of its high profile, violent history, martyrs, and legacy of enduring folk songs, the IWW earned a place in labor and radical history that the IWO, lacking these elements, never achieved. The IWO, by contrast, was not a union but a fraternal benefit insurance organization, legitimized by its state-regulated insurance programs.

Figure 1. IWO membership certificate issued in 1937. Note logo in corners.

This set it apart, giving it a distinct place in the history of left-wing organizations and movements in American history. What has generally been overlooked is that the International Workers Order was the largest left-wing organization in U.S. history.

What Was the IWO? A Juxtaposition of Views

The IWO in its *IWO Declaration of Principles* described itself in the following terms:

The IWO provides sick, disability and death benefits. It organizes for its members medical aid and other forms of fraternal services. It pledges aid and comfort to its members in case of need. The ranks of the International Workers Order and its societies are open to all regardless of sex, nationality, race, color, creed or political affiliation.[2]

The U.S. Government (House Un-American Activities Committee) *Guide to Subversive Organizations* offered a radically different characterization:

One of the most effective and closely knitted organizations among the Communist-'front' movements. It claims a membership of 150,000, bound together through an insurance and social plan. . . . It has contributed large sums of money to Communist Party campaigns, and . . . regularly sponsors Communist Party endorsed candidates for public office. In 1944, its president and general secretary respectively were William Weiner, former Communist Party treasurer, and Max Bedacht, former party secretary.[3]

From its birth in 1930 to the litigation over its right to exist more than twenty years later, the IWO was a controversial organization. Born in a battle between elements of an existing fraternal benefit organization, the Workmen's Circle, it achieved a size and financial success that was unattained by any other left-wing, non-union organization in American history. Most left-wing organizations of the thirties through the fifties were small in numbers and short in duration; the IWO was neither.

Just what it really was, other than the obvious—a fraternal benefit insurance company—continues to engender debate. Political labels have been used: Communist front, Communist affiliated, Party-led auxiliary, left-wing, progressive, radical workers group, subversive. In 1949, the IWO called itself "an interracial federation of national group societies," but in its early years, its attachment to the political leadership of the Communist Party was open and evident.[4]

IWO Origins in the Workmen's Circle

First organized in 1892 and later incorporated as a national fraternal benefit insurance company in 1905, the Workmen's Circle was a Jewish workers' organization that offered the mutual aid and insurance services typical of fraternals—and more. As one historian of the Workmen's Circle has written, the attraction to these Socialist-leaning Jews was "above all a circle of friends . . . a bulwark against lack of acceptance in the established social and economic structure of America and the established Jewish society."[5]

The Workmen's Circle prospered, and by 1915 its membership had reached some 50,000. By 1918, membership was over 80,000; despite frequent raids and arrests during the Red Scare following the First World War, the organization survived.[6]

The split of the American Socialist Party in the early 1920s between Socialists and those who moved to the new Communist Party was reflected in the Workmen's Circle, leading to almost ten years of battle between the left (those favoring the Communist) and the right (those favoring the Socialist) positions within the fraternal organization. These were passionate people and passionate times. Those who supported

Socialist goals as the answer to worker poverty and powerlessness followed the lead of the Jewish *Daily Forward,* while the left had its voice in the Communist Party's Jewish Section daily, the *Morning Freiheit.* Involving vituperative rhetoric and backed by their respective papers, the battle for control of the Workmen's Circle raged through the 1920s. Charges and countercharges flew between the groups: whose program truly represented the working class interests of the members? Dissolution of left-wing branches (lodges) and even physical attacks were mounted as the right wing strove to maintain control; the left wing retaliated with proclamations and demonstrations denouncing Workmen's Circle leadership. Even the children's schools established by the Circle were split, with the left maintaining control of most schools as well as the Circle's summer camp, Kinderland.

The final break in 1929 coincided with a new "line" of Communist international policy which turned away from a "boring from within" to encouraging independent workers' organizations. The manifesto issued by the left-wing after leaving the Workmen's Circle National Convention in October recited in part:

. . . the time has come when everyone who takes the interests of the workers seriously must shake off the dust of the Workmen's Circle.

The Workmen's Circle, originally organized under the banner of the class struggle, writing into its program the abolition of the capitalist order, thus winning the love and respect of the broad working masses in the United States, has been transformed in the last few years into an instrument of capitalist politics. . . .

Therefore, we call upon all the members of the Workmen's Circle who take the interests of the working class seriously; we call upon all those workers who cannot bear any longer the black reactionary rule of the Workmen's Circle; we call upon all class conscious and progressive members of the Workmen's Circle no matter what economic organization they may belong to; we ask them to leave the Workmen's Circle and to help build a real proletarian Order.[7]

Twenty-two years later, the leading figure behind the left-wing split in the Workmen's Circle, Rubin Saltzman, would be cross-examined on the witness stand by the State's lead prosecuting attorney, Paul W. Williams, on these words and on the motivations behind the creation of the International Workers Order.

Historical sources are in general agreement that the leadership of the new Order was composed of Jewish Communists; the majority of members and even of the 235 delegates to the initial convention were, however, non-Communist, but still willing to follow the Party line.[8] At the conclusion of its founding convention, the National Executive Committee of the newly formed Order issued the following statement:

The International Workers Order is a fraternal organization. Its primary purpose is to insure its membership against sickness and death. In other words: the Order is an organization of mutual aid.

. . . But this is not the whole story. The International Workers Order is more than an insurance organization. It is part of the fighting front of the working class. It helps the workers not only to insure themselves for the emergency of sickness and death, but it helps them to improve their lives. It helps them to fight for a better living.[9]

Both the General Secretary, Saltzman, and the first President, William Weiner, were open and prominent Communist Party members as were the initial Executive Committee of the General Council (the day-to-day operational body).[10] Yet, from inception, elements of the Party recognized that the Order did and should have a life of its own.[11]

As the IWO grew in strength, size, and complexity and matured into an organization offering a variegated program of cultural, educational, health, sports, and social activities to its members, its functioning belied any narrow intention that it was simply a Communist Party appendage. While its politics followed the Party line, the maturing Order became more and more mainstream in what it offered its members, prospective members, and its "public face."

But twenty years later, the rhetoric of those early years would come back to roost in a judicial proceeding where the politics of the IWO, and not its operation as a fraternal benefit insurance company, would become of paramount importance.

An early pamphlet issued by the Order in 1932 stated about the Communist Party:

The two major classes of our times are the capitalists and the workers. . . . The International Workers Order realizes that the only party that leads the working class in its struggle against capitalism is the Communist Party which unites the best and proven militant members of the working class and which is bound to become ever stronger until the moment will come when the workers under its leadership will overthrow the capitalist system and establish Soviets. It follows therefore that the International Workers Order is part of the battle front of the working class. . . . We find that the Communist Party is the only party that fights for the workers' interests. We therefore endorse the Communist Party.[12]

Much of this language and position was reflective of two factors: the desperate times of the early Depression years, and the belief among Communists as well as a broad spectrum of non-Communists that capitalism had failed. For Communists, the answer to the terrible ills of American society was in moving to a Communist system of economy, government, and society; they believed the Russian Revolution had brought the ultimate answer of a Marxist state to pragmatic fruition under Lenin and Stalin.

But the revolution did not come. The New Deal stole the thunder of the left and the Second World War ended the catastrophic Depression. During the 1930s, while the Communist leadership at the top of the Order remained intact, the programs the IWO adopted, its involvements, and its attitudes were fundamentally similar to those espoused by liberals or progressives of the times. Thus the Order was actively engaged in the struggle for Social Security legislation, including unemployment insurance, for minority rights, particularly of blacks (then "the Negro people"), and support for militant labor unionism as well as campaigning for a national program of medical insurance.

Movement toward the mainstream of a liberal domestic agenda was undoubtedly a result of the "Popular Front" position of Communists, who took their cue, if not direction, from Russia and its fear of the rise of Fascism in the mid-thirties. There was also the competition for members with the Workmen's Circle: whatever it offered, the IWO argued that its insurance and social programs offered more.[13]

The IWO developed into an integrated multinational and multiracial organization with some thirteen ethnic groups plus a "general" group of English-speaking members. No other fraternal association attempted to attract and organize ethnics and blacks into one organization, while at the same time promoting the identity of each group and, by 1944, allowing a measure of autonomy to each. The IWO was the only national insurance carrier of that time to offer blacks an insurance program at the same rate as to whites; blacks had always been charged more. Furthermore, the IWO offered its insurance program to all working people, regardless of occupation, at the same rate. For this reason, it became strong among West Virginia and Pennsylvania coal miners where its affordable insurance program was most welcome for those in that high risk occupation.

The costs for term life insurance were exceptionally low; for a small additional premium, protection against sickness and tuberculosis (then prevalent among workers in many occupations) could be had. Since the Order employed no paid sales representatives and paid no commissions, depending instead on members to recruit others to join the IWO and enroll in its insurance program, costs were kept low.

Different sections of the Order (e.g., Italians, Ukrainians, Jews) published news in their own languages. Singing societies, sports teams, marching bands, dance and theatre groups were available. The largest and best organized section was the Jewish section, which took on the formal name of Jewish People's Fraternal Order (J.P.F.O.) of the IWO in 1944. Here schools were an added feature; after the public school day ended, children could attend a J.P.F.O.-run school where Yiddish and Jewish oriented secular subjects were taught.

Some of the political and economic positions taken by the Order: support for a broad Social Security system and a form of national health insurance, endorsement of the cause of industrial-type unionization—do not appear from the vantage point of the 1990s, to be very radical. But for the 1930s and 1940s it was exactly that; yesterday's radicalism has become today's received wisdom.

The IWO has been credited for its active and at times crucial role in the early history of the CIO, particularly unionization of the steelworkers. IWO lodges supported strike efforts, raised food, clothing, and money for strikers, and frequently provided the only available meeting halls for unions. As Roger Keeran has noted, "no community organization gave so much to so many unions for such an extended period of time as the IWO gave to the CIO struggles between 1935 and 1941."[14]

It is, however, in the field of race relations that the Order's domestic agenda stands out. Although the IWO failed in an effort to recruit large numbers of blacks, its position in favor of racial equality, anti-poll tax and anti-lynch legislation, and for the establishment of a fair employment practices commission placed it on the cutting edge. And it practiced what it preached: blacks were hired and promoted to positions of responsibility within the Order's work force, a rare practice in those days; a system of incentives existed in order to move blacks into supervisory positions. The Order deliberately set out to reverse the accepted custom that blacks would be the last hired, first fired, and never have more than the most menial positions. In addition, its National Recording Secretary and one of its national organizers were black.[15]

Every official position of the IWO, from discrimination matters (support for the defendants in the Scottsboro case) to social legislation, from militant industrial unionism to support for the Spanish Republican cause, mirrored the position of the Communist Party. This was never overlooked by those who attempted to discredit the organization by sole virtue of that fact, regardless of the merit of such positions.

It must be remembered that these were decades of open and blatant racism, anti-Semitism, isolationism, and xenophobia despite the liberal position of the New Deal and the unity engendered by the Second World War. Members of Congress openly harangued against immigrants, blacks, and other minorities with relative impunity in racist, sexist, and anti-Semitic pronouncements. There was a great deal of pressure on citizens to homogenize into white Protestant America. Hyphenated citizens (e.g., Italian-American or Jewish-American) were suspected of violating the cherished "melting pot" theory of America. When blacks were portrayed in any media, it was invariably as menials. Employment was subject to open discrimination on the grounds of race, religion, country of origin, sex, or any other basis the employer deemed appropriate. The IWO, which emphasized ethnic pride and fostered a diverse cultural base—in effect, a deeply pluralistic society—went against the accepted value system.

The Order was a haven for Communists as well as those foreign-born Americans who were, as Harvey Klehr has noted, "too timid or frightened to join the Communist Party, [while] membership in the IWO enabled them to participate in the 'progressive' movement without suffering any serious consequences."[16] Beyond politics, the appeal of low-cost, nondiscriminatory insurance was a major factor for tens of thousands of its members. The opportunity to share experiences, build friendships, speak a native language and share a sense of fellowship was undoubtedly a drawing component. The range of involvement for members of the IWO, as in most other organizations, varied from simply paying dues in order to maintain insurance (the majority) to deep involvement with all the Order's activities. Analysts who have studied the organization agree that the number of actual Communists was always small; even one who called the Order a "Party-led auxiliary" and a "Communist Front" has recognized this fact.[17]

The attractiveness of the IWO was evidenced by its rapid growth. From the small three- to five-thousand-member group that formed its nucleus in 1930, the organization grew 300 percent between 1933 and 1935, with a membership of some 67,000 by 1935. One-third were Jewish; the balance was divided among different ethnic groups, youth, and English-speaking clusters. The Order also grew by amalgamation with smaller left-wing ethnic fraternal orders and associations. The first to join was a Hungarian group in 1932; thereafter, the Russian Mutual Aid Society and the Slovak Workers Society also linked arms with the IWO. One result was that the Order had to overcome blatant anti-Semitism in evidence among some amalgamating groups.[18]

During the 1930s, the IWO became the fastest growing fraternal order in America; it increased at about double the rate of the second fastest growing fraternal. In 1936, it accounted for more than 10 percent of the total of new members in fraternal organizations throughout the country. In 1935 the General Secretary issued the call, "Forward to One Hundred Thousand Members!" Two years later, he reported membership of over 136,000 and reserve funds of over a million dollars. By 1938, after eight years of existence, the Order had over 141,000 members, double that of four years before, and had paid out close to two million dollars in death and sickness benefits.[19]

Almost all this growth (the exception being increase by amalgamation of small ethnic fraternal groups into the Order, a practice ended in 1936) was the result of individual and small group efforts to recruit members, made all the more remarkable since the Order had no sales staff and paid no commissions. With pride, the IWO leadership explained:

> Our workers' fraternal Order has no profits to provide, no high salaries to pay, no agencies to maintain. It is built by the enthusiasm of its members. Its dues are collected by voluntary functionaries. Most of its organization work is done by volunteers.
>
> The necessary enthusiasm for such volunteer work is generated by the services of the Order to the workers.[20]

Members who recruited others were designated as "Builders." Formal leadership training for them began in 1933; the Order thereafter conducted programs for Builders in ten different geographic sections of the country.[21]

Ignoring the wider pragmatic reasons for this growth, the authors of *Five Years IWO* insisted on explaining it in class conflict terms. In reality, most members were attracted to the low cost and nondiscriminatory availability of insurance and the willingness to take on as insureds anyone who worked, even those in dangerous or high risk employment, as well as the mutual aid benefits of the Order. As Thomas J. E. Walker has observed, "Compared to other fraternal organizations the mutual aid benefits that the Order provided are quite astounding."[22] Solicited by a Builder who spoke his or her language, who offered a chance for cheap insurance, mutual aid benefits such as low cost medical programs (in certain geographic areas), and the friendship of like-situated people, the IWO held much appeal for prospective members. That it was also dedicated to left-wing, "progressive," or indeed Party-supported causes and rhetoric cannot and should not be ignored or glossed over; nevertheless, for most of its members, the IWO met pragmatic needs in an economic and social framework. The result was an organization that grew from a few thousand Jewish dissidents who had left the Workmen's Circle in 1929 to one that, by the Second World War, was licensed in eighteen states and the District of Columbia and could count among its friends and members such notables as Paul Robeson, Langston Hughes, Rockwell Kent, Jimmy Durante, Irwin Corey, and Zero Mostel.[23]

During the 1930s in the area of foreign policy, the IWO (in line with Communist Party policy) promoted the ideas of collective security against Fascism, thus supporting the Spanish Republic in its battle against Franco. The Order urged its members to collect money to aid the victims of the war, and a number of members actually went to Spain to fight in the Abraham Lincoln Brigade on the side of the Spanish Republic.

Domestically, the IWO promoted Social Security legislation, aid for the Scottsboro defendants (black men accused of raping a white woman), and anti-poll tax and anti-lynch laws, and defended the rights of aliens to gain and maintain citizenship. The Order was also consistent and active in its support of pro-union labor legislation. If the cause could be labeled "progressive," "liberal," "anti-discriminatory," or "pro-labor," IWO support was there. Delegations of IWO members could be found in anti-Fascist, anti-war, left-wing, "progressive," and Communist front organizations, committees, causes, and groups.

For the most part, its positions on international and national issues presented no serious problems for the Order's leadership or general membership. Although it was often accused of being "leftist" and tied to the Communist Party line, accusations alone posed no particular threat to the Order; other fraternals had an openly political orientation, so there was no reason for the IWO to make or alter its political viewpoint. Regularly audited by the states in which it operated, the prevailing attitude among IWO leadership was that, so long as it ran the insurance aspects of its business in strict conformity with the law (which it did), its right to function would not be challenged.

The Nazi-Soviet pact of August 1939, a clear reversal and apparent betrayal of the concept of collective security against Fascism, presented the first major issue-oriented problem for the Order. Regardless of any justification by Stalin, the Pact opened the way for Hitler's and then Russia's invasion of Poland, and thus for the commencement of the Second World War. Prior to the 1939 pact, the IWO had maintained solid support for collective security against Hitler, highlighted by its participation in the American League Against War and Fascism and its successor, the American League for Peace and Democracy. The Order's monthly publication, the *Fraternal Outlook,* attacked "Fascist enemies of world peace" and supported President Roosevelt's efforts to awaken the American people to the threat of Hitler and his Fascist allies.[24]

The shock of the Nazi-Soviet Pact caused consternation not only in IWO ranks but throughout the nation, for all who had perceived Stalin's Russia as the bulwark against Fascist aggression in Spain and the appeasement of Hitler at the 1938 Munich Conference sellout of Czechoslovakia. The IWO, not without considerable opposition within its ranks, particularly in the Jewish Section of the Order, followed the Communist Party line of justifications for the Nazi-Soviet Pact. The Order took on and maintained an anti-war, anti-involvement position between August 1939 and June 22, 1941, when Germany suddenly invaded Russia. Then an immediate "flip-flop" took place: all efforts were made to aid the Allies, Britain, and Russia (France had been defeated) and to support FDR's international position—a complete reversal from the accusations against him of warmonger that had immediately preceded the attack on Russia.

The hypocrisy of these reverses, which followed those made by the Communist Party, was not lost on observers and would be highlighted at the trial a decade later, when it was still fresh in the mind of those who had lived through the times.

Not only did the IWO experience internal problems with members who objected to this position, but in 1940 membership itself slipped from some 161,000 to 155,000—the first decline ever. Blistering attacks on the Order came from the Workmen's Circle and its newspaper voice, the *Forward*. More ominously, the Insurance Commission of Massachusetts had the year before (1938) refused to renew the Order's insurance license in that State. The IWO appealed to the Massachusetts Supreme Judicial Court, which found in its favor and in 1940 rescinded the court order denying license renewal. The Dies Committee on Un-American Activities of the U.S. House of Representatives (commonly known as HUAC) investigated the IWO. In October 1939, Max Bedacht, then General Secretary of the Order, testified before the Committee for about four hours. That same year, the U.S. Department of Justice returned an indictment against William Weiner, then IWO President, for passport fraud. After his conviction, the New York Insurance Department insisted on his removal from office, and the Order complied.[25]

A most egregious development followed Bedacht's appearance before the Dies Committee. Without warrant or other authority, Chairman Dies ordered a raid of the Philadelphia headquarters of the IWO. The raiders removed all the files and records they could find and immediately set to copying them. Within hours, the IWO's attorneys were in federal court obtaining an order for the return of the material. The Dies Committee operatives complied, but not before completing the copying.[26]

The war years, 1941 through 1945, were in many ways the best years for the IWO. The nineteen months of promoting a "militant neutrality" were over; now that the "peace loving people of the USSR"[27] were allied with Great Britain in the war effort, the IWO could join in the more comfortable posture of anti-Hitlerism by demanding all-out efforts to aid these Allied powers and backing the President's interventionist moves. William Goldsmith has assessed the IWO role in the following manner:

The IWO quickly elbowed its way back into the vanguard of the anti-Nazi, anti-Fascist movement. Of all the organizations that were dominated by or even sympathetic to the interests of the Communist Party and the Soviet Union, the IWO was perhaps in the most strategic position to wield influence during this period, for it had access to and standing with many important foreign-language groups. . . . Many of their members had relatives in the countries of Europe under Nazi and Fascist subjection.[28]

Composed generally of highly motivated people who had a more personal stake in Hitler's conquests in Eastern Europe than most Americans, the IWO pulled out all stops in favor of the Allied war effort, encouraging everything from picnics with a war theme to blood donations and knitting groups for women. When America entered the war in December 1941, the IWO's efforts in support of the Allies were prodigious. Ten thousand IWO members served in the American armed forces; some 300 lost their lives during the war. The Order participated in War Bond drives, raised money for the Red Cross and USO, set up its own fund for gifts to members in the services, and, until June 1944, urged the opening of a Second Front.[29]

Representatives of major American institutions acknowledged the IWO's contribution to various home front efforts. For example, Harold Ickes, U.S. Secretary of the Interior, praised the Order at a Congress for Soviet-American Friendship at Madison Square Garden in December 1943. Other prominent speakers at that meeting included William Green, president of the American Federation of Labor, and Donald M. Nelson, chairman of the War Production Board. The Adjutant General of the United States publicly endorsed the work of the Order's Russian Section, which had financed the cost of a Flying Fortress bomber. Senator Robert Wagner of New York complimented the wartime activities of the Jewish Section of the Order.[30]

To a significant extent, U.S. alliance with Russia as a crucial wartime partner combined with the American Communist Party's role as a voice calling for full support and vigorous prosecution of the war led many Americans to look differently upon Communists and left-wing organizations such as the IWO. Exemplifying this view, the "Dean" of the House of Representatives, Adolph J. Sabath of Illinois, commended the *Daily Worker* for "having rendered valuable service to the Country in urging harmony and united action."[31] In 1944, the Communist Party, under Earl Browder's leadership, changed from a political party to an "association" as part of a new strategy of at least temporarily accepting the existing two-party system and having American Communists work politically in and through this system.[32]

The IWO, too, underwent a reorganization toward the end of the war; in 1944 it was reorganized, giving even greater emphasis to its membership's divergent backgrounds by creating semiautonomous groups that more sharply reflected the diverse ethnic and racial nature of the Order. This reorganization strengthened the policy of encouraging ethnicity and nationalism; leaders hoped it would yield even greater access to ethnic communities while allowing sectional leaders like Saltzman greater freedom of action and responsibility. Max Bedacht, who had opposed this move, was eased out of a leadership position. In a sense, this increase in group autonomy was more consistent with the founding principles of the Order than the centralized control exhibited to that time.[33]

Although activities in support of the Allied war effort dominated the 1941 to 1945 years, the domestic agenda of the IWO was not forgotten. The need for social legislation, economic security, and an end to racial bias continued as policy and on the Order's action agenda. Rallies, publications, and appeals for support for its positions continued. Most prominently, the IWO worked to promote passage of the Wagner-Murray-Dingell Social Security Bill, the contents of which included broadening Social Security coverage to make benefits available to millions more people and for medical care and compensation while out of work. Further, the Order's pro-industrial-union stand did not diminish.[34]

With the end of the war in late 1945, the prospects for growth of the IWO seemed encouraging; pre-war "Builders" would be back from the Armed Services and the mainstream activities of the Order, along with the wartime alliance with Russia, would make the IWO more acceptable to many prospective members. The Jewish People's Fraternal Order (J.P.F.O.—the Jewish Section of the IWO) gained admission to the American Jewish Congress, a long sought after symbol of community acceptance that lasted until its expulsion in 1949. Membership significantly increased in 1946–47, peaking at almost 200,000, with Jewish Section membership at 29 percent—the highest percentage since the early 1930s.[35] Black membership grew, stimulated by a separate, semiautonomous section named Lincoln-Douglass that removed for blacks any negative perception of being part of an immigrant organization.[36]

Two new leaders also took prominent positions with the Order; Rockwell Kent, the famous American illustrator, was named President of the IWO and the writer Albert Kahn became President of the J.P.F.O. Neither were Party members; both reflected an era when many liberals or progressives were willing to see democratic motives and worthwhile objectives in leftist, even Communist, positions. Kent and Kahn represented the continuing mainstreaming of the IWO.

High hopes for the growth of the Order in the post-war years clashed with the developing Cold War and the Red Scare. When, on December 5, 1947, U.S. Attorney General Tom C. Clark issued his list of subversive organizations with the IWO on it, the Order was hit hard.

Despite attacks by some legal authorities and public officials on the listing of organizations without a hearing or due process procedures and despite the lawsuit filed by the IWO to have its name removed, the listing hurt recruitment of new members and caused a loss in prevailing membership as the pall of guilt by association descended on the Order. It also awakened enemies of the IWO and, as will be seen, the special attention of a minor bureaucrat in the New York Department of Insurance, James B. Haley, who happened to be involved in a financial audit of the Order's books.

During the war years, the U.S. Civil Service Commission and the Immigration and Naturalization Service (INS) had both taken the official position that IWO membership would not render a person "unsuitable for government employment" or be a valid basis for objecting to alien naturalization proceedings.[37] With the war over, the INS began a vigorous campaign to deny citizenship, revoke citizenship status, and deport a number of IWO leaders and members, solely on the basis of belonging to the Order. Among the leaders arrested for deportation were Andrew Dmytryshyn, Vice-President of the Ukrainian-American Fraternal Union (an IWO Section), and Samson Milgrom, National Executive Secretary of the Order.[38] The role of the INS, particularly with respect to the Dmytryshyn case, would prove vital in the trial of the Order itself.

Thus these post-World War II years were destabilizing to the growth of the IWO, and, in the light of the mounting Cold War and Red Scare, portended developments that would challenge the legal existence of the Order. The citadel for the Order was its insurance company status; that the walls of this fort could be breached and the citadel itself put in jeopardy is the basis for the balance of this drama.

Notes

1. Patrick Renshaw, *The Wobblies: The Story of Syndicalism in the United States* (Garden City, NY: Anchor Books, 1967).

2. From the *IWO Declaration of Principles*. IWO Archives.

3. Quoted in House Documents, 136–37, *100 Things You Should Know About Communism and Guide to Subversive Organization and Publication*, 82nd Cong., 1st sess. (Washington, DC: U.S. Government Printing Office, 1951), p. 66.

4. David Greene, *History of the IWO*, dated September 1, 1949, IWO Archives.

5. Judah J. Shapiro, *The Friendly Society: A History of the Workmen's Circle* (New York: Media Judaica, 1970).

6. Maximilliam Hurwitz, *The Workmen's Circle* (New York: The Workmen's Circle, 1936), p. 55.

7. Rubin Saltzman, "First Struggles for a Proletarian Order," in *Five Years IWO 1930–1935* (New York: IWO National Executive Committee, 1935), p. 14.

8. See William Goldsmith, "The Theory and the Practice of the Communist Front" (Ph.D. diss., Columbia University, 1971); Melech Epstein, *The Jew and Communism* (New York: T.U.S.C., 1959), pp. 151–55; Thomas J. E. Walker, "The International Workers Order, a Unique Fraternal Body" (Ph.D. diss., University of Chicago, 1987), pp. 22–29; "International Workers Order," in *Encyclopedia of the American Left,* ed. Mari Jo Buhle, Paul Buhle, and Dan Georgakas (New York: Garland, 1990).

9. Quoted in Walker, "International Workers Order," p. 27.

10. Goldsmith, "Communist Front," p. 503.

11. Ibid., p. 506.

12. *A New Workers' Stronghold: What is the International Workers Order and Why Every Worker Should Join It,* issued by the National Executive Committee International Workers Order, New York, 1930, IWO Archives.

13. Jerry Trauber interview, July 23, 1987.

14. Roger Keeran, "The International Workers Order and the Origins of the CIO," 30 *Labor History* 3 (Summer, 1989).

15. A description of its black hiring and promotion practices will be found in the review of court testimony on this subject.

16. Harvey Klehr, *The Heyday of American Communism: The Depression Decade* (New York: Basic Books, 1984), p. 385.

17. Ibid., p. 385.

18. Goldsmith, "Communist Front," p. 515.

19. Ibid., pp. 524–25; Max Bedacht, "Five Years IWO," in *Five Years IWO 1930–1935* (New York: IWO National Executive Committee, 1935), p. 12.

20. Peter Shipka, "Our Order and Its Benefits," in *Five Years IWO,* p. 33.

21. Walker, "International Workers Orders," p. 40.

22. Ibid., p. 44.

23. "International Workers Order" in *Encyclopedia of the American Left* (note 8), p. 379.

24. Goldsmith, "Communist Front" (note 8), p. 546; Walker, "International Workers Order" (note 8), pp. 52–55.

25. Ibid.

26. Ibid.

27. Quoted in Goldsmith, "Communist Front," p. 550.

28. Ibid., p. 551.

29. David Greene, *History of the IWO,* dated September 1, 1949, IWO Archives.

30. Goldsmith, "Communist Front," p. 563; Walker, "International Workers Order," p. 57.

31. *Fraternal Outlook,* January 1944, p. 11.

32. Goldsmith, "Communist Front," pp. 564–65.

33. Walker, "International Workers Order," pp. 60–63; Goldsmith, "Communist Front," pp. 567–79.

34. Walker, pp. 59–60.

35. Ibid., pp. 61–65; Table of membership, pp. 31–32.

36. *Fraternal Outlook,* September 1945.

37. Trial Record, Exhibits attached to a *Memorandum Re: IWO*; letters dated September 16, 1943 and December 8, 1942, IWO Archives, Box 2.

38. *Memorandum: Attacks on the IWO,* dated June 19, 1950, apparently written by David Greene for Order use, IWO Archives; see also Goldsmith, "Communist Front," p. 626.

Chapter III
The Place and the Players

Courtroom trials have historically been a form of theatre. Although theatre forms developed later than trials, people are frequently unaware that at their core both civil and criminal trials have theatrical elements. It is not by accident but by ease of association that for hundreds of years trials have been a focus for theatrical performances.

Trials have a place comparable to a stage, with a formal set—the courtroom. The actors in the courtroom drama have assigned roles: the judge, the prosecution, the plaintiff or petitioner, the attorney or attorneys for each side, the defendant or respondent, the jury (if one is used), clerks, bailiff, and court reporter. At the opening moment of a trial, the characters are recognizable by virtue of where they stand or sit in that scene.

The court setting where the IWO trial took place, Room 300 at 60 Centre Street in Manhattan, fits this stage setting description in all details. The building is the Supreme Court for the County of New York; despite its name, it is the trial level court, the lowest in the state court system. It is located at the lower end of Manhattan, near the Brooklyn Bridge, in an area dominated by courthouses, federal, state, and municipal government buildings, and New York's historic City Hall, an old district of New York developed as far back as the days of Dutch control in the seventeenth century. Significantly, as will be seen, it is adjacent to the U.S. Courthouse on Foley Square, where trials involving alleged federal crimes and controversies take place.

Taking the elevator to the third floor, one exits to find Room 300, the largest courtroom in this massive building. It is remarkably the same today as in 1950; very little has changed in forty years, and what has changed looks strangely out of place: a computer terminal on a table, and window air-conditioning. Otherwise all is the same, including the furniture; even the judge's chair has not been replaced. Today this

Figure 2. Judge Henry Clay Green-berg, who presided over the trial IWO in New York County Supreme Court.

Figure 3. Paul W. Williams, Special Assistant Attorney General of the State of New York, appointed by Governor Thomas E. Dewey to prosecute the case against the IWO.

Figure 4. Raphael H. Weissman, lead trial attorney for the IWO from December 1950 through April 1951.

Figure 5. Arthur Kinoy, one of the lead IWO attorneys, now Professor of Law, Rutgers University School of Law.

particular courtroom is seldom used for trials, instead serving primarily as the courthouse's ceremonial courtroom.

Entering from the double swinging, padded doors, one encounters a room some seventy feet long by forty-five feet wide. Carved wood Corinthian pillars flank the doors. Two life-sized murals to the left and right of a large clock on the rear wall of the courtroom immediately greet the eye, depicting respectively Dutch and early English courtroom scenes of New Amsterdam and New York. There is no jury box; the room was designed for non-jury, "bench" trials.

Into this imposing courtroom, with its ornate displays of inlaid and carved wood and murals, came the opposing sides in the IWO case. Because the IWO trial was both a non-jury, bench trial and an important case, this large room was assigned as the stage upon which this drama would be played out during the four months of late December 1950 through April 1951. Over this long, intense period, onto this imposing set, would come the actors in this theater of trial. During the course of the trial, the courtroom would from time to time be filled with spectators, including reporters; at other times, barely anyone but the attorneys and the witnesses testifying would be present. Such is the frequent fate of protracted legal proceedings, these theatrical plays where public interest ebbs and flows.

In a bench trial, all attention is focused on the judge. He not only rules on the key evidentiary questions (e.g., what is permissible in terms of documents, testimony, cross-examination, and motions) throughout the trial, but is also the ultimate determiner of fact—of guilt or innocence, of having proved or failed to prove the case. When a jury is present, by contrast, the judge is limited to questions of law (e.g., whether the witness must answer the question, whether a document is relevant or not), leaving the jury to determine the credibility of a witness or the persuasiveness of a particular document. The judge instructs the jury on what the law is (e.g., defining murder, treason, sedition), and the jury then decides whether the acts or omissions of the defendant match this legal definition.

In the IWO case, the judge combined both roles. He made the legal rulings, and decided the ultimate "guilt" or "innocence" of the Order with respect to the State's charges. This confusing scenario can result in some broad misconceptions; it may also result in some unusual situations. Frequently during the trial, for example, the judge took on the role of questioning witnesses, at times quite extensively. The attorney for the side that had called the witness or, more likely, opposing counsel would at times object to the judge's question. The judge would then have to rule on the admissability of his own question!

Because of the additional dramatic element attendant to a jury trial, theatre trials use juries, in effect asking the viewers to act as surrogate jurors as the trial progresses. The major Red Scare trials of the Cold War years—the trials of Communists, the perjury trial of Hiss, the Rosenberg atom spy case—all involved juries. The IWO trial was perhaps the only major trial of the Red Scare era that was a bench trial. It was not that either side of the case did not want a jury; rather, according to the applicable law, the nature of the proceeding was such that it could not have jury participation.

The Judge

In his *History of American Law,* Lawrence M. Friedman observes the following about judges asked to rule on politically sensitive issues:

The judges were themselves middle-class; they could easily empathize with professionals and artisans. Their constitutional antennae were much more sensitive when they picked up vibrations of class struggle or proletarian revolt, things which they barely understood and desperately feared.

On March 9, 1965, at the age of sixty-eight, Judge Henry Clay Greenberg, on his way by train to Florida to recuperate from an operation, died of a heart attack in the main concourse of New York City's Pennsylvania Station. He collapsed while walking with his wife and was pronounced dead upon arrival at the hospital. All the major New York papers reported his death, most with an extensive obituary reviewing famous cases where he had rendered the trial decision. The obituaries in the *New York Herald Tribune* and the *New York Times* both made reference to the IWO case. The former reported that Judge Greenberg had referred to this case as his "toughest decision," the latter that it was his "most difficult case."[2] Why Judge Greenberg found the IWO case deserving of these descriptions will become evident.

Born in Durham, North Carolina, to Lithuanian Jewish immigrant parents who operated a very modest store outside the city, Henry Greenberg showed early academic promise. His mother was an exceptionally brilliant woman who had high ambitions for her children. In high school, Greenberg was a skilled debater and at age fourteen adopted a middle name, Clay, in honor of orator Henry Clay.[3] One of his sisters married a lawyer and later, while raising three children, went to law school and became the first woman admitted to the Virginia bar.

Greenberg attended Trinity College, now Duke University, graduating with honors in 1917. His primary interests during his undergraduate years were debate and journalism. During the First World War, he saw sea duty on a submarine chaser and on his return from service worked as a reporter for the Richmond *Times Dispatch,* reflecting his first love—newspaper work. This interest in the press never left him and would play a role in the IWO trial.

His mother's insistence that he give up a journalistic career for one in law, along with her belief that her son's future would best be served outside the South, took him to Columbia Law School, where he has been described as a brilliant student. He also apparently fell in love with New York and, after graduation in 1921, remained in that city. Thus, he entered the practice of law as an accomplished speaker and writer with polished Southern manners, along with a degree from a first-rate law school. This resulted, not surprisingly, in a successful career. For the next eight years, until 1930, Greenberg practiced law, working in various firms, achieving an excellent reputation as a civil trial attorney, and scoring a number of successes at the trial court and appellate levels.

But politics was also part of his life. Throughout his law career Greenberg was politically active, joining the local Democratic club as a young practitioner. His family confirms that it was his legal talents combined with his excellent interpersonal skills that led him to win a position as legal secretary to Judge Bernard L. Shientag. A job such as this was an acknowledged stepping-stone to a judgeship.

For some fifteen years, from 1930 through 1945, Greenberg served as Judge Shientag's legal secretary. In 1945 he was slated by the Democratic Party for election. Members of his family have explained that Tammany Hall was under attack at that time, and that Greenberg, a "clean," intellectually capable person, was promoted as a "prestige" candidate. They acknowledge, however, that he was also in the right place at the right time and thus got his chance to win the position for which he longed—a judgeship.

In 1945 at age forty-eight, he ran on the Democratic ticket in the counties of New York (Manhattan) and the Bronx. His popular support, along with the unanimous endorsement of area newspapers, resulted in 300,000 more votes than what the Democratic mayor received in those two counties. Greenberg was elected for a fourteen-year term; in 1959, with the endorsement of the Democratic, Republican, and Liberal Parties, he was easily reelected.

As legal secretary to Judge Shientag, Greenberg did research, reviewed pleadings, and worked to acquaint the judge with cases brought before him by discussing the legal issues presented. At times, the secretary (often called a clerk in other jurisdictions) would write memoranda on points of law, analyze a case, and prepare draft orders or even opinions. Judge Shientag was a well-respected judge who had the pick of young lawyers seeking these posts. At Henry Clay Greenberg's induction as a judge on January 2, 1946, presided over by Judge

Harold R. Medina (whose subsequent controversial handling of the trial of the eleven top U.S. communists would place him in the national spotlight), the main speaker was, appropriately, Judge Shientag.

Judge Greenberg was a small, physically slight person, not hand-some, but one who carried himself with dignity. He loved clothes and always appeared well dressed. He was courtly of manner and speech, and very well liked by the bailiffs, clerks, and secretaries who served the court system. Though from the South, which in that generation gener-ally implied an anti-black attitude, during his career Greenberg him-self appointed two black legal secretaries. His cultivated Southern accent and manners, however, set him apart in the New York law scene.

Raised in Judaism, he had rejected orthodox practices but was well versed in Jewish history. Although he did not attend religious services on a regular basis, he was on the board of directors of Temple Rodeph Sholom. He also served on the board of a hospital and belonged to two New York clubs. While not a wealthy man, Greenberg found himself in comfortable circumstances and lived well.

There is general consensus about the man who was to judge the IWO case at the age of fifty-four, with five years experience on the bench: he was intellectually capable, scholarly, and a good lawyer. In the legal profession, being a "good lawyer" before becoming a judge is a distinct qualification; thus, when one of his former legal secretaries, who him-self went on to be a judge, was asked whether Greenberg was a good lawyer, his response was, "He sure was. Otherwise he wouldn't have been with [Judge] Shientag, and he wouldn't have done work for various judges in the civil court at the time."[4] Judge Shientag was considered a brilliant lawyer and judge.

Judge Greenberg's reputation was as a kind and considerate person, well connected politically and hard working as a judge. He was an excellent, careful writer who was very diligent in researching and preparing his opinions. He was neither a man of prejudice nor one without compassion. He appears to have been both patient and toler-ant, qualifications of highest importance to the lawyers presenting their sides of a case. He was also willing to go against the tide, to be controversial in his written opinions and not easily intimidated.

Finally, he was a judge with ambitions. In the world of judges, prestige, recognition, and power attend advancement beyond the trial level to an appellate court for those who seek this goal. Judge Green-berg never advanced to the appellate level, despite his talent as a jurist; he was, throughout his life as a judge, a trial judge only. That Green-berg had higher ambitions is confirmed by his family members, who express both a bitterness that he did not advance and a deep personal affection for the man. They have attributed this failure to be promoted to "certain politicians," who, on the basis of political animosity, feared and were jealous of his abilities.

Toward the end of his life, Judge Greenberg wrote a book he titled *A View from Foley Square*. Unfortunately, it was never published (Bennett Cerf, publisher at Random House, though a friend, turned it down) and is lost, denying us greater insight into his life and views as a judge. What he would have said about his "toughest decision" and "most difficult case" would have been invaluable, along with his views as to why he failed to advance beyond the trial level as a judge—if indeed he even addressed that issue.

The Lawyers

The legal secretary serving Judge Greenberg during the IWO trial has stated that the Judge was assigned this case on a random basis or, plainly put, just by chance. Others involved are adamant that the assignment was not random but came from an administrative judge who handpicked Greenberg. But by whatever the means Judge Greenberg got the case, the choice of prosecuting counsel was anything but random.

When the State of New York's Department of Insurance decided to prosecute the International Workers Order, Inc., the officials in charge took an action that, while unusual, was by no means unique: they reached outside their own pool of lawyers within the Department for an attorney to prosecute the case. The state administration in 1950 was Republican, headed by Governor Thomas E. Dewey.

Governor Dewey placed a call to his friend, Paul Whitcomb Williams, a former Assistant U.S. Attorney who had been an unsuccessful Republican Congressional candidate from the Eighth New York District in 1946. In 1950 Williams was a partner in the prestigious Wall Street law firm of Cahill Gordon and Reindel. With the agreement of his firm partners, Williams accepted the assignment. His title became Special Assistant Attorney General of the State of New York and Special Counsel to the Insurance Department, State of New York.

In an interview conducted with one of the IWO's defense lawyers in the late 1980s, I inquired about Williams and the possibility of contacting him or his chief associate on the case, James B. Henry, Jr. The recollection was that Paul Williams was middle-aged when the case was tried (he was 47) and hence probably deceased, but that the associate was a much younger man, and therefore more likely in the late 1980s to be alive. As it turned out, Williams was still alive and Henry had died.

Tracked down in retirement in Florida in 1988, Williams agreed to be interviewed in the offices of the Cahill Gordon and Reindel firm from which he had retired. He maintained a home on Long Island, spending a portion of the year there. Williams had kindly intervened to make the office files on the IWO case available and entered the room for an interview while they were being initially reviewed. At age eighty-five, he gave the appearance of a man twenty-five years younger; firm of hand and eye, noticeably straight in posture, Williams brushed off the obvious amazement in greeting him with the statement that it was "all in the genes," clearly giving the impression that his amazing physical and mental attributes were not a matter for further discussion.

Paul W. Williams, son of a Baptist minister, was educated at a number of fine schools; he graduated *magna cum laude* from Harvard in 1925, where he majored in government; thereafter, on scholarship, he attended Emmanuel College in Cambridge University for a year, studying international law, and later returned to Harvard to study law, graduating in 1929. He worked as a Harvard undergraduate instructor while attending law school, an indication of his exceptional talent and the high esteem in which he was held by the faculty. Invited to join Harvard College as an assistant professor, he also was offered a position at Cambridge as a law tutor. Instead of an academic career, however, he chose to practice law.

After two years with a large law firm in New York, and a period as an assistant U.S. Attorney, he began, in 1933, his long association with what is now the Cahill firm, becoming a partner in 1939. During World War II he served as a naval officer, returning to his law firm in 1945.

When Williams entered the profession, he seemed most interested in corporate law, but his experience became much broader. He consequently tried four prohibition cases while Assistant U.S. Attorney and won all four, after some eight years where the New York office had not won a single prohibition case.

From his early interest in politics through his higher education in government and law, Paul Williams clearly intended a career that, while grounded in the practice of law, kept the political option open. As a young prosecutor, he worked with Thomas E. Dewey, whose prosecutional skills would win him public acclaim, the governorship, and failed chances at the presidency. Williams maintained close contact with Dewey, acting as his aide on an unofficial basis and was with him at his nomination for the Republican presidential candidate in 1948.

After the IWO trial and his work as special prosecutor in a political corruption case, Williams was appointed by Governor Dewey in October 1954 as a Supreme Court judge, where he joined Greenberg as a colleague. He preferred the other side of the bar, however, and when he was offered a federal judgeship by President Eisenhower, he turned it down, a very rare event, stating he would prefer to be U.S. Attorney for the Southern District of New York; within a year he was appointed to that important and powerful post. He remained there until 1958, when he resigned to return to private practice with the intention of actively pursuing the Republican nomination for Governor of New York. President Eisenhower accepted his resignation by letter of July 25, 1958, deleting, because of the upcoming primary fight, the traditional language of wish for "future success" so as not to appear partisan in the matter. Williams did not win the nomination, and returned instead to a long, successful career as a partner in the prestigious Cahill Wall Street firm.[5]

When he entered the IWO case in 1950, Williams was a man who reflected the "old guard." Later, his political credentials were checked and found "correct" when he was nominated by the President as U.S. Attorney by then Deputy Attorney General (later Secretary of State) William P. Rogers. He was, however, anything but a political hack. His talent as a courtroom lawyer, as a published writer on legal matters, and as a successful criminal prosecutor are all soundly evident. To these attributes must be added his political connections as well as his personal good looks. He was also a man of high ethical and moral standards. That he was repelled by the radical politics of the IWO leadership is reflective not only of the times, but also of the "blue blood" Protestant Republican establishment, of which he was a stellar example. He belonged to the "right" law firm, clubs, and organizations. But Williams was not a witch-hunting zealot, and in fact professed genuine disdain for Senator McCarthy, his tactics, and his followers.

Another factor is evident and important: Paul Williams was, and is, a man of great energy. A case of the magnitude involving the liquidation of a fraternal benefit insurance company, with all its unique features, is not for the slight of heart, strength, or energy. Yet, in the midst of the IWO case appeals, Paul Williams was inducted as President of the Manhattan Council of the Boy Scouts of America, rewarding years of devoted service to scouting. That Williams had the needed energy and commitment to engage in the task of the IWO trial was evident.

According to Judge George Postel, Judge Greenberg's legal secretary at the time of the IWO trial, the Insurance Department chose Williams, "a prominent Republican," in order to send a political message. "To them," Postel explains, "it was a political issue. . . . They too were fighting the Communists." Postel believes that the Insurance Department wanted to pursue the IWO because it was on the Attorney General's Subversive list.[6]

Looking back some forty years, Paul Williams has said he viewed his handling of the case as "just a cold surgical job"; his self-described approach was to "always go for the jugular." Williams's success and strategy as a litigator reflected his vast trial experience; from the time he returned after war service until retirement in 1977, he tried more cases and argued more appeals than all the other firm partners put together.[7]

A different assessment of Williams comes from Rockwell Kent, who was President of the International Workers Order at the time of the trial. Kent authored a number of books about his life as an artist as well as his social and political views. In a portion of *It's Me, O Lord,* he reflects on his participation in the IWO trial:

> Our chief defense attorney, Raphael Weissman, was no match in looks and stature or sartorial elegance to Mr. Williams. A small man [Weissman] and, at first, quite unimpressive, he had, nevertheless, an extraordinary mastery of all the nuances of speech and expression, while in their exercise to the annihilation of such a witness as Budenz he was inspired by a loathing that he was at no pains to conceal. Deftly, yet utterly without mercy, he led his victim into one glaring contradiction after another to the final deep embarrassment of even those who had employed so low a tool to serve their ends.
>
> Going up to the State's attorney during an intermission of the court, I introduced myself and said: "Mr. Williams, a man of your position should be ashamed of himself for getting mixed up with such characters."
>
> And Williams, obviously taken aback, replied: "I know. But you see, Mr. Kent, I'm just an employee. I have to do as I'm told."[8]

The Budenz referred to is Louis Budenz, at the time of trial a former editor of the Communist Party paper, the *Daily Worker,* who had become a professional anti-Communist and one of the lead prosecution witnesses. Budenz had stated under oath during the trial that Kent was a Communist.

Paul Williams strongly denies Kent's report of their conversation, stating that it is incredible "on its face" since he was never told what to do by anyone.[9] Whatever the truth of the matter, Kent's recollection gives a glimpse of the chief trial counsel for the IWO, Raphael H. Weissman. Judge Postel, asked to describe Weissman, remembered only that "he was short, I think a bald-headed guy with a mustache, slightly rotund; he had a good sense of humor."[10] Marshall Perlin, another lawyer on the IWO side, remembers Weissman as a rather small man, baldish and in his fifties, with a curved-up mustache, who was, he felt, a bit pompous.[11]

Just how the IWO chose Weissman as their lead trial counsel is unclear, but he was not the organization's first choice. The IWO had approached John W. Davis, a top Wall Street lawyer and former Democratic candidate for the presidency in 1924 against Calvin Coolidge, but he turned them down.[12]

Perhaps IWO thinking was in line with a friend of Davis, attorney

Charles Burlingham, that, "If the Commies had any sense they would try to get conservative lawyers to argue their cases. I had got this off several times to Roger Baldwin [of the American Civil Liberties Union], and once he did call my bluff . . . and I told him that the best man in the United States for them was named Davis, John W."[13]

The IWO made another, albeit fruitless attempt to have the law firm that included Edward Flynn, Democratic Party powerhouse, represent the Order. The strategy was obvious: to get a lawyer who would have prominence and political clout.

This search for counsel cannot be understood without heed to the times: it was very difficult to find lawyers who would represent any person or organization where the charges were political in nature. Although the American Bar Association Special Committee on Individual Rights in 1953 stated that, "American lawyers generally recognize that it is the duty of the Bar to see that all defendants, however unpopular, have the benefit of counsel for their defense," in fact, few lawyers at this time were willing to represent political clients.[14]

In 1952 Supreme Court Justice William O. Douglas took realistic note of the difficulties faced by unpopular defendants:

Fear even strikes at lawyers and the Bar. Those accused of illegal Communist activity—all presumed innocent, of course, until found guilty—have difficulty getting reputable lawyers to defend them. Lawyers have talked with me about it. Many are worried. Some could not volunteer their services, for if they did they would lose clients and their firms would suffer. Others could not volunteer because if they did they would be dubbed "subversive" by their community and put in the same category as those they would defend. This is a dark tragedy.[15]

Factually, Douglas was correct: getting counsel for those under attack as subversives was very difficult. Because of hearings before the House Committee on Un-American Activities (HUAC), deportation board hearings, and criminal prosecutions of Communists and Communist-affiliated organizations, a significant demand was created for lawyers willing to defend accused individuals and groups. It soon followed that lawyers who answered such calls were subject to criticism at least, and sometimes to worse: every lawyer who represented the top Communist in the *Dennis* trial was found guilty by Judge Medina of contempt and sentenced to prison. All five were thereafter brought up for disbarment in the state where each was licensed. The tragic story of their broken lives has been well documented.[16]

A major attack was leveled against the National Lawyers Guild, an organization of liberal lawyers that provided many attorneys for the accused;[17] HUAC in 1950 labeled the organization an "appendage to the Communist Party" and accused it of serving as a "legal bulwark" of the Party.[18] That same year, the American Bar Association House of Delegates, for the first time in its history, supported the requirement of a test-oath for all lawyers in the form of a non-Communist affidavit, including "whether he is or ever has been a member or supportive of any organization that espouses the overthrow, by force" of the government. If this test-oath process revealed anything "negative," a "fitness to practice law" proceeding would follow. The following year, the American Bar Association adopted more resolutions calling for the expulsion of Communists and advocates of Marxism-Leninism, urging state and local bar associations to commence disbarment proceedings. While there was, given the times, brave opposition to these resolutions, the atmosphere was one of chill, if not panic, among lawyers called upon to act as counsel to those accused people and organizations.[19]

Thus, representing unpopular people, causes, or organizations was not for the faint of heart; an attorney's career might be on the line merely for fulfilling his or her professional obligation to a retaining client. The "red brush" was very broad in the hands of bar associations, elements of Congress, government agencies, and the media as well as those private groups who made a crusade—and a business—out of anti-Communism.

The International Workers Order, upon its inclusion in the Attorney General's Subversive Organizations list in 1947, had to find competent lawyers to represent it, since a decision had been reached to file suit against the Attorney General for this listing. While that battle was being waged in Washington, D.C., the Order's leadership had to find counsel to deal with the more immediate attack in New York by the Department of Insurance. In these battles, the Order suffered from the same disadvantages that denied a wide range or free choice of counsel as described above; the IWO was clearly not a popular cause. On the other hand, the Order had money, one very important advantage, and because it was an organization, not an individual, there was no personalized threat of deportation, jail, or fine by the federal or state government—just liquidation.

Raphael H. Weissman was born in Europe in either 1901 or 1902 and arrived in the United States between 1914 and 1916. His father was Austrian, his mother was Hungarian; both were Jewish. The family had moved around Europe quite a bit and, just before coming to this country, lived in the Netherlands. There Weissman learned English, adding that language to a working knowledge (if not fluency) in German, Dutch, Hungarian, Polish, Russian, Yiddish, and Hebrew. He also knew Latin and Greek.

In the United States, the family settled in the Brownsville section of Brooklyn, where Weissman finished high school in two years. Within four years thereafter he had completed his studies at New York University, which included graduation from law school; he spent one and one-half years as an undergraduate and two and one-half in law studies. In those times, an abbreviated pre-law education was common; in fact, in some states a person could go from high school directly into law school. Weissman was apparently just old enough to qualify for admission to the bar.

Raphael Weissman married a woman raised in England and parts of the British Empire; her mother was an Afrikaner and her father German, neither was Jewish. His wife also graduated from law school but had to wait a year before entering the bar because of her youth.

Young Weissman found early success as an attorney. He became in-house counsel for an insurance firm and then served as an attorney for several major banks in the New York area; for a time he was a partner in a large law firm on Wall Street. Beginning in 1936, he practiced with an uncle by marriage, William J. Wilson, until Wilson's death in 1957. Thus, during the IWO case, while Weissman held himself out as a sole practitioner, he was in fact associated with his uncle.

Weissman's son Richard, also an attorney, has described his father's politics as that of a "Cadillac Communist," a term he explained as meaning, "what he didn't need for himself, everyone could change." One key to understanding Raphael Weissman seems to be that this basically conservative person was secure enough in his professional abilities and success to be willing to undertake risks that others might not. Thus, his representation of the leftist IWO was not an apparent threat to his career. He did not lose clients as a result, and in fact is reported to have added bank clients after his work on the case ended. According to his son, Weissman "wasn't vulnerable to anything, as far as he was concerned. He had a substantial practice in which he was well thought of. . . . I know most lawyers of the time also felt he was recognized in the bank and in the business community in our area."[20]

Physically, Raphael Weissman was a very powerful man, having worked as a stevedore on the New York docks as a youth. Bald by his mid-twenties, he was short, wore glasses, and had a strong, well-modulated voice that, as with most successful trial attorneys, was a finely tuned and rehearsed tool of his trade. By contrast to Rockwell Kent's report, Weissman's son describes him as an impeccably dressed person.

There remains the question of who recommended Weissman to the IWO officers as a trial attorney. Weissman's expertise in the field of insurance company litigation was probably what brought him to their attention; perhaps Nathan Witt, a lawyer with strong leftist connections who played a behind-the-scenes advisory role for the Order, suggested Weissman, although this cannot be confirmed from the records, archives, or personal memories of participants.

Raphael Weissman was a "lawyer's lawyer," an accolade that he sought and apparently earned. Most of his cases were referred to him for trial by other lawyers. Yet, unlike many successful lawyers, he had no interest in being a judge. His son recalls that his father told him, "he could never afford it." This anecdote reflects both the financial success of Weissman and the generally low pay of judges, who are still prohibited from supplementing their pay with practice.

After the IWO case, Weissman returned to his trial and appellate practice and, from the number of reported cases in which he acted as counsel, continued to lead a vigorous life as an attorney. There is no record that he ever took another leftist, civil rights, or accused subversive case. Certainly the IWO was unique as a leftist insurance company, and this lawyer, already deeply involved in insurance litigation law, must have found the opportunity to represent the Order exciting and challenging. He continued to practice for almost fifteen years after the IWO case; during the last five years of his life (he died in 1965, the same year as Judge Greenberg) he fought a final battle with cancer.[21]

Weissman entered the IWO case as lead trial counsel just as it was filed in the New York Supreme Court in December 1950. Prior to that time, the State of New York Insurance Department had instituted an examination of the "fraternal" activities, meaning the politics, of the IWO. This political investigation commenced in 1949, following an earlier determination that the financial status of the IWO was in proper order. In January 1950 the insurance examiner in charge of both the financial and political aspects of the IWO, James B. Haley, filed a 145-page *Report on Examination* (the Haley Report), which called for the liquidation of the IWO because of its politics. When that document was served on the Order, the officers realized, apparently for the first time, that a very serious problem was before them. The Order's General Secretary-Treasurer, Peter Shipka, notified the Department that, pursuant to law, a formal hearing had been requested, accompanied by the filing of some twenty-three specific exceptions to the Report.

Before this Shipka had taken a step known only to a few top IWO officers: within a month after receipt of the Haley Report on the politics of the Order, he had retained the legal services of New York attorney Saul E. Rogers, an older practitioner, to represent the Order before the Department. Shipka kept this move secret from most of the IWO officers and even from other attorneys who then and later represented the Order. Rogers had apparently been retained to see if he could obtain an amicable administrative resolution. In effect, Shipka was seeking a compromise with the State in order to avoid a formal hearing which, if the results went against the IWO, would necessarily lead to litigation. While the retention of Rogers (he was ultimately paid $5,000) was kept quiet, there was nothing illegal or underhanded in the strategy; in doing battle with any bureaucratic agency, it is common sense to attempt such an informal resolution. In fact, this process has recognized legal formalities wherein the parties enter into a consent decree or an assurance of voluntary compliance, not unlike a plea bargain in the criminal case area.

Rogers began his work by telephoning William C. Gould, Deputy Superintendent of Insurance, asking that he be allowed to meet on behalf of the IWO to discuss "certain matters." Gould reminded Rogers that he could discuss the contents of the Haley Report only in the context of a formal hearing. Accepting this limitation, Rogers nevertheless pressed for a chance to present "some ideas" to Gould. The next day they met, along with Examiner Haley.[22]

Rogers did almost all the talking. He explained that the Order had retained him in a "limited capacity," adding that he was a corporate lawyer with a background in the motion picture industry. He then explained his attempt to act as a "conciliator" who would try to resolve the matter to the satisfaction of the Department by correcting the "situation" described in the Haley Report, thus avoiding a long hearing and court review which could go on for possibly two years. According to Gould's memorandum of the meeting, Rogers explained that "he knew it was not the policy of this Department to destroy business enterprise," adding further that a liquidation of the IWO "would merely serve to force the activities we have criticized into underground operation."

What Rogers offered Gould and the Department of Insurance was that in accepting the case, he had insisted as a precondition that those "responsible for the conditions criticized in the Report" be removed from office. Rogers was prepared to offer a "housecleaning" in order to remedy matters. Although this was the essence of his proposal, in an obvious attempt to strengthen his credentials with the Department he surrounded his posture with vehement anti-Communist statements. Rogers pointed out that he was never an IWO member, thus distancing himself personally from his client. He ended by asking that his proposal be brought to the attention of the Superintendent. While not discussed at this meeting, both sides knew that under New York insurance law it was within the power of the Department to recommend a "rehabilitation" of an erring insurance company by mandating changes that, if accepted by the company, would avoid an ultimate liquidation.

The penned notes at the bottom of Gould's memorandum indicate that he promptly followed through. Alfred A. Bohlinger, the Superintendent of Insurance, requested some material for review and, four days later, "insisted that I [Gould] fix [a] hearing date approximately 30 days hence." Thus, for the first but not the last time, attempts at some sort of settlement were made.[23]

Rogers was not yet finished. He tried selling the idea directly to Bohlinger in a meeting with him, but Bohlinger remained steadfast. Rogers made one last effort, just as the formal hearing began, by going to see Williams and Arthur D. Emil, a Cahill associate assigned to work with Williams.[24]

What Rogers proposed to Williams was essentially the same as that advanced earlier to Gould and Bohlinger, embellished by a few specifics: the Department could either recommend or approve the replacement personnel; the IWO would cease contributing to any political campaigns or activities; either it would cease publication of its magazine *Fraternal Outlook* or the magazine would be completely "sanitized"; and it would "dispense" with any "taint" of Communism the Department alleged that the Order contained.[25] These proposals might be viewed as admissions, and perhaps in a sense they were, but not admissions which could be introduced in court. The most serious from a legal standpoint was the matter of contributions to political campaigns or activities, because insurance laws prohibited such a use of policyholders' payments. In a sense, what Rogers was offering was, point for point, exactly what the State would attempt to prove in order to achieve its goal of destroying the IWO. By rejecting compromise, the State in effect sought the most severe remedy: to establish these allegations as grounds for a liquidation order rather than participate in any supervised "rehabilitation."

It is also evident that a mixture of politics and law would be generated by litigating the issue of liquidation, with the IWO taking the position that, by law, the politics of its leadership were irrelevant and that no laws governing fraternal benefit insurance companies had factually been violated by the Order (including the matter of money contributions). The State, in turn, would contend that the politics of the Order were inextricably interwoven with that of the Communist Party, and that such an association created a "hazard" to its policyholders, thus justifying the destruction of the IWO.

Rogers garnished this proposal with his anti-Communist, Republican Party credentials. Williams's response was direct: he was in no position to contradict the Superintendent, and for his part (good trial lawyer that he was) he "would be looking forward" to the litigation of these matters. Emil, who memorialized this meeting, felt that "it was Mr. Williams' thought that he could not do anything about it even if he wanted to." Williams had made it clear that he would not compromise the matter.[26]

Rogers then directed his efforts toward delaying the formal hearing date. His aim this time was to delay the hearing until after January 1, 1951 because of an unusual monetary incentive given by Shipka; in a letter spelling out the terms of their contract, Rogers would be paid $12,500 by the IWO if he could arrange such a delay. The reason, not specified in the letter but gleaned from correspondence and actions taken by the IWO's leadership, was to enable it to call an emergency National Convention in order to marshall the strength of its leadership and most active members and perhaps make some changes that would improve its chances of prevailing in its impending battle with the State.

Rogers was also promised a large fee, totaling $55,000 (an amount equivalent to perhaps $300,000 in 1990s dollars) if he could succeed in getting the liquidation proposal withdrawn and orchestrate a compromise satisfactory to both sides.[27] The amount of money involved reflects the IWO's appreciation of the danger posed by Examiner Haley's report and recommendation. The retention of Rogers may also reflect a behind-the-scenes struggle in the IWO between those who were willing to compromise their own leadership positions and the Order's political posture (at least until the political climate changed) to save the IWO and others who would not accept such changes. Shipka and another officer, Samson Milgram, represented that first position.[28]

When Rogers failed to obtain a delay in the formal hearing beyond October 1950, much less sell a plan of negotiated settlement, he notified the IWO that he was ending his representation of the Order because of "certain very pressing commitments that I have undertaken."[29]

Irony pervades trials as it does all of life; at the very time that the Insurance Department was moving to destroy the organization, it gave formal approval for the IWO to move from rented space at 80 Fifth Avenue and purchase a building for its new home at 635–39 Avenue of the Americas. The move never took place, as it was preempted by the IWO's fight for its existence.[30]

Attempts through Rogers having failed, the IWO turned to the law firm of Donner and Kinoy. In his autobiography, *The Odyssey of a People's Lawyer,* Arthur Kinoy recalls his first meeting with Peter Shipka:

One afternoon Donner called me into his office and introduced me to an older man who was sitting there with an overflowing folder of papers and looking particularly grim. He was Peter Shipka, one of the national officers of the International Workers Order (IWO), a highly successful cultural fraternal benefit society, built primarily by groups of immigrant working people to provide inexpensive insurance and other medical benefits for people whom the commercial insurance companies would not touch. I could not imagine what Peter Shipka would want from us.

Shipka, it developed, wanted to know if we would represent the IWO officers. He pulled out of his folder a legal-looking bunch of papers and handed it to us, saying, "They want to liquidate us." The petition was from the New York State Superintendent of Insurance, asking the New York courts for an order "liquidating" and "dissolving" the IWO.[31]

Engaging this firm marked a turning away from the attempt to secure politically prominent or well-connected counsel for the IWO toward lawyers known for their representation of unions, civil rights causes, and leftists. Weissman's engagement for the actual trial was an additional turn, this time putting aside these well-known left-wing lawyers for a highly skilled trial man, politically unconnected and not known for any leftist or civil rights representation. In the language of that era, Weissman was not known as a progressive. He was, however, an experienced trial attorney who had been involved in at least two complex, nonpolitical insurance liquidation proceedings prior to the IWO case. Donner and Kinoy were unhappy with relegation to assisting Weissman, though they appear to have sustained an amicable working relationship with him.

By 1950, Frank Donner, at age thirty-nine, had already achieved prominence as an attorney involved in labor law and civil rights matters. He was part of the team of lawyers that had worked on behalf of the defendants in the Smith Act prosecutions of leading Communist Party members in 1949, the *Dennis* case. During that work, Donner invited Arthur Kinoy, then an attorney for the United Electrical Radio and Machine Workers of America, one of the largest industrial trade unions, to join the *Dennis* defense team. Kinoy found this an "irresistible offer" from a man whom he describes as "one of the most creative brilliant legal thinkers in the practice of people's law."[32] Kinoy, a Harvard graduate who had completed his law degree at Columbia in 1937, was twenty-nine years old at the time.

Two additional points about all of the lawyers involved must be made. The attorneys for both sides, the State and the IWO, were first-class lawyers, totally involved with their clients. A case of this magnitude allows an attorney to concentrate and direct all his or her energy in pursuit of the client's needs. Although Raphael Weissman, who was called into the IWO case just as litigation commenced, was unfamiliar with the organization, he nonetheless threw himself into the matter with full heart and head; this can be strongly sensed from reading the trial record.

The degree of dedication on both sides was so intense, compelling, and overriding that the scenes which would later unfold come close to a trial as portrayed by the media, where a single case dominates the professional and even personal lives of the lawyers involved. In the

IWO case that usual distortion of reality was in fact evident and real—this, despite the absence of a threat of jail, fine, deportation, or execution for the defendant. A major factor explaining such a total concentration of attorneys on a single case was money; the State of New York had it and so did the IWO, with enough at stake for both sides to spend liberally.

The other point is this: lawyers like Williams would not likely be induced to represent defendants like the IWO or any other acknowledged Communist or radical. The same was true of Donner, Kinoy, and Perlin; they would not likely be comfortable representing the government or, in a broader sense, the "establishment." In the decades following the IWO case, these lawyers stayed on their side of the fence for their practice: Williams as a judge, prosecutor, and litigator; Donner, Kinoy, and Perlin in their representation of the underdog, the radical, labor unions, and generally, the accused. Donner's books and articles bespeak of that life.[33] Kinoy, now a law professor at Rutgers, has lost none of his zeal and fire; the San Francisco Bay Area Chapter of the National Lawyers Guild recently honored him for his "steadfast solidarity with progressive movements here and abroad."[34] Perlin is still involved in the Rosenberg atom spy case, on behalf of Morton Sobell.

Note should be taken that these lawyers and in fact all of the attorneys involved were bright, competent, and really quite exceptional. The case that generated the legal arena in which these talents would meet and clash was, likewise, in the words of the equally bright, competent, and dedicated judge, "an unusual and extraordinary proceeding."[35]

In kaleidoscope fashion, politics from many angles would obviously play a major role in these proceedings: the politics of the Cold War, of the Red Scare, of the State of New York, of the IWO, of its officers, and even of the attorneys. Judge Greenberg and the prosecuting attorney Williams had political ambitions, and attorneys like Donner, Kinoy, and Perlin were in the political arena as combatants against the "establishment," while this and other Red Scare cases and events held center stage in the nation's domestic life.

Notes

1. Lawrence M. Friedman, *A History of American Law*, 2nd ed. (New York: Simon & Schuster, 1985), p. 457.

2. *New York Journal American*, March 11, 1965; *New York Herald Tribune*, March 10, 1965; *New York Times*, March 10, 1965.

3. The information here is gathered from obituaries and from an interview conducted with Judge Greenberg's daughter Jean (Mrs. Emanuel Lewis

Greene) and his son-in-law, Emanuel Lewis Greene, on July 13, 1989, and from interviews conducted with court personnel as well as memorabilia loaned and shown to me by Mr. and Mrs. Greene.

4. Hon. George Postel interview, on October 27, 1989.

5. Paul W. Williams interview, July 25, 1988; also, Dwight D. Eisenhower Library documents on Williams's nomination and resignation as U.S. Attorney: Office of the Attorney General, Washington D.C., July 13, 1955, Letter by Herbert Brownell, Jr. to President Eisenhower; Department of Justice, Office of the Deputy Attorney General, Washington D.C., July 13, 1955, Letter by William P. Rogers to Edward Tait; The White House, Washington D.C., July 15, 1955, Memorandum by Edward Tait to Governor Adams; United States Attorney's Office, New York, N.Y., September 9, 1957, Letter by Paul Williams to Herbert Brownell, Jr.; Office of the Attorney General, Washington D.C., September 12, 1957, Letter by Paul Williams to President Eisenhower; Office of the Attorney General, Washington D.C., July 18, 1958, Memorandum by William Rogers to William J. Hopkins; The White House, Washington D.C., July 21, 1958, Memorandum by Robert E. Hampton to Governor Adams; The White House, Washington D.C., July 25, 1958, Letter by President Eisenhower to Paul Williams; *New York Times*, January 4, 1952; January 23, 1952; January 24, 1952; September 19, 1952; September 29, 1952; October 8, 1954; December 9, 1953; *Who's Who In America* (Chicago: Marquis, 1981).

6. George Postel interview, October 27, 1989.

7. Williams interview, July 25, 1988.

8. Rockwell Kent, *It's Me, O Lord: The Autobiography of Rockwell Kent* (New York: Dodd, Mead & Co., 1955), pp. 597–98.

9. Letter to author from Paul W. Williams, February 8, 1989.

10. Postel interview, October 27, 1989.

11. Marshall Perlin interview, October 27, 1989.

12. Trauber interview, July 23, 1988.

13. Quoted in William H. Harbaugh, *Lawyer's Lawyer: The Life of John W. Davis* (New York: Oxford University Press, 1973), p. 441.

14. Quoted in *Report*, "The Independence of the Bar," 13 *Law. Guild Rev.*, p. 158, 1953.

15. William O. Douglas, "The Black Silence of Fear," *New York Times Magazine*, January 13, 1952, p. 1.

16. *Report*, "The Independence of the Bar," pp. 159–61; Benjamin Dreyfus and Doris Brin Walker, "Grounds for Discipline of Attorneys," 18 *Law. Guild Rev.* 67, 1958; "Weissman, Sacher and Isserman in the Courts," 12 *Law. Guild Rev.* 39, 1952.

17. Harper, "Loyalty and Lawyers," 11 *Law. Guild Rev.* 705, 1951.

18. House Committee on Un-American Activities, "Report on the National Lawyers Guild, Legal Bulwark of the Communist Party," H.R. Rep. No. 3123, 81st Cong., 2nd Sess., 1950.

19. Proceedings of the House of Delegates, 1950, 36 *A.B.A. Journal*, 948, 972, 1950; see also "The Lawyers Loyalty Oath," 37 *A.B.A. Journal*, 128, 1951 and Proceedings of the House of Delegates, pp. 309 ff.

20. Richard Weissman interview, July 25, 1990; information and quotations from that interview.

21. Ibid.

22. Williams Office Files, Memoranda, Vol. I, Memorandum for File—W. C. Gould, dated June 22, 1950.

23. Ibid.

24. Williams Office Files, Memoranda, Vol. I, Memorandum for File—Arthur D. Emil, dated October 18, 1950.

25. Ibid.

26. Ibid.

27. Letter by Peter Shipka, IWO General Secretary-Treasurer, to Saul E. Rogers, Esq., dated June 16, 1950; accepted by Rogers signature appended thereto, IWO Archives.

28. Trauber interviews; telephone conversation of March 1, 1990.

29. Letter, Rogers to Shipka, October 18, 1950, IWO Archives.

30. Williams Office Files, Correspondence, Letter by Superintendent of Insurance to Shipka, September 7, 1950.

31. Arthur Kinoy, *Right on Trial: The Odyssey of a People's Lawyer* (Cambridge, MA: Harvard University Press, 1983), pp. 86–87.

32. Ibid., p. 74.

33. Frank J. Donner, "Hoover's Legacy," *The Nation* 218, 22 (June 1, 1974); *The Un-Americans* (New York: Ballantine, 1961); "The Informer," *The Nation* 178, 15 (April 10, 1954).

34. "Testimonial Dinner Announcement," National Lawyers Guild, San Francisco Bay Area Chapter, held April 21, 1990.

35. Trial Record, p. 746.

Chapter IV
The Formal Hearing

Fraternal benefit insurance companies were children of necessity. Companies selling life and other kinds of insurance were in business prior to the American Civil War, but these were profit-operated businesses that generally reached only the relatively affluent. In 1868 the first fraternal benefit insurance society was organized, the Ancient Order of United Workmen. Modeled in part after semi-religious societies in Ancient Greece and Rome, the Guilds of England, and the British Friendly Societies, these fraternal benefit organizations developed to fill the need for life insurance and sickness benefits for working people. Always more than just insurance companies, these societies offered a support system at a time when Social Security, Workers' Compensation, and Medicare-Medicaid did not exist, much less employer-sponsored plans. A few unions did begin to provide some of these services, but the vast majority of working people were never unionized.

The "more" offered by fraternals included an umbrella concept expressed by the word "fraternalism." In contemporary parlance, these organizations offered a mutual aid network that might include giving payments while a member was out of work, running an old people's home, and offering a place where people of a similar ethnic, religious, or racial background could meet, share, and enjoy each other's company. In lieu of "passing the hat" when a family or person experienced trouble, the fraternal offered insurance. To the sick, the society offered caring friends. To its members, it offered educational, charitable, patriotic, and sometimes religious activities.

Fraternal insurance organizations are still regulated by state law. Although each fraternal is unique, under law all must:

- Conduct fraternal programs for the benefit of their members and the general community.
- Be not-for-profit.

Figure 6. IWO logo as it appeared on membership certificates from 1930 through 1939. Note the presence of a hammer, a sickle, and a white, a black, and a woman laborer. The use of the belts and gears in the logo were to come into question with respect to Communist symbolism during the trial. Rockwell Kent's 1940 lithograph (Figure 7) replaced this logo.

- Have a representative form of government.
- Have a system of local lodges.
- Provide insurance and other benefits to members.

According to an umbrella organization of American fraternals, some ten million people currently belong to over 200 fraternal benefit societies. Some are well known, such as the Catholic Order of Foresters, Polish National Alliance, the Shriners, and the Loyal Order of Moose. Traditionally, however, most have been small in membership and tied to religious or ethnic groups, such as the Aid Association for Lutherans and the Western Slavonic Association.

The largest growth period for fraternals was in the post-Civil War era when urban populations were swelled by the gigantic influx of immigrants who fed labor to the mines, mills, and factories of the new industrial America. These ethnic fraternals held out the promise of urgently needed insurance policies for those who otherwise would not be insured by commercial companies and offered ethnic and religious comradeship to its members. Often, native languages were spoken and cultural traditions emphasized in an attempt to preserve each group's ethnic heritage. Though formed late in the era of the fraternals, the IWO also emphasized the cultural identity of its members, yet was unique in that many different ethnic groups, each organized into a fairly autonomous unit, belonged to one large fraternal order.

Because of the potential for fraud, exploitation, and mismanagement, the insurance business traditionally has been one of the most regulated areas of American economic life. By 1870 most states had undertaken some sort of insurance regulation. In the face of some insurance companies using every device and trick to avoid paying claims while others collapsed, leaving policyholders without recourse, the government sought administrative control by departments or boards which functioned under state statutes. In the United States, only railroads were more regulated than insurance companies.

Even before the Civil War, the state of New York had begun some regulation of insurance companies; by 1859, it had a separate Insurance Department. In state after state, a steady flow of legislation inflated the powers of insurance departments. Its basic aim was to check on the solvency of the carriers, insist on reserves, and monitor the payment of claims; state governments sought to accomplish these goals through the bureaucracy of administrative departments.

The onset of regulation did not automatically eliminate all problems in the industry. By the mid-twentieth century, however, administrative control of all insurance companies including fraternals was quite effective. Not only were periodic audits and reviews established, but, using the sweeping powers granted it by the legislature, the New York Department of Insurance could and did move efficaciously when serious problems arose. Until the IWO case, these moves were invariably for the purpose of protecting the fiscal integrity of the insurance carrier on behalf of the policyholders.

Because fraternal benefit insurance companies operate differently from commercial enterprises, New York, like many states, established a separate Bureau within the Insurance Department for the regulation of fraternals, known as the Mutual and Fraternal Bureau; at the time the IWO became the focus of its attention, the division was headed by James B. Haley.

Haley, a long-time Civil Service employee, had begun a routine examination of the IWO under instructions for his superiors in Albany; although he had been with the Department of Insurance for almost all his adult working life, he had never before audited the IWO.

The Bureau had first audited the IWO in 1932 and had done so once again immediately prior to the Haley appointment in late 1947, under which he was to start a new cycle of regular audit procedures on the IWO and produce a completed report in 1949.[1]

A month before Haley filed an initial report on January 25, 1949 covering the usual financial review of the Order, he had already received another appointment to make a further report "upon the fraternal activities of the Order."[2] The financial report contained no unusual or critical information. In fact, throughout both the formal hearing that was to follow his second report on the IWO and the subsequent trial, the State never claimed any legitimate basis for action against the organization on financial grounds; the IWO was in excellent financial shape, running efficiently as an insurance company. As will be seen, this became a classic "Catch 22" for the Order.

The second part of the report on the IWO would focus on its "fraternal activities," in effect its politics. That Report on Examination, which contained the recommendation for liquidation pursuant to New York insurance law (the Haley Report), was filed on January 15, 1950, almost one year after the financial report. Just how and why Haley went beyond the initial inquiry concerning finances into the realm of the Order's politics would become a leading issue when he and his supervisor took the witness stand in the trial phase of this story.

A copy of the Haley Report went to the Order; under law the IWO had the opportunity to file exceptions (objections) and to call for a formal hearing. As the Order began to deal with the crisis created by the Report, the State made further moves as well. In anticipation of the filing of exceptions and request for a formal hearing, Governor Thomas E. Dewey called his good friend Paul W. Williams and offered him the job as Hearing Officer, a responsibility which in effect would entail hearing the case and ruling on issues and evidence brought before him. Williams turned him down, instead preferring to prosecute the case on behalf of the Insurance Department. As he has recalled telling Governor Dewey:

> I like fighting in court. I'm a lawyer and . . . I would prefer to be counsel and take it all the way to the Supreme Court of the United States if I had to, and do the investigating myself. And he said all right, we'll appoint Manny [Manuel Lee] Robbins as the Commissioner for the Insurance Department and you can be counsel for the Insurance Department and I'll deputize you also . . . as Special Assistant Attorney General for the State of New York. So I said all right.[3]

Williams recounted the motivation for the Governor's call as the result of a *New York Times* article Dewey had read saying "there was a Communist front insurance company in New York called the IWO, chartered in New York"; from that "Tom [Thomas E. Dewey] said he had been getting a lot of letters from people complaining about it."[4] The record and sources do not bear out Williams's account; it must be remembered, however, that Williams was relying on his memory, not his records, for a time some forty years before. More likely, the Haley Report was politically "hot," and the question of a Hearing Officer and counsel for the State had come to the Governor's desk. In response, Dewey called Williams, offering him the job as counsel for that formal hearing. Under the assumption that the matter would end up in court, Dewey also appointed him as Special Assistant Attorney General to pursue this task.

Political pressure reflecting the power of the Red Scare was certainly not new in New York politics. In the 1948 Presidential Campaign, where Governors Dewey and Warren (of California) made up the Republican ticket, Attorney General Tom Clark, a Democrat, stated that New York and California had more Communists than any other state and that little was being done about it. Earlier in that year Clark had stated, "those who do not believe in the ideology of the United States should not be allowed to stay in the United States."[5] It was a time when toleration of alleged Communists, left-wingers, and liberals (who were also considered susceptible) was not politically wise; here was Dewey, Governor of a state which contained the home office of the largest non-union, left-wing organization in the country. The IWO was, as one historian has observed "the most conspicuously successful Communist front in the United States, and obviously a prime target for the authorities. . . ."[6]

Fees were set by Insurance Department Superintendent Bohlinger at $150 per day for Williams and $50 per day for each of his assistants; he was allowed as many of these as he felt necessary. Bohlinger knew such a figure was far less than Williams's usual rate of compensation. Williams needed, and got, approval from his senior partners to take this job, which would inevitably require heavy involvement on his part and thus draw him away from regular firm work. Williams began his work as Special Counsel to the Insurance Department on August 17, 1950.

With the retention of Williams as Special Counsel, the appointment of attorney Manuel Lee Robbins as Deputy Superintendent of the Insurance Department for the purpose of conducting the Formal Hearing, and the rejection of Saul E. Rogers's efforts to resolve the matter without such a hearing, the stage was set for the first act in this drama pitting the State of New York against the IWO.

The basic document was the Haley Report on the "fraternal activities" of the Order. In accordance with New York insurance law, the Superintendent sent a copy to the IWO, granting a reasonable "opportunity to obtain further details and to demand a hearing with reference to facts, conclusions or recommendations therein contained."[7]

The Haley Report became the crux of all that was to follow; in some 200 printed pages, he set out to review the history of the IWO, beginning with basic information about the Order as a "fraternal insurer" in the State of New York and concluding with a recommendation for liquidation—the severest penalty that could be levied under New York insurance law and the one most rarely used.[8]

He recited that the IWO was licensed by the State on July 16, 1930 and had grown to some 185,000 members by December 31, 1946 with licenses to act as a fraternal insurance company in seventeen other states and the District of Columbia, and also noted that the Order wrote life and disability (accident and health) insurance in these jurisdictions. Haley also noted that subsequent to the November 1947 listing of the Order as a "subversive organization on the Attorney General's list," membership had declined by approximately 25,000 by the end of 1949.

Haley also recited the Charter powers, the statement of IWO aims and purposes; these included promotion of "fraternal intercourse among the members," assistance in cases of sickness or disability, the carrying on of altruistic, educational, fraternal, and recreational activities (all of which were stock phrases), and the aim of allaying poverty among its members. Nationality groups, he explained, made up the backbone of the Order. These ranged from the Jewish People's Fraternal Order (the largest, consisting of about one-third of IWO membership) to affiliates of Hungarians, Poles, Italians, and Finns—in all, some fourteen of these nationality groups, each separate but bound under the IWO umbrella.

There followed the charge that the IWO was "subversive," based on its listing as such in November 1947 by the United States Attorney General. Haley reprinted portions of a letter dated November 24, 1947 from Tom Clark, Attorney General of the United States, to the head of the federal Loyalty Review Board regarding the famous subversive organization list which was supposed to be used only by federal government agencies in "connection with consideration of employee loyalty." This list got national publicity and use; in fact, it became a cornerstone for Red Scare prosecutions, deportations, and job dismissals throughout the country, ranging from Hollywood personalities to teachers on all educational levels, and even to the most pedestrian of employees.

Haley had written to government agencies asking for specific reasons why the IWO had been included in the list of "proscribed" organizations; he was informed that agencies "were not at liberty to divulge their evidence." Because he could not get their evidence, and "in view of the extremely serious nature [of the charges] which can vitally effect [sic] the stability of this fraternal insurance corporation," Haley made his own inquiry.[9] The bulk of his report was an attempt to prove his belief that the IWO was a subversive organization.

He first attacked the officers of the IWO. After a detailed naming of the leadership of the Order drawn mainly from these nationality groups, Haley attempted to link many of these names to alleged Communist or otherwise "subversive activities" and organizations. He noted, for instance, that the President of the IWO from 1935 to 1944, William Weiner, who had been convicted of passport violations, was, "at the instance of this Department" replaced in 1944.[10] He included officials and officers who either were formerly or presently (1950) "known, publicly, as advocates of Communist doctrines and for their support of, or affiliation with (or both), organizations which proclaim such doctrines." Included in this list were the former President, Weiner, and the then current President, Rockwell Kent, along with two Vice-Presidents and several General Council members.

For each named person he used material quoted from the *Daily Worker* and other newspapers to establish the validity of his charge. For example, he cited Kent as having addressed a rally protesting the trial of the leading Communists and Rubin Saltzman, a Vice-President, as having stated that "the Communists in the Order (the IWO) not only were not ashamed of belonging to the Communist Party, they were proud of it. They gave their best years in the fight for Communist ideals."[11]

Quoting from an article that he had read in the *Pittsburgh Press*, Haley pegged Samson Milgrom, General Director of Organization for the Order, as the "possible new No. 1 Kremlin agent in the U.S." He drew this conclusion from the testimony of Matthew Cvetic before the House Committee on Un-American Activities (HUAC), where Cvetic is quoted as saying that Milgrom "is a member of the Communist Party's national commission—the arm which directs Red Infiltration of nationality groups in America."[12] When he later testified at the IWO trial, Cvetic would represent himself as an undercover agent for the FBI; the film *I Was a Communist for the FBI* was based on his character.

Under a heading entitled "Activities of the Order," Haley detailed payments over three years by the Order of some $3,638.57 to eleven organizations, all of which had been designated subversive by the Attorney General. This money was paid as donations, for pamphlets and copies of speeches, and for tickets to events.

Haley moved to his review of the Order's monthly magazine, *Fraternal Outlook,* concentrating on the years 1946–47. Although his survey of the *Outlook* "disclosed no affirmative evidence of subversive acts of the Order," Haley found a "publication policy" that sharply criticized the U.S. government's foreign policies but supported the policies of the U.S.S.R. by intensive propaganda."[13] He provided examples from the magazine, dividing them into two categories labeled "Critical of America" and "Laudatory of the U.S.S.R." Under the former heading, Haley pulled excerpts from articles criticizing U.S. foreign and domestic policies, and followed these with explanatory notes from newspapers linking the author of that article to the left. He quoted, for instance, from articles by U.S. Senator Glen H. Taylor and U.S. Representative Vito Marcantonio criticizing the Marshall Plan and red-baiting in America, laying blame for it on President Truman, HUAC, and the FBI, calling the Truman foreign policy a war policy which was paralleled domestically by a repressive, anti-union, red-baiting agenda. The articles also praised F. D. Roosevelt's policies in contrast to Truman's Cold War tactics.[14] In the category "Laudatory of the U.S.S.R.," Haley quoted from articles that praised the Soviet Union as having done everything possible to maintain peace and cooperation with the West. As before, he linked each writer to some leftist or Communist tie.

Haley dealt with expenditure for publications and motion pictures, listing twelve more titles "selected at random," almost all of which dealt with Russia. He also examined "Press Publicity" advertisements placed by the IWO in newspapers, such as the *Daily Worker* and the Jewish voice of the Communist party the *Freiheit,* stating the Order had spent $123,000 over three years. He cited articles from *Fraternal Outlook* praising the space given by the *Daily Worker* to "activities and struggles of the labor unions, the International Workers Order and its national societies and progressive organizations generally." He discerned direct as well as the indirect support for the *Daily Worker* in news coverage about the IWO.[15] Rubin Saltzman, Vice-President of the Order, was noted as a Vice-President of the *Freiheit* association, a position linking him to this "Jewish language counterpart of the *Daily Worker.*"[16] Saltzman, one of the founders of the IWO, would later become the lead-off witness for the defense at the trial.

Haley concluded this section with his reactions stated as "Comment on the Foregoing":

By approving for publication such intemperate remarks as those quoted above under the heading "Critical of America", the editors of the Order's magazine give sanction to the doctrines set forth therein by those to whom these expressions are accredited. Such a policy impresses the examiner [Haley] as sharply in conflict with the Order's "General Declaration of Principles" quoted in full earlier in this report, one paragraph of which will bear repeating at this point:

"By these fraternal and civic means the Order strives to contribute to the unity and equality of the American people and to strengthen their fighting power against foes of American democracy from within and without."

It is the opinion of the examiner that the excerpts from the Order's publication, submitted above, make the foregoing declaration a sham. The publication policy pursued by this magazine appears to be one calculated to create disunity among the American people, a condition which surely would weaken their fighting power against foes.[17]

This was not only a criticism of the Order's politics, but also a legal attack in terms of insurance law, which translated IWO politics into an alleged violation of its Charter. Criticism of foreign and domestic policies and personalities, along with association with Communists and left-wing politics was, in the view of Examiner Haley, somehow a violation of insurance law.

Haley analyzed speeches from the Order's 1947 General Convention, characterizing them as evidence of subversive utterances. Samson Milgrom, for instance, delivered an indictment of American postwar policy; his basic thesis was that F.D.R.'s program had been shattered by "Wall Street and the monopolies, the traditional enemies of the American people." Milgrom also warned of global imperialism by the U.S., quoted former Vice-President Henry A. Wallace on world reaction to the Truman Doctrine and Senator Claude Pepper on his anti-Dulles (John Foster Dulles) position, attacked the European Recovery Program, commonly called the Marshall Plan, and called on the convention to go on record against "the [U.S.] policy of intervention."

Domestically, Milgrom decried "the most flagrant denials of civil liberties [caused by] Red-Baiting, smearing of individuals and of organizations, [and] the establishment of a new police concept in America." (Interestingly, he made these remarks shortly before the IWO was, in Milgrom's words, "smeared" by being listed as a subversive organization.") He warned of "a new form of regimentation" that was "a prelude to planned concentration-camp regimentation" which he described as "policies borrowed from the Hitler arsenal." Milgrom concluded by calling for a return to the policies of F.D.R.[18] With regard to this and other speeches, Haley concluded:

that a concerted effort is being made by the Order to impugn the integrity of our country's President, his Cabinet and the Congress, specifically in their conduct of foreign policy, and particularly in that policy as developed since the close of World War II.

While the foregoing may not represent an affirmative subversive act, yet there may be discerned therein a plan to accomplish by indirection the same result as would be achieved by a direct subversive act.[19]

Since the 1930s the House Committee on Un-American Activities had, from time to time, taken testimony from various witnesses with direct or indirect ties to the IWO. For fifty pages, the report reviewed both excerpts from this testimony and documents presented to HUAC. Appearing before HUAC in September and October 1939 five men, four of whom were under subpoena, testified before this Committee, in part about the IWO. In its continuing investigation of Communism, HUAC called Earl Browder, the leading Communist party official in the United States. Haley noted that Browder had named the members of the National Committee of the Communist Party, U.S.A., which at that time included Max Bedacht, former Secretary of the IWO, and William Weiner, former President of the Order. Browder's lengthy testimony of 1939 covered many areas of Communist activities, positions, and beliefs, including the subject of the IWO. As digested by Haley, the highlights of Browder's testimony included:

- that the IWO as such was not connected with the Party;
- that only about 3% of the IWO membership was Communist;
- that while Communists were involved in the creation of the IWO, and most of the organizers were Party members, that is [in 1939] no longer the case ". . . and the Communists are now in a minority in the organization";
- that while the Communist Party did not establish the IWO, it considered the organization a "transmission belt" for the Party. For many pages, testimony was taken and articles cited about the meaning of "transmission belt" in Communist parlance. In essence, it is a mass (that is, proletarian based) organization either set up by or independent of the Party, susceptible to Party influence, as well as a potential pool for Party membership recruitment.[20]

Max Bedacht's Communist credentials were recited; these included high Party office and spokesperson in written materials for the Party. He was also General Secretary of the IWO from 1933 until his replacement in 1947. Haley highlighted Bedacht's 1939 testimony before HUAC at length and also included a large portion of an article by Bedacht entitled "The Place of the IWO in the Revolutionary Movement" from the *Daily Worker* about which Bedacht was questioned. In it, the basic theme was that the Order must help workers solve their need for social insurance by providing an insurance program, thus promoting worker class consciousness, leading them to the ultimate realization that their problem "is beyond their control, is in reality a fundamental political problem—the problem of establishing a working-class rule in place of the existing capitalist-class rule."

Thus, the IWO helped solve an immediate problem—the lack of some measure of social insurance—as the means to a greater end, which Bedacht expressed as follows: "By leading our members into the struggle for social insurance, we merely extend our members' conception of mutual help to the individual worker, to a conception of help to the whole working class." He also emphasized the need to make members militant trade unionists; from these struggles would spring class consciousness and involvement, and "revolutionary leadership."[21] With respect to these statements, the Committee had pressed Bedacht as follows:

Q. Then, the basis of this immediate need is to involve the members of the organization in what you call class-consciousness, or for the purpose of developing class-consciousness or revolutionary consciousness. Is that the attitude and purpose of the I.W.O.? Is that the thing you are trying to do in the I.W.O.?

A. I try to do it everywhere. That is what we are trying to do.

Q. That is a role of the I.W.O.?

A. It is not a role of the I.W.O. I mean that is a role of the Communist Party. The role of the I.W.O. is to insure. . . .

Q. Again speaking of the I.W.O., I read: "It is an organization that allows Communist leadership to drive its roots into the uncharted depths of the American working masses, where class consciousness has not yet penetrated."

Q. Is that the object of the I.W.O.?

A. That is my policy.

Q. Do you say that the International Workers Order is an organization that allows Communist leadership to drive its roots into the uncharted depths of the American working masses?

A. Any organization that has—

(The Chairman, interposing): That is not responsive to the question. You have identified an article as having been written by you and this language has been read to you from the article. You can either repudiate it, or say whether that is your view. Is that your opinion now?

A. I will answer the question but he puts it in such a way that I cannot answer it.

(The Chairman): You wrote that, did you not?

A. Yes, sir.

Q. Does that express your views? Is that correct?

A. It does not express my views from what he has read into it.[22]

More sharp questioning followed about this and other statements. Some six years after he wrote this article, Bedacht took the position before the HUAC that he was being misinterpreted, that these written statements had been merely personal opinions and beliefs, not those of the Order itself.

A final sally was made by the Committee with respect to the emblem or logo of the IWO:

A. The emblem of the International Workers Order is a group of two or three people with wheels of industry, transmission belts, and holding tools; several of the figures in the emblem hold tools.

Q. Yes. What tool does the figure on the left hold (indicating)?

A. Oh, I don't know. One holds the hammer and one holds the sickle.

Q. Yes—

A. If I may state, the sickle is an agricultural instrument and not a political weapon.

Q. But the emblem, is the hammer and sickle, is it?

A. The emblem is a group of people with wheels, with transmission belts, a woman, a man and a child. I believe one figure is to indicate the unity of the people in a fraternal organization and the instruments and machinery indicate that it is primarily for workers.[23]

The IWO replaced this emblem in 1940 with new artwork created by Rockwell Kent.

Under the heading "Additional Data Examined," Haley selected speeches, articles, and publications which appeared to him to contain "authoritative commentary" on IWO activities. In this section of the Report covering some thirty-three pages, he quoted portions of articles from a Party magazine, *The Communist,* political campaign materials, pamphlets, speeches made to Communist Party conventions, reports to IWO conferences, and reports of participation in May Day parades by the IWO. All this material reflected the first years of the Order's existence.

Election brochures issued by the IWO in 1932 encouraged its members to vote for Communist candidates, with the caveat that the IWO "cannot and does not enter the political campaign" itself. "Of all the parties in the field," the brochure concluded, "we find the Communist Party to be the only one that concerns itself with the welfare and interests of the masses."[24]

A July 1934 article in *The Communist* termed IWO membership "under Party influence," but noted that the "splendid" increase in that membership was more the result of efforts by non-Communist members of the Order than by the efforts of Party members of the IWO. Using Communist parlance, the article further criticized the Communist "fractions" for not emphasizing the class struggle aspects in IWO recruitment, in effect stating that the Order had placed too much emphasis on the insurance program. "Fractions" related to a Party technique wherein, within an organization or union, Party members would meet, perhaps get Party orders, and generally decide on what plans they should carry out to further Party objectives within the larger organization or union.[25] (The matter of "fractions" would reappear during the trial.)

The report quotes Max Bedacht's 1933 address to the Communist

Party, in which he chastised those Communists who failed to recognize the political importance of the IWO. "Without these mass organizations," Bedacht explained, "the Party could not have leadership over these masses in a permanent organization form." He defended his work as a Party member involved in the IWO by concluding:

> I want to assure the comrades that while I am in the I.W.O. I am not away from the Party, but on the contrary when we succeed in putting all leading members of the Party into active positions of leadership of real organized masses of workers, only then their leadership becomes reality and ceases to be an abstraction.[26]

In 1934 Bedacht addressed a New York City Conference of the Order, noting that the Conference date was near the date of Lenin's death, and that no better memorial to Lenin could be had than growth of the IWO as well as "a Leninist understanding of the tasks of our Order among all our members." He emphasized the importance of the mutual benefit aspects of the IWO for its worker-members:

> When we come to a worker and invite him to join our organization, what do we tell him? Your organization, the Elks and the Eagles and all the other capitalist orders are not revolutionary; you should not stay with them; you are a worker; you should come to us. If the winning away of the workers from capitalist leadership were that simple, we would not have any problem of making a revolution.[27]

And further:

> We do not make revolutionists out of workers so we can take them into the Order—we take them into the Order so that we may get a chance to make revolutionists out of them. . . .
> We can demonstrate to them the difference of the purposes of a bourgeois benefit society and the IWO as a proletarian benefit society.[28]

In this 1934 speech, Bedacht referred to his listeners and fellow officers as "Comrades." Later, as the IWO matured, this form of address was dropped, and the language of fraternal organizations adopted; thereafter members were referred to as "Brother" or "Sister."

Haley also pointed out that the IWO was a "consistent supporter of and participant in the 'May Day' parades," listing thirteen parade groups that were all "units" (nationality sections) of the IWO. Haley also focused on a mass meeting held to protest the trial of the top Communists under the Smith Act at which Rockwell Kent and another IWO officer had spoken. Haley recited that IWO lodges raised some $18,000 for the Civil Rights Congress, a subversive-labeled organization that was the main source of funding for the defense of the Communists.[29]

Haley's review of IWO magazines and periodicals published from 1931 through 1939 led him to conclude that some were "violently revolutionary," noting however that as time passed, "their subject matter seems to have assumed a more cautious tone. At all times, however," he added, "it favored the Soviet viewpoint."[30] Haley flavored his conclusions with excerpts from these periodicals. Max Bedacht wrote a "Birthday Greeting" to the *New Pioneer*, the Order's youth magazine that was one year old in 1932. In part it read:

The ogre of capitalism was not satisfied merely to rob the larders of the workers' children. The capitalist masters of the land also stopped the building of schools. They punish workers' children in school whenever they show a lack of enthusiasm in swearing allegiance to the capitalist ogre and his emblems.

Working class fathers all over the land must organize with the working class mothers and the working class children into one grand army. This army will grow strong enough to challenge the capitalist ogre. It will grow strong enough to tumble the capitalist ogre off his throne.[31]

In the issue for September 1936, Haley found a full-page feature on the forthcoming national election featuring Browder's candidacy for President, which contained the following:

A National Committee for the support of the Communist Party Presidential ticket has been formed within the I.W.O. by outstanding leaders of our organization. The officers of this Committee are as follows:
   Rubin Saltzman, Campaign Manager
   Max Bedacht, Treasurer
   Rebecca Grecht, Secretary.[32]

This feature was followed by an appeal urging IWO members to vote Communist and advising that the Committee was sending out material to Order branches for fund-raising purposes. Haley reprinted the caveat that appeared to the effect that the Committee "is not an official body of the National Executive Committee [of the IWO], but an independent Committee set up by these IWO leaders."[33]

Haley then turned to a review of the Order's political position from the Nazi-Soviet Pact of August 1939 through the Nazi invasion of Russia in June 1941. Under the heading, "Attitude Toward World War II," he gave his account of the great "flip-flop." When the Nazi-Soviet Pact was entered into, it sent shock waves throughout the world. Hitler, the implacable foe of Communism, had agreed to be reconciled (temporarily as it turned out) with Stalin, the leading anti-Fascist. IWO support of the Pact caused a split in the IWO over this issue. Many also left the Communist Party over its support for Stalin's action; the IWO leadership followed the Party line, attacking Roosevelt as "war mongering" and his attempt to aid the Allies as imperialism. In American politics, it was a time of strange bedfellows: many of the sentiments and arguments of the right-wing, sometimes pro-Fascist, isolationist America First Committee were echoed by the Communist Party and IWO leadership.

The invasion of the Soviet Union called forth an immediate and complete change, a "flip-flop" from which, in some respects, the ultra-left never recovered. Haley addressed this point with these thoughts:

CHANGE IN WAR ATTITUDE REFLECTED SIMILAR CHANGE BY
COMMUNIST PARTY.

The examiner finds that the sudden "switch" by the Order in its attitude toward World War II, from one (prior to Hitler's attack on Russia) of vehement condemnation of any Allied aid offered by the United States, to one (subsequent to Hitler's attack on Russia) of hearty support of the Allied cause, exactly paralleled an equally sudden change of position in this matter by the Communist Party.[34]

Haley then exemplified the "switch" with contrasting positions expressed in IWO and Communist Party publications and speeches.[35] He followed with the charge that IWO lodge facilities were used for activities by the Communist Party, supporting this by articles announcing Party speakers at lodges.

The balance of the Report consisted of twenty-five pages of material drawn from a book edited by Rubin Saltzman entitled *Five Years IWO* and published by the National Executive Committee of the Order in May 1935 that also contained articles written by leaders of a number of the nationality sections. In the book Saltzman recounts his version of the origin of the IWO. Haley's reading of the extracts of the book and a later Saltzman pamphlet led him to conclude:

The examiner observes that Mr. Saltzman's explanation of the origin of the I.W.O. confirms the testimony of Mr. Browder, set forth hereinbefore that at the inception of the I.W.O. most of its members were members of the Communist Party; and the testimony of Mr. Gitlow [an ex-Communist testifying 1939 before HUAC] that the Communist Party had 'set up' the I.W.O.[36]

Haley moved to his recommendation, based on his investigation, for liquidation of the IWO. He found one conclusion inescapable: the Order has exceeded the powers inherent in its Charter (the basic corporate document issued by the state of New York entitling the Order to function as an insurance company). As with any corporation, this creature of the state must conform to the statements in its Charter.

The provision cited by Haley was the basic undertaking to promote "fraternal intercourse" as the IWO had itself defined its fraternalist activities. Haley was alleging that the Order had "been employed for other purposes." He then stated that, regardless of whether the Communist Party had "set up" the IWO (a question he deemed unresolved), the Order was from its inception controlled by Communists "who have formulated its policies and directed its affairs," and therefore was not employed for its members but for Communist purposes. He added, "in the opinion of the examiner these activities and purposes are alarming."

Haley contended that the IWO was indeed a "transmission belt" for conversion of members to the Party and that the Order "exploited" people seeking insurance through "intensive class consciousness propaganda designed to convince them that their interests and those of the Communist Party are identical." His interpretation of what he had quoted from Bedacht was that members must be "disabused" of the idea that their economic status could be improved through peaceful means; thus Haley concluded that by exposing members to Party aims, the IWO was involved in a procedure that "would seem to amount to a deception upon the public."

For Haley, the material in the Report "[seemed] to establish, indisputably, that the Order is a medium of Communist propaganda." This, he maintained, was violative of insurance law because fraternal benefit societies "are insurance corporations and the law never contemplated that insurance corporations could espouse any political party—Communist, Democratic, Republican, Socialist or other." He concluded that by "using its corporate structure and/or funds for support of a political party," the IWO was breaking the law.

Beyond recruiting and propagandizing for the Party, Haley believed the IWO went even further by urging its members to "hate" elected and appointed officials, including the President, Congress, and Justices of the Supreme Court. Portrayal of government officials as "perfidious and tyrannical" offended Haley. He was certain that "this propaganda of hate is not fraternalism as conceived by the Insurance Law and as expounded by the Order in its charter." His "fear" was that the IWO, by "inflaming its members' minds . . . may well become a threat to America's peace." He speculated that this may have been the chief factor which led the U.S. Attorney General to declare the Order "subversive," adding that "the business of an insurance organization should be so conducted that not even the suspicion of being subversive to America's interests will be given."

Here, for the first time, Haley used the crucial word "hazard," stating:

Membership in an order charged as disloyal could hold a definite hazard for a member of the public also, who because of such membership may be subjected, likewise, to a charge of disloyalty.

In the hands of Williams and his legal team, this word would take on a new meaning with respect to the politics of the IWO and insurance law.

Haley closed his long Report by stating:

It is, therefore, the conclusion of the examiner that the method of operations of the International Workers Order, as herein described, constitutes a hazard to the public. Consequently, he recommends that the Order be liquidated in accordance with the provisions of Article XVI of the Insurance Law.

Respectfully submitted,

JAMES B. HALEY,
Examiner.[37]

With the delivery of the Report to the IWO on May 18, 1950, both sides were galvanized into action. The State, represented by Williams and his associates, began preparation on behalf of the Insurance Department; Donner and Kinoy moved to prepare their response before the Hearing Officer, Manuel Lee Robbins.

Those unacquainted with the work of lawyers do not generally understand or appreciate that most of the actual work in preparation for any public aspect of a legal proceeding goes on behind the scenes. Legal research begins, investigations are undertaken, interviews conducted, sources checked out, witness prepared, documents obtained, memoranda written, and anticipated legal issues and procedural moves are plotted out, all as part of the lawyers' work. Additionally, an overall strategy for the case must be worked out that reflects the goals and obstacles involved; pleadings have to be prepared, and statements to be orally delivered must be drafted, critiqued, revised, and polished. Again, because of the importance of this case and the ability of clients to afford total dedication, the efforts put forth by the attorneys with respect to all these facets were prodigious.

The IWO moved for more time to respond. In part, as earlier explained, this reflected the strategy designed to give Rogers time to make his settlement proposals as well as to delay long enough to enable the Order to call a special emergency National Convention. The Department of Insurance pressured the IWO for a list of exceptions to the Haley Report and an agreement as to a date for the start of the formal hearing. Finally, on June 8, 1950, a seven-page single spaced list of exceptions (objections) to the Report was hand delivered by the Order to the Department, along with a plea for more time to prepare for the formal hearing, pointing out that while the Haley Report was dated

January 15, 1950, the IWO didn't receive a copy of it until May 18, 1950.

In those pages, the Order cited some twenty-three specific exceptions to the findings and opinions set forth by Haley. The IWO quoted from the Report, simply noting that it took exception to each statement, opinion, or conclusion cited, with the overall promise of a more elaborate and specific rebuttal to come at a later date.

Williams's team of associates then reviewed the allegations in the Haley Report and the validity of the exceptions. The early analysis made by Arthur Emil, Williams's associate, was discouraging for the State. As he stated in a memorandum to Williams:

> My impression, still unchanged, is that the materials which we have on hand are sufficient to prove only that the organization is Communist run, but not that it has done any acts which would be *ultra vires* [beyond their charter powers] or hazardous to the public interest, aside from whatever may be gained by showing that Communists are sworn to overthrow the Government.[38]

In a later memorandum to Williams, Emil detailed a breakdown of each exception listed by the IWO, concluding that most of the grounds advanced for dissolution by the State were inadequate under the law.[39]

It must be understood that this represented the detached, hard-nosed assessment of good lawyers coolly examining their legal situation vis à vis insurance law and communicating among themselves about what perhaps from an evidentiary standpoint could and could not be proven. The State, however, obviously was not planning to concede any grounds as inadequate. The legal burden, under State insurance law, was on the IWO, because the Report under the name of and with the approval of the Insurance Department was *presumed* sufficient for its liquidation remedy. If the Hearing Examiner approved of the Haley Report, the burden would remain with the IWO, as the State moved into court asking for an order "directing such insurer [the IWO] to show cause why the Superintendent should not have the relief prayed for."[40]

The Williams team of lawyers moved in many directions to strengthen their case and prepare for the formal hearing. They researched case and statutory law, gathered articles from the *Daily Worker*, and got copies of every publication mentioned in the Report and some that were not. The team contacted the U.S. Attorney General, the New York District Attorney, and the Attorney General's office of the State of New York in order to solicit information and advice. They also contacted a reporter for the *New York World Telegram* who had won a Pulitzer Prize for "exposing Communism" to see what his files might reveal and what leads he could produce; an extensive interview with the reporter was reported as "not very helpful."[41]

Much more helpful was a conference with the U.S. Immigration and Naturalization Service (INS). Emil reported that the INS had been investigating the IWO for some two and one-half years. In the summer of 1950, the INS had presented an extensive case for deportation against one Andrew Dmytryshyn on grounds that he was a member of the IWO, an organization they felt advocated the violent overthrow of the government. The INS took the position that his membership in the Order was enough, since it was "affiliated" with the Communist Party.

Significantly, Dmytryshyn conceded, and in fact was willing to stipulate membership in the Communist Party, but the INS chose to ignore that fact and prosecute him on the grounds of IWO membership to get at the IWO. The INS introduced twelve witnesses and eighty-five documents at his deportation hearing. These witnesses, all paid by the INS, linked the Communist Party to the IWO. In the report on this meeting, Emil concluded that:

in my estimation, the Department of Immigration and Naturalization is in an excellent position to render us all sorts of assistance through their files, through their documents and through the witnesses whom they have lined up and whom Mr. Parr [an INS official] thought would be willing to testify for us. Parr had gotten something of a run around from the Insurance Department at the time when he knew they were preparing the report on the IWO and it would seem that, had the Insurance Department consulted with this branch of the Department of Justice at the time when the offer to help was made, the examiner's report would be stronger.

Parr stated that he would be more than willing to help us in anything that we do. His expertise, having worked on this matter full time for so long, will be invaluable to us if we utilize it.[42]

In a 1988 interview, Williams confirmed that the INS did indeed prove invaluable in terms of providing almost all of the State's witnesses used in the IWO trial—the same people who testified at the Dmytryshyn deportation hearing—and documents in the form of pamphlets, books, newspapers, and magazines used at that trial. To a significant extent, the IWO trial would be a rerun of the Dmytryshyn case.[43]

Preparation continued on a daily basis. Case law research moved forward; the federal Smith and McCarran Acts were reviewed for potential relevance. Every reference in the Haley Report was indexed and cross-referenced. The Williams team also kept an eye out as to what judge might be assigned the case, under the assumption that it would end up in court. Detailed analysis was made as to how the formal hearing would be conducted, including how and what evidence would be introduced. A barrage of correspondence with the Insurance Department and other relevant agencies was maintained.

Of particular interest was the desire of officials from Pennsylvania to attend and perhaps intervene in the hearing; a zealous anti-Communist activist in the state bureaucracy was kept advised. This carried a serious portent for the IWO since it was licensed in so many states, each of which had full regulatory powers. Generally, any significant action taken by the home state, the state which issued the Charter for business and audited the home office books of the company, would be followed by similar action in other states. In 1950 and 1951, zeal in pursuing anti-Communist activities was a politically safe course, which made the IWO particularly vulnerable throughout the United States.

The cycle of audit of the IWO's financial status that began again in late 1950 provided the Williams team with an unusual fact gathering opportunity. Emil called in the new Examiner, a man named Edward Tiger, and asked him covertly to look for certain things in the Order's files. Tiger reported it would be "very difficult to get any such information without tipping our hand." Nevertheless, he did provide information as requested and was told to "keep his eyes and ears open" as to any plans for the Order's upcoming 1951 convention.[44] This use of a "mole," in effect, shows the extremes to which to State was willing to go in preparing its case.

The matter of a National Convention of the Order became an important side issue in the midst of the formal hearing matter. The IWO, as all fraternals, was required to have a convention of its membership on a regular basis. The last one had been in 1947; in accordance with the Order's four-year convention cycle, the next was due in 1951. The first strategy of the IWO officers was quickly to call a Special Emergency National Convention to be held in late 1950; we have seen that part of Rogers's task was to accomplish sufficient delay in the hearing process, and therefore any court action that might follow, in order to allow such a Convention to meet. Thus, the Order pressed the Insurance Department in October 1950 for permission to call a Special Emergency National Convention for November or December of that year.

The six-month notice requirement for any such convention proved problematic for the IWO. Despite all the arguments and pressure the Order could muster, the Insurance Department refused to approve a Special Emergency National Convention. The interests of the Department were best served by denying the convention call, a power they possessed and used to their advantage.[45] Without permission for the earlier convention, the Order could only plan its regular National

Convention for, they hoped, early 1951. The proper notice for this regular National Convention had already gone out.

With awareness of the need to counter the legal presumption of correctness of the Haley Report, Donner and Kinoy's basic defense strategy was to question the power of Examiner Haley to make recommendation for liquidation. This approach involved consistent appeals to the law, avoidance of the emotional content of political issues, and a firm insistence that, regardless of all extraneous (i.e., political) issues, State law must be strictly interpreted and followed.

This strategy (which was in part to be followed into the trial of the case) mandated that the IWO would make no major attempt to disprove the State's allegations with witnesses or documents, but instead would challenge at every step the underlying issue of the legality of the proceeding under New York insurance law and constitutionally protected rights of belief. In turn, the State would at every step attempt to link the specter of dangerous political heresy to the Order and call for liberal and expansive interpretations of existing law for the greater goal of suppressing the "Communist menace." How successful each side was will be seen in this unfolding drama.

Initially Donner and Kinoy filed a *Motion to Dismiss the Proceedings Herein* and a separate *Motion to Strike the Examiner's Report and Recommendation,* both addressed to the Hearing Officer, Manuel Lee Robbins, Deputy Superintendent of Insurance, when the formal hearing commenced on October 16, 1950.

The *Motions* urged that Haley's recommendation be stricken and the entire proceeding dismissed on the grounds that "the Examiner's Report is illegal and contrary to law." Buttressing this demand were arguments to the effect that the examination must be limited as recited in applicable insurance law to the "books, records or other documents of such insurer or other person or as ascertained from the sworn testimony of its officers or other persons examined concerning its affairs." This was not, they contended, what Haley had done; rather, he had gone far beyond this limitation in that he based his recommendation of liquidation "upon alleged facts beyond and outside the statutory limitation" of the law. Here they meant the use of newspaper articles, HUAC testimony, and speeches before the Communist Party.

The argument was advanced in the *Briefs* that the evidence used by Haley was "legally irrelevant and incompetent," followed by recitals that the report was largely hearsay; that nothing had been produced relevant to an accusation of "public hazard"; that the Order's activities were not proscribed by insurance law; and that, in any event, the activities went beyond the administrative control of the Department.

Stripped of legal verbiage, these *Briefs* further alleged:

- that the basic definition of "public hazard" was being twisted beyond its plain and intended meaning relating to financial solvency;
- that what Haley quoted was misleading;
- that much of what he recited involved the activities, beliefs, and actions of individuals who happened to be IWO officers or members but not official actions or positions of the Order;
- that a great deal of what was stated occurred some twenty years before and therefore were irrelevant in terms of 1950;
- that a large portion of the activities were known to and approved by the Insurance Department for the past twenty years and that a large portion of the activities were constitutionally protected by the federal and State of New York Constitutions;
- that the remedy of liquidation is "designed exclusively" to meet financial loss risks to policyholders, while here it was being applied to a solvent insurance company;
- that the State was obliged to remedy any problems and keep the company alive, not destroy it.[46]

With certain variations and refinements, these arguments expressed the fundamental and unchanging position of the IWO in response to the liquidation remedy sought by the State. The legal issues raised would remain essentially the same throughout the course of the Order's struggles to survive through all the impending court battles.

The formal hearing before Robbins began on October 16, 1950 and ran four full days. Williams, relying on the Haley Report (which he had modified over the strong objections of IWO counsel who claimed he was covering up defects in Haley's work), used the Examiner as his sole witness, plus additional written materials of the same type Haley had cited.

The Order, consonant with its strategy, called no witnesses in rebuttal, instead relying solely on cross-examination of Haley and introduction of documents showing the broad scope of the IWO's cultural, civic, and social activities. In effect, the Order challenged the legality of the proceeding on the premise that its political activities could not lawfully be the basis for liquidation and, further, that Haley had distorted the IWO by his narrow selection of materials.

As a result, both sides were drawn into legal arguments over the meaning and intent of specific sections of state insurance law. Those arguments were presented orally and later in writing to Robbins. The IWO, as Respondent, filed a 37-page *Brief* in support of its *Motion to Strike* and a 62-page *Brief in Support of Motion to Dismiss the Proceedings*. Williams, as Special Counsel to the Insurance Department, filed his *Brief in Opposition to Motion to Dismiss Proceedings and Motion to Strike*

Examiner's [Haley's] Report, some 57 pages long combining into one *Brief* his response to the two-pronged attack by the IWO. IWO counsel then filed a 35-page *Respondent's Reply Brief* that attacked the position and material in the State's *Brief.* Although this was not a court proceeding, the briefs were prepared and printed with the same format as those used in formal court proceedings.[47]

All three IWO *Briefs* argued that Haley violated specific provisions of the insurance law and ignored the only legitimate basis for such an action against an insurance carrier: that policyholders, both present and prospective, were *financially* at risk, and therefore the carrier constituted a "hazard" if the insurance company continued to operate.

In the IWO *Briefs,* the financial status of the Order was reviewed, showing its growth from assets of some $31,000 in 1930 when it began, to over $6 million as of December 31, 1949. Insurance in force jumped from some $3 million to $110 million in that same period. In those twenty years, the IWO had paid out over $13 million in benefits and by 1950 had almost $2 million in surpluses, an amount far above legal requirements. The assets were secure and liquid with over 97 percent in cash and government bonds. *Dunne's Insurance Report,* the most prestigious insurance rating firm, gave the Order an "A plus" (excellent) rating, placing it among the top five fraternals out of 200 nationwide. *Dunne's* stated that the IWO "is worthy of public confidence and we so recommend it."[48]

Having established the financial solvency of the Order, the *Briefs* then forcefully argued statutory interpretation; that is, relevant or governing portions of the State insurance law were carefully examined to support the conclusion that there was no legal authority for Haley's recommendation. The *Briefs* concentrated on the definition of "hazardous," arguing that it "refers exclusively to financial loss or risk of loss out of the business operations of an insurer."[49] Case law was extensively quoted to buttress this key contention.

The *Briefs* even reviewed the history of insurance law to examine the question of legislative intent in order to show that this was the only meaning given to the "hazardous" concept when the law was written, and followed that with interpretation of similar phrases from the insurance laws of other states. The arguments called for a strict interpretation of New York law consonant with the legislature's intent when it wrote the law regulating insurance companies, as well as case law interpreting the statutes involved. On these issues, the IWO stood on firm grounds and should have prevailed, provided the Hearing Officer took a literal and conservative view of the law. If, however, he was willing to engage in new and broader interpretations on these key issues—in effect to inject politics and political content into the insurance law—then the State would prevail.

The IWO *Briefs* pointed out that, from the inception of modern insurance company regulation, "the Insurance Superintendents have uniformly held that the statutory remedy of liquidation is designed to meet *financial problems* in the operation of insurers." The history of the Department itself as well as case law interpreting litigation on insurance matters was used to back this contention.[50] Moving beyond case law, State statutes, and regulatory interpretations, the *Briefs* concentrated on state and federal constitutional law dealing with administrative powers, and the First (freedom of speech, press, assembly, political association) and Fourteenth (due process) Amendments.

By utilizing a two-pronged approach—*Motion to Dismiss, Motion to Strike*—the IWO Attorneys tried to cover all the legal bases. Thus in the *Brief* on the *Motion to Strike,* specific attacks were made and arguments advanced designed to convince Robbins that the Haley Report, as a matter of law, must be stricken as a basis for the liquidation recommendation. Here the lawyers argued over the legal meaning of "other person" in the permissible scope of Haley's investigation. The IWO argued that Haley was limited to persons responsible for the running of the Order, thus excluding newspapers, pamphlets, speeches, and "extraneous" individuals and writings, contending that only the books and records of the IWO were relevant. Twenty-three pages were devoted in one *Brief* to this sole legal issue of interpreting the phrase "other person"; the conclusion was then reached that "the command of the legislative intention is thus clear that the Examiner's Report must be stricken as violative of Section 29 of the Insurance Law."[51]

After fourteen pages of additional arguments, the *Brief* ended with a direct appeal to the broader political issue with these words:

> This case involves a fraternal benefit society composed of working men and women whose every thought and action may not conform with the personal predilections of the Superintendent. The next case may involve an insurance company whose Republican officers do not hold the same beliefs as a Democratic administration. If this country is indeed a government of law and not of men, then the basic rules designed to protect insurance companies and their policyholders must be applied to this case as to the next. If the long established and fundamental rules heretofore adhered to are abandoned in this proceeding, then no fraternal benefit society and no insurance company will be secure.[52]

In some ninety-nine pages in two IWO *Briefs,* neither the word "Communism" nor the words "Communist Party" were used. The State's *Brief,* on the other hand, devoted itself from start to finish to the

Communist issue. Thus, in its opening statement, the Williams team asserted:

> The essence of this report [the Haley Report] is that the IWO, far from being a simple fraternal benefit association, is in fact a powerful and important agency of the Communist Party in the United States. Its insurance business is simply a sideline to attract prospective proselytes to the doctrines of communism and to entice them into joining the Communist Party or supporting its policies. The Examiner recommended that the IWO be liquidated pursuant to Article XVI of the Insurance Law, principally on the ground that its further transaction of business constituted a hazard to the public.[53]

Pointing out that the Order had not introduced any witnesses or other evidence to contradict the factual statements relied on by Haley, the State was implicitly arguing that since there was no factual rebuttal, all Haley had produced as the basis for his liquidation recommendation was true. The *Brief* stated:

> It is apparent that its large membership and financial backing make it a formidable tool in the hands of the Communist Party. That it is in fact a Communist tool will be amply shown below.[54]

This was followed by a twenty-one-page condensation of the "juicier" parts of the Haley Report; the words "Communist" or "Communist Party" appear on every page. The fact that the IWO was listed as a "subversive organization" by the U.S. Attorney General was also emphasized.

The balance of the *Brief* was devoted to responding to the legal issues raised by the IWO. As would be expected, the State called for a broad interpretation of the insurance law on the points of "hazardous" and "other person," citing as many allusions to case law as they could find for such liberal interpretations. One aspect of the State's reasoning is particularly noteworthy: since the IWO was financially solvent, and that solvency was in the form of liquid assets (97 percent in cash and government bonds readily convertible to cash), and because many of its officers were primarily loyal to Russia, "the possibility is not to be ignored that in the event of war or threatened war with Russia, the organization would find some means to transfer its assets to that country."[55] Thus, the financial health of the Order was made a detriment—a "hazard" to the policyholders and public since the officers could "take the money and run." Williams himself takes credit for devising that argument.[56]

The State admitted that while some of the Haley Report "may not . . . have been technically proper," nevertheless enough was there, including admissible hearsay, to support the liquidation recommendation, since the Hearing Officer could modify the Report and then adopt it, excluding the "technically defective" material.[57] In fact, the *Brief* went so far as to cite grounds for liquidation not even proposed in the Report.

The State, denying that any constitutionally protected rights were involved in the case, concluded its arguments with the following statement:

Its only position is that although it may be an organization disloyal to the United States which seeks to destroy the United States, nevertheless there is nothing that can be done about it. Although it uses the facilities provided by law for insurance companies in the State of New York to further its subversive aims, we are told that the Superintendent of Insurance is powerless even to adopt a report for filing which sets out these facts, let alone to proceed for the liquidation of the organization. It is submitted that the officers of the democratic government of the State of New York are not thus powerless to resist attack.[58]

The lawyers for the IWO did not have to respond to the State's *Brief*; they could have simply relied on their two *Briefs* as the presentation of their legal arguments. Instead, they filed a *Reply Brief,* apparently angered if not outraged by what the State had recited. This *Brief* opened:

We will show that at every point at which Special Counsel [Williams] finds it impossible to answer a legal, statutory or constitutional consideration which would compel the dismissal of the proceedings, he has resorted to one of two techniques: Either he urges the Superintendent to ignore the legal obstacle, or he attempts to rewrite the Report of the Examiner to overcome whatever hurdle in the statute, the case law or the constitution, he is then faced with. The entire brief is permeated with these two approaches, often offered simultaneously. As we will point out in this memorandum, it is not possible to either ignore the law or rewrite the report.[59]

The polite, legal language of the two previous IWO *Briefs* was thrown aside in this *Reply Brief.* Additionally, the Communist issue was tackled. The lawyers pointed out that the State's *Brief,* not the Haley Report, had found the Order to be an affiliate of the Communist Party or an advocate of the overthrow of the government by force and violence. The Order accused Williams of seeking to "overcome the illegality of the proceedings" by replacing "the Examiner's Report with a new one of his own writing."[60]

It also accused Williams of twisting and turning to escape the plain meaning and effect of the relevant statutory sections and of engaging in a "desperate attempt to explain away the patent illegality of the Examiner's Report . . . [leading] the Department beyond the looking glass into a statutory wonderland."[61] With the gloves off, the IWO attorneys accused Williams of "distortion," and the use of "absurd" approaches, concluding that "the simple fact of the matter is that the insurance law was never designed to permit or authorize political inquisition of insurers or their officers."[62]

The reaction to the proposition of "take the money and run" was predictably harsh:

> In his transparently unsuccessful effort to conjure up some justification for the Examiner's recommendation, Special Counsel swings from the extreme of one absurdity to the extreme of another. Special Counsel paints simultaneously a hazard flowing from solvency and insolvency. Suffice it to say the incredible suggestions of Special Counsel have no support in the record and were never even intimated by the Examiner or mentioned in the hearing. It should be sufficient to point out that a finding of potential hazard which flows from the fact that the assets of an insurance company are *too liquid,* is simply too incredible to dignify with discussion.[63]

Whether the argument was "simply too incredible" remains to be seen.

Using acerbic language, the IWO lawyers accused Williams of ignoring case law, misstating cases as precedent where no such precedent existed, and of illegally seeking to expand the powers of the Insurance Department beyond those ever intended by any reasonable interpretation of statutory or case law.

The State did not respond to the *Reply Brief*; the Williams team was content to let the matter rest with their one *Brief* and await the opinion of Deputy Superintendent Robbins, which was filed on December 14, 1950.

After a brief review of the process leading to the formal hearing and noting that the Order made no attempt to disprove factually or to rebut the Report, Robbins turned his attention to what he considered to be three issues raised by the IWO:

(1) that the Report was illegally violative of Section 29 of the Insurance Law,
(2) that as hearsay it was incompetent proof, and that in any event,
(3) there was no statutory authorization to recommend its liquidation as "a hazard to the public," absent any proof of financial insecurity.[64]

On the first issue, Robbins came down on the side of the State, confirming a broad interpretation of the key phrases in the law regarding "other person," thus justifying Haley's use of materials and testimony that were not part of the books and records of the IWO as a reasonably implied power of the Examiner. Taking what he labeled a "common sense" approach, Robbins was willing to concede to the State anything relating to the examination of an insurance company that wasn't clearly a "fishing expedition."[65]

As to the second issue, hearsay, he put the question this way: "Whether there is sufficient relevant and competent proof in the Report to establish that the Order is a Communist 'medium' and 'propaganda unit.'" Although finding that there was, he nevertheless substantially reduced the evidence Haley had included to what he felt was legally relevant. Like Haley, Robbins was impressed with the views of the IWO which "blatantly vilify our foreign policy and public servants entrusted to guide it."[66] He quoted extensively from portions of the Haley Report that contained material politically critical of American foreign policy.

This led Robbins into the final question of "hazard." From a fair reading of the balance of the Robbins opinion, it becomes clear that once politics enter, they predominate. Avoiding all of the case law cited by the Order's three *Briefs*, Robbins relied on the Report as proof of Communist control. He put it this way: "Hence, the ultimate question remains whether solely because it is a medium or unit of Communist propaganda and organization [which he takes as proved] 'its further transaction of business will be hazardous.'"[67]

Robbins believed the State was not limited to financial hazards, stating, "it seems inconceivable that all other serious hazards must therefore be ignored." Asserting that the "law is a living thing," he willingly extended it to cover politics and political hazards, concluding:

It is now apparent that the eve of hostilities has passed and the dawn of actual firing is upon us, and in the light of that dawn it would be foolhardy, to say the least, to hold that a vast, well-controlled and secure organization presently devoted to furthering a revolutionary class war and supporting a Party working toward the overthrow of our Government, does not present a serious hazard not only to the public but to its present policyholders, many of whom conceivably, are loyal American citizens.[68]

The "dawn of actual firing" referred to was the Korean War and the fear that Communist China, having joined its North Korean allies with Russia behind this effort, presented imminent conditions for a new world war. The thrust of the Robbins argument was, how could you let the law protect the domestic enemy? Speaking with the urgency of what he called "the present emergency,"[69] he also cited with approval the "take the money and run" argument.

The State's efforts proved victorious. Not one argument had been won by the IWO attorneys, although the striking of a portion of the materials cited by Haley implicitly confirmed in part their hearsay argument. On the other hand, Robbins had gone further than Haley by accepting the Williams argument that the Order was an "affiliate of the Communist Party," and "advocates the overthrow of the government by force and violence," conclusions that Haley had not even drawn.

It may well be questioned whether Robbins could be expected to have ruled in favor of the IWO. He was specifically selected by the Governor for the job as Hearing Officer and designated as an Assistant Superintendent of Insurance for this purpose. Although he was formally bound to objectivity, the circumstances of his appointment must be kept in mind. Favoring the IWO would have meant disputing the finding of a Chief Examiner in his own Department. Moreover, Robbins's views reflected conformity with the Cold War–Red Scare times.

The IWO had been named as a subversive organization by the U.S. Attorney General. The Korean War was going badly; on December 1, 1950, President Truman stated that the United States was in a fight for national survival. Russia had vetoed a United Nations resolution ordering Red China out of Korea. There was serious talk about using the atomic bomb. The threat of domestic "Red" sabotage in war industries was discussed. In New York, the highest state court had backed the state's ban on "subversives" teaching in the public schools. Espionage trials were making headlines.[70]

If Robbins was attached to the concept of the law as a "living thing," it can reasonably be assumed that the impact of these events impinged on his views; the willingness to flex the law to achieve a designed greater goal must have been irresistible under these circumstances and times. Put another way, it would have taken a great deal of courage to have favored the legal arguments of the IWO, to have told the Insurance Department and thus the State that it did not have a sound legal basis in insurance law for attacking this politically "dangerous" organization.

It was certainly the safer course to go with the tide of public and legal opinion. Here was an organization that since 1947 had been on the Attorney General's Subversive List. The list was the result of a federal Loyalty Program, instigated by President Truman's Executive Order number 9835. The Truman administration, under pressure to be more aggressively anti-Communist, had issued this Order. The list, formally and publicly published in March 1948, listed some seventy-eight organizations. Historian David Caute has assessed its impact: "From the outset, the list was used to intimidate and morally outlaw the Left, to pillory and ostracize critics of the Truman administration and to deter potential critics."[71]

In 1950 the IWO was in the midst of fighting that designation. It had already lost in the Federal District Court for the District of Columbia and in the Court of Appeals. But the U.S. Supreme Court had agreed to hear an appeal of the case so that, while ultimate disposition of the subversive listing issue was still open when Robbins made his decision, his blow against "subversiveness" was consistent with the legal tenor of the times.[72]

An additional weapon in the Red Scare war was the use of the Internal Revenue Service to deny tax-exempt status to any listed organization; the IWO was one of the organizations so affected. This meant that any funds collected for charitable purposes would not be tax deductible to contributors. Caute comments that this move "punctured the claim that the purpose of the list was solely to assist the federal Personnel Loyalty Program," concluding that "America now had a government of men, not of laws."[73]

Notes

1. Trial Record, pp. 2867–3106.
2. Trial Record, p. 41.
3. Williams interview, July 25, 1988 and letter to author, February 27, 1990.
4. Williams interview, July 25, 1988.
5. David Caute, *The Great Fear: The Anti-Communist Purge Under Truman and Eisenhower* (New York: Simon and Schuster, 1978), pp. 15, 33.
6. Ibid., p. 173.
7. Trial Record, p. 248.
8. Trial Record, pp. 41–246.
9. Trial Record, p. 54.
10. Trial Record, p. 53.
11. Trial Record, pp. 55–56.
12. Trial Record, pp. 58–59.
13. Trial Record, p. 65.
14. Trial Record, pp. 65–78.
15. Trial Record, pp. 84–87.
16. Trial Record, pp. 87–88.
17. Trial Record, pp. 88–89.
18. Trial Record, pp. 89–97.
19. Trial Record, p. 107.
20. Trial Record, pp. 109–21.
21. Trial Record, pp. 122–36.
22. Trial Record, pp. 138–39.
23. Trial Record, p. 146.
24. Trial Record, pp. 160–65.
25. Trial Record, pp. 165–76.
26. Trial Record, p. 178.
27. Trial Record, pp. 180–81.
28. Trial Record, p. 182.
29. Trial Record, pp. 189–93.
30. Trial Record, p. 193.

31. Trial Record, pp. 194–95.

32. Trial Record, p. 201.

33. Trial Record, p. 202.

34. Trial Record, p. 209.

35. Trial Record, pp. 204–11.

36. Trial Record, p. 219.

37. Trial Record, pp. 220–44.

38. Williams Office Files, Memorandum of Emil, dated September 27, 1950.

39. Ibid.

40. New York Insurance Law, Article XVI, paragraph 526.

41. Williams Office Files, Memoranda, Vol. I, Memorandum from Emil, dated September 27, 1950.

42. Ibid.

43. Williams interview, July 28, 1988.

44. Williams Office Files, Memorandum from Emil, dated November 13, 1950.

45. Ibid.

46. Williams Office Files, Documents, *Motion to Dismiss the Proceedings Herein; Motion to Strike the Examiner's Report and Recommendation.*

47. Williams Office Files, Documents, IWO *Brief in Support of Motion to Strike the Examiner's Report*; IWO *Brief in Support of Motion to Dismiss the Proceedings*; State's *Brief in Opposition to Motion to Dismiss Proceedings and Motion to Strike Examiner's Report*; IWO Respondent's *Reply Brief.*

48. Quoted in IWO, *Brief in Support of Motion to Dismiss the Proceedings,* p. 2.

49. Ibid., p. 3.

50. Ibid., p. 21. Emphasis added.

51. IWO *Brief In Support of Motion to Strike Examiner's Report,* p. 23.

52. Ibid., p. 36.

53. State *Brief In Opposition to Motion to Dismiss Proceedings and Motion to Strike Examiner's Report,* p. 1.

54. Ibid., p. 3.

55. Ibid., p. 32.

56. Williams interview, July 25, 1988.

57. State *Brief in Opposition,* pp. 36, 39–40.

58. Ibid., pp. 56–57.

59. IWO *Reply Brief,* p. 1.

60. Ibid., pp. 3–4.

61. Ibid., pp. 7–8.

62. Ibid., p. 19.

63. Ibid., p. 24. Emphasis in original.

64. Trial Record, p. 249.

65. Trial Record, p. 256.

66. Ibid.

67. Trial Record, p. 260.

68. Trial Record, pp. 260–61.

69. Trial Record, p. 263.

70. *New York Herald Tribune,* December 1, 1950.

71. Caute, *The Great Fear* (note 5), p. 169.

72. *International Workers Order v. McGrath,* 182 F.2d 368 (D.C. Cir. 1950); Cert. Granted, 71 Sup. Ct. 39 (1950).

73. Caute, *The Great Fear,* p. 180.

Chapter V
Into Foley Square

On Thursday, December 14, 1950, the same day Robbins issued his decision sustaining the conclusions of the Haley Report, denying all IWO motions and confirming the liquidation recommendation, the Acting Superintendent of Insurance approved the Robbins Opinion and Findings. Williams, having anticipated a favorable ruling, wasted no time. On that same day he was in Room 300 of the New York County Courthouse before Judge Henry Clay Greenberg with a *Petition* from the Insurance Department asking for an *Order to Show Cause* why the IWO should not be liquidated.

The *Petition* laid out the history of the Haley Report and Robbins review, with the Haley Report and Robbins decision attached as Exhibits. The *Petition* itself stated four grounds for liquidation. The first was that the IWO was organized "under the auspices" of the Communist Party, advocated the violent overthrow of the government, encouraged disloyalty to the United States through propaganda, and, *because* it was financially successful, was "hazardous" to the policyholders and public.[1]

The second ground was that it was listed as subversive by the U.S. Attorney General; here the petition cited the "take the money and run" argument. The third was, it invoked the Smith Act, the federal statute which made the teaching of overthrow or destruction of the government a crime; the criminal anarchy statute of New York was also thrown in for good measure. The final ground was the *ultra vires* accusation: that contrary to its application for a charter from the State, its true purposes and functions had not been stated. The prayer for relief asked the Court to proceed to a full hearing on the merits of the *Petition* on Monday, December 18, 1950.

Judge Greenberg read the *Petition* and the very next day, Friday, December 15, 1950, signed an *Order to Show Cause* directed to the IWO. This meant that on Monday the court would hear arguments and testimony as to why the Department of Insurance should not proceed with the dissolution of the Order, the liquidation of its assets, and reinsurance with another carrier. The burden was now on the IWO "to show cause" why the State should not get what it wanted—in effect, the Order now had to prove its innocence, since the *Petition* and the attached Exhibits were being taken as a presumption of guilt.

The legal burden imposed here reflected the need built into insurance law to protect policyholders and the public (who may be induced as customers) where the supervising administrative agency had, through an examination process, found wrongdoing. The entire procedure was designed to ensure that the State could act swiftly to protect the innocent policyholders and public. To this date the law and this accelerated procedure had always been used to stop financial wrongdoing; now it was being invoked by the State to stop alleged political "wrongdoing."

More importantly, however, the Court *Order,* drafted by Williams and signed by Greenberg, took the further step of stopping, as of that day, any attempt to enroll new members in the IWO or issue new policies, in effect freezing the operation of the Order. Furthermore, it put the Department of Insurance into actual control of the IWO because from that date, while the court hearing (really a trial) went on, no money could be spent—literally nothing done—without *joint* agreement of the Order and representatives of the Insurance Department.[2]

The power of insurance regulators to invoke and exercise this kind of legal muscle, predicated only on an examination process, is comparable to federal regulatory powers over banks and savings and loan institutions. These governmental agencies must be able to act swiftly and decisively in order to protect the public. With the exception of the IWO case, action like this to protect the public had always been taken where the financial position of the business, whether insurance, banking, or savings and loan, seemed in jeopardy. (Actions taken by federal agencies in the current banking and savings and loan crisis illustrate the point.)

The Cold War-Red Scare times of late 1950 encouraged the Insurance Department to use the authority vested in it by the State of New York to crush this politically radical insurance company. When asked whether the result in the IWO case would be the same if brought today, Williams responded that in current times there would have been no case brought in the first place, much less the result, although he believes the initiation and decision in the case were correct in 1950.[3]

The impact of Judge Greenberg's *Show Cause Order* was immediate, wide reaching, and devastating for the IWO. Without any opportunity to oppose the action, based as it was on existing insurance law, a group of Insurance Department staff members entered the offices of the Order on that Monday morning at its 80 Fifth Avenue headquarters. There was confusion and disorder. Essentially, the IWO was paralyzed. It could not solicit new members. It could not issue new policies. Every check, whether for benefits, payroll, or supplies, and all other pertinent documents, had to be countersigned by Insurance Department personnel.[4]

Pursuant to New York State law, the formal hearing had been a confidential one; no public announcements concerning it were made. Williams was correctly circumspect in this regard. Despite the lack of publicity about the hearing itself, news of its result spread quickly and generated inquiries noted by Williams's office. One was from a Mr. F. J. McNamara of American Business Consultants in New York. Arthur Emil, who took this call for Williams, recognized McNamara as the publisher of *Counterattack*, which Emil described as "a real red-baiting outfit," and gave him no information, stating, "my suggestion is that we do not [send him any information] and that we stay as far away from this particular organization in this case as possible." Emil's advice appears to have been followed.[5]

Williams's office, anticipating Judge Greenberg's *Show Cause Order*, was primed to move quickly and efficiently to spread the word through all legal channels and offices. Thus the banks where the IWO had funds were notified that checks must have the signature of an Insurance Department representative. Every state where the IWO did business was contacted and sent a copy of the *Show Cause Order* signed by Judge Greenberg. Copies of the *Petition* and *Show Cause Order* were also sent, with Court permission, to 1,673 IWO lodges. The U.S. Department of Justice was kept apprised, as was the Immigration and Naturalization Service. Newspapers were supplied with relevant documents.

One state, Illinois, wasted no time in beginning legal action against the IWO. On January 8, 1951, the Director of Insurance filed a *Petition for an Order to Take Possession of Assets,* reciting that the New York Superintendent of Insurance had "concluded that the defendant International Workers' [sic] Order, Inc. is 'a recruiting and propaganda unit for the Communist Party' and a 'medium of communist propaganda' and that the continuing operation of said defendant would 'constitute a hazard to the public.' "[6] There were 118 IWO lodges in Illinois, with some 14,000 members and some $9,375,000 in insurance issued. Once again, the financial status was unquestionably good.

Illinois insurance law paralleled that of New York; thus, following that state, the Illinois court issued a *Show Cause Order,* placing the IWO's local assets into the sole custody of the Illinois Department of Insurance (a step further than New York had gone with its joint custody), and moved to liquidate the IWO in Illinois. Frank Donner and Arthur Kinoy hired local counsel and entered their own appearances, obtaining delays in the question of liquidation pending the outcome of the New York trial.[7] Most of the other states where the IWO operated were willing to wait and see what would happen in the New York courts before making a move to liquidate the local assets of the Order. Williams kept them all advised.

From out of the woodwork came diverse people and organizations which, having learned about the *Show Cause Order* in New York, sent messages of inquiry and congratulations as well as pleas from IWO members to stop the process. Directed to the Insurance Department or Governor Dewey, all were dutifully forwarded to Williams's Wall Street offices for response if Williams felt it necessary. One inquiry of particular interest was from the American Civil Liberties Union. In response, the Insurance Department sent copies of documents using a letter drafted by Williams, but the ACLU never entered into the case or lent its support in any form. Another inquiry of note came from an insurance company interested in taking over the insurance business of the Order.

Confusion and fright permeated the Order's underlying lodge organizations when each received a copy of the Court's *Show Cause Order* from the New York Insurance Department. The IWO attempted to calm the waters with letters approved by the Department explaining what was happening; here the IWO stressed the need to continue collecting dues so that members' insurance would remain in good standing. One of these letters concluded:

While we are fighting this injunction against the Order in the courts, we will continue to do our utmost to serve our brothers and sisters as efficiently and as promptly as in the past. We are sure that you will do your part to do the same.[8]

Within the IWO headquarters, Insurance Department representatives monitored all activities of the Order. William Karlin, the head Insurance Department agent, reported to Williams, sending him copies of materials issued by the Order and requesting instructions as to the limits of his ability to control what the officers of the Order were doing. Arrangements were made for Karlin to have a secret phone installed in the basement of the building housing the IWO for speedy, direct confidential contact with Williams's office.[9]

During the weekend following issuance of the *Show Cause Order*, the IWO retained Raphael H. Weissman as its lead trial counsel; he had to be "educated" at breakneck speed by Donner and Kinoy as to what the case was about and a strategy had to be developed. There was general agreement that the judge assigned to the case was capable and knowledgeable, one who could understand and deal with the legal issues involved.[10]

On Monday morning, December 18, 1950, in Room 300 of the New York County Courthouse, The Honorable Henry Clay Greenberg, Judge of the Supreme Court, had before him for the first time the attorneys representing both the State and the IWO. In essence, the fact that the matter was out of the hands of the Insurance Department and now in a court of law gave the IWO its first objective opportunity to get its arguments across. Weissman directed his opening remarks to Judge Greenberg's power to have entered the *Show Cause Order,* arguing that the Court lacked jurisdiction of the case on the grounds that the *Petition* for the *Show Cause Order* was defective. In effect he was telling the Judge that the State had no just grounds at law for seeking the *Show Cause Order* and therefore his entry of that *Order* should be vacated. Greenberg assured him that he was not ruling on any of the issues, including his own jurisdiction; he set the matter over to January 8, 1951 in order to give both sides time to prepare motions and briefs on these issues.

Before adjournment to that date, Williams introduced Mr. Donegan, a representative of the local office of the U.S. Attorney and suggested that the Judge ask this man why he was in court, to which Donegan answered:

Mr. Donegan: Yes. If your Honor pleases, I am appearing here as a Special Assistant Attorney General, and as a representative of the Attorney General. I merely wish to state that the Department of Justice is cooperating with the Attorney General of the State of New York in this proceeding, and also to state that this organization is on the Attorney General's list as a subversive organization—that is the purpose of my appearance here—and that the Department of Justice will continue to cooperate with Mr. Williams and the Attorney General's office.

To which Weissman responded: This is the most extraordinary thing that ever happened in my life.[11]

Weissman went on to object that since this was, on its face, a state proceeding having nothing to do with the federal government, the move was merely an attempt to impress the Judge with the fact that "important people are here." The State also introduced a representative of the Attorney General of Pennsylvania who asserted his reason for being there was to cooperate with and assist Williams. With a few more preliminaries, including confirmation that Greenberg was assigned as the judge to hear the entire matter, there was an adjournment to the IWO case to January 8, 1951.[12]

Robbins had justified his liberal approach to New York insurance law on the basis that the "law is a living thing"; he had argued that legal interpretation must reflect the reality of the times and not leave government impotent in the face of threat and evil. The IWO, in turn, advocated the "strict constructionist–original intent" position, an argument that takes as its ultimate precept the notion that the legal system must reflect a nation of laws, not men.

This classic argument, sometimes revolving around the phrase "judicial activism," has existed in one form or another throughout American legal history. Generally, those discontented with the direction courts have taken argue either for or against strict constructionism and judicial activism, depending on which position most favors their cause. Thus, unions and labor sympathizers argued against liberal interpretations and the judicial activism that created and enforced labor injunctions that in effect outlawed strikes and boycotts in the late nineteenth century. Conversely, attacks on the New Deal and Warren Supreme Court have been made on the grounds that liberal law interpretations and judicial activism yielded undesirable welfare state and pro-criminal defense postures. To a significant extent, the politics of judicial power—who is being favored by its use—determines the critical position.

In its clash with the legal system, first in terms of administrative regulation and then the courts, IWO was forced to rely on a strict construction, conservative approach to the law. In order to further its arguments with statutory and case law, and even constitutional protections, an approach of administrative and judicial conservatism was needed. Here, the irony of radicals dependent on a conservative legal approach is evident, but American legal history also demonstrates the converse—conservatives relying on a liberal, if not radical posture of interpretation by the courts to achieve desired results.

In its *Briefs* addressed to Robbins and now before Judge Greenberg, and in its challenge to the Haley Report, the IWO was insisting on obedience to strictly construed meanings and interpretations of applicable law; it demanded, for example, that the original intent of the legislature be followed in construing such phrases as "other persons" and "hazard." To the degree that it obeyed the insurance law, which under strict interpretation it had, the IWO expected to be protected by the law. Years later, when directly asked why the Order failed to recognize its vulnerability, one officer reflecting an apparent consensus among IWO leaders responded by explaining that so long as they ran the insurance company properly, the officers felt they were safe, in effect protected, from any challenge by such compliance.[13]

What the IWO leadership failed to realize and properly assess was that the times could influence and shape the law, that administrative and judicial activism and liberal interpretations of the applicable law could place in danger the entire structure they had built for over twenty years. The times had created a milieu where strict construction might not shield them.

Peter Steinberg, while researching another case of the Red Scare era in the Federal District court next to where the IWO trial took place, found the words "dirty commies" written on the official case docket sheet. Reflecting on this he has observed:

The judicial system came to be used as one element in a campaign which spread a sense of political fear throughout the United States and threatened to destroy the delicate balance which has always existed between individual freedom and the perception of national security.[14]

The law, as a "living thing," functions through and acts upon people and their institutions. Nothing alive can be sustained in a vacuum; therefore the times create the milieu in which the system operates. Stability in the law, however, is to a great extent linked to the willingness to recognize and apply overriding legal principles which impose limitations on the actions of government, individuals, and the courts themselves. It is this balance—the recognition of the needs of the times against the importance of stability—which yields predictability that was in focus in early 1951.

J. Edgar Hoover's role in generating the domestic Red Scare has been the subject of scholarly attention in recent years. There is little question that he influenced President Truman to believe that an internal "fifth column" of Communists and their fellow-travelers were at the core of domestic problems. As Peter Steinberg has stated, "the president's reaction [blaming domestic Communism] indicates that the cumulating of FBI memoranda and other reports, supplemented by the rising international crisis, had been most effective. No one had been more responsible for this effect than J. Edgar Hoover."[15]

The result was an anti-Communist program by the Truman administration, soon overwhelmed by the McCarthyism that followed. Thus Truman and McCarthyism, which was to go far beyond these two powerful men, constituted two "isms" that created the Red Scare, fused together into what one chronicler of the times has called "The Great Fear."[16]

Encouraged by elements in the Catholic Church, right-wing groups, the American Legion, the U.S. Chamber of Commerce, the House Committee on Un-American Activities, conservative intellectuals, sensation-seeking newspapers and magazines, all the post-war, Korean War frustrations seemed to focus on the simple explanation of an internal enemy—domestic Communism. Hollywood writers and personalities came under attack. The perjury conviction of Alger Hiss, who had been with the State Department and even appeared at Yalta, gave credence to the existence in high places of Communists spies and plots.

The anti-Communist hysteria permeated important institutions of American life. Unions were torn over the loyalty oath issue. Many academics were fired. The atmosphere was one of fear—fear as to one's past associations, politics, or even family. Loyalty to America was no longer presumed, but had to be proven by anti-Red acts or statements. Even what one read could make one suspect.

"Anti-Communism has become so pervasive in American society since World War II that it has become an integral part of our culture," wrote Peter Buchingham.[17] Paperback books, films, television, and the theater became outlets for anti-Communist sentiment. Being a former Communist and willing to say so became a profitable way of life, producing confessional books, magazine articles, and paid testimony. These ex-Communists, a number of whom were to testify against the IWO, did not initiate the Red Scare, but certainly "helped turn attention away from the global competition between the United States and the Soviet Union and provided a rationale for domestic redbaiting and witch hunting."[18]

As already noted, the bad war news from Korea was fueling popular fears of the Soviet menace here and abroad. It was almost a year since the initial 1950 McCarthy speech, and while his theme echoed that of many others such as Richard M. Nixon, Robert Taft, John Rankin, Karl Mundt, and J. Parnell Thomas, "McCarthy's bombastic and outrageous style was singularly newsworthy, and the era's lingering images of paranoia are dominated by the accusatory Senator from Wisconsin."[19] In the years that followed, until the Army-McCarthy Hearings and his subsequent condemnation by the Senate on December 2, 1954, McCarthy's power as the leading spokesperson in what he termed "a final all out battle between Communist atheism and Christianity" was unsurpassed.[20] Thus, the bad war news from Korea was combined with a witch hunt for subversives that severely intimidated prominent segments of the entire country.

The media were relentless; anti-Communism, exposures, and accusations all made for saleable news. Careers were smashed. Hurried deportations of aliens raised little concern; after all, they were not U.S. citizens entitled to the protection of the American legal system. School boards could ban books and discharge teachers for what they read, what they thought, or with whom they associated—in effect, intimidate them as they themselves were being intimidated by the cry for conformity. Congressional committees created headlines, trampling over anyone who failed to cooperate by refusing to name names, admit having believed in or belonged to the Party, or even having known someone who in any way was "suspect." The same was true of many state and local governments who carried on anti-Communist crusades.

That the legal system also could and would be used as a Red Scare weapon was clearly intended by some. In an August, 1949 article in *Look* magazine, U.S. Attorney General Tom C. Clark, just before his appointment to the Supreme Court, wrote under a headline: "Why the Reds Won't Scare Us Any More." He stated that, although it was costing as much as one million dollars a trial, the Justice Department had Communists "on the run," pointing to "a record of real accomplishment against subversives in our midst . . . coupled with full regard for civil liberties." Claiming that "our score is high," he recited the case of eleven top Communists being brought to trial in New York (the *Dennis* case), thirty-four alleged Communists convicted for contempt of Congress, twenty-five more found in contempt of state bodies in California, and seven more in Colorado.

Furthermore, Clark stated that under the President's Employee Loyalty Program launched March 21, 1947, the FBI "had checked over two and one-half million people, resulting in prosecution of seven Federal employees. As of April, some 3,278 aliens were in the process of being deported," with more promised. Clark then called for stronger peacetime laws to strengthen the hand of his Department and excoriated "Red" lawyers.[21]

Today, some forty years later, historians now able to look behind the scenes have found that it was J. Edgar Hoover and his FBI who pushed for the indictment and trial of the top Communist Party leaders against his doubting and reluctant boss, Attorney General Clark. Hoover wanted his crusade against Communism to bear the fruit of convictions, as well as justify his direction of the enormous expenditure of money, time, and effort. The Attorney General knew that no evidence existed establishing Communist efforts in this country as a genuine threat, and doubt was expressed that the Smith Act was legally sufficient for a successful prosecution of the top Communist Party members. Hoover, however, by exerting pressure directly and through powerful intermediaries, got his way. He apparently had a better feeling for the mood of the country—that the courts and law would bend to the anti-Communist crusade that he had been so involved in creating.[22]

Clark got what he wanted from Congress in the form of the Internal Security Act of 1950, commonly known as the McCarran Act, passed over Truman's veto on September 23, 1950. Encompassing registration of Communist "organizations" and strengthening espionage laws, the Act also provided for forced detention of potential spies and saboteurs in time of national emergency.[23]

As the IWO case was working its way to Judge Greenberg, the stormy trial of the eleven top Communist Party members that lasted nine months in 1949 and had resulted in eventual conviction before Judge Medina, was on appeal before the U.S. Supreme Court. Along with the Hiss perjury case, Judith Coplon was convicted for espionage; these were three of the more famous trials dominating the news. Additionally, the Rosenberg atomic spy case was about to be tried in the federal court adjacent to the state court where Judge Greenberg was hearing the IWO matter.

Henry Clay Greenberg was a devoted newspaper reader; his first love and vocation had been print journalism.[24] During the IWO trial he had published a long essay entitled, *The Bench, the Bar and the Press,* a critical review of the role of each in the reporting of trials, and the influence of the press on the bench; as will be seen, this writing came up during the IWO trial.[25]

Judge Greenberg had been reading about the same foreign and domestic events of late 1950 that were evident in the Robbins Opinion. In mid-December 1950, news of the Korean War continued to be bad, with United Nations forces (mainly American) continuing to retreat; on January 4, 1951, Seoul, the capital of South Korea, fell to North Korean and Communist Chinese forces.

Just as the IWO case came before him, the *New York Times,* which the Judge read regularly, had carried an advertisement from an AFL local that recited, "Communism Is Treason, Wake Up America." Earl Browder, former head of the Party, and four others had been jailed for contempt of Congress for refusing to answer questions put to them by Senator McCarthy; Judge Greenberg's friend Judge Medina was honored by the American Legion for his work in presiding at the Communist trial; a rabbinic group had called for a moral crusade against Communists; twenty-nine more people were indicted for contempt of Congress, while the Supreme Court heard arguments on the Smith Act Communist convictions; Coplon's conviction was overturned, but not the indictment; and Hiss's conviction was unanimously upheld by the U.S. Court of Appeals.

The government asked for a 25 year sentence for a spy for Russia who instead got the maximum of 30 years. Writer Howard Fast, having served three months for contempt of Congress, was barred from speaking at New York University. Eight teachers were fired for refusing to answer whether they were Party members. These news items all appeared in the two weeks preceding Judge Greenberg's entry of the *Stay Order.*[26] The day he signed the *Order,* Governor Dewey was quoted as asking for total mobilization to combat Communist aggression, President Truman was reported as ready to proclaim a

State of National Emergency, and Secretary of State Marshall warned that "[a] single word from the other side" could start an all-out world war.[27]

By January 8, 1951, when the IWO matter resumed, not only had Seoul fallen but American casualties in Korea had risen to over 40,000 in dead and wounded. The parade of contempt cases and accusations of subversion and Communist leanings against people from all walks of life continued unabated. Senator McCarthy was maintaining his accusations in rapid-fire declarations. The perjury trial of William Remington, former Commerce Department aide, had commenced. All CBS employees, including radio and television performers, had been asked to take a loyalty oath. Judge Greenberg's colleague on the bench, Judge Samuel Dickstein, had sustained the refusal of a New York hotel to rent a room to a group seeking to honor actor Paul Robeson, an IWO member. A local New York bar group had endorsed disbarment for two lawyers who had represented convicted Communist Party members.

At Christmas, President Truman had called for "all [to] join in the fight against the tyranny of Communism," while on New Year's, the Soviet press had boasted that in the second half of the twentieth century "all roads [would] lead to Communism."[28]

Other judges on the bench with Greenberg had already shown antiradical colors: Justice Aaron Levy, in apparent disregard of the law as interpreted by the U.S. Supreme Court, had refused to extradite the perjurious ex-Communist professional informer, George Hewitt, thus protecting him from trial in the state of Washington; this matter would come up later in the IWO trial. In May, 1950 Judge E. L. Hammer had handed down the first decision supporting the right of a union to discipline its members solely on the grounds of Party membership. He laced the opinion with quotations from Hoover, Truman, and General Douglas MacArthur. Citing the Attorney General's List, Hammer concluded that the alleged activities of those forced out of the union were "anticountry and antiunion and completely political."[29]

Another factor to be weighed as the IWO case came before Judge Greenberg was politics. In the Congressional elections of November 1950, Republican Party candidates were frantic in their attacks on the Truman administration, particularly against Secretary of State Dean Acheson who had dared to state that he would not turn his back on Alger Hiss.

Representative Robert Rick (R.-Pa.) charged that Acheson was on Stalin's payroll. Representative Harold Velde (R.-Ill.) recited that "Soviet spies were infesting the entire country, like gypsy moths," while Senator William E. Jenner (R.-Ind.) called General George C. Marshall a "front man for traitors, a living lie who had joined hands with this criminal crowd of traitors and appeasers who, under the continuing influence of Truman and Acheson, are still selling America down the river." President Truman was denounced in the Senate as one of the "egg-sucking liberals" whose pitiful squealing would "hold sacrosanct those Communists and queers" who had "sold China into atheistic slavery."[30] Seven thousand Republican party workers received a newsletter accusing the government of covering up for traitors, subversives, and sexual perverts.[31]

Liberals were under attack; many lost primary and general elections for Congress and local governments. Red-baiting was successfully used by candidates in both parties. Vito Marcantonio, Vice-President of the IWO and a member of Congress, went down in defeat in 1950 after casting the sole vote in opposition to the Korean War. In the Congressional session prior to the election, members of both Houses had tried to outdo each other in sponsoring anti-Communist bills. To anyone with political ambitions, the message, regardless of party, was very clear.

In January 1951, the Senate established its own investigating committee—the Senate Internal Security Subcommittee (SISS)—in an attempt to steal the limelight from HUAC with its special brand of investigations. This Committee was in addition to McCarthy's own Subcommittee on Investigations. Thus by early 1951 there existed at least three investigating committees, each demanding the attention of the national audience, and each vying for attention with simultaneous state and local "investigations."

Congress had authorized a total 285 investigations between 1789 and 1925; between 1950 and 1952 it authorized no fewer than 225, thirty-four of them on the subject of Communism. Parenthetically, during the same years in England there were no legislative investigations, tribunals of inquiry, or royal commissions investigating Communism, subversion, or disloyalty.[32] The Red Scare was to remain a peculiar American virus.

By 1951 even physical violence attended the anti-Communist crusade, with the breakup of Party meetings and a riot in Peekskill, New York, in 1949 following a meeting of leftists, including Paul Robeson, who had been conducting an interracial rally. Little wonder that William L. Shirer, reflecting on this era, has written:

As I struggled through my first years back home, trying in my broadcasts and newspaper columns to make some kind of sense of what was going on, I began to wonder if my beloved country was turning into a lunatic bin. I had lived through the nightmare years in Nazi Germany. Were there to be nightmare years at home?[33]

Because Henry Clay Greenberg was a diligent judge knowledgeable about major trends in the law, he was familiar not only with the *Dennis* case tried by his friend and mentor Judge Medina, but also with its appeal to the Federal Court of Appeals for the Second District, located in New York. In October 1949 this trial of the eleven top Communist Party leaders had resulted in guilty verdicts for all, with fines and prison terms. When the appeal came before the Appeals Court, its Chief Justice was the venerable 79-year-old "legal saint," Learned Hand.[34] His 20,000 word judgment, giving the Court's unanimous affirmation of the convictions, has been described by David Caute as "deeply biased in favor of the prevailing political assumptions of the day,"[35] and as "a product of hysteria."[36]

Judge Hand had found a "clear and present danger" in the Communist Party and that the "gravity of the 'evil' discounted by its improbability, justified such invasion of free speech as is necessary to avoid the danger." With an opinion laced with extensive references to the world situation in 1950, Hand put his own and his court's prestigious seal on these political convictions.[37] While the case would proceed to the U.S. Supreme Court on appeal, the impact of Hand's decision on the legal community was important. Significantly, both Frank Donner and Arthur Kinoy, standing before Judge Greenberg in January 1951 as backup to Weissman, were both on the defense team in the *Dennis* case.

We now return to the courtroom setting on that Monday morning, January 8, 1951, some three weeks after the initial hearing. In attendance were Williams, Weissman, Donner, and three lawyers representing the U.S. Attorney General, the Department of Insurance of Pennsylvania, and the Attorney General of Massachusetts. In addition two new attorneys, Milton H. Friedman and Thomas R. Jones, made their appearance before Judge Greenberg.

Friedman and Jones were there to present a petition to intervene in the proceedings on behalf of a group known as the International Workers Order Policyholders' Protective Committee. Friedman explained in his presentation to the court that he and Jones represented a group of over 2,000 IWO members who had organized to intervene in the proceedings, which they asserted were prejudicial to their interests; this group opposed the liquidation.

Behind this move was a bit of trial strategy, probably conceived by the IWO lawyers and immediately endorsed and acted on by the Order's leadership. The idea was to have a separate entity—this Committee—apart from the IWO itself protest the proceeding to liquidate on the grounds of their *property interest* in the policies issued to them by the IWO. It would mean another basis for objection and another voice in opposition, which it was hoped would cement the membership to the cause and perhaps open up some legal avenue that could save the Order in the name of the contractual rights of its policyholders. Jerry Trauber, National Director of the Junior [Youth] Section of the Order, resigned from the IWO to head up this Committee.[38]

In arguing the merits of this intervention, Friedman, a bright and articulate attorney, pointed to statutory authority for such a move, explaining that the "very essence" of the State's position was that the policyholders' interests were not being represented by the IWO (rather, it was representing the political interests of the Communist Party), so the policyholders themselves had joined together to guard their interests. Weissman, of course, had no objection, so the Judge turned to Williams. Williams argued that the interests of the Order and of the policyholders were identical (to which the Judge disagreed) and that allowing the application might bring a number of other intervening groups which would clog the proceedings. Assured by counsel that there would be no further interventions by other policyholder groups, the Court granted the application to intervene.[39]

Behind these legal arguments, and in fact behind all that was to follow, was the long shadow of the *Dennis* trial with its histrionics. All parties including Judge Greenberg wanted to avoid the circus-like atmosphere that had frequently pervaded that trial; a reading of the trial record in the IWO case bespeaks this air of caution. The vital fact that this proceeding did not include a jury helped keep it from becoming more "theatrical" than would have been the case had a jury been involved. On the other hand, given the milieu in which the IWO trial took place, the highly charged emotional content of who and what was involved was always present: twelve jurors might not have been there, but two more powerful factors—prejudice and passion—certainly were evident.

On December 18, 1950, Judge Greenberg had assured Weissman that he would have "full freedom of action" on January 8, 1951; this meant Greenberg would entertain any motion or challenge to his own act in issuing the *Show Cause Order* and injunction that had put the State in joint control of the IWO, especially since it was done "ex parte" (without the presence or argument of the other side), on the basis of the State's *Petition*.[40]

For almost two hours, interrupted only by brief comments and questions from the Judge, Weissman spoke in support of the IWO's request to vacate the judicial actions of December 18, 1950. Ranging over all the issues and allegations contained in the State's documents, Weissman attempted to focus attention on what he believed the Judge should find relevant: that the Order was financially solvent, that the Haley Report and Robbins Opinion related to what a few officers or members thought and said, in main, many years before, and that to liquidate the Order because of the politics of some individuals was unprecedented in the legal history of New York (or of any other state). He pointed out that the "subversive" listing by the Attorney General had been thrown out by Robbins as irrelevant, yet had reappeared in the State's *Petition*.

Weissman moved smoothly from point to point, examining all aspects of the Haley Report and the Robbins Opinion, responded with cogent arguments, and demanded that the Court focus on what he stated was genuinely relevant and admissible under the law. He did not duck the political issues of the times, pointing out that the recitation of evidence of the Order's politics was "just the examiner's own way of trying very hard to identify these people with something [i.e., Communism] that happens to be unpopular now," and commented that, the "Superintendent of Insurance has no business whatever to interfere with this corporation."[41]

He also went into depth on the "hazard" issue, arguing that it is in the province of the State legislature to change the plain meaning of "hazard," explaining that the Superintendent cannot "arrogate to himself legislative power." Quoting from Robbins's Opinion wherein he had stated that "In the face of a danger clear and present, the state can use all its visitorial power to remove the threat to its own life," Weissman observed that the last time "we heard that kind of talk was from Louis XIV, who said the state was he," to which Judge Greenberg quipped, "you forgot Frank Hague [a famous political boss who had said he was the law] of New Jersey." But both men knew that Robbins had been paraphrasing Learned Hand on the Court of Appeals decision in the *Dennis* case. What Weissman was attempting to do was paint a picture of bureaucratic arrogance, of a judicial system acting in total disregard of statutory and case law.[42]

With his knowledge of insurance law from his practice in this area, Weissman delved deeply into the problem of interpreting the meaning of "hazard." Judge Greenberg interrupted his presentation to ask, "assume a case where its political activities would endanger its financial structure, what would you say of such a situation?" Weissman responded by arguing that the Superintendent is limited to financial hazard; to broaden the definition to pure politics, he explained, would be an unconstitutional delegation of power to an administrative official.[43]

Ranging into every corner and question presented by the State's *Petition* and Exhibits (the Haley Report and Robbins Opinion), Weissman attempted to meet every argument raised by the State. That he could speak at such length without losing his train of thought and essentially without written notes reflects the training and abilities of this highly skilled trial professional.

Weissman grew impassioned on the subject of the crippling effect of Greenberg's *Show Cause Order* and injunction on the IWO. He made the point that the *Show Cause Order,* placing the Superintendent in joint control of the IWO and stopping all new business, constituted "nine-tenths of [an] instantaneous liquidation." He could understand how the Judge, in responding to a "presumably . . . responsible official of the state," could have been led to sign the *Order* but was now asking for immediate relief on the grounds that there was no emergency support-ing such drastic action. He ended by asking for the Court's consent to the General Convention call, for which monies had already been ex-pended.[44]

Having completed his lengthy argument and having called for the vacating of the Court's earlier *Order,* Weissman sat down. Judge Green-berg turned to Friedman and asked whether he wanted to speak; Friedman began by essentially supporting Weissman's position. and then focused on the impact on the IWO of the December *Order.* Specifi-cally, his concern was for the General Convention call. Reciting the democratic procedure mandated by law and followed by the IWO, Friedman asked that the Court instruct the Superintendent of Insur-ance to cooperate by permitting the holding of the convention and the further expenditure of monies for that purpose.

Paul Williams had not said a word all morning; he had remained silent throughout both Weissman's and Friedman's presentations. Now Judge Greenberg turned to Williams for a response; Williams asked to begin in the afternoon, and the Court adjourned.

Using an outline to stay on track, Williams was, in effect, mustering arguments to convince the Judge that he had not erred in issuing the *Show Cause Order* which had put the Superintendent in joint control of the IWO and frozen the Order's business. He reviewed the back-ground of the Haley Report and Robbins Opinion in order to dispel any intimation that this proceeding could be compared to the conduct of a Louis XIV. Going into a brief description of how the IWO func-tioned as a fraternal benefit organization, Williams wasted no time in linking the IWO to the Communist Party, calling it "the financial backbone of the Communist Party in this country."[45]

Contending that the IWO was organized "by the directions or in-structions from the international Communist Party in Russia," Wil-liams reviewed all the allegations made by Haley and accepted by Robbins. He spiced his arguments with references to the Attorney

General's List and the fact that IWO membership had been grounds for deportation of unnaturalized aliens. He stated:

In less desperate times, I might point out also, our people could afford to be lax and permit the existence of such an organization as this one, which advocates the violent overthrow of the government, but, today, it is a luxury that we cannot afford, and I will argue that the time has long since past when a well-recognized publicly labeled Communist front can operate under a charter from the State of New York.[46]

By explaining the State's version of "hazard," Williams pointed out that a large percentage of IWO funds were liquid and in the hands of officers who were Communist Party members or who owed their first allegiance to a "foreign power."[47]

There followed this colloquy between the Judge and Williams:

The Court: Has this liquid position of the organization been something that has existed for a long period of time?

Mr. Williams: Yes, your Honor. I believe they have always been liquid.

The Court: Is that something for which they should be condemned? I always thought an organization that is not liquid was more to be condemned than one that is in a liquid financial position.

Mr. Williams: That is true. I don't say they should be criticized for that, but I say in the event of war, and I don't think I can say or your Honor can say we won't have war with Russia within a year, to have these funds in the hands of men who espouse a loyalty to the Soviet Union ahead of any loyalty to the United States is extremely hazardous to the public, to the State of New York, and to the policyholders.

The Court: Is it as bad as that?

Mr. Williams: It certainly is. I had no idea until I got into this case and talked to the witnesses whom I will put on the stand, as to the extent and direction and control and discipline of this organization, and of the Communist party, and I am certainly no novice.[48]

The Judge wanted Williams to respond to the argument that the Department of Insurance was limited to dealing with a financial hazard. He did so by arguing that indeed the Superintendent of Insurance had that power. Williams also implied that while the U.S. Attorney General and the Governor would like to liquidate the IWO, such a move was not within their discretion, but it was within the broad powers of the Department of Insurance. Judge Greenberg then summed up Williams's argument as follows:

The Court: Your argument about the financial hazard is really predicated on the assumption that since this is a Communist-dominated organization, and since further we are apt to go to war with Russia, the controlling interest will take the money of the treasury, which is liquid, and thus it will financially affect the structural status of the corporation and hence this is a hazardous undertaking.[49]

In essence, it was the "take the money and run" position once again. Under questioning by the Court, Williams admitted there was no legal precedent for his interpretation of "hazard" in New York or elsewhere, arguing instead that the language should be broadly interpreted so that this "Frankenstein monster," as he called the IWO, could be dealt with effectively. He then proceeded with the theme of Communist creation and control of the IWO, insisting that liquidation was the only answer.

The Judge asked whether reorganization in lieu of liquidation might not serve the purpose, but Williams objected, describing the IWO as "cancerous" and "rotten" and on a quest to overthrow the government; he added that one of the reasons the State objected to allowing the Order to hold its convention was in order to avoid any "change of face" or "new facade." By openly boasting that the federal government was fully cooperating in his effort, Williams was urging Judge Greenberg to do his patriotic duty and rule in the State's favor. Williams pulled out the stops by describing the organization as "evil" and by alleging that the top members of the organization, as well as those in charge of local lodges, were "Commies."[50]

Judge Greenberg, who had often injected questions and comments during the speeches of both Weissman and Williams, interrupted when Williams began to portray the IWO as a recruiting ground for the Party:

The Court: I met a doctor the other night who said he holds a policy in this organization, and he was surprised to find out that it was Communist-controlled, as you put it.[51]

Good trial attorney that he was, Williams bounced right back, agreeing that there are "probably many such people" (surely the Judge would not associate with "Commies"), using this to illustrate how a "front organization," as a tool of the Party, brought people to the point of being critical of the government and ultimately so indoctrinated them that they were selectively asked to join the Party. Williams flatly stated that the IWO was "the great recruiting ground for the Communist Party."[52] He added, "I am ashamed to think that the State of New York has permitted such a condition [the existence of the IWO] to exist since 1930."[53]

Williams promised the Court the testimony of "very distinguished and well-known ex-Communists" who would identify the IWO as the "financial backbone" of the Communist Party. This brought the following reaction from the Judge:

The Court: Let us not forget we are not trying the Communist party in this lawsuit.

Mr. Williams: No.

The Court: We have one big question before us, and that is whether or not the Superintendent of Insurance has the power to invoke the jurisdiction of the Supreme Court to dissolve and liquidate the IWO on the ground that it is a hazard to the public welfare which, as you say and which Mr. Weissman disputes, goes beyond a financial hazard, or the reasonable likelihood of it becoming a financial hazard. Let us say that they have been using their money improperly or something to that extent.

Mr. Williams: That is right.

The Court: I don't want this case to go off on a tangent of Communism during the trial. I think we should try to adhere closely to the narrow legal issues in this case, and, as I see it, with all due deference to the very persuasive argument presented by Mr. Weissman, I think the one big point of the case is just what I mentioned a moment ago; does what you claim they have been doing come within the definition of the word "hazard" in the light of the history of the enactment and in the light also of the realities of a given situation.

Mr. Williams: That is correct, sir.

The Court: And I confess it is a troublesome question. Maybe not so much to you as it is to me.[54]

This question of testing in the light of "the realities of a given situation" was a clear indication that Judge Greenberg felt it necessary to operate not in a "legal vacuum" but in response to the times; his characterization of the question as "troublesome" led him to state that he was taking that issue under advisement, which meant delaying any decision on the IWO motions to strike and dismiss.

Judge Greenberg followed that statement by taking up the question of whether to allow the IWO to hold its convention. He pointedly asked Williams what harm would come if the convention were held in New York City as planned. Williams argued that, despite what Weissman had stated, the Order *was* receiving the cooperation of the Insurance Department in its daily activities, but that to allow more money (it had already spent $20,000) would be wrong because "this is a subversive organization and they are working against the Government of the United States." "Why give them an opportunity" he asked, "to do the very things they are enjoined from doing, and [carry] on . . . a campaign which I have no doubt will be directed against the Superintendent and against your Honor."[55] The Judge reacted by telling Williams not to worry, that he could take care of himself. What Williams had attempted to play on was Greenberg's knowledge of the left's vilification of Judge Medina during his conduct in the *Dennis* trial.

Again the Judge pressed Williams to agree to allow the Order to hold its convention. Williams responded by reiterating the State's position that the IWO was subversive and organized to "defeat the Government of the United States and overthrow it by force" and, on a more mundane level, argued that a convention would allow it to put in new officers or "try to change their face."[56]

One gets a clear sense from the record that the Judge, in the name of fairness and equity, literally pleaded with Williams to give in on this point. Weissman argued that $20,000 had already been committed and the convention call had been issued prior to the *Show Cause Order.* Williams and Weissman also argued over whether the deposits could be returned.

More heated debate followed, ranging away from the convention issue back into the matter of lifting the *Show Cause Order,* and then back again to the convention issue as Friedman joined in on behalf of the Policyholders' Protective Committee. The result was that Judge Greenberg refused to rule on either the convention matter or the more important motions to strike and dismiss the entire proceedings; he said he wanted more time to think over and study these issues.[57]

What each side wanted was clear. Williams, representing the State of New York, wanted to try the issue of whether the Superintendent could proceed to liquidate the IWO; as an ancillary, he did not want a convention which might muddy his waters. On the other hand, the IWO wanted the Judge to rule on its motions to lift the hand of the Department of Insurance from the operation of the Order, hold a convention to rally the membership to its cause, and allow it to take such action as might improve its position while demonstrating with a convention the democratic nature of the organization.

But there was more at stake for the IWO and its legal position: if Judge Greenberg ruled against the Order on its motions to strike and dismiss, it could appeal those rulings immediately, thus delaying any trial on the liquidation issue; if he favored the IWO motions, the State would lose its hold on the Order and *they* would have to appeal Greenberg's decision.

While these arguments were being heard in court, some 500 IWO members, organized by the Policyholders' Protective Committee, traveled to Albany, New York, to meet with Governor Dewey in order to protest the Insurance Department's action. Dewey had his "confidential law assistant" meet with representatives of the group. The group urged the Governor to stop a "usurpation of power" that the "people and the legislature never gave" the Insurance Superintendent, adding that such a proceeding had happened "only in Hitler Germany in the years 1933 to 1945 when confiscation of property for political, social, racial or religious reasons was recognized as a legitimate function of government," and never to an organization that was outstandingly "financially stable."[58]

At the same time, the news of the Korean War continued to be bad for United Nations forces. The Eighth Army headquarters had imposed full censorship on news from the front and banned the use of the word "retreat," threatening to court-martial any correspondent who used it. At home, McCarthy had accused nationally known columnist and radio personality Drew Pearson of being a Communist, and self-confessed Soviet spy courier Elizabeth Bentley had testified that William Remington, a former State Department employee, had passed secrets to her. An official of the Civil Rights Congress (another organization on the Attorney General's list) was arrested and charged with violating the Subversive Activities Control Act.[59]

On Wednesday January 10, 1951, Judge Greenberg once again heard extensive arguments of counsel, as representatives of the U.S. Attorney's office and the Attorneys General of at least two states listened; the Judge characterized them all as "watchful observers."[60]

The Judge then ruled that no convention would be allowed except under the joint agreement and supervision of the Superintendent of Insurance; since the Superintendent would not allow one prior to the trial, the Court's position effectively barred the Convention. Judge Greenberg also refused to vacate the *Show Cause Order,* or to dismiss the proceedings. It should be noted that he did not rule against the IWO; he refused to rule one way or the other. This move effectively prevented any appeal at that point to any higher court. He simply held these crucial motions in limbo, promising a decision when he had read and heard enough to allow him to rule.

He promised to read the *Briefs* filed on these motions as submitted by the IWO (which they had already prepared, running some 97 pages) and that the State would provide (some 23 pages), and dangled the possibility of a ruling (which would then be an appealable order) at any time thereafter. Meanwhile, Greenberg wanted the trial to commence and evidence to be presented, stating once again that after he heard the evidence he might ultimately find that the Superintendent had acted outside the scope of his authority and thus favor the IWO motions.[61] This crucial victory for the State meant that the IWO was locked into a trial; its efforts to focus on the statutory and case law involved, divorced from the politics of its leadership and of the news of the day, had failed.

Judge Greenberg's rulings made news. The *New York Herald Tribune* headlined its coverage "Court Forbids Convention of IWO Saturday; State Says Aim is Election of New Officers Less Easy to Identify as Reds." Williams was quoted as stating:

> It is clear that the sole function of the convention will be to carry out the instructions of the Communist party. It may also be assumed that the entire aim of the convention will be to whitewash the International Workers Order.

These words were spoken outside the courtroom, and do not appear in the trial record. The paper also quoted IWO President Rockwell Kent as follows:

> The superintendent's action has the purpose of confiscating the savings and insurance of our members and turning them over to the large insurance monopolies. His action represents a fundamental attack on the well established and democratic principle of fraternalism.[62]

Under the heading, "Court Ban Issued on Workers Order; Fraternal Group, Classed as Subversive, is Forbidden to Hold Convention Here," the *New York Times* joined in the news of Greenberg's decision. Williams was again quoted on the Communist connection.[63] In both instances, neither newspaper revealed the more important though technically complicated ruling that meant the trial of the case would begin.

Judge Henry Clay Greenberg had exercised a power that, while not unique in character, was nevertheless unusual. Plainly put, he could have gotten rid of the case and the burden of what both sides assured him would be a long and difficult trial by ruling on the IWO motions. If he ruled in favor of the IWO and the higher court or courts affirmed him on appeal, then the matter would be over. If he ruled in favor of the State and was affirmed on appeal, he would most likely have gotten the case back to try but with the major issues of law already decided, so that he would only have had to apply his fact-finding to the legal interpretations of higher courts, thus considerably lessening his task and his vulnerability to criticism. Why Greenberg chose to deny a basis for appeal by refusing to rule on the motions is subject to speculation. His reasoning may have been clarified in the lost memoirs he wrote some years later.[64]

By trying this case, Judge Greenberg would have the opportunity to engage in the kind of case that quickly caught the eye of the public, the bench, the bar, the press, and the government. A case like this could make a judge's reputation, possibly opening the way to advancement up the judicial ladder. It had happened to others. In addition, this trial, with the complex issues and the characters involved, presented an opportunity that was undoubtedly intellectually stimulating. This was to be Judge Greenberg's first and last Red Scare case.

The suave Williams challenged by the feisty Weissman would certainly make for some exciting days ahead. Whatever his motives, Greenberg insisted that the presentation of evidence proceed and, despite vigorous objection from Weissman, stuck to his position, refusing to rule one way or the other on the crucial testing motions. He got the parties to agree to start presenting witnesses six days later.

The intervening days brought continued bad news on the Korean War front. Domestically, McCarthy and the Red Scare predominated: thirteen AFL officers were barred for three years from participation in union affairs for "Communist activities"; a call was issued by the government for civic leaders to assist in the battle against "Red Ideology"; and Attorney General McGrath (who succeeded Clark) urged calm and warned against labeling "the constructive critic" disloyal or subversive. The morning of the January 16 carried news of President Truman hinting that the atomic bomb might go into mass production.[65]

Instead of hearing witnesses present testimony, Judge Greenberg heard four lawyers engage in lengthy legal arguments. Weissman would not give up on his attempt to force the judge to rule on the crucial IWO motions, with Friedman and Jones joining in on behalf of the Policyholders' Protective Committee. Williams took the position that he was ready for trial and ready to present evidence through witnesses to support the *Petition for Liquidation.*

The arguments presented by Weissman basically challenged the standing of the State to seek liquidation of the IWO on both procedural and substantive grounds. Williams retorted by urging that all Weissman's arguments had been heard before and that the statutory and case law did in fact support both the substance and procedure of the State's position. Judge Greenberg questioned Williams closely, forcing him to argue the points Weissman had raised; this is frequently done to make the responding lawyer stay on track and to elicit exact responses instead of simply a counterspeech.

Attorney Thomas Jones asked to be heard. He was black, and the Policyholders' Protective Committee had apparently retained him in part to send a message to the Judge: IWO members act on their beliefs; they believe in racial equality and have retained a black lawyer in a case where blacks made up a relatively small portion of the organization whose cause was at issue.[66] This move was highly unusual for its time.

Addressing what must have been on the minds of all, Jones argued that this entire matter was an attempt to "dissolve a going concern on

the basis of the hysteria which surrounds us." Judge Greenberg immediately broke in to deny that this would influence him. But Jones
persisted, stating that "In normal times this [the suit to destroy the
Order] would never happen," urging the Court to "stand firm" against
this attempt. Arguing that "irreparable damage" had been done to the
policyholders "simply because the Superintendent of Insurance decides he doesn't like the politics, perhaps, of some of the leaders of the
organization," Jones concluded by characterizing the proceeding as
nothing more than a "witch hunt."[67]

Williams had to respond to this and promptly did so, stating that the
action was "not the result of any impetuous or momentary desire of the
Superintendent to follow any course of conduct based on a current war
scare, or the present emergency," pointing out that the listing of the
IWO as subversive by the Attorney General occurred long before the
current [Korean War] crisis.[68] Weissman retorted by pointing out that
what was truly unprecedented about this case was that the attempt to
liquidate "[was] based on political grounds, and [that] never in the
history of this country, not only this State," had such an attempt been
made.[69]

After further lengthy arguments surrounding the issue of the pending motions by the IWO, Judge Greenberg again stated that he would
not rule; he would hold the IWO motions "in abeyance" and direct the
Superintendent to proceed. Weissman again pleaded for a ruling but
the Judge, while acknowledging that this was "an unusual and extraordinary proceeding," demanded that the case be tried before him, at the
same time promising that the trial would be "completely removed from
the hysteria which may exist today, altogether separate from the hue
and cry which unfortunately exists to a great extent in the country at
this present time."[70]

Yet Weissman renewed his arguments. He tenaciously clung to
the demand that Greenberg rule so he could appeal (if against the
IWO), reminding the Judge that, in his view, by signing the *Show Cause
Order* Greenberg had "struck this organization a blow from which it
will never recover and it is lying prostrate now," then adding in
extension of this metaphor: "Our corporation is barely breathing. It
has the foot of the Superintendent on its neck." Weissman concluded
by saying:

What I am asking your Honor to do at this time, and what I am most respectfully demanding of your Honor is that you sign an Order indicating your
decision on this motion, so that we may take an appeal and find out whether
the Court or the Superintendent has a right to drag us in here on a political
matter before we have to go through a long and arduous trial.[71]

If the ruling on the motion went against him, he had prepared a *Notice of Appeal*. Weissman's "respectful demand" was an unusual tactic in a case that was already moving in unusual ways.

Friedman then addressed the court, reiterating the political argument with these words:

Political differences are not new. They are as old as politics, and the reason that never in the history of this country has an administrative officer ever attempted to liquidate and dissolve a private corporation, an insurance corporation or any other corporation, on the basis of political grounds, is that such grounds are not recognized as proper for either an administrative or a judicial officer to act upon in that manner.[72]

But the Judge would not be moved. When it became clear that no amount of argument would sway Greenberg, the parties turned to the matter of when the trial would start. Weissman explained that he had been brought into the case just as the Judge had signed the *Show Cause Order*, had worked seven days a week since then (about a month), and needed at least three weeks to go through thousands of pages of documents. Williams argued against any such delay; the Judge adjourned the case to January 22, 1951, some six days later. Appeals for more time were rebuffed, and thus what has been described as a "long and arduous trial" finally began.

Notes

1. *Petition* and *Order to Show Cause*, Trial Record, pp. 23–35.
2. Ibid.
3. Williams interview, July 25, 1988 and correspondence with the author.
4. Trauber interviews, March 8 and 10, 1988, July 23, 1988.
5. Williams Office Files, Memoranda, Vol. I, Memorandum from Emil dated December 18, 1950.
6. *People of the State of Illinois ex rel J. Edward Day, Director of Insurance for the Department of Insurance of the State of Illinois v. International Worker's Order, Inc.*, Case # 99156, State of Illinois, County of Sangamon, 1950. Chancery.
7. Ibid.; Court File and Donner and Kinoy Office Files.
8. Williams Office Files, Memoranda, Vol. I, Letters to Lodge Financial Secretaries, December 28, 1950 and January 5, 1951.
9. Williams Office Files, Memoranda, Vol. I, Letters to Lodge Financial Secretaries; undated handwritten memo, Karlin to Williams.
10. Kinoy, Perlin, and Trauber interviews, March 10, 1988; July 23, 1988; June 28, 1989; October 27, 1989.
11. Trial Record, pp. 597–99.
12. Trial Record, pp. 600–601.
13. Trauber interviews, March 10 and July 23, 1988.
14. Peter L. Steinberg, *The Great "Red Menace": United States Prosecution of*

American Communists, 1947–1952 (Westport, CT: Greenwood Press, 1984), p. ix.

15. Ibid., pp. 9–10. Also see Kenneth O'Reilly, "The FBI and the Origins of McCarthyism," *The Historian* 45 (Spring–Summer 1983), pp. 372–93.

16. Peter H. Buchingham, *America Sees Red* (Claremout, CA: Regina Books, 1988); see also David Caute, *The Great Fear: The Anti-Communist Purge Under Truman and Eisenhower* (New York: Simon and Schuster, 1978).

17. Buchingham, *America Sees Red,* p. 216.

18. Harold Josephson, "Ex-Communists in Crossfire: A Cold War Debate," *The Historian* 44, 1 (Winter 1981), p. 69.

19. Michael J. Strada, "McCarthy's Wheeling Speech: Catalyst to Mayhem," *Upper Ohio Historical Review* 15 (Spring–Summer 1985), pp. 33–41.

20. Ibid., p. 38.

21. Tom C. Clark, "Why the Reds Won't Scare Us," *Look Magazine,* August 30, 1949, pp. 51–53.

22. Steinberg, *The Great "Red Menace"* passim.

23. Internal Security Act of 1950, 64 STAT. 987 et seq.

24. Mr. & Mrs. Greene interview, July 13, 1989.

25. Henry Clay Greenberg, *The Bench, the Bar and the Press* (Kingsport, TN: Kingsport Press, 1951).

26. *New York Times,* December 1,2,3,5,6,8,10,12, 1950.

27. *New York Times,* December 15, 1950.

28. *New York Times,* December 19,20,21,22,25, January 1,4,6, 1951.

29. Quotes appear in Caute, *The Great Fear* (note 16), pp. 141–42.

30. Quoted in William L. Shirer, *20th Century Journey: A Memoir of a Life and the Times* (1976; reprint Boston: Little, Brown and Company, 1990), p. 90.

31. Caute, *The Great Fear,* p. 37.

32. Ibid., p. 85.

33. Shirer, p. 90.

34. *United States v. Dennis,* 183 F. 2d 201 (2nd Cir. N.Y., August 1, 1950).

35. Caute, *The Great Fear,* p. 193.

36. Steinberg, *The Great "Red Menace"* (note 14), p. 198.

37. *Dennis,* Court of Appeals Decision.

38. Trial Record, pp. 603 ff.; Trauber interview, July 23, 1988.

39. Trial Record, pp. 605–11.

40. Trial Record, pp. 611–12.

41. Trial Record, pp. 612–33.

42. Ibid.

43. Trial Record, pp. 636–50.

44. Trial Record, pp. 650–53.

45. Ibid.

46. Ibid.

47. Trial Record, p. 665.

48. Ibid.

49. Trial Record, p. 668.

50. Ibid.

51. Trial Record, pp. 669–82.

52. Trial Record, p. 682.

53. Trial Record, pp. 683–84.

54. Trial Record, pp. 684–85.

55. Trial Record, pp. 688–89.

56. Trial Record, p. 689.

57. Trial Record, pp. 690–707.

58. *New York Times,* January 9, 1951.

59. *New York Times,* January 9, 10, 1951.

60. Trial Record, p. 708.

61. Trial Record, pp. 709–27.

62. *New York Herald Tribune,* January 11, 1951, p. 3.

63. *New York Times,* January 11, 1951.

64. Mr. & Mrs. Greene interview, July 13, 1989; correspondence with Mr. Greene.

65. *New York Times,* January 12–January 16, 1951.

66. Trauber interviews, March 8 and 10, 1988; July 23, 1988; October 27, 1989.

67. Trial Record, pp. 737–38.

68. Trial Record, pp. 738–39.

69. Trial Record, pp. 739–40.

70. Trial Record, pp. 745–46.

71. Trial Record, pp. 747–51.

72. Trial Record, p. 753.

Chapter VI
Trial Strategy and the Paid Informer

The January 17, 1951, edition of the *New York Times* carried a report of the IWO case under the headline, "Trial Date Set in Insurance Case; Action Against Workers Order, Accused as Communist, to Go Before Court Monday." The article featured Weissman's comments on the "witch hunt-hysteria nature" of the action and Williams's emphasis on the Communist angle, including his statement that the Order was "founded on orders from Moscow and was run by and for Communists."[1] Trial by newspaper reports had begun.

The courtroom scenes, however, relate only part of the story. The offices of the Williams team and, on the other side, Weissman, Donnor, Kinoy, Friedman, and Jones, were devoting full-time efforts to the preparation of every aspect of the case. Weissman may have been guilty of hyperbole in his language depicting the foot of the Superintendent of Insurance on the neck of the IWO, but there was no exaggeration in his claim about the time and efforts he and the other lawyers were exerting.

That which is presented in court in terms of argument, testimony, cross-examination, and thereafter written briefs constitutes merely the "tip of the iceberg" in terms of the work underlying all phases of a major litigation. Certainly, what the public sees or reads about—the decision after a major trial—is the end product of a mountain of work. Such preparation includes not only the fundamental research into case and applicable statutory or constitutional law, but also the matter of devising a strategy for framing the legal issues into cogent, convincing arguments supported by a fair reading of those cases and statutes.

Then there is the trial strategy itself. Questions include: Who is available to testify about what? Will that witness withstand sharp cross-examination? What trial moves by the other side are to be anticipated? Knowing where our side is vulnerable, how do we limit the damage? In this bench trial, what will convince the Judge from an evidentiary standpoint?

Thus hours are spent. Books of cases, statutes, and constitutional interpretations are examined; witnesses are interviewed and evaluated; documentary evidence such as correspondence, pamphlets, magazine articles, books, and newspapers are examined. Then it all must be organized, digested, written, rehearsed, and polished. All these steps and more are found in abundance in the office files of both sides. The "more" includes the mundane task of accounting for and reporting literally every penny spent by each side and chargeable to their respective clients: taxi fares, overtime for secretaries, outside photocopying services, meals while traveling or interviewing witnesses or for office help held over past the work day, books, pamphlets, and newspapers purchased—all were carefully accounted for by the firms, together with the underlying professional fees.

Williams's office files reveal that a clippings file was maintained on every article in the *Daily Worker* relating to the case or anyone in the IWO whose name was in any news article or editorial. The same was done for the *Freiheit* and the *Forward*, both in translation from Yiddish. Every other foreign language paper that might mention the IWO was reviewed by translators, and articles clipped, translated, and mounted in chronological order. All major New York papers were carefully reviewed for any coverage of the litigation; these articles also were clipped and mounted in dated order. This work went on prospectively not just for a few weeks or months but for *years* as this case and any related developments became the focus of news media attention.

Additionally, Williams's office received copies of all letters, minutes, reports, and notes generated by the Order. These were gathered by the head of the Superintendent's staff, William Karlin, who was working at IWO headquarters, and forwarded to Williams's office. From the number and variety of reports, memoranda, and copies of internal documents that found their way into the State's files, it becomes evident that there was little that the officers of the IWO could do, decide, or even discuss which, if written, would not be known to the Williams team. This certainly gave the State an unusual advantage.

Just how thorough was the State's work is illustrated by a lengthy memorandum to Williams from James B. Henry, who replaced Emil as Williams's chief assistant. Henry reported on the May Day parade of 1951 which he described as run by the Communist Party, as distinguished from the Socialist Party or the Socialist Workers' Party (the Trotskyites). He noted entertainment by a "white boy and girl and a colored boy and girl." He recounted lyrics of "militant" songs he heard sung. Of course, Henry most carefully noted the presence of IWO officers and members and the signs they carried, such as "Governor Dewey—Confiscation of the People's savings is illegal—Hands off the IWO." Henry also reported that he was "alarmed" by the large number of young people of high school and college age attending and participating.[2] Williams himself included in this file a sheet he had obtained with a sample of Weissman's handwriting, even though no explanation for needing this bit of information was given; the one word in Weissman's handwriting was "anxiety."[3]

Little of the vast amount of information and materials gathered, cataloged, and digested ever found its way into court or into the written briefs of the parties. What this vast amount of background material does indicate is thoroughness in preparation, the leaving of few unturned stones in the search for evidence and information that would yield understanding.

Another dimension of this drama was the IWO's attempt to rouse various outside organizations and members, as well as nonaffiliated individuals who might support the Order in its struggle for survival. As noted, a delegation of IWO members made a trip to Albany in early January 1951 to see Governor Dewey. This was followed later that month by a call for an "Emergency Conference" on February 10, 1951 to protest the liquidation effort. Under the signature of Rockwell Kent as President, a pamphlet was distributed announcing a mass meeting in New York City. The basic appeal made in the pamphlet was to the effect that if this could happen to a financially healthy insurance company, it could also happen to "trade unions and fraternal societies; all organizations of the people are threatened with thought control by confiscation." The pamphlet assessed the underlying cause for the State's action as war hysteria, concluding that:

Once war hysteria permits such precedents to be set, then there are no limits. Only in Hitler Germany can we find parallels to this situation—the smashing of organizations and the confiscation of private property in order to control social, civic or political thought!

The members of the IWO are working people. They are in many cases your fellow union members, or the co-members with you in other organizations. We ask you to defend their interests. We ask you to defend the IWO in order to safeguard their security—and your own American rights![4]

What was not discussed were the State's allegations of ties to the Communist Party and the presence of Communist Party members as leaders of the Order.

On the other hand, every article that appeared in major New York newspapers emphasized the "Red" connection. Thus, when the initial *Petition* was presented in court in December 1950, the headlines read:

State Suing to Disband Red Insurance Unit.[5]

State Insurance Dept. Files Suit to Dissolve I.W.O. as Red Front.[6]

Insurance Lodge Sued as Red-Ruled.[7]

Throughout the course of the trial, the IWO attempted to rally its own members to its defense, essentially on the basis that the suit was an illegal attempt to deny them their insurance for political purposes and that the loss of the Order would destroy their fraternal, social, and cultural benefits. In early 1951, elderly and disabled IWO policyholders picketed the New York Insurance Department offices.[8]

A letter over Kent's signature went out to some three hundred prominent persons urging them to recognize the implicit threat to political liberty and the right of association in the attack on the IWO. Those who received the letter had endorsed the Henry Wallace-Progressive Party campaign in 1948. The result of this effort was a dismal failure; practically no positive responses were received. Especially galling was the lack of positive response from union leaders who for many years had sought and received vital support from the IWO and its members. These were times when many were unwilling to attach their name to any cause that had been labeled "Red," regardless of the broader implications to basic freedoms.[9]

Hundreds of letters and telegrams were, however, sent to the Department of Insurance or to the Governor's office from lodges and members throughout the United States, arguing that the prosecution should be ended. Each was duly forwarded to Williams's office and cataloged. Generally, no answer was sent to the writer; where one was deemed worthy of answer, it was usually composed by Williams's office.[10] Overall, however, the IWO was never able to create a cause célébre out of its battle with the State. While the mood of Red Scare times explains to some extent why the Order's leadership was ineffective in this area, the inescapable fact was that the threat posed was to a fraternal benefit insurance company, not to an individual or small identifiable group, and thus lacked the drama of impending prison, death, or expulsion from the country as a potential punishment. The issues were less human when corporate martyrdom was involved.

Despite the apparently firm order to start the trial on January 22, 1951, by consent of all counsel and with Court approval, it was delayed another week to January 29, 1951. While the record does not reveal just who asked for this delay, such an occurrence was certainly not unusual. The opposing lawyers were, in fact, very civil and courteous with each other throughout this entire case; that did not mean there were not to be bitter clashes—there were indeed—but both in court and out, the attorneys respected each other and each other's word; although they clearly disagreed, they were not disagreeable. Undoubtedly, they all knew how terrible and recriminatory the battles had been between the lawyers in some of the other Red Scare cases of the day; it is apparent from the record and office files that all involved sought to avoid this in the IWO case. To a great extent, this task was made easier by the absence of a jury, where "theatrics" might have brought unnecessary clashes between them that would have been counterproductive in a bench trial.

On January 29, appearances were filed by the Attorneys General of New Jersey and New York, which were duly noted. Judge Greenberg then asked that Williams call his first witness.

Weissman, however, was not going to give up. His tenacity in cajoling the Judge to rule on the pending motions was more than a trial tactic; his real aim was to avoid a trial on witnesses' evidence that would inevitably focus on allegations, facts, and personalities instead of legal issues. No gain could come to the IWO side from a parade of witnesses and written materials expressing leftist political positions in the supercharged atmosphere of 1951. Regardless of Judge Greenberg's assurances, the times, pressures, and volatile nature of politics of the IWO leadership constituted a spark that could bring on a conflagration that might burn down the house that had been built over the Order's twenty-year existence.

Weissman again asked the Judge to rule, and again Judge Greenberg refused. After further arguments of a technical pleading nature, Williams called his first witness, George E. Powers.[11] Over the following days that would stretch into weeks, the State called thirteen witnesses and introduced 171 exhibits, mainly articles, pamphlets, and books. Every State witness except one claimed to be an ex-Communist, that is, a person who had either voluntarily attached him—or herself to the Party as a member and then had quit or been thrown out or, in one case, claimed to have joined the Party as a spy for the FBI. Almost all the State's witnesses were supplied by the Immigration and Naturalization Service (INS), which, as noted earlier, had been prosecuting and deporting aliens on the basis of IWO membership prior to the New York State action.

Williams, it will be remembered, credited the INS with providing witnesses and exhibit material for his prosecution. Contacts with the New York Office of the INS led to trips by Williams and his associates to

Washington, D.C., where they met with INS Central Office officials. One early meeting took place the day after Christmas, 1950; its importance is apparent from the fact that an official of the INS New York office traveled to Washington with Henry and Emil, Williams's chief associates.

In a memorandum to Williams about this meeting dated December 27, 1950, Emil reported that he received a pledge of "full cooperation" from the INS. The Williams team indicated their need for witnesses, documents, and assistance, detailing eight specific areas of help desired. First and foremost, they wanted access to all the witnesses used by the INS in the Dmytryshyn deportation case. Williams's team also wanted assistance in "gaining the confidence of witnesses used by the Immigration Service previously." Emil then reported that he had received a call from the INS in Washington confirming that he would have everything requested.[12]

Gaining access to INS witnesses was of vital importance in the State's case because it gave Williams an identified body of ready-made testimony from a stable of rehearsed, professional witnesses with which to prosecute. Almost all the State's witnesses had testified in the Dmytryshyn case, and thus a full-dress rehearsal of the pending case against the Order had already taken place.

The description "professional witness" requires explanation. In the Red Scare-Cold War era a group of ex-Communists appeared who described themselves as experts on the Party in terms of its operations, fronts, and affiliates and whose testimony became headline news as they described the aims and methods of the Party to Congressional committees, "named names" at Smith Act trials, and assisted at deportation hearings. This group not only testified, they became professional witnesses in the sense that they were under contract (usually written) to the Department of Justice and its subordinate agencies, such as the FBI and INS, who paid them to travel where they were needed. Depending on whether full-time or part-time witnesses are counted, the number under contract has been estimated as ranging from 35 to 83 during the early 1950s.[13]

Most people who came into the Party in the 1930s and left in the 1940s simply became "former" Communists and never anti-Communists crusaders; they must be distinguished from certain ex-Communists who, as part of their anti-Red crusade, also became professional witnesses. A few of these paid witnesses claimed to have become Party members at the behest of the FBI, and then assisted in prosecutions; one of the most notorious, Matthew Cvetic, testified at the IWO trial.

The phenomenon of the government-paid professional informer

was unique to the Red Scare era. The paid informer per se is as old as human history and can be found in trials for treason, subversion, and many forms of criminality. What was different in this era was that these people held themselves out as experts on Communism and the Party, moving from trial to trial, from committee to committee, using their "expertise" and naming names on behalf of the U.S. and state governments. They are distinguishable because they were not part of only a single trial and did not give information as to one occasion of alleged criminal conduct. As described by historian Richard Rovere, "It is a novel arrangement, this hiring of people to take a solemn oath and testify favorably to the government. American history offers no precedent for it."[14] These witnesses claimed to have been part of the "evil" and that, having seen the wrongs of their ways, they alone could expose the evils they had forsaken, pointing the finger to those who had been or were still a part of the apparatus of the terrible empire of Communism. Their willingness to level these accusations put them on U.S. and state government payrolls.

The use of paid informers of this type was troublesome. The government argued that these people were valuable in order to achieve the greater goal of attacking the Communist conspiracy and that they must be telling the truth because so many juries had believed them enough to render guilty sentences.[15] The testimony that came from these ex-Communists was often clothed in quasi-religious language: terms like "resurrection" and "escape from the devil" were frequently heard. Ironically, these witnesses first had to justify their worth and credibility by convincing the court of their complete devotion to the Communist cause, which had resulted in their being trusted with Party secrets, Party policy, and exposure to Party members. Then came the conversion. Ex-Communists frequently took the following stance: "I was a liar and deceiver before, because I was part of this nefarious Communist conspiracy which taught me that to lie and deceive was appropriate; now I am free to tell the truth and now you must believe me." Louis Budenz, the most prominent ex-Communist of the times to testify in the IWO case, expressed this idea:

I think the most truthful people in the world are the ex-Communists, on the whole, and for this simple reason: They have learned how utterly incorrect is the morality of Lenin, the morality of deceiving for a cause. They have learned in pain and suffering. I want to assure you . . . they certainly have a resurrection within themselves, on the whole.[16]

Or, as the eminent historian Bernard DeVoto has expressed the ex-Communist stance:

Understood, I am right now *because* I was wrong then. *Only* the ex-Communist can understand Communism. Trust me to lead you aright *because* I tried to lead you astray. My intelligence has been vindicated *in that* it made an all-out commitment to error.[17]

This questionable logic was enough for so many Americans that Elmer Davis, a prominent radio commentator of the time, remarked that "Ex-Communists are more highly regarded in some quarters than people who were never Communist at all."[18]

But the question remains. Should such ex-Communists have been believed? Should they, as in the IWO trial, have been the backbone of government testimony? A major problem presented by a number of critics, including those of strong anti-Communist bent, was that these people were "kept witnesses" whose worth depended on their *continuous* ability to make identifications, in effect to be useful to prosecutors in naming Communists and describing the Party's operation in case after case. David Caute has described the problem in the following terms:

This goes to the heart of the matter. The informers as a group made a living out of pretending to an encyclopedic knowledge of the Communist movement across the face of a vast country. On a nod from prosecutors, they sold hunches or guesses as inside knowledge, supporting their claims with bogus reports of conversations and encounters.[19]

That these kept witnesses did lie, that they did use a "creative" memory as to events and people, has been well established.[20]

Probably the best-known exposures relate to Harvey Matusow, Louis Budenz, Matthew Cvetic, Paul Crouch, Manning Johnson, and two relatively minor characters who lied about prominent businessman Edward Lamb. In his book *False Witness,* Matusow detailed how he had lied in order to serve prosecutorial purposes as well as his own ego and pocketbook. Budenz, Cvetic, Sylvia Crouch (Paul Crouch's wife), and Manning Johnson were among the other paid witnesses used in the IWO case.[21]

Exposures about these paid professional informers came, for the most part, shortly before and would continue after the 1957 Supreme Court decision in the *Yates* case; a side effect of ending Red Scare prosecutions was to discontinue the use of paid witnesses. One angry response to these exposures as they were made came from William F. Thompkins, then United States Assistant Attorney General in charge of the Internal Security Division, who stated in testimony before a Senate committee that, "It has become increasingly clear that the current attack against government witnesses . . . has its roots in a Communist effort."[22]

A rather egregious result of exposure was the occasional perjury indictment of ex-Communist professional witnesses. Matusow was indicted after admitting he had lied. This is the same man who at one time told reporters that "This is a good racket, being a professional witness."[23]

The federal government's ability to contract with and pay these ex-Communist witnesses was the result of a curious though not unique application of a reform-minded statute for purposes other than that intended. A portion of the General Services and Administration Act of 1939 sought to allow the government to retain the part-time service of American specialists in such fields as science and education; with no other means then available, the Act allowed the government to contract for services on a per diem basis. This 1939 Act was the opening for the retention of professional witnesses from the ex-Communist pool.[24]

The money earned was generous by government standards for that time, usually $25 a day plus $9 "in lieu of expenses" and paid travel. Payment was made not only for actual trial appearances, but also for travel and for preparation with lawyers prior to taking the witness stand and for time consumed in waiting to be called. It should be noted that the usual fee paid to an ordinary witness under subpoena was only $4 a day. Furthermore, in comparison to what was earned as a full-time Communist Party functionary or in private employment prior to becoming a professional witness, the amounts earned were substantial. The notoriety—being sought after (and paid by) the media as well as lecturing on Communism to a variety of audiences—was a further reward. There was clearly the pressure to "remember" more, to make increasingly dramatic accusations that ensured the continuance of the contract position as a paid professional.

Use of such paid witnesses certainly marked a move away from the rule of "disinterestedness" supposedly present in the giving of testimony, a concept that goes back to Roman times and before. Giving disinterested, truthful testimony is one duty of citizenship; it must be done freely and in good faith. The power of a court to command the appearance and testimony of parties who have knowledge by subpoena was then and still is basic to court operation. The use of paid, professional witnesses to testify in political trials seems in retrospect to have violated the spirit of our legal system.

Payment for true expert testimony (e.g., medical, engineering, accounting testimony) to help the court and jury understand that which is normally beyond the average layperson's knowledge, must be distinguished from these Red Scare "professionals." In the rendering of such expert testimony, payment is an accepted practice, and such payment can never be contingent on the result obtained in the case. It is self-evident that the use of ex-Communists under the circumstances described was a substantial deviation from the norm applicable in American legal proceedings. It involved, as Richard Rovere has written, "the use of subsidized perjury."[25] "[T]he kept witnesses," he concludes, "have been given the opportunity to foul American due process and quite a bit else besides."[26]

The famed ex-Communist Whittaker Chambers, who gave testimony but never became a professional witness, said of the paid witness:

He [the ex-Communist, anti-Communist witness] risks little. He sits in security and uses his special knowledge to destroy others. He has that special information to give because he knows those others' faces, voices, and lives, because he once lived within their confidence.[27]

The Williams team apparently had few if any second thoughts about using these paid witnesses. It is clear from the records that they eagerly sought their services from the INS, set up special accounts to pay them, reviewed their line of testimony, and prepared them as the backbone of the State's case against the IWO.

Notes

1. *New York Times,* January 17, 1951.
2. Williams Office Files, Memoranda, Vol. I, Report of Henry dated May 4, 1951.
3. Ibid., Sheet inserted in this file.
4. Ibid., Copy of "IWO Call . . ." inserted in this file.
5. *New York World Telegram,* December 14, 1950.
6. *New York Herald Tribune,* December 15, 1950.
7. *New York Times,* December 16, 1950.
8. *The Daily Worker,* January 21, 1951.
9. Trauber interviews, March 8 and 10, 1988; July 23, 1988; October 27, 1989.
10. Williams Office Files, Correspondence and Memoranda.
11. Trial Record, pp. 771–78.
12. Williams Office Files, Memoranda, Vol. I, Memorandum from Emil dated December 27, 1950.
13. Quoted in Richard H. Rovere, "The Kept Witness," in *The American Establishment and Other Reports, Opinions and Speculations* (London: Rupert Hart-Davis, 1963), p. 61; David Caute, *The Great Fear: The Anti-Communist Purge Under Truman and Eisenhower* (New York: Simon and Schuster, 1978), p. 120.
14. Rovere, "The Kept Witness," p. 64.
15. Walter Olney III, "The Use of Former Communists as Witnesses," *Vital Speeches of the Day* 20, 21 (1954).

16. Quoted in Joseph Alsop, "The Strange Case of Louis Budenz," *Atlantic Monthly* 189 (April 1952), p. 29.

17. Bernard DeVoto, "The Ex-Communists," *Atlantic Monthly* 187 (February 1951), p. 61.

18. Quoted in DeVoto.

19. Caute, *The Great Fear,* p. 137.

20. Rovere, "The Kept Witness," p. 61; DeVoto, *The Ex-Communist,* p. 61; Alsop, "The Strange Case," p. 29; Murray Kempton, "The Achievement of Harvey Matusow," *The Progressive* 19, 4 (April 1955); Joseph L. Rawh, "Informers, G-Men and Freeman," *The Progressive* 14, 5, (May 1950); Edward Lamb, *No Lamb for Slaughter: An Autobiography* (New York: Harcourt, Brace and World, 1963).

21. See Caute, Alsop, Lamb, Rovere, Kempton, Rawh; also Herbert L. Packer, *Ex-Communist Witnesses: Four Studies in Fact-Finding* (Stanford, CA: Stanford University Press, 1962); Harvey Matusow, *False Witness* (New York: Cameron and Kahn, 1955).

22. Quoted in Rovere, "The Kept Witness," p. 60.

23. Ibid., p. 58.

24. Ibid., pp. 62–63.

25. Ibid., p. 69.

26. Ibid., p. 73.

27. Ibid., p. 66.

Chapter VII
Ex-Communist, Ex-IWO Vice-President

The choice of George E. Powers as the State's lead witness was an obvious one: Powers, a former Vice-President of the IWO, was an admitted ex-Communist. Thus he was a witness who had credentials bridging the Order and the Communist Party over a number of years. Since the Williams strategy was to tie the two together, Powers was an ideal first witness even though he had been out of the IWO and the Party since 1939, making his association with both organizations some twelve years old by the time he took the stand in 1951.

As Williams began to question Powers, the strategy of Raphael Weissman, lead trial counsel for the IWO, became evident. Weissman wished to limit Powers's testimony to matters strictly having to do with his membership and offices held with the Order; he did not even want any background information on the witness, such as his occupation (he was a sheet-metal worker) or the fact that Powers had used aliases during his life. Most importantly, Weissman's objections to questions Williams put to Powers were designed to block testimony on the politics of the IWO.

The problem with this strategy was twofold. First, with no jury, the Judge was able to have evidence presented to him that might otherwise be objectionable before a jury. Second, it was obvious that Judge Greenberg was interested—in fact, evidently anxious—to get at the facts of the political side of the IWO. Weissman's difficult task, carried out by his objections to questions, was to try to focus the Judge's attention on the operation of the Order as an insurance company and on the legal issues involving limitations on the State's power as an insurance regulator—not on the IWO's politics.

Inherent in this matter was the comingling of what the IWO stood for as an insurance company, that is, how it operated as a corporation that simply offered insurance, and the politics of its officers. The State was out to prove that a corporation could have a political position and that this one was dangerous—thus "hazardous"—under the law in a new, very broad sense. A corporation can only act through its agents—its officers, directors, and employees. The defense wanted the court to focus on what the officers had done in the official name of the IWO in running it as an insurance company, thus concentrating on its insurance and other fraternal offerings. Williams would attempt to show that the officers' politics permeated the Order—and that those politics were so radical, so tied to the Communist Party, that the corporation itself should be destroyed.

In the supercharged political atmosphere of early 1951, maintaining a clear line of separation was simply impossible. A taste of this can be gained from the following, as Powers is questioned:

Q. Were you ever a member of the Communist party?

A. I was.

Q. When did you become a member of the Communist party?

Mr. Weissman: I object to that. That has nothing to do with the issues in this case. We are not trying the Communist party.

The Court: That is right, but it is part of the proceeding here, and I cannot determine at this stage of the proceeding, Mr. Weissman, whether it will become material or not.

Mr. Weissman: What has his lurid background got to do with the issues in this case? We are trying a corporation on specific allegations.

The Court: I understand.

Mr. Weissman: Exception. [Adding a few moments later:]

Mr. Weissman: My point is that this man's background has nothing to do with the issues. Let us find out what he did or knows, or what was done in connection with IWO.[1]

By way of explanation, the word "exception" means that counsel was asking the court to recognize that he objected to the Judge's ruling ("taking exception" to that ruling), thus preserving the objection for potential review on appeal as reversible error.

Another aspect of trial lore is that an extensive trial takes on a life, so to speak, of its own. As it begins, the attorneys on each side attempt to move it in a direction favorable to eliciting the issues they wish highlighted and proved. One way this manifests itself is in the need to develop a specific trial strategy and tactics; the attorney must decide, early on, how he or she will get evidence before the court to make that important first impression and direction. The countertactic is consistently to object to the testimony and evidence in order to block that impression and direction. How effective all this will be depends on the skill of the attorneys involved and the judge's view of the case. The judge, the ultimate determining factor, signals the direction it will take by his rulings on the testimony being presented and on what documentary evidence he deems relevant.

The unfolding of the IWO case was initially slow, with a great deal of probing by each side. Judge Greenberg made it clear on this first full day of trial that he wanted to hear it all, consistently reassuring Weissman that he had reserved the right within himself to determine what ultimately was and was not relevant. In effect, Greenberg was saying, there is no jury here that might be swayed by passion or prejudice—so I will dispassionately filter out that which is irrelevant and incompetent. To this Weissman could not object, and the result was that Williams could and did press to present everything that might suggest the role of politics as the key issue in the case.

Williams's aim was to tie the radical politics of the officers (most of whom he maintained were Party members) to the policies of the IWO to show that the Order in turn was directed and driven by the Communist Party. Weissman pushed in the opposite direction: the officers, he reasoned, are citizens who have the right to whatever political opinions they choose; when they express political views it is as individuals; where the Order has taken an official position, it is within the officers' right to determine the fraternal policy of the IWO, and, unless the policy threatens the financial stability of the insurance program, the State has no right to interfere.

The testimony of George Powers was brought out over the bitter objections of Weissman; Williams, Powers, and Weissman clashed so violently that Judge Greenberg had to warn Weissman that he, Weissman, would have high blood pressure before the first day was over. If the alleged link between the Communist Party and the IWO was indeed to be a major legal issue and Powers was in fact believed, his testimony would be devastating.

Powers testified that the Party had sent him to the IWO in 1934 with instructions to take up an executive position with the Order; prior to his journey from Party headquarters to the IWO home office, Powers had not been an Order member. His initial work, he said, was to be that of secretary of the English-speaking lodges in New York City and in that capacity to recruit members for the Party's Workers' School as well as circulate Party propaganda. Not only did he identify a number of the IWO officers in the courtroom as Party members, he stated that when he was in the Order, he was a member of the Communist "fraction" for the IWO. Powers explained that certain trusted Party members who were also in the IWO would meet separately in what was known as a "fraction" (in Party terminology) to receive Party instructions regarding the Order. Asked about the location of these fraction meetings, he said they were held mainly at Party headquarters, but occasionally on the IWO premises. Powers portrayed himself as a Party functionary who carried out Party directives within the Order and reported directly to his supervisor at Party headquarters.

Powers related that he was charged with finding potential Party member recruits as part of his work, for which he had quotas; he described part of this process in the following terms:

> To the best of my recollection, he [his Party supervisor] said, "George, what is going on? Are you getting many party members in? Are you forgetting about the party? Are you just becoming an IWO man or are you really carrying out the party work in the IWO," and I answered him, telling him what I was doing, that I had it in heart to build the Communist party, so far as my connection with the IWO; and so far as recruitment is concerned, he mentioned quotas.[2]

Powers described the Order as a "transmission belt" for the Communist party. He defined this term as Party language for the idea of the Party as the "central motor" over a mass organization such as the IWO, where the organization is directed for Party purposes by the fraction and thus moved along the path (the transmission belt) laid out by the Party, even if the majority of Order members are not Party members.[3]

Williams's questioning moved to the distribution of Party literature at IWO lodges and support for Communist political campaigns in 1934 and 1936 through IWO member contributions. Powers consistently portrayed himself as being berated by this Party supervisor for not doing enough for the Party in his IWO job. Whether deliberate or not, Powers's testimony blurred the distinction between his Party activities and those of his IWO job.

He also testified that he personally spoke at lodge meetings. In a tense moment, Williams asked whether he ever advocated the violent overthrow of the government. Before Powers could answer, the Judge interrupted, asking Williams whether he wanted Powers to answer; the warning signal sent to Williams was clear—Powers may be waiving his Fifth Amendment rights if he answers, and thus potentially incriminating himself by violating the Smith Act. But Powers insisted on answering "No," he had never so advocated.[4]

As the day's testimony continued, Judge Greenberg took a more and more active role. He broke through a number of "logjams" when Williams could not ask a question to which Weissman did not validly object, when Powers did not understand what was asked of him, or, most importantly, when the Judge wanted answers to his own questions. This last is important because it gives a clue to the Judge's thinking. For example, Greenberg asked whether Powers ever noted any objections from members about Party literature at meetings (none that he could remember) or whether the majority of the lodge members were Communists (no—only leaders). He also elicited descriptions of what went on at the usual lodge meetings, for example, presence of a "hospitaler" for liaison with the sick and a cemetery committee.[5]

Moving to his advancement within the Order to the vice-presidency in 1935, Powers identified all the other top officers in that year as Party members; he described them all as part of the Communist Party fraction taking Party orders on various issues. Recalling the fraction meetings, he detailed arguments over how closely the IWO should appear to follow the Party line on national and international issues.[6]

The first full day of testimony ended with Powers recalling fraction meetings where the agenda had included ways to enhance support for the Soviet Union within the Order. According to Powers, Russia was to be projected as peace-loving and with no warlike or aggressive intentions. The counterpart was to "spread distress in our leadership in this country" if their political positions were disfavorable to the Soviet Union.[7]

Newspaper accounts of the first day's proceedings carried the titles:

I.W.O. TRIAL TOLD
6 OFFICERS ARE FORMER REDS[8]

EX-RED AIDS STATE IN INSURANCE SUIT—TELLS OF COMMUNIST CONTROL OF INTERNATIONAL WORKERS ORDER AND ITS OFFICERS[9]

In their coverage, both reports emphasized Powers's identification of Order officers as Communists. If Judge Greenberg had missed it during the Powers testimony, the *New York Herald Tribune* had identified Jack Stachel, one of the eleven convicted top Communists, as present at fraction meetings attended by Powers. Because Greenberg was an avid newspaper reader as well as naturally curious, newspaper accounts of the trial most likely came to his attention.

News of these days carried stories of the Korean War, atom bomb test explosions in Nevada, inflation, and Red Scare events. In the last category, the Remington perjury trial continued; twenty-two people, including Earl Browder, were appealing Congressional contempt citations; Hiss was appealing his conviction to the Supreme Court; Pearl S.

Buck, the famous novelist, was banned as a commencement speaker at a high school because her record with the House Un-American Activities Committee (HUAC) was "not clear"; and the Subversive Activities Control Board was to open hearings by demand of the U.S. Attorney General that the Communist Party and its members register as agents of Russia. A bill funding the Senate Judiciary Subcommittee investigating the enforcement of the Internal Security Act of 1950 was passed over President Truman's veto; Truman had called some of the bill's provisions "hysterical."[10]

In a follow-up article on January 31, 1951, the *New York Times* delved further into the case under a column titled, "Six Officers In I.W.O. Identified As Reds; 3 National Vice Presidents Are Among Those Named In Court By Powers, Ex-Communist." The fact that Powers could not state whether Rockwell Kent and Vito Marcantonio, then present officers of the Order, were Communists, was noted. The article ended by stating that New Jersey officials had joined with New York in the legal effort to liquidate the IWO.[11]

When the trial resumed the next day, Williams attempted further to qualify Powers, this time "as an expert on Communist matters and Communist doctrines." Williams needed this "expert" qualification so that he could explore Communist doctrine and Party methods and link both to the IWO. Weissman strongly objected, reminding the Judge that "this is not a Communist trial, and this is not a red-baiting trial. . . . There is no issue here in [terms of] trying the Communist Party." But Judge Greenberg was willing to hear more evidence on the basis that "at least one theory of the proceeding [is] that the IWO was dominated and controlled by the Communist Party." "It may be somewhat of a handicap to you," he explained, "but until I decide the basic issue, I will have to admit some of that testimony."[12] (Given the times, calling any testimony relating to Communism a "handicap" is a vast understatement.)

This turn of events meant that Williams could now use Powers to introduce evidence involving a broad area (the doctrines and operation of the Communist Party) and then attempt to factually to tie the Party's operation to the Order, in support of his need to stretch the insurance laws of the State in order to get at the "great evil" behind the politics of the IWO—the Communist Party. Williams's early strategy and tactics were working.

After lengthy, unenlightening detail of Powers's relationship to the Party (positions held, etc.), Williams asked Powers, as an ex-Communist now an expert on Communism, what the Party's fundamental aim was. Weissman got the question limited to the Party's aim as of 1939, when Powers left the Party. The answer of Powers was predictable: "to advocate and counsel and guide the steps necessary for the forcible overthrow and destruction of existing so-called bourgeois governments, capitalist governments and to set up on their ruins . . . a Soviet form of government . . . controlled by . . . the Communist Party."[13] Williams's questions led Powers to delve more deeply into Communist Policy; he stated that this "forcible violent overthrow" was not to be openly advocated until the time was right, adding:

The immediate aim is to entrench the Party wherever possible in other organizations, and gain control of other organizations on the basis of the transmission belt system which I described yesterday in order to give the Communist Party a tremendous far-reaching control over many, many organizations involving many people who are not Communists.

Q. Was the IWO one of those organizations?

A. It was and it is.[14]

Williams, pushing for a "kill" on the issue, was at first rebuffed, but Powers saved the point in response to the Judge's own question:

By the Court:

Q. Can you recall any meeting from the first occasion that you attended. where the question came up in connection with seeking to gain control, if such was discussed, of the IWO, insofar as the fraction meetings are concerned?

A. It was not a question of gaining control, but of exercising the existing control, and that was discussed.[15]

Powers went on to state that the General Secretary of the Order reported to the Communist Party in fraction meetings; this was in addition to reporting and being responsible to the General Executive Board of the IWO.[16]

It must be understood that none of this came into the record without a fight from the IWO lawyers. Shouting matches took place and sarcasm entered as objections were made and points of the law of evidence were argued.

When a judge asks questions, intervening in the proceeding, he is indicating that which most interests him. At this stage of Powers's testimony, Judge Greenberg appeared to be most interested in the fraction meetings—who was there, where they were held, and what was discussed. Powers related meetings during the early 1930s, specifically emphasizing (under Williams's prodding) Jack Stachel, the convicted Communist, as the Party leader who was involved.

Williams was also using the press to further his cause: he had been giving copies of exhibits—specifically pictures of IWO leaders whom Powers had identified as Communist Party members—to newspaper reporters. Weissman accused him of trying the case in the press. Judge Greenberg ordered Williams to stop giving copies of exhibits to reporters.[17]

Judge Greenberg took a more aggressive role in questioning as the second day of Powers's testimony continued. He wanted to know more about the campaigns carried on by the IWO surrounding social and political issues. Powers told him that the role of the Communist Party fraction was powerful in directing which campaigns would be sanctioned.[18] Powers also related how the Party sought to gain members from the IWO under fraction direction.[19]

As the theme of ties to the Communist Party developed, Weissman attempted to reduce its impact and impugn Powers's credibility through objections and demands for specifics. The problem he faced, which would grow as the trial moved on and as Judge Greenberg took over questioning witnesses, was the strategic difficulty for Weissman to object to the Judge's own questions; therefore, much more got into the record than might have otherwise.

The relationship with the Party was never far from view, particularly as the Judge, who was free to explore as he wished, questioned Powers. It must have been particularly frustrating for Weissman as Judge Greenberg asked Powers about the use of IWO members as "good timber for the Communist Party." Here, Weissman could not effectively attack the Judge's line of questioning—not only because he was the judge, but also because objections to his questions could be viewed as an attempt to hide the truth.[20]

During the second day's afternoon session, the focus shifted to introduction of books and pamphlets as State's exhibits, starting with the *Communist Manifesto* by Karl Marx and Friedrich Engels and V. I. Lenin's *State and Revolution,* through to pamphlets by Joseph Stalin and Communist periodicals. Also introduced into evidence were IWO teaching materials and books such as *5 Years IWO.* The significance of these exhibits was that they contained Communist doctrine and because Powers stated that "literature tables" at lodge meetings offered these materials for sale to members. Williams would later refer to the exhibits in cross-examining witnesses for the Order.[21] Significantly, Judge Greenberg stated he would have to and indeed promised to read all of these exhibits.[22] The direct examination of George Powers ended on this note, and the witness was turned over to the IWO team for cross-examination.

In almost two full days of testimony, Powers and Williams had done a remarkable job of putting forth the ties of the past and many of the present leaders of the IWO to the Communist Party, as well as Party influence on the Order's politics. A layperson reading this record would be hard-pressed to imagine how or on what basis this ex-vice-president of the IWO and ex-Communist could be challenged. As Weissman took up the task, the answer would promptly unfold.

Weissman mounted an attack on Powers from a number of angles, moving rapidly from one topic to another, frequently in seemingly random fashion. This technique is used to break down the witness's confidence, to get him or her to admit inaccuracies at various points of testimony, to demonstrate the validity of different interpretations with respect to prior testimony, and to show the inadequacy of the witness's memory. Weissman did all of this as he hammered on different areas of Powers's testimony. For instance, he got Powers to admit that a number of the books and pamphlets he had identified were materials readily found in public bookstores and libraries, not just at IWO lodge meetings; that there was little connection between his running for public office while an IWO officer and the fact of his officer status in the IWO; and that he had testified differently on some of the same matters when he was a witness in the earlier Dmytryshyn case.

Weissman then attempted to discredit Powers as a paid witness, eliciting the fact that he was earning $25 per day for court testimony and $20 per session when "consulting" with attorneys in this case; this was then contrasted with his top pay of $40 per week when employed by the IWO. Powers had testified for the authorities in another matter under a written contract at $25 per day; he stated he had also testified in still other matters without pay.[23]

Weissman continued to press. Under his questioning, Powers stated that he had left the Party and the IWO in 1939 because of the Nazi-Soviet Pact.[24] He admitted that later that same year he had testified falsely before a grand jury on the identity of the Communist leader Earl Browder. Weissman, having established these facts, tried to get Powers to admit that he had become a government-paid witness giving testimony in another case before an investigating committee in exchange for not being indicted for perjury, and that this was the real reason he left the IWO and the Party. Powers would not admit this as his motivation and denied that the threat influenced him in his attitude towards "this question of the IWO and Communism." Weissman baited him with sarcasm when Powers asserted his only motivation in giving testimony was "public service . . . determined to help [my] country."[25]

Weissman continued the pressure by turning to Powers's standing as an IWO member. After Powers stated that "my presence as a functionary of the IWO was dependent mainly upon my being a Communist Party member rather than being a member of the IWO" and after describing himself as a disciplined Communist, Weissman asked why he had been suspended twice from the Order for nonpayment of dues.[26]

While the State's advantage was the "rehearsal" of the IWO case in the Dmytryshyn deportation hearing the previous summer, the IWO attorneys had the counter-advantage of using a transcript of the record in that case with which to cross-examine the State's witnesses. As noted, Powers had become one of the paid witnesses who testified for the Immigration and Naturalization Service. Now Weissman was trying to show discrepancies between what he had said there and what he was now saying here. With respect to the matter of being dropped from Order membership, Powers's responses were evasive, apparently angering Williams as well. Unfortunately for Weissman, the matter in question did not implicate any substantive portion of Powers's testimony; cracks alone do not bring down the edifice. It did serve to illustrate, however, something of the "selective" nature of the witness's memory. To the trained observer—most importantly the Judge—it also indicated a witness well rehearsed in the ways of testimony, who could be evasive in his responses.[27]

For what was left of the day, Weissman probed Powers's background as a labor union functionary and his attachment to Communist Party fractions in those unions. The climax came when Weissman got Powers to admit that the Party fraction in the IWO had no authority over the Order as such. Williams quickly interrupted to ask for and got an adjournment to the following day.[28]

Weissman opened the next day with formal motions to the Court to strike all of Powers's testimony on fraction meetings and related conversations, based on that important Powers admission on the role of fractions obtained at the close of the previous day. Judge Greenberg denied the motions because of some potential "binding effect" on the Order these fraction meetings may have had, and invited Weissman to renew them at a later time.[29]

Returning to the cross-examination, Weissman's initial attack was on Powers's memory; in effect he was asking how he could remember with such clarity persons and events of many years before. Using the Dmytryshyn transcript, Weissman pointed out that what Powers failed to remember in this proceeding he had clearly remembered six months before at the Dmytryshyn hearing, and vice versa. Demonstrating his skill in a frequently used cross-examination technique, Weissman showed the Court that Powers could not remember a salient date and some numbers or persons he had just referred to the day before. Weissman's objective was to signal to the Judge that Powers's testimony about happenings years before could not be believed if he could not even remember what he testified to yesterday.

In grueling fashion, Weissman attacked Powers's veracity and competence, using as tools the prior days' testimony (though expensive, a record can be transcribed overnight so that the attorneys and judge can have it the next day) and the Dmytryshyn transcript. Sarcastically referring to him as a "former big shot Communist," he punched at Powers to admit to inaccuracies, overgeneralizations, and lack of honest knowledge.[30]

Using an article Powers himself had written for the Order's magazine on the subject of literature available through the IWO, Weissman got him to admit that no mention was made of Communist literature. Turning to Powers's election to the vice-presidency, Weissman obtained admissions about the democratic nature of the IWO convention and voting process.

Because recruitment was one of Powers's duties in the Order, Weissman made him reexamine what he had said in order to place a different, more benign face to his use of the word "penetration" of unions—that it was simply to get IWO members. While Powers admitted that was primary, he nevertheless added that his role was to make it a three-step process: "penetrate" unions to get IWO members, recruit IWO members to the Party cause, and "penetration" of unions by Party-IWO members. Powers showed he was adept at turning a question back to where he wanted the focus: Party interest in the growth of the Order.[31]

Hours of intensive cross-examination were devoted to reviewing selected elements of Powers's direct testimony. What Weissman appears to have achieved was to establish that, notwithstanding Powers's position in the Party and the IWO, his alleged Party-driven directives were not always followed in the Order. Powers admitted that the IWO campaigns on behalf of the accused in the Scottsboro case and of the Loyalists in the Spanish Civil War (1936–1939) were not "sinister" in nature and represented a rather broad spectrum of political support. Weissman also obtained concrete admissions that no IWO funds were involved in these campaigns—only monies contributed by individual members.[32]

Weissman's last shot at Powers concerned the circumstances of his termination from his IWO post. Powers had testified on direct examination that he left over the Nazi-Soviet Pact. Weissman got him to admit that in fact he was fired prior to the date of the Pact, and then closed as follows:

Q. And before you disassociated yourself with the Communist Party you had been, let us say, let go from IWO, isn't that so?

A. From an official post, yes.

Q. I put it to you as a fact, Mr. Powers, that you left the Communist Party because you had been thrown out of IWO. Do you agree?

A. No, I do not.

Mr. Weissman: That is all.[33]

When Weissman finished, Williams had the right to obtain more testimony from Powers on redirect examination. He immediately returned to the matter of Powers's termination from the Order, and through his questioning got Powers to testify that the Party fraction had decided he should not run again for office and that, for whatever reason, "as a good disciplined Communist" he abided by that decision.[34]

Because the Policyholders' Protective Committee constituted a separate entity in the litigation, Friedman, as attorney for the group, had the opportunity to cross-examine Powers. With speed and deftness (everyone involved was getting tired of this one witness for this long period of time, in part because he tended to make speeches rather than answer questions) Friedman used the Constitution of the IWO to elicit from Powers that, during his years with the Order, there were no departures from the principles stated in it. Then he got Powers to state that the IWO fulfilled its promises to its members by providing low-cost insurance, paying sick benefits, and providing a full range of social activities.

The major thrust of Friedman's cross-examination was to challenge the most damaging aspect of the Powers testimony: the power of the Communist Party to direct and control the IWO through the fraction device. What he accomplished were admissions that major campaigns and policies of the Order were taken up or implemented *before* any "directive" from the fraction; this was true of the case of support for the Scottsboro defense, support for Loyalist Spain, endorsement of black civil rights, endorsement of the social legislation of the New Deal, and support for the unionization efforts of the CIO.

Delving into the matter of the Scottsboro defense, Friedman established that the IWO involvement was consistent with its overall position of support for black civil liberties, including anti-lynch laws and anti-poll tax legislation. He used Powers to confirm that the Order had adopted a resolution at its 1938 Convention calling for the National and American League baseball clubs to hire black players, long before the hiring of Jackie Robinson. Powers agreed that the IWO had worked to increase black members and had offered blacks its insurance programs at the same rates as whites and that blacks fully participated in the Order.

On issue after issue, Friedman gained concessions from Powers that these and other policies and activities of the Order were in place from the origin of the IWO and not dependent on any "directives" from the "fraction." He delved deeply into IWO support for the CIO, developing how the Order had encouraged its members to join CIO unions; a letter from Philip Murray, President of the CIO, was introduced, which recognized and complemented the contribution of the IWO in this regard. Friedman was able to make a telling point when he established that Powers, in preparation for this case and for testifying before the Immigration and Naturalization Service, had at least fourteen conferences with government personnel and attorneys; he wanted the Judge to understand that Powers's testimony was very well rehearsed.

One way of determining when a very sensitive point has been reached in a trial is the reaction by opposing counsel to a question put to a witness; when Williams asked Powers on redirect examination, "Do you know of any campaign of the Communist Party of the United States that was not also a campaign of the IWO?" Weissman was immediately on his feet to object. This objection resulted in a lengthy debate with the Judge as to the relevance of the question and whether the witness was competent to testify on this point. The Judge overruled his objection, explaining at length that he felt that it was relevant to the issue of domination of the IWO by the Party and that he understood "perfectly well what the question [was] driving at."[35] The Judge then tried his hand at phrasing the question; Weissman and Friedman objected to the Judge's phraseology, and Greenberg overruled the objection to his *own* question. (Once again this illustrates the unusual situation where, in a bench trial, the judge must rule on his own questions.)

The answer by Powers was finally reduced to the one word "No"; he did not recall any Communist Party campaign that was not participated in by the IWO.[36] Judge Greenberg wanted to know whether IWO members referred to each other as "comrade"; Powers answered "yes," but that in about 1936 this had changed to "brother and sister."

The Judge wanted to know about Powers's involvement with a federal grand jury and how he had purposely misidentified Earl Browder in his testimony before it. Browder had been indicted on passport violations by that jury. Powers explained that he had falsified a document while in the Party and later when Browder was tried on these passport violations. Because the government refused to grant Powers immunity, he continued at that trial to lie about the identification of Browder.

With the testimony of Powers coming to a close, the IWO lawyers had a final opportunity to challenge his credibility and attempt to establish that, as a result of this admitted perjury, he had become a paid witness for the government. Jones and Friedman concluded with motions to strike all of the testimony of "an acknowledged and avowed perjurer and liar before the Grand Jury," but Judge Greenberg denied these motions.[37]

Before moving on to the next State witness, it should be pointed out that not only did Judge Greenberg takes notes, as most judges do during a trial, but also went over the day's testimony and exhibits each night. He told the lawyers he was doing this, demonstrating not only his diligence but also equipping himself with material and information which would allow him to inject himself still further into the actual proceedings of the case.[38]

Notes

1. Trial Record, pp. 781–82.
2. Trial Record, pp. 814–15.
3. Trial Record, p. 852.
4. Trial Record, p. 853.
5. Trial Record, pp. 854–55.
6. Trial Record, pp. 857–66.
7. Trial Record, p. 867.
8. *New York Herald Tribune,* January 31, 1951.
9. *New York Times,* January 30, 1951.
10. *New York Times,* January 27,28,29,30, 1951.
11. *New York Times,* January 31, 1951.
12. Trial Record, pp. 869–71.
13. Trial Record, pp. 871–90.
14. Trial Record, p. 892.
15. Trial Record, p. 895.
16. Trial Record, pp. 905–7.
17. Trial Record, p. 926.
18. Trial Record, pp. 928–30.
19. Trial Record, pp. 934–36.
20. Trial Record, p. 940.
21. Trial Record, pp. 943–61.
22. Trial Record, p. 948.
23. Trial Record, pp. 961–72.
24. Trial Record, pp. 973–77.
25. Trial Record, p. 977.
26. Trial Record, pp. 979–81.
27. Trial Record, pp. 981–87.
28. Trial Record, pp. 988–96.
29. Trial Record, pp. 997–98.
30. Trial Record, pp. 1020–46.
31. Trial Record, pp. 1047–69.
32. Trial Record, pp. 1071–1102.
33. Trial Record, pp. 1107–11.

34. Trial Record, pp. 1111–12.
35. Trial Record, pp. 1153–58.
36. Trial Record, p. 1157.
37. Trial Record, p. 1177.
38. Trial Record, p. 1179.

Chapter VIII

The State's Case Continues

The second witness for the State was not only obtained from the Immigration and Naturalization Service, but was also an employee of the INS. Manning Johnson, who was black, called himself an "analyst" for the Service. Like Powers, he was an ex-Communist Party member.

At the time of the IWO trial, Johnson was forty-three years old. His opening testimony established his theme—he knew the IWO through his work as a Communist Party functionary. Over an ever-increasing crescendo of objections from IWO lawyers, most of which Judge Greenberg overruled, Johnson testified that he had never been a member of the IWO, but had joined the Party in 1930, quitting in 1939 over the Nazi-Soviet Pact. He described a "secret national training school" run by the Party where he had been taught to embrace its singular objective—the overthrow of every capitalist government.[1]

Williams used Johnson to introduce Party pamphlets of a revolutionary nature and to identify Stachel and other top Communists as his teachers. Johnson testified that William Weiner and Max Bedacht, both IWO officers, had lectured to them on the Order. When Johnson was asked by Williams what Bedacht had said, Weissman injected:

Just a moment, if your Honor pleases. This is a conversation by an official of IWO somewhere else, obviously acting in the capacity of a teacher of the Communist Party. This much I think is perfectly clear, that is not binding on IWO. It is just conversation he had or instructions somewhere else.

The Court: Overruled; exception.[2]

Johnson testified that in 1932 Bedacht had explained the origin of the IWO as a decision by the Party after it failed to get the Workmen's Circle to accept the "revolutionary class struggle line of the Communist Party." He explained the fraction as a control device and the use of low-cost insurance as an appeal to bring masses of workers into the organi-zation, and thereafter as a "transmission belt" for Party recruitment.[3]

Johnson then explained how he spoke at IWO lodge meetings as a Communist, lecturing on unemployment, soliciting support for Party and Party-front organizations, distributing leaflets, and promoting the sale of the *Daily Worker*. He then dropped a "bomb": the IWO sup-ported the Communist Party financially in Buffalo, New York, by donating 20 percent of all monies raised at IWO affairs. In addition, the IWO paid all Johnson's expenses.[4]

This accusation caused considerable chaos in the courtroom. Law-yers interrupted, the Judge interjected questions, and vigorous argu-ments flew from both sides:

By the Court.

Q. Do you know how many lodges there were of the IWO in what you call the Communist district of Buffalo?

A. We had lodges, if I recall correctly at that time, in Buffalo—

Q. Do you know how many there were in Buffalo?

Mr. Weissman: I move to strike out the answer, "We had lodges." Who is the "we"?

Q. There were lodges?

A. There were IWO lodges.

Mr. Weissman: Did you own the IWO lodges, sir?

The Witness: The Communist Party did.[5]

Williams used Johnson to come at the fraction issue from another angle: that the Communist party had in Johnson a non-IWO operative whose responsibilities included meeting with the Party fractions in IWO lodges in order to carry out Party decisions. Williams also used him to identify Party and IWO literature distributed in 1932 at the Order's lodges and rallies which specifically involved Order support for Communist candidates.[6]

When the matter of raising money for Communist causes again came up, just where the money was coming from was clarified for all parties, including the Judge, as solicitations that had nothing to do with IWO insurance or dues monies. Williams, in fact, conceded the issue, and the Judge stated:

It is conceded that the Order was solvent financially, at least so shown by the investigations and reports of the State Insurance Department, and also from a business point of view, it was conducted satisfactorily to the Insurance Department and to those who were interested.[7]

Johnson claimed that in one extraordinary meeting in 1933, the top Party leaders decided to discontinue the taking of 20 percent Party funding from IWO affairs because such "piratical" ways of raising monies could cause problems, agreeing that other means would have to be found. Friedman objected to this testimony as the "rankest sort of hearsay" but was overruled.[8]

Tempers flared and words of anger from the attorneys filled the courtroom as Williams pressed Johnson to relate what substituted as the means for Party support by the IWO. What came out, over the chorus of objections, was Johnson's story that the Party directed quotas for monies to be raised to help finance the *Daily Worker,* adding that the quota for the Order was "substantially larger than that of other organizations."[9]

Thereafter, Johnson was led by Williams through an identification process. Using lists and photographs, Johnson "named names," stating which IWO leaders were known to him as Communist Party members. Those of whom Williams failed to inquire, the Judge himself, using his own references, asked about.[10]

Johnson then went to the limit by declaring that the directive of the Party included the following:

The membership of the International Workers Order must be willing to make any and every sacrifice in order to defend their fatherland, the Soviet Union; that they may be possibly called upon eventually to take up arms by the United States Government against Russia, and that they must do all within their power to prevent the shipment of arms, ammunitions, and to bring about a general demoralization of the armed forces of our nation, and to agitate within those armed forces that the American armed forces shoot their own officers, desert, and go over on the side of the Red Army.

Friedman responded:

You see how far this has taken us. This witness is testifying to what was said, as he claims, at some Communist party meeting, not at an IWO meeting, at which someone, still unidentified, expressed some aspirations about what he wanted the IWO members to do; no statement made that that was at an IWO meeting.[11]

He continued:

Here we have had presented to us exhibits showing what transpired at the conventions of the IWO, the publications of the IWO. That is the place to show whether anything was said about killing officers in the American army, not what he says he heard at some meeting of some other organization. Let him show what the IWO did.[12]

It takes little imagination to envision the impact of these alleged words counseling treason when uttered in the tense Cold War days of early 1951.

On January 31, 1951, the first day of Manning Johnson's testimony ended. On that same day, William W. Remington, an economist with the U.S. Department of Commerce, was found guilty of perjury for denying he was a Communist and was given the maximum sentence of five years in prison. That evening, the New York Board of Education fired eight teachers who refused to answer Loyalty Oath questions.[13]

The next day Johnson's testimony basically involved filling in details by naming more IWO officers who were Party members and stating what these people had said at Communist Party meetings or conventions many years before. The thrust of this testimony was that the Party recognized the significance and value of the Order, used the Order for all its purposes, and counted on the Order to do its will.[14] The State's final role for Johnson was to use him to identify Communist Party literature that was sold or distributed at lodge meetings. Henry, Williams's chief assistant, acted as attorney for the State in this phase. The record indicates Henry was not nearly as skilled as Williams; Weissman and Friedman were able to "rough him up," and at times Williams had to intercede.[15]

Weissman's cross-examination began with a memory exercise. He immediately established that while Johnson claimed to be able to recall names, meetings, and speeches going back to the early and mid-1930s, he could not accurately remember dates in his own life of the 1940s or how he had responded to a question Judge Greenberg had asked him only the day before. But this was more than a memory exercise. Weissman showed that, in recounting his employment for the Judge, Johnson had left out a key period of his life in 1947 when he had supported himself and his family by working as a paid informer for the U.S. government. By the time of the IWO trial, Johnson already had been a paid witness for some four years. He had been granted an unpaid leave by the INS in order to testify in this trial, with the State paying him $25 per day for court testimony and $20 per day for preparation.[16] As a witness Johnson became easily flustered when he was not rendering one of his apparent "set pieces" of testimony.

What Weissman and Judge Greenberg were able to elicit was that Johnson turned informer initially in the Gerhart Eisler deportation case and, on the basis of his past services, was given a full-time job with the INS. Judge Greenberg's questioning confirmed that Johnson could not have gotten the job had it not been for his prior services as an informer. Weissman developed this theme:

Q. So that it is a fact that your work consists chiefly in connection with matters relating to persons or organizations with whom or which you formerly had intimate relations, or relations?

A. Yes.

Q. Do you now, I ask you again, repel the suggestion that your work consists chiefly in acting as an informer?

A. I say that, in the strictest sense, no.

Q. You mean you do not repel the suggestion?

A. I say this, that my position, as I stated before, is to assist the investigators in establishing the facts with regard to subversiveness, individuals and organizations, that are seeking the violent overthrow of the Government of the United States. That is my job.[17]

Weissman's aim was not only to establish Johnson as a paid professional informer, but to show that he was also a liar. To do this, Weissman had to rely on transcripts of testimony from prior trials or hearings where Johnson had testified. The technique Weissman used was first to throw the witness off by taking him in rapid-fire succession from one topic to another and then come down hard on specific discrepancies in testimony. For several hours, Weissman did just that with respect to an identification Johnson had made in a prior case and the dates he had attended the alleged secret Party school. In the first instance, Johnson claimed that the transcript was wrong in that it left out some of his testimony. With respect to the dates, he passed off the discrepancy in time by claiming he had simply been in error about when he had attended the school.[18]

Research into Johnson's background as a professional paid informer had yielded some results; his veracity and credibility had been challenged, bringing him close to a charge of perjury. In addition, his role as a paid witness informer—a role he accepted as a matter of making a living and being "patriotic"—may have tarnished his testimony in the Judge's mind. A fair reading of the record indicates that Johnson had a very selective memory—one well rehearsed as to events of some ten or more years before but unable to deal with events, for example, as recent as the previous summer, when he had testified in the Dmytryshyn matter.

By the time of the IWO trial in 1951, Johnson had testified in hearings on deportation, in at least twenty trials, and before state loyalty or Congressional subversive activities committees. He would continue in the role of professional ex-Communist until his usefulness diminished in 1954, when the government stopped using him after he swore that Ralph Bunche, the famous black statesman, was a Communist, and Johnson was caught in flat disproof of that testimony. In another matter, his testimony on the Communist Party before the Subversive Activities Control Board (established by the federal Internal Security Act) was thrown out by the U.S. Supreme Court as "tainted."[19]

That Manning Johnson would and did lie is borne out by his record of testimony. To Johnson, the power to hurt, imprison, and deport people he hated and feared was more important than the truth. Johnson was questioned before the Subversive Activities Control Board about lying under oath:

Q. In other words, you will tell a lie under oath in a court of law rather than run counter to your instructions for the FBI. Is that right?

To which he responded:

Johnson: A. If the interests of my government are at stake. In the face of enemies, at home and abroad, if maintaining secrecy of the techniques of methods of operation of the FBI who have responsibility for the protection of our people, I say I will do it a thousand times.[20]

When cross-examined during a sedition trial in Pennsylvania about testimony he had given in an earlier deportation hearing, Johnson again admitted to having lied under oath:

Q. That testimony was not correct, was it, Mr. Johnson?

Johnson: A. No, it wasn't, precisely, because I could not at that time reveal that I had supplied information to the FBI. . . . I think the security of the government has priority over . . . any other considerations.[21]

To Johnson, serving his country, as he interpreted such "service," meant that lying under oath was justified.

Manning Johnson's testimony earned him $9,096 in one two-year period during the early 1950s, and the Justice Department continued to pay him $4,548 a year even after he admitted that he had perjured himself in a deportation case. After the Ralph Bunche affair, the Justice Department finally announced it was investigating him for perjury. He promptly quit as a paid informer and began to sell insurance. Prior to his death in 1959, he had become an early recruit to the John Birch Society.[22] However, these events, bringing Johnson into disrepute, came too late to help in the IWO case.

Williams's next witness, Joseph Zack Kornfeder, admitted to having used at least five different names, stating "these are a few that I can remember at this time."[23] He was fifty-four years old in 1951, and told the court he made a living as a writer and lecturer. He had also been a member of the IWO for two years, from 1932 to 1934.

More importantly for Williams, Kornfeder was an ex-Communist who professed expertise on Communism and its relationship to the Order. Williams stated that, "Most of the evidence this witness will give will be from the Communist point of view toward the IWO." Weissman's objection to his testifying at all was reflected in his question, "How many experts do we need on this one point?" Weissman added that he might testify to "debatable and highly inflammatory and utterly irrelevant" matters. Judge Greenberg brushed aside these objections, stating, "Don't worry about the inflammatory character."[24]

Under Williams's questioning, Kornfeder recited how he was a charter member of the Communist Party and became a Party functionary in the 1920s, moving through a number of positions until leaving the Party in 1934. He claimed to have been on its Central Committee for some years and on the Anglo-American Secretariat of Communist International, the worldwide governing body of English-speaking Communist Parties. He stated that from 1927 to 1930 he attended the Lenin School in Moscow and later taught at a Party school in America.[25] Judge Greenberg joined in the questioning as the witness told of lectures in the Moscow School by famous Soviets including Molotov and Stalin. Kornfeder also stated his knowledge of and connection with men who were involved with the IWO after 1930 such as Bedacht, Weiner, and Saltzman; all were identified as Party members in the 1920s and 1930s.[26]

Kornfeder's testimony followed along the lines of both Powers's and Johnson's as he detailed the close ties between the IWO and the Party through the "fraction" system and how in specific instances the Party dictated policy for the Order. "Yes," Kornfeder claimed, "the IWO was considered a basic prop of the Communist Party. It was a subject of discussion at important meetings."[27] What he added however, was that from the lodge to the national level, the Communist Party, through the fraction device, controlled who would be the leaders of the IWO, even though the majority of its voting members were not Communists. He testified that a proposed slate of national IWO officers was submitted to the Central Committee of the Party for approval.[28]

Courtroom "heat" really turned up when Williams questioned Kornfeder about the origins of the IWO, because Kornfeder would testify, in effect, that Moscow Communists actually *ordered* the break with the Workmen's Circle and the formation of the IWO. When this line of questioning developed, the following colloquy took place between the Judge and the lawyers:

By the Court.

Q. Did you ever attend any of those gatherings of the American section of the secretariat, or the International secretariat where the proposal with respect to forming the IWO was discussed?

A. Yes.

Q. Tell us what happened?

Mr. Weissman: Who was present, your Honor? . . . Was anybody from IWO present?

Q. All right. There couldn't have been anybody present in 1929 because it was not formed until 1930.

Mr. Weissman: You see, this illustrates one of the inherent vices in trying political issues in a courtroom.

The Court: No.

Mr. Weissman: We have no rules of evidence. Here is a man who says he read something in a report—

The Court: That is why I asked him and he said he was present, and I want to see what happened.

Mr. Williams: We have qualified this man as an expert on the Communist Party affairs and he is telling us how something works. There is no violation of any rule of evidence, as far as I know.

Mr. Weissman: [Being] an expert will cover some vices, but not all the vices.

Mr. Williams: I know counsel would like to keep out political matters here, but we have got to find out how the thing was set up, that is one of the charges here.[29]

Kornfeder then declared that the Moscow Politburo issued "directives" to form the IWO by relaying a message to the Central Committee of the Communist Party in the United States. When pressed about the nature of these "directives," Kornfeder could not recall any written or any oral ones—yet he insisted that such "directives" did exist.[30]

Williams's apparent strategy was to duplicate as much testimony about the alleged connection between the Communist Party and the IWO as possible, thus risking the inevitable boredom of such repetition to accomplish a greater goal: convincing Judge Greenberg that there must be truth to the underlying "hazard" argument by establishing a political link between the IWO and the "evil" of the Communist Party. Thus, the repeated characterization of Bedacht, Weiner, Saltzman, and others as Communist Party members who functioned for the Party through the fraction system effectively served the State's purpose. Only a few other points came out of the rest of Kornfeder's testimony, in large measure elicited by the Judge's own questions: that the Party paid his IWO dues, that he knew Powers and Johnson, and that he had testified in other matters.[31]

The *New York Times* carried the major Kornfeder accusation under the headline:

IWO Formation is Laid to Moscow
Kornfeder, Former Communist Testifies Politburo Ordered Group be Set up in '29.[32]

In a bench trial, counsel and the judge may freely discuss issues and the direction of evidence; with a jury present, by contrast, all discussion in open court must be much more circumspect. Thus, when Williams asked Kornfeder to identify a single member of the Communist Party who had subscribed to the initial Certificate of Incorporation of the IWO in 1930, Friedman and Judge Greenberg began the following exchange:

Mr. Friedman: That is objected to as irrelevant and immaterial. This certificate has been filed and has been officially approved. It has been on file for 20 years. What difference could it make in this proceeding who the signers of that were?

The Court: One of the issues tendered by the papers is that the IWO was founded by the Communist Party, or by Communists, and on that issue I think it is relevant and competent.

Mr. Friedman: Of course, that issue—

The Court: That may not have any ultimate bearing on the outcome of the litigation . . .[33]

Friedman's objection reflects what he considered to be the heart of the matter: who these people were and why their politics were irrelevant. What *was* relevant is what they did that may have been violative of a sound, conservative interpretation of the law. Yes, the Judge indicated, you may be correct as to the *legal* consequences, but I am willing to allow the State to develop a *factual* basis—that of Communist Party domination—that may create certain legal consequences.

Weissman's cross-examination of Kornfeder began with the question, "Mr. Kornfeder, are you a fictionalist?" Thus began a line of questions laced with sarcasm designed to impugn the testimony he had already given.[34]

Weissman developed that Kornfeder was a professional anti-Communist who made a living writing and lecturing as an ex-Communist. Kornfeder bridled under Weissman's questioning; he reluctantly admitted that he really had no occupation other than that of ex-Communist. He stated that in recent years he had testified in nine or ten cases for the federal government and also at Congressional hearings and in state matters. He was now getting "the usual" fee of $25 per day plus $9 in expenses. When Weissman asked Kornfeder whether he thought it was a "noble and patriotic way of making a living," Kornfeder replied that "It was a noble and patriotic way of fighting a major evil."[35]

Weissman then turned up the heat, showing by his examination and documents that Kornfeder had given different versions of when and where he was born and whether or not he was an alien. Weissman also suggested a link, which Kornfeder denied, between the INS dropping a deportation case against him and his quitting the Communist Party and testifying thereafter for the government.[36]

Weissman became even more effective in attacking Kornfeder's account of Communist Party discussions about the IWO and approval of a slate of officers. Kornfeder continually backpedaled on when and where these discussions were held. Weissman pointed out the logical inconsistencies in his testimony, showing that in other cases he had testified the opposite as to voting on an officer slate for the IWO as part of his Party work. Now, in the IWO case, he was changing his testimony again, claiming he had attended meetings and had voted. Even under Judge Greenberg's questioning Kornfeder could not deliver a cogent story.[37]

Bitterness between witness and cross-examiner erupted several times as Weissman turned to Kornfeder's story about a Moscow meeting where a "directive" was sent to break with the Workmen's Circle and form the Order. Weissman caught him on the matter of when this meeting took place; Kornfeder had changed the time of year of the meeting from his testimony in the Dmytryshyn case, but still insisted such a meeting had occurred. Kornfeder had testified in another case in 1948 that the decision to break had been made in 1923–24 with no mention of Moscow; he now claimed he had been in error in the earlier testimony.[38]

When Weissman finished with Kornfeder, Jones, Friedman's associate, took over the cross-examination. He developed that Kornfeder really had little knowledge of the workings of the IWO at the lodge level and that he had attended only a few lodge meetings and never an IWO convention. Thus Jones attempted to poke holes in the witness's assertions of Communist domination of the Order by showing how little he knew about its operation. Jones plodded through aspects of lodge activities, focusing on the apparently democratic election process and, in turn, Kornfeder's lack of involvement with or knowledge about them.

On a personal level, Jones established that the witness was living with a common-law wife and had never obtained a divorce from his first wife, who was still in Russia. Furthermore, Jones brought out that Kornfeder had no regular employment after 1946 and lived off wartime savings, lecture fees, and his salary as a paid professional witness.[39] No major New York newspaper carried any story reflecting the effective cross-examination of Kornfeder.

On February 7, 1951, the distaff side of one of the strangest couples to leave an impact on American history during the postwar decade took the stand as the next State's witness, forty-four-year-old Sylvia Crouch, wife of Paul Crouch. The Crouches were the only husband-wife team of professional paid informers in American history. Unknown to the defense, the State had arranged for both husband and wife to testify, but only Sylvia appeared. Williams's office files yield no explanation for Paul Crouch's failure to appear. So important was the lining up and preparation of these witnesses that an investigative agent of the Immigration and Naturalization Service, Laurence G. Parr, was on detached service with the Williams team, occupying space at the Wall Street law firm and assisting in the handling of witness matters. This was the same Parr who had been the subject of earlier contact by the Williams team as they sought INS cooperation. Not only did they get cooperation, but they got the actual "in-house" services of an INS official.[40]

Paul Crouch, a native of North Carolina, was a Socialist when he joined the army in 1924 or 1925. Within a year, he was court-martialed for offenses serious enough to result in a sentence of forty years' hard labor on Alcatraz Island, where he was released after three years with a dishonorable discharge. After release from prison, he joined the Communist Party and visited Russia. Thereafter, his Party assignments were in minor areas of Party work in Utah, the Carolinas, Virginia, Tennessee, Alabama, and California. Sylvia and Paul Crouch probably left the Communist Party in 1942. By the end of the decade, they had begun a joint career which would make them two of the best known and among the most financially successful paid professional ex-Communists of the time. Before becoming a professional paid-witness, Paul Crouch had earned eighty-five cents an hour as an airline employee; by the time of the IWO trial he was earning about $5,000 a year from his testimony.[41]

Sylvia Crouch and her husband were said to have approached their witnessing careers "in a thoroughly professional manner." Calling herself "acting executive secretary," Sylvia Crouch attempted to organize the "Federation of Former Communists." She wrote to other informers asking that they join her in seeking higher status, recognition, and fees for their group through organizational efforts.[42]

Historians who have dealt with the subject of paid informers frequently use Paul Crouch as an example of all that was evil about the system. David Caute has described him as "one of the most brazen and colorful liars in the business" and as "a political vampire" because of his record of wild accusations that harmed, even destroyed, many innocent people.[43]

The influential conservative columnists Joseph and Stewart Alsop exposed the Crouch taint by mid-1954, forcing the U.S. Attorney General to promise an investigation. Crouch reacted hysterically, demanding an investigation of the Attorney General's aides by the FBI and later petitioning Senator McCarthy to investigate Attorney General Brownell himself. In August 1954, Crouch filed a libel suit against the Alsops and the *New York Herald Tribune,* but the suit got nowhere and the Crouches' career as professional paid informers was at an end. As the years wore on, cases were reversed or dropped where the accused could point to the perjury of Crouch, Harvey Matusow, or Manning Johnson—allegations the Attorney General did not deny.[44]

On the witness stand, Sylvia Crouch, who had been flown in from Florida, testified that she, like her husband, had used many aliases. She claimed membership in the IWO for a little over a year, joining in 1932 and then rejoining in June or July of 1941 for a few months. She also claimed Communist Party membership from 1929 to 1942. With no more than an elementary school education, she had married Paul Crouch in 1928 and had two children.[45]

The first few hours of direct testimony by Sylvia Crouch yielded little that was new or pertinent. She testified that she was taught in a Communist Party school (where her husband was one of the teachers) that the IWO would carry out the Party's functions and be a haven for Party members if the Party were ever forced "underground."

Crouch claimed the Party ordered her to join the IWO, that she never had insurance with the Order, and that she was only a "social member." She also stated her dues were paid by other Party-IWO members.[46] In addition, she testified that she attended executive committee meetings of one IWO lodge where she obtained pledges of financial support to aid the Party in the 1932 national elections, and that she recalled seeing Party literature at IWO meetings.[47]

In later testimony, Crouch described two visits by Max Bedacht, whom she claimed addressed the IWO lodge in Norfolk, Virginia, in 1932 in order to raise money for the Communist Party campaign and again in 1933 to benefit the *Freiheit* (the Party's Jewish newspaper). When asked whether she knew Bedacht, Crouch responded that she did, but then misidentified George Powers as Bedacht from a photograph.[48]

The questioning was not without tension and rancor. After Williams described her as "a little frightened," this colloquy followed:

Mr. Weissman: Excuse me, madam, and your Honor: I don't think we ought to leave that [in the] record in that context without stating, in my opinion, and perhaps that of my colleagues at the table, that the lady has been speaking with a heavy, deep breathing since she identified George E. Powers as Max Bedacht and it was quite obvious to everybody in the court room that she was seriously embarrassed by that attempted identification, and if she has any difficulty about speaking freely, that is what is bothering her in her mind and conscience and not anything that happened in this court room.

Mr. Williams: Mr. Weissman, that is a very clever maneuver, but I don't submit that she was embarrassed or breathing heavily.

Mr. Weissman: I make no pretense of clever maneuvers. I don't want the record to show there was ever a suggestion on the ground for fear except of her own conscience.

Mr. Williams: That statement called for a comment by me that she is not embarrassed by anything that she has said.

Mr. Weissman: She ought to have been.

Mr. Williams: I have no comment for that remark.

The Court: Go ahead, counselor.[49]

In substance, Mrs. Crouch added that the Party decided to end the Young Pioneers, a Party youth organization, and transfer all members to the IWO's Youth Division and that David Greene, who was IWO Youth director as well as a Party functionary, was to carry this out.[50]

When Crouch testified that some officers of a lodge she belonged to were Communist Party members, Judge Greenberg asked whether anyone at a lodge meeting ever objected to discussions relating to Communism and the Party. She stated there had not been objections, and that while not all members of this lodge (some twelve to twenty) were Communists, they were all "sympathetic" to Communism.[51] This matter of possible objection to Communist topics, speakers, or literature was a recurring theme of Greenberg's about which, as has been seen, he inquired of several witnesses.

The cross-examination of Sylvia Crouch took longer than her direct testimony. Weissman wanted to elicit that she was barely literate and not to be believed. Having elicited that Crouch had no more than a seventh grade education, he demonstrated that she did not understand words that she used or books on Communism that she claimed to have read. For instance, when questioning her on her pay for testimony, she could not define "per diem," did not understand the word "curriculum," and confused "directive" with "decision." The harder Weissman pressed, the angrier she got and the worse her English became. At one point Weissman remarked, "I wish your snarl could be recorded on the record."[52]

Using the 1940 IWO Convention Proceedings, he showed that she could not have been a "social member" in 1932 since that category of membership began in 1940; nonetheless, Crouch insisted she was a "social member." Weissman also got her to concede that she and her husband earned most of their livelihood as paid witnesses, as she stated:

I am not ashamed of the fact that I am being paid as a witness. I am not a wealthy person and I have to live. I would not be able to pay my expenses to testify. And, I am not ashamed of the fact that I receive $25 a day.[53]

She also received $9 per day for expenses, plus paid travel and hotel accommodations.

A good deal of Crouch's testimony on cross-examination dealt with the 1930s when she, her husband, and their children wandered from state to state as minor Party functionaries, rarely staying more than a few months or a year at one place. It was a story of deprivations, wandering, and family illnesses. The family fortunes did not change until they quit the Party and found jobs in industry.[54]

Weissman returned to Crouch's having joined or rejoined the IWO in 1941. On the application card was a question about whether the applicant had ever belonged to the Order before. Crouch responded that she could not remember what or how she had answered, nor could she remember how she had answered these same questions under examination in the Dmytryshyn hearing. As Weissman questioned how she could remember exact conversations, persons, and events of 1932, but could not remember her responses under oath just a few months before, she gave this account of her memory:

A. I don't remember the exact words I answered. I know what was said, the text of what I said. I know what I remember. Maybe I don't remember at this moment just exactly the same thing I remembered at that moment.[55]

The application card also asked for the nature of employment; Sylvia Crouch had answered "housewife." Weissman challenged the answer, to which she responded, "Well, now, I wouldn't put down anything like that I am a member or organizer of the Young Communist League." The idea that Crouch would "hesitate to put [that] down on an application to the IWO" was very appealing to Weissman, since it ran counter to everything she had said about the ties between the Order and the Party.[56]

Friedman then took over the cross-examination, developing the fact that Sylvia Crouch had acted as a spy by reporting the names of persons she recognized as Communists in the defense plant where she worked. He also got Crouch to admit that she was not an expert on the IWO, even though the INS had contracted with her as such an "expert."[57]

Friedman then did a masterful job of moving through her testimony to impugn her reliability as a witness. It had been some eighteen years since Crouch claimed she had attended several meetings a week in her various functions, and she wanted the Court to believe she could remember exact items and details of who said what at certain of those meetings. Yet upon questioning, she could not remember very basic matters relevant to those same occurrences. Crouch acknowledged that part of the IWO meetings she attended were not in English, her only language. Furthermore she admitted that, although a great deal of other lodge business took place, she could not recall anything other than that relating to the Party, even failing to remember the name and location of the lodge or the names of any of its officers.[58]

Using Sylvia Crouch's testimony on cross-examination, Friedman introduced a number of documents drawn from the 1941 period when she was an IWO member living in Oakland, California. His twofold purpose was to demonstrate to the Court the number of social and cultural activities (drum and bugle corps competitions, basketball teams, a folk festival) sponsored by the Order as well as literature on a number of social and cultural topics disseminated by the IWO and that this witness, though claiming to be active in the organization, could identify only one matter (the folk festival) that did not pertain to her testimony on Communist ties. After Friedman elicited that she could remember only unnamed Communist literature but none of the many pieces published by the IWO, Friedman closed in on Crouch with this question:

Q. Is it possible that the reason you don't remember those publications is that you are being paid to testify that you saw Communist publications and you are not being paid to testify that you saw IWO publications; is that the reason?

Mr. Williams: That question is improper in form.

The Court: No, I think I will allow that, Mr. Williams. Objection overruled, exception.

A. No.

Q. That could have nothing to do with it?

A. Nothing whatsoever.[59]

Of the State's witnesses thus far, Sylvia Crouch was clearly the least effective, least credible, and least knowledgeable about the IWO. One clue to her apparent deficiencies in building the State's case is the paucity of involvement by Judge Greenberg, who asked her very little in contrast to earlier witnesses. Not only did Friedman's cross-examination challenge the validity and persuasiveness of Crouch's testimony, but her direct testimony was objectively unconvincing. On the other hand, she did not seriously damage the earlier testimony of the State's witnesses.

Until Crouch's testimony, the IWO's press releases had not specifically attacked State witnesses. On February 8, 1951, however, a news release attacking her testimony read, in part:

Mrs. Sylvia Crouch, mother of two children, who in deportation hearings has helped send mothers to jail and tear fathers from their families, is the state's current witness in the liquidation trial of the International Workers Order.

This marks the fifth time Mrs. Crouch has appeared as a paid government witness against working men and women. After a lifetime of trying to raise a family on ten or twelve dollars a week, Mrs. Crouch now earns twenty-five dollars a day plus nine dollars in expenses as an "expert" informer. With her husband, Paul Crouch, she is part of a husband-and-wife team testifying jointly before the Un-American Activities committees and in deportation trials. Their joint income, then, becomes fifty dollars a day plus expenses. This is the kind of money the Crouches use to put meat on their table and clothes on their backs.

But for all her willingness, the lady proved a poor witness for the prosecution. A fellow informer in the trial, George E. Powers, had "identified" from a page of photographs, Max Bedacht, former IWO official, as a Communist. Shown the same page of photographs, Mrs. Crouch fingered a photo of Powers and said, "This is Max Bedacht."

A shocking thing about her attack on the Order is her admission that when she and her family were destitute in Norfolk, Virginia, in 1932, IWO members gave them bread, shoes, clothes and money. She offered no explanation for turning against the Order except to voluntarily testify that her present career as informer "pays her way."

Mrs. Crouch who sells her testimony with a Southern accent, left the stand today and will undoubtedly make other appearances in witch hunting trials.[60]

When Sylvia Crouch left the witness stand on February 8, 1951, the IWO lawyers renewed their application to the Judge for permission to hold the planned National IWO Convention. In turn, the Superintendent of Insurance vigorously renewed his opposition through Williams. Judge Greenberg reviewed the facts and, essentially relying on the argument that since the Order was in court with its legal existence under challenge, "It [the convention] would interfere with the orderly process of the law and serve no useful purpose," and once again denied the application.[61]

The Judge went on to assure the IWO that this did not prevent its "right of assembly" or the privilege to "freely express their views" or take any alternative action short of an official convention. He pointed out that communication between the national office and the local lodges remained "free and unhampered" and that protests were still permitted.[62] Weissman reacted to the Judge's decision by arguing that, without a convention, the IWO membership of some 162,000 could not express their reaction to the Haley Report or this legal action.

Friedman then argued that the Court's position was in fact in "sharp derogation of [the Order's] rights to assemble and to express their views. There is no way in which these 162,000 people can express themselves except by the method provided by statute [a general convention]." Weissman pleaded for the Court to reconsider, offering to withdraw any request for the further release of monies to pay for the convention; delegates would pay their own way. He argued that the entire proceeding "is part of the Cold War, and also, unfortunately, a witch hunt."[63]

Judge Greenberg's final answer was to tell the lawyers for the Order and Policyholders Protective Committee to go "up to 25th Street and Madison Avenue" to test if he was wrong. This was a reference to the Appellate Division; he was, in effect, telling the IWO lawyers to appeal his denial of their application. The problem, however, was that the denial of this application for a convention was probably not appealable since it was within the trial court's discretion.[64]

From Sylvia Crouch, Williams now moved to Charles H. White, a thirty-eight-year-old black ex-Communist (1930–1936), and ex-IWO member (1934–1935) as his next witness. Williams's purpose in having White testify was to tie the operations of the Young Communist League (YCL) to the IWO. White testified that he went to the Lenin School in

Moscow in late 1931 and early 1932 and there learned about the place of the IWO in the Party's scheme. White also spoke of having received military training while in Russia, and when Weissman objected, Judge Greenberg took the matter lightly. Weissman, however, took a more serious view, stating, "I hardly think the record nor the press will take it that light, I move to strike out all of this business of firearms." The Judge refused.[65]

White testified that the IWO was discussed at the school, along with advice on how to build "fractions." He stated that young people "who were not quite ready yet to recruit in the Young Communist League directly" were to be targeted for recruitment into the IWO's Youth Division. In summary, he described his duties as involving organizing youth sections of the IWO, recruiting prospects from there to the YCL, and getting IWO contributions for Party election campaigns.[66]

Judge Greenberg cut short White's testimony, because it was evident that Williams was covering areas about which prior witnesses had already testified. The Judge understood the trial technique of reinforcement through repetition: get enough cross-collateralization of an idea or theme and the point is made. Even though cross-examination weakens the credibility of each, the whole of the testimony stands.

When White claimed he was "ordered" to join the IWO by the YCL, Judge Greenberg questioned him closely:

The Court: It was an assignment for you to join?

The Witness: Yes.

The Court: You are sure of that?

The Witness: It was an order, it came from the Young Communist International.

Mr. Weissman: Was the last answer, "It came from the Young Communist International?"

The Witness: Yes.

The Court: Did you pay your dues?

The Witness: I recall paying some moneys. I was told that the party would take care of the dues; I didn't have to worry about it. I was a full-time functionary for the Young Communist League.[67]

The testimony most damaging to the IWO was White's description of his assignment by the Young Communist League to build a youth section for the Order in Harlem, controlled by a YCL "fraction." He described how, with the permission of IWO officers David Greene and

Louise Patterson, he used the Order's Harlem headquarters for his organizational efforts. Using IWO lists, he told how he visited members' homes to induce young people to join the Youth section he was organizing.[68]

Williams took him deeply into the use of literature—Party books and pamphlets—sold and given out at IWO meetings. White himself claimed to have written one pamphlet distributed at these meetings.[69]

Tempers flared when White went beyond what was asked in order to state what he apparently wanted the Judge to hear. Although not specifically asked about the matter, he broached the topic of the collection of monies at lodge meetings where he had spoken. Everyone understood that contributions by *individual* Order members to any cause White was promoting constituted individual acts, but use of *lodge* monies for political purposes would be violative of the insurance laws. At best, White could remember only that he collected cash, not checks, and could not remember whether he got any money directly from any lodge treasury.[70]

At this point Judge Greenberg took over the examination of White, asking him a series of questions: did he know the other witnesses? (Powers—no; Johnson—yes; Kornfeder—yes). He asked about William Weiner, IWO President at the time White was a member. White said Weiner, who then was also the Party treasurer, gave him money to go to Moscow. White told the Judge he had dropped out of the Order because he had no need for insurance; the Party, he claimed, paid for his needs, adding "I was in there for other purposes."[71] In anticipation of and even perhaps in an attempt to cut short the cross-examination to follow, Judge Greenberg asked White about his work as a paid witness. White stated he had testified for the government about twelve times since 1937 at the usual $25 per day.[72]

The cross-examination of White demonstrated an increasing bitterness on the part of Weissman. He must have known the influence upon the Judge of the parade of witnesses repeating the same story, from different angles, of Communist Party connection with the IWO. When early in the trial Judge Greenberg made the crucial ruling denying the IWO motions to dismiss, he had, in effect, shown his willingness to hear the "political" theme presented by the State.

In his cross-examination, Weissman as before used White's testimony at the Dmytryshyn hearing, pointing out discrepancies about dates, particularly as to when White joined the Order. White admitted he might have been as much as a year off in his testimony. Weissman also got White to admit he was wrong about the payment of dues. Just how bitter this exchange became is reflected in the record:

Q. What about this business you were telling us, you gave somebody money and somebody did something for you? That was a lie, wasn't it?

A. That was not a lie.

Q. It wasn't the truth, it was an invention, wasn't it?

A. It was a hasty recollection.

Q. An invention. Was the story told here on direct examination also a hasty recollection? Let me put it to you as man to man. Was it also an invention; yes or no?

A. I don't know what you mean, counsellor.

Mr. Williams: What story?

Q. The whole story you told on the witness stand.

A. (No answer.)

Q. Let us go back to the Dmytryshyn hearings. Listen to me and look at me, if you please. How long ago were the Dmytryshyn hearings, do you remember?

A. Let me think about it so I will get it as close as possible.

Q. Think about it, think hard.

A. It was sometime around September or August, I am not sure.

Q. Of what year?

A. Last year.

Q. Was that so difficult to recall, Mr. White?

A. It was.

Q. But you had no difficulty in being very fluent and even offering details about matters that occurred eighteen years ago; isn't that so?

A. I do have difficulty recalling what happened eighteen years ago.[73]

White was pummeled by the questions Weissman fired at him in rapid succession. The examination revealed discrepancies and inconsistencies as White hung on to his essential story of YCL-IWO activity. The fact that he was a paid, professional informer was elaborated upon. That he had lied when he wrote on his IWO application that he was a "laborer" resulted in this colloquy which brought laughter to the courtroom:

Q. And you were a laborer at the time?

A. I was an organizer for the Young Communist League, to the best of my recollection.

Q. Then, when you put down the statement you were a laborer, it was false; is that so? Have you an answer, Mr. White?

A. It was false and there was a purpose for that.

Q. Now, what purpose did you think up in the last three minutes, tell us that.

Mr. Williams: If your Honor, please, it was not three minutes; there was a pause, but it was not three minutes.

A. I will tell you.

Q. You tell me now, you have the purpose in mind, tell me right away.

A. As a Y.C.L. functionary it was my duty to tell many official and unofficial lies; it was a lie. On applications, no matter.

Q. Excuse me, have you gotten out of that habit yet?

Mr. Williams: I thought it was something like that. Let the witness finish his answer and then you can ask another question. This is not for the amusement of the gallery.

Mr. Weissman: This is hardly amusing.

Mr. Williams: They seem to think it is amusing.

Mr. Weissman: I am talking about what is happening on the witness stand. We have no gallery here; we have a performer in the front.

Mr. Williams: You elicited laughs from the gallery here.

Mr. Weissman: Are you making the suggestion on the record I was playing to any gallery?

Mr. Williams: I am not suggesting what you were doing, that you were playing to any gallery. Let the witness answer the question. That is all I am asking you to do.

The Witness: We were not permitted to write anywhere that we were paid organizers of the Young Communist League at any time . . . for the purposes of economic security for the future.

Q. It was necessary to conceal it from IWO?

A. From anybody, everybody.

Q. It was necessary to conceal it from IWO?

A. From the IWO, too.[74]

In an apparent strategic move, Weissman abruptly stopped his cross-examination and Jones, the lawyer who in association with Friedman represented the Policyholders' Protective Committee, rose to his feet to continue. Jones began by asking White what IWO lodge he belonged to in 1935; White said he didn't recall belonging to any lodge. When Jones challenged this response by pointing out that every member is required to belong to a lodge, White responded:

A. The functionaries of the Young Communist League weren't; we were exceptional people. We could walk in any of those lodges any time we got ready.[75]

The problem for Jones was that to rebut this assertion he would have to wait for the testimony of someone from the Order or specific documentary evidence that would disprove what White had just said.

White was apparently given to hyperbole. He asserted that in 1934 he attended about 1,000 meetings, approximately ten of which were of IWO lodges. White claimed he remembered those Order meetings and the titles of Party literature sold there. Jones took him through a long interrogation on the matter of literature and his ability to recall what was available at those meetings some seventeen years before in order to demonstrate, in effect, the impossibility of what White claimed to remember.[76]

Moving to the subject of his status as a witness, Jones asked White the loaded question, "When did you begin to be an informer for the Government?" White responded that he was never an informer. Jones re-phrased the question into "When did you begin putting the finger on your former friends for the Government?" Williams was at once on his feet objecting, and Judge Greenberg stepped in:

The Court: Let us not quibble. When did you start testifying as an expert on Communism and the Communist party, whether it is for the Government, the State, or any Congressional or legislative committee?

The Witness: As an expert, I began in 1947. Prior to that I hadn't qualified myself as an expert, but just stating my background and experience.

The Court: You had testified before?

The Witness: Yes.

The Court: You have been testifying since 1937; is that it?

The Witness: Since 1937.[77]

The Cold War and Red Scare had improved White's status from "witness" to paid "expert."

Notes

1. Trial Record, pp. 1180–85.
2. Trial Record, p. 1190.
3. Trial Record, pp. 1190–93.
4. Trial Record, pp. 1199–1200.
5. Trial Record, pp. 1202–03.
6. Trial Record, pp. 1212–17.
7. Trial Record, p. 1218.
8. Trial Record, pp. 1222–28.
9. Trial Record, pp. 1229–33.
10. Trial Record, pp. 1233–41.
11. Trial Record, p. 1243.
12. Trial Record, p. 1244.
13. *New York Herald Tribune,* February 1, 1951.
14. Trial Record, pp. 1263–79.
15. Trial Record, pp. 1279–88.
16. Trial Record, pp. 1288–97.
17. Trial Record, p. 1301.
18. Trial Record, pp. 1307–21.
19. Johnson's record on these matters is stated in Murray Kempton, *America Comes of Middle Age* (Boston: Little, Brown, 1963), pp. 13–14.
20. Quoted in Richard H. Rovere, "The Kept Witness," in *The American Establishment and Other Reports, Opinions and Speculations* (London: Rupert Hart-Davis, 1963), p. 70.
21. Ibid.
22. David Caute, *The Great Fear: The Anti-Communist Purge Under Truman and Eisenhower* (New York: Simon and Schuster, 1978), p. 129.
23. Trial Record, pp. 1163–64.
24. Trial Record, p. 1365.
25. Trial Record, pp. 1365–73.
26. Trial Record, pp. 1374–80.
27. Trial Record, p. 1389.
28. Trial Record, pp. 1390–1400.
29. Trial Record, pp. 1406–07.
30. Trial Record, pp. 1409–10.
31. Trial Record, pp. 1412–24.
32. *New York Times,* February 6, 1951.
33. Trial Record, pp. 1425–28.
34. Trial Record, p. 1430.
35. Trial Record, pp. 1431–38.
36. Trial Record, pp. 1439–43.
37. Trial Record, pp. 1460–63.
38. Trial Record, pp. 1465–77.
39. Trial Record, pp. 1486–1505.
40. Williams Office Files, Correspondence, Vol. I.

41. Harvey Klehr, *The Heyday of American Communism: The Depression Decade* (New York: Basic Books, 1984); Rovere, "The Kept Witness" (note 20), p. 61.

42. Caute, *The Great Fear* (note 22), p. 127.

43. Ibid., pp. 126–27.

44. Ibid., pp. 128, 171.

45. Trial Record, pp. 1506–10.

46. Trial Record, pp. 1530–31.

47. Trial Record, pp. 1532–45.

48. Trial Record, pp. 1549–55.

49. Trial Record, pp. 1560–61.

50. Trial Record, pp. 1561–65.

51. Trial Record, pp. 1566–70.

52. Trial Record, p. 1580.

53. Trial Record, p. 1585.

54. Trial Record, pp. 1606–19.

55. Trial Record, pp. 1620–21.

56. Trial Record, p. 1622.

57. Trial Record, pp. 1640–47.

58. Trial Record, pp. 1650–59.

59. Trial Record, pp. 1660–69.

60. *IWO News Release,* February 8, 1951. Williams Office Files.

61. Trial Record, p. 1682.

62. Trial Record, pp. 1682–83.

63. Trial Record, pp. 1685–87.

64. Trial Record, p. 1688.

65. Trial Record, pp. 1692–1705.

66. Trial Record, pp. 1705–07.

67. Trial Record, pp. 1715–16.

68. Trial Record, pp. 1716–17.

69. Trial Record, pp. 1719–20.

70. Trial Record, pp. 1720–23.

71. Trial Record, pp. 1723–25.

72. Trial Record, pp. 1725–26.

73. Trial Record, pp. 1727–36.

74. Trial Record, pp. 1747–49.

75. Trial Record, pp. 1749–50.

76. Trial Record, pp. 1750–59.

77. Trial Record, pp. 1760–61.

Chapter IX
The Role of the Press; The State Continues its Case

Before the State called its next witness, Williams addressed the Court, advising the Judge that Mrs. Crouch had reported she had been threatened as she left the courtroom after her testimony. He immediately added that he didn't think "[the IWO lawyers] would have permitted any such thing." Friedman then asked why Williams would even raise the matter "unless it was for the purpose of casting an imputation on the defense."[1]

Tensions ran high as Sylvia Crouch took the stand again to explain what had happened. She stated that she had been followed out the door of the courtroom by a man who said, "You better get out of here as fast as you can, witness [or paid witness—she was not certain]; if you know what is good for you, you had better get out of here." Upon questioning, she added that the man did not follow her into the elevator nor did he make any gesture toward her. All of this was reported to Henry and Williams, who asked her to stay another day to see whether the man showed up. Crouch admitted she was not afraid. Weissman responded by addressing the Court:

> The incident is not remotely connected with anything which would be something like a threat. It might have been something which was in bad taste, as it would be, for anybody to talk to a witness who leaves the court room, but I can't for the life of me, see what this melodramatic business about calling it to the attention of the Court on the record was for.
>
> The effect of it is to create the same kind of air of mystery and violence. . . . It is more than a regrettable incident and I think your Honor ought to take some action with respect to it. This record should not be cluttered up with such unfortunate incidents. The lady said the man was never [closer than] either 20 or 25 feet away from her. He made some remark which, as I said, was probably in bad taste.[2]

Judge Greenberg stated that he attached no significance to the incident and considered it "closed or forgotten." Jones asked the Judge to "see to it that the press does not abuse this particular situation," to which he responded:

You, of all people, should be the last person to want me to censor the press.

Mr. Jones: No. An admonition with respect to the subject will protect this proceeding from becoming a political football.

The Court: Let me say this to you, Mr. Jones. In about two weeks time an article is coming out over my pen, for better or worse, and perhaps I am exposing myself to dangers, in which I have certain comments to make about the function and the position of the press in a democratic society. There are some things stated in there that I am not sure will be met eye to eye by the members of the Fourth Estate, so you need not have any concern about my being influenced either by the press or by those two ever present witnesses referred to by a friend of mine, "Hue" and "Cry." You see, the press is even taking that down. We will now adjourn to Tuesday at 11:00 o'clock.[3]

Newspapers, as predicted, did pick up the story. On February 10, 1951, the *New York Herald Tribune* summarized the event under the headline, "Witness For State in I.W.O. Suit Tells Court She Was Threatened."[4]

What Judge Greenberg was referring to was an essay he had composed for a series entitled "The Main Currents of Our Democracy." The essay, published in April 1951, was a forty-page composition on *The Bench, the Bar and the Press.* Judge Greenberg, a legal scholar as well as an active trial judge, had an avid interest in the press; newspaper work had been his first love and occupation. In this essay, he explained the role of each component in the operation of a modern court system, with special emphasis on the role of the press in reporting legal matters, particularly pending lawsuits.[5]

Recognizing the power of the press to shape public opinion as well as influence judges, lawyers, and juries, Greenberg argued for the approach used in England where, he maintained, a satisfactory balance had been achieved without the need for dangerous legislation. There, an agreement had been reached, promulgated in a code of journalistic ethics which included the prohibition on editorial comments pending the outcome of a trial and guaranteed that allegations would be clearly stated and treated as allegations only. Furthermore, any defense against such allegations would be given "equal and prominent" place.[6]

Judge Greenberg recognized the power of the press in the light of the Red Scare. About this, he wrote:

It is interesting to analyze various newspapers for their manner of reporting. A critical subject is the one of current investigation into subversive acts. Some newspapers announce in big type that an investigator has called someone a Communist. Then some days later, if at all, these newspapers print a reply, perhaps on an inside page. Reputations are destroyed without the grant of an adequate defense. People are tried in a diabolical sense without due process law. . . .

Yet who can be tried these days for a crime having political implications, protected by the sanctity of a fair trial, when attitudinizing about the trial destroys the very safety the accused is alleged to have attempted to destroy?[7]

While Greenberg obviously was admonishing against the trend of the times being influenced by and in turn influencing the power of the press, he was also aware that no one—including the bench—was immune from its influence; thus, he stated:

Think of the power of this creation! Who is not affected by the press? The child finds his comics there; the historian his premises; the financier his market. Everyone is touched, and however intellectually free one says he is, no one puts his paper down without taking forever a part of it with him.[8]

As an avid newspaper reader, could Judge Henry Clay Greenberg rise above the "Hue and Cry" in his own courtroom on the hottest domestic subject of the day—the role of Communism in American life? It was indeed a neat piece of irony that Judge Greenberg, the legal scholar, had written such a piece, apparently completed before the IWO case began, and that he himself would now put to the specific test of rising above media coverage during Red Scare times.

Williams's next witness, Charles Baxter, was another "consultant" to the Immigration and Naturalization Service, brought from Cleveland to testify. Now aged forty-four, his background was that of a Party member and functionary from 1927 to 1945 who had operated primarily in the field of seamen's union activities. Williams's questioning yielded responses that placed Baxter in Moscow at the Lenin School in 1929 and 1930 where, once again, part of the training he received was in firearms and guerilla warfare. Baxter testified that the concept of a Communist split in the Workmen's Circle, which led to the formation of the IWO, had been discussed at the school.

The basic premise advanced by Baxter in his testimony was that his Party role "was to see that the IWO functioned correctly." As Judge Greenberg explored this matter, taking an ever-increasing role by his direct questioning, the IWO attorneys objected to some of the Judge's questions, thus once more forcing him to rule on objections to his own questions. The Order's attorneys had to do this without antagonizing Judge Greenberg's ego or leading him to believe they were attempting to limit the search for truth. Williams played the matter from the vantage point of silence: ask any witness whatever you wish, even if it might hurt my case. He was in the position to benefit by rarely, if ever, challenging the Judge's questioning.[9]

Baxter claimed that, as a Party functionary moving from place to place across the country, he was in contact with Party members who were in the IWO—that, in effect, he had played liaison between the Party and the Order. Of particular interest to the Court, Baxter stated that after the Nazi-Soviet Pact of 1939 his task was to help IWO lodges explain the Pact and get members who had dropped out to rejoin. Judge Greenberg asked, "The Stalin-Hitler Pact didn't shock you?" Baxter answered, "No, it didn't shock me, very frankly."[10]

The balance of Baxter's direct testimony was an identification process. The Judge began by running through his list of names of IWO officers to see whether Baxter knew them and could identify them from photographs. Williams then took him through the same list to elicit whether he knew them to be Communist Party members, most of whom Baxter did so identify.

Baxter had been a full-time employee of the Immigration and Naturalization Service since February 1950. On cross-examination, Weissman probed the exact nature of his work for the INS, boiling the matter down to the question, "You mean you sell your former Communist connections; is that right?" Baxter answered with a simple "yes." When Weissman then asked "What else do you do?" Baxter responded, "Well, that is the main outline of my duties."[11] Weissman elicited that Baxter made more money on the days when he testified than when he was simply on the government payroll. He had, in fact, testified between ten and fifteen times in less than a year. The major admission Weissman obtained was that, in a prior hearing, Baxter admitted that he had been promised steady employment with the INS in exchange for his agreement to testify for the government.[12]

By asking about the circumstances surrounding Baxter's having left the Party, Weissman opened up a fruitful area in his quest to discredit the witness. Tempers flared and the Judge, apparently becoming angry, stepped in with a number of pointed questions, as Weissman demonstrated that the witness had been accused of accepting a bribe from an employer or at least of being the courier for a bribe when he was a union officer. Weissman did a credible job in tying together Baxter leaving his union job with his being thrown out of the Communist Party over the bribe matter. Judge Greenberg was apparently so incensed by Baxter's testimony that he told him to step down, only then remembering that it was still Weissman's right to continue the cross-examination.[13]

Weissman's continued questioning revealed that Baxter had been arrested on charges of illegally selling liquor and maintaining a house of prostitution. Under further questioning by counsel and the Judge, there was considerable erosion of his story about the formation of the IWO as it related to what he heard while at school in Moscow. Weissman, in a spurt of sarcasm, followed up by contrasting Baxter's ability to remember the titles of pamphlets he claimed to have seen on tables at lodge meetings eighteen years ago with his inability to recall his testimony at the Dmytryshyn hearing only six months before.[14]

One of the attributes of a good trial lawyer is the ability to listen carefully and remember what has been said. Weissman demonstrated this ability upon Baxter's return the next day to the stand, when he challenged Baxter's earlier claim that he had collected money for the Party at IWO social affairs on two or three occasions and that the money had come from "lodge treasuries." Baxter denied that he had said that. The record of earlier testimony was produced, showing that Weissman was correct—Baxter had so testified. Confronted with this, the witness then backed away from this assertion.[15] Williams did not ask for any redirect testimony from Baxter after Weissman finished his cross-examination. The legal implication was that Baxter's credibility had been effectually challenged, and Williams could not rehabilitate his witness.

In a press release dated February 14, 1951, the IWO covered part of Baxter's testimony as follows:

In addition to bribe-taking, Baxter was arraigned in Cleveland in 1947 on the charge of renting out a room for purposes of prostitution and illegally selling alcohol. He was convicted on the latter charge.

Baxter's participation in a $2,000 bribe scandal and his unsavory court record were concealed by the Insurance Department, who presented him to the court as an "expert" witness.

Spectators who thronged the courtroom evidenced disgust with Baxter, several leaving for a breath of fresh air. Even Judge Henry C. Greenberg, who has listened most patiently to the testimony of stoolpigeons, displayed distaste with the conduct and record of the witness and angrily ordered him from the stand. This occurred when the judge took over the questioning and received shifty answers from Baxter. IWO counsel, however, said he had further questions to ask and the cross-examination continued. . . .

In startling contrast with his paid attempt to portray the IWO as a "tool" of the Communist Party, Baxter blurted out that the IWO was and is "basically non-political. It supports working class struggles. Campaigns are presented in the IWO as being in the interest of the working class, not the Communist Party."[16]

Howard Rushmore, thirty-nine years old in 1951, was the State's next witness. His testimony was of apparent interest to Judge Greenberg because he was a journalist who had worked for the *Daily Worker* and other Communist publications between 1937 and 1939. The major points of Rushmore's testimony were, in effect, two: First, that as a reporter for the *Daily Worker,* he had interviewed Max Bedacht, then general secretary of the Order, who told him—as Communist to Communist—that, as the IWO expanded and enlarged, "it could prove an excellent recruiting ground for the Party" and that Bedacht appreciated the *Daily Worker*'s efforts to bring the IWO to the attention of its readers. His other major point was that he had been ordered by his superiors at the *Daily Worker* to carry out the policy of the paper, which was to publicize and give favorable treatment to the IWO. Judge Greenberg then asked, "Did you carry out these orders?" to which Rushmore replied, "Yes, your Honor."[17]

Early into the cross-examination, Weissman developed that almost immediately upon leaving the Communist Party Rushmore had gotten a job with the *New York Journal American* newspaper, where he specialized in articles about Communists. Asked, "Didn't you start right in with articles against your former associates of the Communist Party?" Rushmore answered, "Oh, yes, very happily; I love to do it." Later, he acknowledged, "I am assigned exclusively to handle Communism, more or less, on a roving assignment basis."[18]

Rushmore had already testified in a number of cases involving alleged Communists and the Party. Weissman, throughout his cross-examination, attempted to paint this obviously articulate person as so thoroughly blending his anti-Communism with his newspaper work that he was willing to say anything to make the IWO appear more sinister if it would make the State's case sound better. Thus Rushmore denied it when Weissman asked, "Isn't it because of your anti-Communist policy to shove in anything you can in an answer?"

When Simon Weber took the stand for the State on February 19, 1951, this constituted a direct confrontation of old enemies. Weber was the city editor of the *Jewish Daily Forward,* the voice of the Workmen's Circle, and a longtime implacable enemy of the Jewish leftists who had founded the IWO. Through the *Freiheit,* the Communist Party paper of the Jewish left, the battle between the radical leftists and Communists and the Socialists, whose voice was the *Forward,* had raged for some twenty years. These groups and their respective papers took their politics as a matter of utmost seriousness and for years had heaped mutual vituperation upon each other.

Weber had been in touch with Williams's office when word first came out about the State's prosecution. He had made telephone inquiries about the case, in response to which Williams had sent him materials about it. Weber sent Williams *Forward* articles denouncing the IWO, which Williams had translated for his files. Weber was to be the only nonprofessional witness used by the State and the only one who appeared in response to a subpoena.

Weber, then forty years old, had changed sides, and therein lay his value to the State. A member of the Communist Party from 1931 to 1937, in the early to mid-thirties he had taught in the IWO schools run by its Jewish section. He had also written for and then worked for the *Freiheit*. He testified that he got his IWO teaching job (he was also an Order member for a couple of years during the mid-1930s) through his Communist Party contacts.[19]

With this testimony concerning teaching, Weber was serving Williams's purpose by establishing close ties between the Party and the IWO. When asked what he had taught to the attending schoolchildren he emphasized the political nature and indoctrination aims of his work:

Q. Was there any basic doctrine that you taught these children?

A. Yes, there was.

Q. What was it?

A. The basic doctrine was to grow up to be Communists.[20]

At a time when the alleged potential of Communist subversion through the act of teaching in schools was in the national spotlight, such statements carried dramatic force. Here was a man who was declaring under oath that he had participated in direct propagandizing of children for the Communist cause with not only the acquiescence but, as he stated in his testimony, under the actual direction of the school administration.

Weber's testimony continued, centering on his activities for the *Freiheit* in Detroit as they related to the IWO. He stated that the Order advertised in modest amounts in the paper and that it ran social affairs where money was collected from individual members to support the *Freiheit*. Of these monies, Weber testified that 80 percent was forwarded to the *Freiheit*'s New York office and 20 percent to the district committee of the Communist Party in Detroit. The Judge in his direct questioning brought out that IWO officials and members did not know about the split of the monies; the contributors were led to believe all monies simply benefited the paper.[21]

Williams used Weber to introduce a pamphlet written in 1931 by then editor of the *Freiheit*, M. Olgin, whom Weber had earlier identified as a Party member, entitled *The International Workers Order—History, Program, Technique*. The problem was that the pamphlet was in Yiddish, and Weber proceeded to translate, "By Commission of National Executive Committee of the International Workers Order by M. Olgin, New York, 1931." A heated argument ensued as to whether Weber had properly translated the words "By Commission." Williams stated:

This book, the witness has identified, as a book which he saw in IWO lodges distributed among the members, and he has read it. On its cover it says, "Commissioned," or "put out," or something else, by the IWO, and on its frontispiece it is identified as an IWO piece of literature. It contains statements which I want in evidence, which I believe are very damaging to the respondent.

The Court: Dealing with Communism?

Mr. Williams: Dealing with Communism and the identification of the IWO with the Communist Party.

The Court: Does it?

The Witness: It does.

Mr. Williams: Furthermore, it deals with the position of the IWO if the Communist Party had to go underground.[22]

Williams had obtained the copy and its translation from the Immigration and Naturalization Service. Weissman and Friedman argued that the translation "contained some very serious divergences from the original." The Court agreed to "hold it in status quo" until the defense had a chance to investigate the translation. Weber further stated that Olgin was neither a member nor an officer of the Order.[23]

Under direct examination in his closing testimony, Weber stated that he had testified for the INS at the Dmytryshyn hearing and had there learned a fact he had forgotten—that he had been for a short time an IWO member and had been expelled for nonpayment of dues. Finally he claimed that he had, at the direction of the Party, made speeches at IWO lodge meetings.[24]

Weissman then rose for his cross-examination of Weber; he was able to elicit from Weber that he had made a twelve-year career of being an anti-Communist, about which Weber stated, "I am very proud of my anti-Communist writings." When Weissman asked Weber whether he had written articles advising *Forward* readers to quit the IWO, the following colloquy took place:

Q. And you advised all the readers who happened to belong to the IWO to leave the IWO, did you not?

A. No, not exactly.

Q. What did you do in that respect?

A. I called attention to the fact that membership in the IWO by people who innocently joined because they thought it was a fraternal order, may lead them, if they are not citizens, to deportation proceedings, and I advised them that IWO was Communist-controlled and if they innocently joined, they better leave.[25]

A lengthy interrogation followed, designed to discredit Weber as a reporter because he had obeyed an order from his superiors to suppress a certain news story and also to suggest, over Weber's objections and denials, that he had taken a bribe as part of that suppression.[26]

Weissman then moved to the matter of Weber's teaching in IWO schools by rapidly firing off questions in an attempt to disturb Weber's balance. Although Weissman obtained admissions that modified how Weber got the job, Weber stuck to his story that Communist doctrine, diluted for reception by children, was taught by him. He did admit, however, that the school was financed not by the lodge treasury but by parents whose children attended.

Weissman took his seat, and Jones resumed the cross-examination. Jones's theme of interrogation was similar to what he had used on other State witnesses—to establish that the major programs and political positions of the IWO were in the mainstream of "acceptable" attitudes. Thus, he got Weber to confirm that there was nothing "sinister" about the Order's support for a broadened Social Security system, Fair Housing law, slum clearance, enlarged unemployment insurance, and civil rights for blacks. Weber conceded that he knew little or nothing about the internal affairs of the IWO since he left it some fifteen years ago and that he could name only one position of the Order (fight against Fascist elements and anti-Semitism demonstrated in the Peekskill riots) since 1935. Weissman had earlier elicited from Weber that not only were all of his articles anti-IWO, but that the official policy of the *Forward* was one of actual hostility toward the Order.[27] Weber would become Editor-in-Chief of the *Forward* following the trial.

The IWO was composed mainly of foreign-born people seeking, at least in significant measure, the company of others of the same nationality. It encompassed not one but over a dozen nationality groups which, by the mid-1940s, had substantial autonomy within the larger national organization. Until this point in the trial, all the State's witnesses spoke English as their native language, or spoke it at least well enough to communicate reasonably in that language.

Williams's use of foreign-born Thadeus Zygmont as his next witness was an attempt to demonstrate that the Communist Party wanted different ethnic groups in the IWO in order to strengthen its base in the masses of workers. The risk Williams ran was the language problem: Zygmont, a Polish immigrant, was inarticulate and thus would present considerable frustration to the Court and the lawyers as they attempted to understand him. What Williams was counting on was that enough would get through to make the endeavor worthwhile; he was willing to take the risk.

Zygmont, a building trades worker, was fifty-six years old in 1951 and had been associated with the Communist movement since his youth. The testimony that boiled down from his many hours on the stand was that as a minor Party functionary he had, under Party direction, helped organize the Polish Chamber of Labor, which was then slowly dissolved in the early 1930s, with those "ready" for Party membership encouraged to join the Party and those "only half class conscious" to join the Polish section of the IWO.[28] As an "organizer at large" for the Order (his task during the early to mid-1930s), Zygmont testified that he was part of the Polish fraction of Party members in the IWO, meeting with other Party members in the Order. What came through with considerable clarity was that he was serving the purposes of the Communist Party by recruiting workers into the IWO. He also stated that, as a Communist, "I have to belong to IWO."[29]

The cross-examination by Weissman appeared curious. He slowly took the witness through intimate details of his life since his arrival in the United States in 1913. To those uninitiated in the art of cross-examination, this might seem irrelevant, but Weissman knew where he was going and why: to show that this witness was mentally disturbed and had an impaired memory. He painstakingly developed that Zygmont had apparently spent time in veterans hospitals (he had served in the First World War) as a mental patient, though the witness protested the characterization of "mental sickness," instead insisting that it was just "nervousness." Weissman, using a transcript of the Dmytryshyn hearing, nailed Zygmont with his prior admission as to his mental illness in that earlier testimony. He also attempted to show that Zygmont was involved in an incident while in the army where he participated in beating up an officer.[30]

The next line of interrogation led to a level of low comedy, the point of which was that Zygmont had drawn federal WPA pay while he was working and earning other monies, in violation of WPA rules. The comedy came into play because Zygmont could not remember what he had said about this matter in his testimony in the Dmytryshyn matter and asked Weissman, in effect, what his answers should be now.

Weissman also got an admission from Zygmont to the effect that he had cheated an employer. The cross-examination continued along these lines:

Q. You had the benefit of the experience in the Dmytryshyn hearing—do you know what I am talking about?

A. Oh, yes, you always get experience.

Q. And yet you came here yesterday and you testified you were a member of the IWO between 1933 and 1937; is that right?

A. Yes, I would say that.

Q. Is that a fact?

A. No, I think that was—maybe I was confused.

Q. What were you confused about? When Mr. Henry [Williams's associate] was questioning you, what were you confused about?

A. I don't remember what I was confused about.[31]

Zygmont persisted, however, in repeating that he was told, "That if I am good Communist I should belong to IWO."[32] After further cross-examination by Friedman, Zygmont was discharged. Williams did not attempt any redirect questioning that might have clarified the matter.[33]

Whatever comedy and confusion entered the courtroom by virtue of Zygmont's testimony, it quickly evaporated as Williams called forty-nine-year-old John Leech to the witness stand. Leech proved to be quite articulate, giving some of the most damaging testimony up to that point in the trial—if the politics of the Order would indeed prove to be determinative. The deadly seriousness of Leech's testimony departed from the buffoonery of Zygmont; his exactitude in naming dates, persons, and firsthand events contrasted vividly with Zygmont's generalizations and barely understandable perorations.

On the afternoon of February 20, 1951, Leech testified that he had been an IWO member for some two and one-half years, from mid-1933 to the end of 1936; he also claimed he was a Communist Party member from 1930 to 1937 and that he had attended Party schools, one of which was conducted at IWO headquarters in New York. Naming names, he stated what he was told by Party members, specifically by Max Bedacht:

That the International Workers Order would be one of the principal organizations that the Communist Party would utilize in the building of a people's front or a popular front in the United States, patterned after the then, very successful, people's front and popular front movements that were taking place in France.

That the mass movements, such as the International Workers Order, were the transmission belts of the Communist Party; that the IWO must be built into an effective mass organization so that the party could then work in it and recruit the most advanced elements out of it into . . . the Communist Party.[34]

Leech, under Williams's questioning, articulated the most direct connection yet given in the trial between the Party and the IWO. He claimed he was a fraction member of the Order on the West Coast and, as a Party leader, had given direct orders as to the running of the Order. Under questioning, he stated:

Q. Did the Communist Party give you any duties with respect to these IWO branches?

A. Yes, sir.

Q. What were your duties?

A. That I was to be responsible for the political life, the campaigns, the organizational activity and the general functioning of this mass organization.

Q. Did you meet with any of the leaders of the IWO in this Los Angeles section?

A. Yes, sir . . .

A. I met frequently, weekly, for a period of a couple of years, with the Southern California district council of the International Workers Order which had its office on the corner of 3rd and Spring Street in Los Angeles.[35]

Leech testified that he regularly collected money from the IWO, claiming that "complete financial and organizational statements" were submitted to him by the Order. Judge Greenberg interrupted him to ask, "Did the IWO do that?" Leech responded, "They did do that." He also claimed checks drawn on the IWO account in Los Angeles were given to him to deposit into the Party account. Again the Judge interrupted him: "You are sure of that?" to which Leech responded, "Yes, sir."[36]

He even went on to describe an incident where, as a member of a Party discipline committee, he witnessed IWO officers—who were Communists—being chastised for purchasing certain printed material "contrary to the orders of the section committee of the Communist Party in that area." Naming the members of this discipline committee, Leech stated that the Order officers were told that "they would be removed from their positions if a decision of the section committee was violated in the future."[37]

Although Leech's testimony continued for some time, delving into areas such as his arranging for Party members to speak at IWO functions and the purveying of Communist literature through the Order, the high point came in his responses to Judge Greenberg's questions:

The Court: According to your testimony up to now, it is your conclusion that the Communist Party actually supervised the work of the IWO?

The Witness: In that territory, in the very closest way.

The Court: Do you know of any instance where any of the officers were removed or were put into office as the result of Communist activity or orders or what-not?

The Witness: I do.

The Court: Can you tell us where and when?

The Witness: Yes sir. [He then detailed two instances].[38]

One way to defuse the effect of cross-examination is to have the witness deal on direct testimony with some adverse information instead of waiting for the information to come out later on cross-examination. Williams did this by asking Leech if he was ever convicted of a crime. He admitted he had been, at age nineteen, for illegally raising the amount of a postal money order, and that he had been sentenced to one hour in the custody of a United States Marshal.[39] By having Leech admit to this during direct testimony, Williams aimed to impress the Judge with Leech's honesty in confessing to this youthful indiscretion. The risk involved in employing such a strategy was that the witness might not have confessed to everything that could bring his testimony into question. With the day almost over, Weissman suggested that the cross-examination begin the next day—to which all agreed.

The following day, with Leech back on the stand, Weissman immediately began to probe matters that the witness had not revealed on direct testimony in order to challenge his veracity, reliability, and worthiness as a witness—in effect, to impeach him. What Weissman faced, however, was an experienced, paid professional ex-Communist witness who had testified for the government since at least 1938, thus having some thirteen years of experience behind him.

Weissman elicited from Leech that he had also at one time been convicted of a prohibition offense; Leech stated that the Party had paid his fine. Then Weissman asked whether he had testified in the deportation case of Harry Bridges, nationally known labor leader who, for many years, was locked in a battle with the Immigration and Naturalization Service over his alleged Communist Party membership and his status as an alien. Leech stated he had testified in 1939 that Bridges was a Communist Party member. Weissman then accused Leech of perjury concerning the Bridges testimony, but Leech denied it. In testifying against Bridges, Leech had appeared before James M. Landis, Dean of the Harvard Law School, who was assigned to hear the testimony. Weissman was able to get a portion of the Landis report into the trial record.[40]

Dean Landis, in writing his report, had accused Leech of "cheating," "lying," "falsification," and "evasion," concluding, "It is impossible accurately even to summarize this day and a half of testimony by Leech. In evasion, qualifications and contradiction it is almost unique. Its flavor cannot be conveyed by a few scattered abstracts from the record, for the evasions are truly labyrinthine." During that hearing, the government attorneys had suggested to Leech that he "withdraw" his earlier damaging remarks about Bridges, which Leech did. Williams, in a rare first, fought to keep the Landis opinion out of the record before the Court, but Judge Greenberg accepted it.[41]

Weissman also gained an admission that Leech had provided an affidavit in the Bridges case to the Immigration and Naturalization Service and had received money from them, and that the INS, in exchange for this help, promised to assist him in finding a job. Judge Greenberg intervened with the witness to confirm that, without the aid and assistance of the Immigration authorities, Leech would not have gotten that job.[42]

Weissman then took Leech into his testimony before the Dies Committee, chaired by U.S. Representative Martin Dies of Texas; the Committee's formal name was the House Committee on Un-American Activities (HUAC). In 1940, before Dies individually and before his Committee, Leech had identified certain people as Communist Party members, including Ellis Patterson, then Lieutenant Governor of California.

It was then developed that Leech had made the same accusation both against a man who later became a Justice of the Supreme Court of California and against Mr. and Mrs. Fredric March, famous movie personalities. March had responded by bringing suit against American Business Consultants, the publishers of *Counterattack*, which had reprinted Leech's accusation, but the case was apparently settled with a payment to March and a retraction and apology by the magazine.[43] (As was earlier noted, this was the same publication whose editor had called Williams's associate, Emil, seeking information about the IWO when the matter had first become public.)

Concerning Leech and his accusations, one critic has written:

Leech was habituated to making strong charges against well-known individuals and then backing down when pressed for evidence or confronted by the accused. Most of his testimony dribbled away like sand. Still the nation was treated to the odd experience of reading that the great stars in whom it had invested so much of its emotional life, those near-mythical figures, were appearing one by one before a Congressman from Orange, Texas, for absolution. Dies, sitting alone, received, heard, and issued his clearances to James Cagney, Humphrey Bogart, and Fredric March, to Franchot Tone, Luise Rainer, and Francis Lederer. . . . Such are the uses of the Leeches among us.[44]

Weissman's questioning of Leech about the many individuals he had identified over the years as Communists was designed to destroy his credibility in Judge Greenberg's eyes. Rational people were aware that wild and unfounded accusations were being made, with the too-frequent result that lives were being destroyed. If Weissman could get the Judge to see this witness as a "wild accuser," the weight of his testimony with respect to the IWO, its leaders, and its politics would be significantly diminished.

Using court records, HUAC proceedings, and other public documents, Weissman questioned Leech about accusations he had made against a man who was later elected to Congress, and then returned to his accusations against the member of the California Supreme Court, all in order to emphasize the unreliability of this witness. In keeping with a consistent theme in his cross-examination, Weissman, using the Dmytryshyn transcript, demonstrated to the Judge that Leech could not remember the questions asked of him or give the same answers he had given to them a few months before, yet still claimed to remember people, events, and even speeches from more than fifteen years before. For instance, the IWO records indicated he was an Order member for about one year, 1935–1936, and then was expelled for nonpayment of dues, but at both the Dmytryshyn hearing and at this trial, he told different versions of how long he had been a member, how and to whom he paid dues, and why IWO records differed from his recollections.[45]

While Weissman had concentrated on Leech's overall credibility, Friedman, when he picked up the cross-examination, assumed the task of dealing with certain specifics of the witness's testimony. Using an intensive questioning technique, Friedman probed the crucial matter of monies Leech stated he received from the IWO for Communist Party purposes. Using Leech's direct testimony from the day before and the Dmytryshyn transcript where he had testified earlier on the same matter, Friedman pounded at Leech to gain admissions of inconsistency. For example:

Q. Isn't it rather your concern about testifying to something where the documentary evidence will contradict you; isn't that what is bothering you?

A. That is untrue; completely untrue.

Q. This $2,000 to $4,000 was made up in rather large denominations; wasn't it?

A. Sometimes.

Q. You have received one payment of $1,200 once, didn't you?

A. Well, I received, I recall, I received money of approximately $1,000, at least one time.

Q. Last August you remember $1,200.

A. All right, I so testified, $1,200.

Q. Yesterday you remember a $700 and an $800 one, didn't you?

A. Yes, I remember several different amounts over a period of time.

Q. Just answer my question. Yesterday, didn't you remember $700 and $800?

A. I don't remember—I can't recall at this time having testified concerning $800; $700, I can, yes.

Q. Do you remember a $700 one, too?

A. Yes.

Q. In more than one of them, more than one $700 item?

A. I can't be sure.

Q. There isn't much room left for more contributions inside this $2,000 to $4,000 total, is there?

A. I don't understand your question.

Q. Well, if you received one $1,200 contribution and more than one $700 contribution, you know what that would equal, don't you, if there were at least two $700 contributions?

A. Yes.

Q. That would be $2,600 in those three contributions.

A. Yes.[46]

Friedman concluded the segment with these questions:

Q. You were familiar with the IWO and its affairs, weren't you?

A. Reasonably so, yes, sir.

Q. As a matter of fact, you were required—it was one of your political duties—to be familiar with it, wasn't it?

A. Right.

Q. And you knew what the legal obligations of the IWO were in California, didn't you?

A. I can't say that I did.

Q. Let us put it this way: Did you know that the IWO had to file financial reports with the State of California showing to whom it had made payments and the purpose of those payments?

A. I may have, but I cannot say that I did.

Q. Didn't you know that the State of California Insurance Department had the right to examine the records of the IWO in California and did so?

A. Well—no, sir, I would have to be presuming; I do not know of my own knowledge.

Q. But nevertheless, you say that the IWO issued checks to you, payable to you as an individual?

A. I do.[47]

Friedman then took up the other most damaging area of Leech's testimony: the matter of Communist Party control over IWO officers and their activities. Through his questioning, Friedman attempted to establish that the IWO itself controlled who became its officers by democratic election methods. Friedman later established that Leech had rehearsed his literature testimony with Henry prior to testifying. Despite a bevy of pamphlets and books put out by the IWO, Leech could not recall any; all he could remember were those put out by the Party. Friedman's final gambit with Leech unfolded like this:

Q. Do you clearly recall that the IWO was a very important organization to implement the Communist Party policy?

A. I do and—

Q. You do, that is your answer. When you testified before the Dies committee, you knew that too, didn't you?

A. Yes . . .

Q. Did you tell the Dies committee about the steps taken by the Communist Party in California to control and dominate the life of the people there?

A. Yes . . .

Q. You said that the Communist Party had tried to take over the Army, the Navy, and the National Guard, didn't you?

A. Not in those words.

Q. But in other words?

A. Yes.

Q. And the Democratic and Republican parties, too?

A. Yes.

Q. And you mentioned many other organizations, didn't you?

A. The EPIC Society—

Q. Yes. Didn't you mention many other organizations?

A. I was trying to name them. I could not say many, but I did identify organizations.

Q. Did you at that time, anywhere in that testimony, mention the IWO?

A. No; these were—

Mr. Friedman: That is all.[48]

Williams then got on his feet to conduct redirect questioning in an attempt to breathe some credibility into Leech's testimony after the vigorous cross-examination by Weissman and Friedman. Most importantly, Williams questioned Leech about whether he had in fact mentioned the IWO during his Dies Committee testimony; he had already answered this in the negative on cross-examination, but now answered that he had. Williams had apparently sent Leech to the New York Public Library where he had read a transcript of his testimony concerning a person he had named as a Communist where he had referred to the Order as "the Party controlled International Workers Order." When Weissman renewed his cross-examination, however, he got Leech to admit that when he was testifying before HUAC on Communist Party finances, he never mentioned the IWO.[49]

Friedman then resumed the cross-examination. This point in the trial contained the longest and most intensive cross-examination, a fact that reflects the importance of Leech's testimony. Friedman dealt with the crucial allegation by Leech that he paid the IWO dues for some eleven or twelve Party members including himself, using Party funds. Leech added four more names during this session of cross-examination. Of those fifteen or sixteen people, Friedman, using IWO records, was able to demonstrate that only four of those named by Leech were ever IWO members and that some were members only after the period from 1933 to 1936 that Leech had claimed Party involvement with dues payment.[50]

Williams had a final chance to shore up Leech's testimony concerning whether he had or did not have the opportunity to talk about the IWO to the Dies (HUAC) Committee. This was important because it went to the heart of the witness's contention that the Party controlled the Order; if so, logically he would have mentioned—in fact, gone on at great length about the IWO. Tension was high as Williams propounded question after question, only to have Judge Greenberg rule them out on Weissman's or Friedman's objection. Finally, the Judge asked:

But you were talking about mass organizations and front organizations and front people of the Communist Party, and as I understand it, your conception of the IWO was one of the largest of the front or mass organizations. Didn't you think it important to call that to the attention of the committee?

to which Leech answered:

I will try, sir, to tell you how I remembered how I understood that. Mr. Dies was examining me on our policy of Communist infiltration of non-Communist Party organizations and I feel, as I still think, Mr. Dies would have reprimanded me had I brought in a discussion of the ILD or FSU or the IWO at that time.

Judge Greenberg, however, was not only reading the trial record nightly, but had also gone through some three volumes of HUAC testimony, and from this he apparently remembered material on one of those named organizations, an alleged Communist front called the ILD. He asked, "The ILD was inquired into, wasn't it?" Williams jumped in before Leech answered, asking, "Were you asked about the ILD?" to which Leech replied:

Only in a very minor way in connection with other front activities. Mr. Dies, sir, as I remember, was inquiring into the Communist position in the Negro field, in the Mexican field and how we were trying to infiltrate in legitimate political parties, and he was not questioning me at all about the mass organizations that we controlled.[51]

The IWO news release on February 21, 1951, reviewing Leech's testimony and cross-examination, concluded:

A frequent government witness in witchhunts and deportation trials, Leech proved too strong for even the stomach of Martin Dies, original chairman of the Un-American Activities Committee. When Leech fingered Frederick [sic] March as a Communist, Dies told him "you don't know what you're talking about," according to committee records. "Dies badgered me," the fingerman complained from the stand today. Others he has "identified" as Communist Party members include a former Lieutenant-Governor of California and a Justice of the Supreme Court of California. He now says the IWO is "Communist-dominated."[52]

Tempers were hot and patience had worn thin among the attorneys on both sides of the battle over Leech's testimony. With Leech and earlier witnesses, Williams had been building a wall around his case, while the IWO lawyers had diligently been attempting to destroy the structure by tearing at its bricks.

The battle being waged in this New York courtroom was part of the larger war against domestic Communism and alleged subversion that had permeated American life. The Red Scare continued unabated as headlines reported other trials, loyalty matters, and sensational revelations against the background of the "hot" war being waged in Korea. One development that may have had an incidental though important impact was the news announcement that on March 6, 1951, Julius and Ethel Rosenberg and Morton Sobell, accused as atomic bomb spies for Russia, would go on trial in a courtroom only a few hundred yards from where the IWO case was being tried.

In other news of the day, the Federal Loyalty Review Board had recommended that "reasonable doubt" be sufficient grounds to dismiss government employees or to bar employment; the Communist Party denied that it was a subversive organization that had to register under the new anti-subversive law; actor Edward G. Robinson asked for an early hearing on charges against him before HUAC; T. J. Fitzpatrick, a former official of the left-wing United Electrical Workers Union, went on trial for contempt charges stemming from his refusal to answer questions posed by HUAC; and HUAC sent two agents to Hollywood with subpoenas for at least ten movie figures. The war in Korea and the war of words in the United Nations between the former World War II Allies continued to dominate foreign news.[53]

Returning to the courtroom, the handling of the State's next witness set off the short tempers that were the result of the long and bitter battle over Leech when John T. Pace, a fifty-four-year-old farmer from Tennessee, took the stand. Immediately after it was established that Pace was a Party functionary for a few years in the early 1930s and not an IWO member at any time, the objections began. In essence, the Order's lawyers argued that Pace's testimony would simply be repetitious. Judge Greenberg asked Williams, "In any event, isn't it reaching a point of being cumulative?" To which Williams responded, "I think so."

When Judge Greenberg responded to Williams's last statement, he gave the lawyers some insight into what he was thinking:

If, at least, you had some [testimony] down for later dates, 1940, 1943 or 1945, even in the nature of being cumulative. I don't see what more you can add to the record. If I am not convinced up to this time as to what is in the record, if the testimony is going to be of a similar character, frankly, it wouldn't add any weight to the record, in my judgment.

Mr. Williams: The testimony, I believe, is going to be of a similar character. Suppose I go right to the IWO meetings and we skip the fraction meetings, and any discussions that might have taken place there?[54]

Plainly, the Judge was telling Williams that he had already built a record for the 1930s and was now asking him in effect, what do you have for the 1940s?

Pace's testimony on the IWO was vague and thin in substance. He had attended only a few meetings in Detroit where he had spoken on behalf of the Party. Williams's attempt to get Pace to identify IWO officers was ineffectual. In fact, there was so little in Pace's entire short testimony that, for the first and only time, the IWO lawyers did not bother with a cross-examination. On direct examination, Pace had admitted that he had testified in a number of loyalty and deportation matters, so that apparently the Order's lawyers were satisfied that the Court understood that Pace was simply another paid professional witness.[55]

Notes

1. Trial Record, p. 1766.
2. Trial Record, pp. 1766–74.
3. Trial Record, pp. 1766–74.
4. *New York Herald Tribune*, February 10, 1951.
5. Henry Clay Greenberg, *The Bench, the Bar and the Press* (Kingsport, TN: Kingsport Press, 1951).
6. Ibid., pp. 34–39.
7. Ibid., p. 30.
8. Ibid., p. 27.
9. Trial Record, pp. 1796–97.
10. Trial Record, pp. 1801–07.
11. Trial Record, pp. 1809–14.
12. Trial Record, pp. 1815–25.
13. Trial Record, pp. 1826–47.
14. Trial Record, pp. 1848–60.

15. Trial Record, pp. 1860–70.
16. IWO News Release, February 14, 1951.
17. Trial Record, pp. 1870–89.
18. Trial Record, pp. 1900–01.
19. Trial Record, pp. 1930–43.
20. Trial Record, p. 1944.
21. Trial Record, pp. 1959–64.
22. Trial Record, pp. 1965–69.
23. Trial Record, pp. 1970–72.
24. Trial Record, pp. 1973–79.
25. Trial Record, pp. 1981–82.
26. Trial Record, pp. 1984–93.
27. Trial Record, pp. 2024–35.
28. Trial Record, pp. 2048–58.
29. Trial Record, pp. 2059–69.
30. Trial Record, pp. 2070–2102.
31. Trial Record, pp. 2110–14.
32. Trial Record, pp. 2115–19.
33. Trial Record, pp. 2120–35.
34. Trial Record, pp. 2136–40.
35. Trial Record, p. 2146.
36. Trial Record, pp. 2149–50.
37. Trial Record, pp. 2153–55.
38. Trial Record, pp. 2158–59.
39. Trial Record, pp. 2173–74.
40. Trial Record, pp. 2175–79.
41. Trial Record, pp. 2180–85; IWO News Release, February 21, 1951.
42. Trial Record, pp. 2234–35.
43. Trial Record, pp. 2243–50.
44. Walter Goodman, *The Committee: The Extraordinary Career of the House Committee on Un-American Activities* (New York: Farrar, Straus and Giroux, 1968), pp. 101–02.
45. Trial Record, pp. 2251–58.
46. Trial Record, pp. 2259–70.
47. Trial Record, p. 2271.
48. Trial Record, pp. 2284–85.
49. Trial Record, pp. 2292–2304.
50. Trial Record, pp. 2304–23.
51. Trial Record, pp. 2324–25.
52. IWO News Release, February 21, 1951.
53. *New York Times*, February 10–23, 1951.
54. Trial Record, pp. 2328–33.
55. Trial Record, pp. 2334–44.

Chapter X
Two Anti-Communist Stars

Williams understood the implication of what Judge Greenberg had in effect stated: present testimony that what your witnesses have alleged took place in the early to mid-1930s continued into the 1940s—that in terms of IWO politics and its connection to the Communist Party, nothing essential had changed down to 1951. Drawn from the comments by and questions from the Judge, his attitude seemed to be that even though some of the early leaders and programs were Communist, this was understandable because those were terrible Depression years. Demonstrate, he seemed to say, that very little or nothing has changed in terms of IWO leadership and politics in the last fifteen years. Williams was in fact ready to do that with his last two witnesses, both of whom had already achieved "star" status by 1951 and were now ready to supply testimony that would carry the allegations down to the trial date.

Forty-two-year-old Matthew Cvetic had "surfaced" as an FBI undercover informer in February 1950. He spent some seven years in the Communist Party in the role—he claimed—of a spy for the FBI. His marathon testimony before HUAC had brought him a great deal of media attention, so that within one year he had become an anti-Communist "star" performer. His carefully prepared testimony before HUAC probably took the record for length of time (some ten days) and for the number of names named (as many as 250). As Frank Donner, one of the IWO lawyers, has written about Cvetic in his book *The Un-Americans*, "he not only named names, but delivered himself of elaborate political commentaries on the evil machinations of his victims. He devised a cabalistic rationale to make the most innocuous document seem fraught with terror."[1]

Two factors merged to send Cvetic's star soaring. First he was one of the first and most prominent of what would prove to be a long line of such undercover agents, spies or informers planted in the Party in order to feed HUAC what it wanted to hear. Second, he had operated in Pittsburgh, Pennsylvania, which David Caute has called "the violent epicenter of the anti-Communist eruption in postwar America."[2] By mid-1950 his story, "I Posed as a Communist for the FBI," was the featured article in a three-part series in the *Saturday Evening Post*, a widely circulated national magazine. Stating it was Cvetic's story "as told to Pete Martin," a contributing editor for the *Post*, the article began:

For nine agonizing years Matt Cvetic listened in on Communist Party secrets. His family—with anger and shame—thought him a traitor. They didn't know he was making regular reports to the FBI. Here is his own exciting story of the tense life of an undercover informant.[3]

Coming into the national limelight just as the Red Scare was moving into high gear, Cvetic's services were eagerly sought by government agencies, loyalty boards, and the media—but nowhere more than in Pittsburgh. Newspaper and radio stations clamored for his "revelations." On March 5, 1950 the *Pittsburgh Press* featured Cvetic's tale of "Red Plots for the Violent Overthrow of the United States" and editorials such as "All Communists Must Be Ferreted Out." The paper quoted Cvetic to the effect that the "Communist Party is no more a political party than a gang of robbers is a political party." Using Cvetic as authority, the *Pittsburgh Sun Telegraph* announced that Pittsburgh Communists were already laying plans for a U.S.-Soviet war; Cvetic claimed to have been given detailed information on a Russian plan to invade the United States through Alaska.

Feeding the press and the airwaves with accusations in 1950 and 1951, Cvetic became a local hero and celebrity. More importantly, he became immensely powerful. Being named by Cvetic could and did cost people jobs, friends, and reputations. A sense of Cvetic's power can be gained from Caute's report of what transpired:

No sooner had Cvetic begun to name his victims than the *Pittsburgh Press*, *Hearst's Pittsburgh Sun-Telegraph*, the *Pittsburgh Post-Gazette* and other local papers joined in the witch hunt by blazoning the names, addresses and employers of the red termites across their pages. Nearly one hundred people lost their jobs in short time, notably at U.S. Steel, Etna Steel, and the Crucible Steel Company.

Many workers were ostracized, were refused credit at local stores, saw their kids abused or attacked at school, were denied state welfare benefits, or were threatened with denaturalization or deportation. As this steel city began to boom with the Korean war orders, the fever rose: perhaps two hundred people had to leave town.[4]

Thus Cvetic was feared by some and hero to a great many. Approximately one month after he testified in the IWO trial, on April 19, 1951, the film *I Was a Communist for the FBI* had its world premiere at the Stanley Theatre in Pittsburgh. That day was declared by the Mayor to be "Matt Cvetic Day"; a parade followed a lunch in his honor. The Governor of Pennsylvania and the then current Miss America pinned the Pennsylvania Legion's Americanism Award on Cvetic.

In the film, a local Communist Party official, Steve Nelson, whose conviction for violation of the state's Subversive Act and later for violation of the federal Smith Act dependent in part on Cvetic's testimony, was portrayed under another name as ordering a murder. Cvetic justified this fictional event on the grounds that Nelson had once told him that the revolution would involve the liquidation "of one third of the United States population." Cvetic was paid some $18,000 for serial and motion picture rights; *I Was a Communist for the FBI* was also serialized on the radio. Of the $18,000, $12,500 was retained by Cvetic and the rest shared by his ghost writer and his agent-manager; the latter was also the local vice-president of an organization called Americans Battling Communism.[5]

In 1983, a film critic wrote about this movie:

I WAS A COMMUNIST FOR THE F.B.I. is a totally repulsive and reprehensible film that portrays labor unions, intellectuals, schoolteachers, and independent-minded people as potentially dangerous Communist dupes who, through their stupidity, could destroy the very fabric of American life. . . . I WAS A COMMUNIST FOR THE F.B.I. is totally self-serving, panders to thoughtless paranoia, and was produced by Hollywood to placate Joe McCarthy and the House Committee on Un-American Activities. In fact, Hollywood was so desperate to convince the public of its sincerity that the film was nominated by the Motion Picture Academy for Best Documentary of 1951. Thankfully, hindsight has taken the edge off the film and it remains a disturbing curio of an era that has—hopefully—passed.[6]

By contrast, in early 1950 the *Pittsburgh Press* had declared,

There has been no room for doubt at any time about the veracity of Matt Cvetic . . . the testimony, background and substance of Mr. Cvetic are too firmly established to justify any reasonable doubt about his story.[7]

In 1951, there was a movement in Congress to award informers like Cvetic metals of gallantry similar to those awarded to soldiers for heroism on the battlefield.[8] Cvetic's star was thus shining brightly by the time Williams brought him to the witness stand and would continue its ascent until the mid-1950s, when his sordid private life, including his long history of mental illness and alcoholism, was made public. Interestingly, as will be seen, facts about his life and problems were actually revealed in the IWO trial, but received no public attention because no major newspaper reported any of it.

Cvetic entered a mental hospital in March 1955, and soon thereafter his testimony was effectively challenged. As Frank Donner put it, his "politically sinister explanations no longer worked their old magic."[9] He left the Pittsburgh area in the late 1950s and moved to California, where he lectured on the John Birch Society circuit and later for the extremist Billie James Hargis's Christian Crusade. By then, courts were beginning to question his testimony. In one case, an appeals court opinion stated that "it is inherent in the findings [of the hearing officer] that he regarded the testimony of the witness [Cvetic] as unbelievable and incredible."[10] But it was 1951, not 1955, when Cvetic took the witness stand in the IWO case.

Cvetic claimed the FBI asked him to join the Party in 1941 after he had applied for a position with U.S. Army Intelligence. Cvetic's main work for the FBI had been with an organization known as the American Slav Congress, which he claimed was taken over by the Communist Party in 1944; it was an active and substantial group of Slavic Americans, and Cvetic claimed to be on its national committee. He stated that, as a Party functionary, it was his duty to carry out Party activities and interests related to this and other nationality groups.

Claiming to have served on the Party's "nationality commission," Cvetic gave names of IWO officers who were also on this commission. In only a minute or two, he reeled off twenty-one names of commission members—most of whom he identified as IWO functionaries. Most importantly, he was dating his work on this commission and his knowledge of these people from the period 1944 to February 1950. Judge Greenberg was apparently impressed enough to ask Cvetic about whether IWO people mentioned by earlier witnesses had been members of this Communist Party commission. Cvetic answered "yes" to every name the Judge inquired about, even though he had previously stated he could not remember any more names of nationality commission members. Friedman's objection to the Judge's line of questioning was overruled by the Judge.[11] That Cvetic's testimony was having an impact is apparent from the following exchange:

Mr. Friedman: The effect of this, your Honor, is to transform this trial into a trial of the Communist Party instead of a trial of the International Workers Order.

The Court: No.

Mr. Williams: The petition charges that the Communist Party dominates and controls the International Workers Order and this is part of the proof of that fact.

The Court: Yes, I think so.[12]

Williams's line of questioning led Cvetic to describe Party recruitment from the IWO as well as Party support of the Order. He characterized the IWO as "the main mass organization of the Communist Party." Over numerous and vociferous objections, Cvetic described his relationship with Sam Milgrom, then Executive Secretary of the IWO, claiming that Party nationality commission meetings (at least one of which he stated was at IWO headquarters in New York) heard reports on the IWO from Milgrom, whom he asserted was also a commission member; he called Milgrom an "international agent" of the Communist Party, but just what that meant was unclear until Williams declared, "I have talked to the witness and I know what he can testify to. I propose to show the head of the International Workers Order [Milgrom] is also the Moscow representative in this country."[13]

Williams, however, had a difficult time trying to get Cvetic to prove what he had announced. He did succeed in getting Cvetic to name Milgrom as the sometime leader of the Party's nationality commission from 1948 to 1950. Cvetic then testified that at a meeting in 1949 Milgrom gave a report:

The Witness: At this meeting Samson Milgrom stressed the importance of recruiting members for the Communist Party and he stated, "Remember, Comrades, the International Workers Order is one of our best reservoirs for recruits for the Communist Party."

The Court: Do you remember he said that?

The Witness: Yes, sir.

The Court: You are sure about that?

The Witness: I am positive about that, not only one meeting, at several.[14]

Judge Greenberg's questioning then opened up an area that would lead to a great deal of controversy: he asked Cvetic about his self-styled description as an undercover agent for the FBI. Cvetic's response was that he was just that, submitting reports in writing to the Bureau. Judge Greenberg, while apparently intrigued with this man, nevertheless pressed him on the question:

Q. Let me ask you this question: Are you sure you were an undercover agent, or weren't just a normal member of the party?

A. Your Honor, I testified that I was asked by the FBI in April 1941 to volunteer my services.

Q. If the FBI representatives were called here, do you think they would sustain you?

A. Under oath, I am sure they would.[15]

Cvetic stated he was paid by the Bureau, that he had testified some twelve or fourteen times since he ceased being an undercover agent, and that he had held a job as a placement interviewer for the U.S. Employment Service in Pittsburgh, remaining "undercover." "Until I went to Washington in 1950 to testify before the committee [HUAC]," he explained, "the Commies never caught on." He added that for this trial he was being paid $25 per day and $9 for expenses by the State of New York.[16]

Judge Greenberg continued to question Cvetic, becoming as frequent an inquisitor as Williams. Under the Judge's questioning, Cvetic admitted that the IWO was only an "incidental" part of his work, though he asserted he had named the Order as "Communist-controlled" before HUAC when he "surfaced" in 1950:

To the best of my recollection I testified before the Committee on Un-American Activities in regard to the IWO.

The Court: You are sure of that now?

The Witness: Yes, sir.

The Court: Specifically, the IWO and not fraternal organizations?

The Witness: Yes.[17]

If Cvetic was to be believed, his testimony would prove very damaging to the Order since he was repeating all the essential allegations of earlier witnesses about the close connection between the IWO and the Communist Party, bringing the time frame to as late as 1950. For instance, with respect to a 1949 Party nationality commission meeting held at IWO headquarters in New York, Cvetic quoted Milgrom as having said:

[It is] "Our Order, and we must build the International Workers Order; that it is our best transmission belt between the party apparatus and the large reservoir of masses we can reach down below."[18]

Cvetic remained on the witness stand longer than any prior State witness. His testimony dealt with the by now familiar grounds of money raising in the IWO for Communist publications and Party political campaigns, speeches he delivered at lodge meetings at the behest of the Party, and Party literature sold at Order meetings. He also testified that the Party ordered him to join the IWO and that he attended Party schools where the violent overthrow of the government was discussed. In addition, he identified active Party members from pictures of present IWO leaders. Asked whether he ever held office in the IWO, he stated that he was offered the job of English Section organizer, but turned it down under orders from the FBI. Having testified as to all of this, Williams turned the witness over for cross-examination.[19]

The February 24, 1951 edition of the *New York Times* carried a story on the Cvetic testimony. Under the headline "Red Fund Plea Laid to Insurance Lodge," his testimony was recounted including his quote of Milgrom recited above.[20] The cross-examination, which would continue for days, was not reported by any major metropolitan newspaper. Throughout the entire trial, no report of any admission or revelation obtained on cross-examination was ever reported in English except in the *Daily Worker*. This astonishing fact dramatizes the temper and biases of the times. Judge Greenberg had written about this phenomenon in his essay on the bench, bar, and press. The question is, did he recognize that it was happening in the IWO case?

Weissman's cross-examination followed his now-familiar pattern of establishing the selective memory of the State's witnesses, the fact that they depended on payments from government agencies for a living, and their attempts to peddle their anti-Communism to the media. Cvetic presented different problems for the IWO attorneys because he claimed that he was never a Communist but always an employee of the FBI during his information gathering. Cvetic also attempted to use his alleged FBI affiliation to avoid answering questions:

Q. How many hours did you spend in the FBI office?

A. I can't answer that, because I am liable to give away something.

Mr. Weissman: If your Honor please, that dodge has nothing to do with this, what is he liable to give away?

Mr. Williams: That assumes he spent any time at all in the FBI.

Q. Did you spend any time in the FBI office?

A. I am sorry, I can't answer that.

Mr. Weissman: Will your Honor direct him to answer that?

The Court: Yes, you will have to answer that.

The Witness: Do I have to answer that?

The Court: Yes.

The Witness: Well, I spent some times back in 1945 and 1946, but after 1946 the FBI thought it was best if I didn't come to the office, because the Commies may catch on to me.[21]

Weissman used the lengthy transcript from the HUAC testimony of the previous year to show the Court the many inconsistencies in Cvetic's testimony, comparing what he had said there to what he had stated in this trial. At one point, having established the inconsistencies, Weissman asked:

Q. What you said here today is also probably correct?

A. You are referring to this one date.

Q. Yes, referring to this one date.

A. Yes.

Q. What you said here today is also probably correct; right? And we take our choice.

A. It is correct, to the best of my knowledge. I am just a human being.

Mr. Weissman: We won't debate that for a while.[22]

Using every scrap of information he had been able to find, Weissman went into Cvetic's background, developing that he was divorced on grounds of "cruel and barbarous" treatment of his wife and that he had been indicted for aggravated assault and battery of his sister-in-law. In an early case where this matter had been raised, Cvetic had defended himself with the comment, "since when . . . was it a crime to beat up your sister-in-law, anyhow." Weissman suggested it was sexual in nature, which Cvetic denied.[23]

Weissman mounted a general attack on Cvetic's role for the FBI. Cvetic had no difficulty with the definition of his role as a paid informer. Weissman also challenged his story of being approached by the Bureau by disputing his qualifications for undercover work (he had none) and suggesting several scenarios as to how and why he became an informer, all designed to punch holes into Cvetic's story. Judge Greenberg was quite protective of the witness, denying any obligation on Cvetic's part to name any agent of the FBI that had dealt with him; this was true even though Cvetic had named agents in previous cases and in articles about himself.

Weissman even challenged whether Cvetic was ever an undercover agent; Williams insisted that since the U.S. Attorney and Attorney General had entered appearances in the case and the State of New York had proffered the witness, that was sufficient; Judge Greenberg stated, however, that the defense had a right to raise the issue.[24]

For days of cross-examination, Weissman challenged Cvetic to report the same answers he had given in prior hearings and trials to the same questions he was now being asked. When he could not, Weissman attacked his memory lapses, his credibility, and, ultimately, his desire to tell the truth. Weissman probed minute areas of his testimony, displaying a remarkable ability—often better than Cvetic's—to remember over numerous occasions what Cvetic had testified to on a particular subject and where he had done so.

Weissman succeeded in getting Cvetic to admit that he had not, in his earlier testimony, mentioned Milgrom as a leader of the nationality commission of the Communist Party and that, until this trial, he had not even identified Milgrom as Executive Secretary of the IWO. Initially on cross-examination Cvetic had stated he had no idea about the amount of surplus held in the IWO treasury; Weissman then showed him that he had in fact testified before HUAC that it was $26 million (it was $6 million). Weissman also emphasized that Cvetic was making a great deal of money as an anti-Communist crusader: $12,500 net to him for the movie rights and $6,500 for the *Saturday Evening Post* articles. He then tied the issue of these substantial monies to Cvetic's failure to provide financial support for his children.

Friedman took over the cross-examination, eliciting from Cvetic that aspects of his life depicted in the *Post* articles were in fact inaccurate. In relentless fashion, Friedman questioned Cvetic's memory on various dates and places, revealing his inability to remember basic facts about his own life, such as when he was married, when he was divorced, when he registered for the Selective Service (the draft), and how many years he had gone to high school. Perhaps the most outstanding feature of this phase of cross-examination was that Cvetic ended up disowning many salient points in the *Post* articles, even though he had proofread them before they appeared.[25] Again, none of this was reported in any of the major metropolitan newspapers.

On direct questioning, Cvetic had reeled off the names of some twenty-one members of the nationality commission of the Communist Party; of the twenty-one, he identified those who were also IWO officers. Friedman then asked about Cvetic's testimony before HUAC, where he had similarly given twenty-one names. Friedman was able to point out through lengthy cross-examination that the lists did not conform: he had not named the same people, and he did not identify as IWO members some that he had earlier named at the trial. Under examination, Cvetic admitted that of all the names he gave to HUAC as members of the Party's nationality commission, he had identified only two as IWO members. This process took all of one morning, apparently exhausting the lawyers, the Judge, and Cvetic himself.

In his further cross-examination, Friedman was attempting to establish that when Cvetic had a number of key opportunities in trials and hearings to mention the IWO in response to questions about Communist Party front organizations, nationality groups infiltrated or controlled by the Party, or organizations where Party literature was distributed, he never did. The logic of Friedman's approach was: you do not talk about the IWO, which you have said here was the leading instrument of the Party, unless you are paid to do it.[26]

Friedman used sarcasm and deprecation of Cvetic's moral values to break down his credibility:

Q. Do you remember you did testify in a proceeding to get a Miss Albert fired from her job as a school teacher last April because you saw her at a Communist Party meeting; do you remember that testimony; would that be the fact?

A. I remember testifying at a hearing for Dorothy Albert, who was a school teacher.

Q. And you were solicitous, then, about protecting FBI secrets, weren't you? Do you remember you refused to answer many, many questions there?

A. Yes, I remember.

Q. You said that you claim privilege to defend national security?

A. That's right.

Q. You were trying to defend the American way of life from its enemies?

A. You bet.

Q. Including American traditions and customs?

A. Yes.

Q. Does that include the custom of breaking your sister-in-law's wrist which you say was an old American custom; is that one of the customs you are trying to protect?

Mr. Williams: I object to that.

The Court: I will allow it.

A. No, sir. I certainly would protect—I meant, defending the customs of the freedoms that we enjoy here in America against an international Communist conspiracy which wants to take over the country and set up here a dictatorship.[27]

Tempers flared as Cvetic was questioned about the background of his initial appearance before HUAC:

Mr. Friedman: How did you arrange to get to the Un-American Activities Committee?

A. The absolute arrangements were made finally by Bob Taylor of the Pittsburgh Press.

Q. What do you mean "absolute arrangements"? Did you understand his Honor to ask you about absolute arrangements, did you understand that?

Mr. Williams: He did. Don't shout at the witness. I am tired of this.

Mr. Weissman: If you are tired, that explains why you are shouting.

Mr. Williams: I am tired of the rudeness of the cross-examination, your Honor.

Mr. Weissman: If anybody is rude, your display here is terrible.

Mr. Williams: His Honor asked the witness a question—

Mr. Weissman: Address yourself to your Honor.

Mr. Williams: I object to the manner of his cross-examination.

Mr. Weissman: Don't shout.

Mr. Williams: Don't you shout, I have as good a voice as you.[28]

It was then revealed that Cvetic had *asked* to be a witness before the Committee in February 1950; this was the platform from which his anti-Communist "star" was launched. Besides his newspaper contacts, he and his agent had spoken to Judge Gunther, a Pennsylvania judge who was a member of Americans Battling Communism, to ask him to intervene on Cvetic's behalf so he could appear before HUAC.[29]

Apparently the IWO lawyers had struck enough cracks in Cvetic's testimony—and thus his credibility—for Williams to use his right to have Cvetic answer further questions in order to "rehabilitate" his witness and thus shore up his credibility. He did this by having Cvetic testify on a number of subjects, asking him questions which gave him a chance to explain or expound on some earlier answer he had given under cross-examination. Of significance was that Cvetic stated he was called on to testify in the *Dennis* case (the Smith Act trial of the top Communists) and had his testimony prepared by two U.S. Attorneys, but for some reason he was never called to the stand. Judge Greenberg, from the nature of his questions, seemed to be impressed that Cvetic had been on tap to testify in the most important Communist case to date and further that he would appear to have been a credible witness to the U.S. Attorneys who worked with him for two or three weeks, though why Cvetic did not actually testify remained unanswered.

With Cvetic's long testimony completed, Raphael Weissman stepped up to the bench to raise and argue an interesting legal issue. Throughout the trial, Judge Greenberg was called on to rule on many issues of law. Prime examples were the IWO motions to *Strike* and to *Dismiss* (where he refused to rule) and the matter of whether the National Convention could be held. For weeks, stretching into months, of this trial, Greenberg ruled on many other questions of law, most frequently (literally hundreds of times) on evidentiary matters (for example: Was a certain document admissible? Could the witness be asked that question? Should an answer—in whole or in part—be stricken from the record?).

A new legal issue now was presented: whether the Judge should, or even could procure copies of the reports Cvetic claimed he filed with the FBI. Though Cvetic had shifted grounds under cross-examination, he had consistently maintained that he had prepared and filed many reports of his activities with the Bureau, but at the same time insisted that he had kept no notes from which the reports had been prepared or copies of the reports themselves.

Such reports would be the best evidence with respect to what in fact Cvetic had actually done, seen, and heard, as well as establish that he was what he claimed to be: only an undercover agent-informer during those years. A U.S. Supreme Court decision had just come down that seemed to indicate inferentially that such reports may be obtained by a court with the judge screening out any security matters. Weissman was asking Judge Greenberg to agree to try to get the reports, or, if he could not obtain them, to strike all of Cvetic's testimony from the record because of the acuteness of those reports as the basis for appropriate cross-examination. If the Judge was willing to favor this position—get the reports or strike all Cvetic had said—an important segment of the State's case would be jeopardized.

So important was this matter that, after preliminary discussion between himself and the attorneys, Judge Greenberg adjourned the trial in order to have counsel brief the issues as well as contact the FBI in order to determine whether they would willingly turn over the reports. Williams took the position that he had not seen the reports, adding, "If your Honor can request—properly request—the U.S. Attorney, and the Attorney General of the United States to compel the Bureau of Investigation to produce the reports, I would be delighted." Judge Greenberg directed Weissman to prepare a letter to that effect, with the assurance that he would initial it.[30]

The letter was sent and J. Edgar Hoover himself replied, denying the request. A U.S. Attorney appeared before the Court to state that the Attorney General, who was Hoover's superior, could not produce the requested documents which were "confidential and privileged."[31] Weissman argued that Judge Greenberg had the right to demand production under the late decision of the U.S. Supreme Court and by the fact that the U.S. Attorney had, at the opening of the trial, filed an Appearance in this case. Therefore, he argued, this Court had the power to order the reports for screening, because the relevant parties had submitted themselves to the Court's jurisdiction.

Both sides had researched the legal questions involved and had prepared memoranda on the issues. Williams argued that the U.S. Supreme Court decision did not support Weissman's interpretation and furthermore that Cvetic's testimony must stand because he had not testified as to the contents of the reports, but rather as to what he had heard and seen. If Judge Greenberg pressed an order on the government to produce the reports, it would be the first time in U.S. legal history that a state court took such action. The Judge took the matter under advisement, which meant he would read and think about it.

The matter of obtaining the alleged Cvetic reports developed over the following weeks. Further briefs were prepared and arguments were made; each time the Judge took the matter under further advisement. At one point, he ordered the U.S. Attorney into court to clarify the government's position. When he appeared as demanded, he argued that the Attorney General had broad discretionary powers for overriding national interests to refuse to produce the reports. To this the Judge responded:

What I can't get into my head is under what authority can the Attorney General delegate to himself the right to decide what should or should not go into evidence in a court of law if he submitted himself to the jurisdiction of that court. [The Attorney General had entered an appearance in the IWO case.]

Mr. Roth: [Representing the U.S. Attorney General] Your Honor, that's a fundamental question and a fundamental thing. The division of powers between the judiciary and the executive is something that's been discussed by the United States Supreme Court, and I think it's beyond question that the Attorney General of the United States can decide—certainly it's beyond question now—what is confidential in his department.[32]

Every relevant issue was examined thoroughly: separation of powers, the effect of the appearance by the government in this State court case, the role of confidentiality in order to preserve national security, and the question of whether Cvetic's testimony relied on those reports. At one point, Judge Greenberg gave Roth the following reminder:

It's more than that—pardon me, Mr. Roth. Mr. Cvetic's testimony is very very important. He touched upon investigations made by him over a long period of time in Western Pennsylvania. He testified as to trips he made for meetings of the nationality commission of the Communist Party and to other activities which could be very crucial in this case.

Mr. Roth: That may be.

The Court: And if his testimony stands uncontradicted or without an opportunity to contradict it, and it is believed and accepted by the Court, it can go a very long ways towards establishing a particular fact in the case. It might not be the deciding factor, but it certainly would go a long way in determining whether or not the IWO was dominated and controlled by the Communist Party. And that is why that is a very very vital factor in this case.[33]

Roth responded that "larger interests" were involved, and that if the State's case suffered by the federal refusal, the administration in Washington was willing to take that risk.[34] The arguments rose to a peak level:

The Court: Don't you think, Mr. Roth, that on elementary principles of justice, where certain documents or certain investigations are made the basis of a prosecution or a litigation, that the documents ought to be produced?

Mr. Roth: Again, I say, your Honor, that we are dealing with matters that go far beyond this courtroom and far beyond this case. These are matters of high policy. Of course, justice would ordinarily require it and that's why there is such an extraordinary measure as that, and why cases have gone to the United States Supreme Court and why the President of the United States has been upheld in his refusal to turn over to Congress and the courts paper—for over a hundred years.

The Court: I think the courts are far superior to the Congress, as a matter of fact. The founding fathers certainly gave them at least equal rank, and since the days of John Marshall, they have had superior rank and could declare laws of Congress unconstitutional. I think without the courts, with all the criticism leveled at them, our liberties would be at greater stake than they are today.[35]

Still, the Judge delayed his decision. In fact, it was not until the last day of the trial, April 13, 1951, moments before the end of the entire trial, that Judge Greenberg gave his decision. Stating he believed he had the power to direct production of the reports (a position which would be sustained in another case some six years later and again decades later in the Nixon tapes case), he nevertheless ruled that he would neither exercise that power nor strike all of Cvetic's testimony; he believed Cvetic's testimony was "solely from recollection and [that he] did not make any reference to any memoranda."[36] Thus the entire record of Cvetic's testimony, direct and on cross-examination, remained and would be considered by the Judge when he rendered his decision.

Recent research has established that Cvetic was never an *agent* of the FBI (a fact that he carefully covered up, leading the public and courts to believe that in fact he was) but only a paid informer. It is also now evident that his extremely neurotic personality, drinking, and womanizing caused serious problems for the FBI. Hoover wanted to get rid of him as early as December 1948, but kept him on to get as much out of him as possible until he became too indiscreet and troublesome; on January 3, 1950, they fired him. The Communist Party had already dumped him the year before. Neither of these two salient facts were known by the State or the IWO at the time of Cvetic's testimony, and clearly he did not reveal the truth with regard to the FBI or the Party when he testified.[37]

The State's last witness was another "star"—probably the one best known on the national scene and the person who earned the most money as a professional anti-Communist, Louis F. Budenz. Budenz had made headlines when he left his position as managing editor of the *Daily Worker*, reembraced Catholicism, and became an Assistant Professor of Economics at Fordham University and a militant, avowed anti-Communist. Budenz's prominence is attested to by the fact that he was the only witness to whom Paul Williams personally wrote to confirm his appearance and set up a meeting with him. Williams also wrote Father Laurence J. McGinley, President of Fordham University, thanking him for allowing Budenz to testify, concluding that "Mr. Budenz's testimony will be most important to us and in testifying he will perform a real public service."[38]

Williams requested that Budenz take the stand while the extensive cross-examination of Cvetic was still in progress. This kind of interruption is disconcerting to all trial participants and disrupts the normal flow of any trial. Still, with the Court's permission and the reluctant agreement of Weissman, Budenz took the stand on February 21, 1951; Williams had explained that Budenz had a "rather complicated lecture schedule," to which Williams had to accommodate.[39]

Then sixty years old, Budenz related his background as a labor organizer which had led him to join the Communist Party in 1935 as an editor for the *Daily Worker*, where he remained until leaving the Party and this employment ten years later. He claimed membership in the IWO from 1940 through 1945. He testified that during his ten years as a Party member, he rose to the position of membership on the National Commission of the Party, a group with high influence in setting Party policy.

Williams's questioning explored Budenz's relationship with the IWO: Budenz claimed he joined the Order at the behest of the Party and that the *Daily Worker* paid his dues. He stated that, as late as 1945, he had spoken scores of times at IWO meetings as a *Daily Worker* editor and Party National Commission member. In response to the usual line of questioning by Judge Greenberg, Budenz stated that no one ever objected to his appearances or challenged what he said.[40]

Budenz was the smoothest and most educated and articulate witness produced by the State. In reading the record, it is apparent that Judge Greenberg was impressed with the man and was barely able to conceal his interest in Budenz's work as a newspaperman, the Judge's own special area of interest.

Like earlier witnesses, Budenz told of meetings—this time of the National Commission of the Communist Party—where IWO officials like Bedacht, John Middleton, (an IWO Vice-President) and, David Greene (an IWO officer) were present because they too were on the Commission. What was new and startling was that Budenz named Rockwell Kent, President of the IWO at the time of the trial, as the chairman of a meeting of Communists. When asked directly, "Is Rockwell Kent a member of the Communist Party, to your knowledge?" Budenz answered, "Yes, sir." Expanding on this, the witness stated that Kent was introduced to the meeting where "only Communists could be present" as "Comrade Kent."[41]

Budenz also testified that at practically all Party National Commission meetings, the IWO was discussed. At one specific meeting he recalled a reference to the Order as "an arm of the Party":

The Court: Who said that? Bedacht?

The Witness: Bedacht, yes, sir, and he dealt, finally, with the financial aid the IWO could give to the party in advancing a particular line, at that time pointing out the participation of lodge members in Communist Party drives for the *Daily Worker* and the like.[42]

When Weissman accused Williams of violating rules of evidence by giving leading questions (questions that indicated what Williams wanted Budenz to say), Williams retorted that this particular witness was "above reproach" in that he "could not be led." This was the first and only time Williams characterized any State's witness in this manner.[43]

Further testimony from Budenz was very damaging to the Order's case. He claimed, for instance, that he attended a meeting of the Party's Politburo (another Party governing body) in 1938 where the work of George Powers, then an IWO vice-president, was reviewed, and that it was decided that "there should be a checkup on the officers and representatives of the IWO throughout the country," to be carried on by a Party member who "was in charge of the IWO."[44]

Budenz established another damaging tie between the Party and the IWO:

Q. Tell us, specifically, about this conference.

A. This conference had to do with advertisements of the International Workers Order in the *Daily Worker.*

Q. Tell us what was said about the advertisements.

A. Yes, sir. Mr. Browder and I took the matter of advertisements up with Mr. Bedacht and he said, as rapidly as possible, these advertisements would be inserted. Mr. Browder and I urged him to put them in as soon as they could because of the financial condition of the *Daily Worker,* and he said they would move as fast as they could; that they had to take into consideration not over-doing it in order not to violate any insurance laws.[45]

Budenz identified Bronislav Gebert as the head of the Polonia Society—a nationality section of the IWO—and a Party member. He stated that in 1945 Gebert had said that the IWO foreign sections "had been used and could be effectively used for contact with Soviet agents in their respective language fields from abroad." Friedman's vigorous objections to this testimony were overruled by the Judge.[46] Budenz also identified Milgrom as "an underground agent of the Communist Party endeavoring to stir up strikes."[47]

The burden on the IWO attorneys to impugn this witness's testimony was onerous given what he, an articulate college professor, had stated on key political issues. The *New York Times* carried a report of Budenz's testimony on Kent, along with Kent's denial to a *Times* reporter that he was a Communist.[48]

Any news interest about the IWO trial was, however, overshadowed by the Rosenberg atom spy trial that began on March 6, 1951 in the federal district court adjacent to the courthouse where the IWO case was entering its third month.

The same day that the Rosenberg trial began, Budenz returned to the stand for cross-examination. Weissman's strategy was to attempt to cut Budenz down to size—to puncture his prestige and present him as just another paid informer who was using his past Party connections for notoriety and personal gain. Thus he immediately attacked the idea that Budenz was an "unwilling witness" (Williams had subpoenaed him) on the grounds that Budenz actually "wanted to get into the act here" in order to promote an article he had recently written for the *American Legion Magazine* entitled "I.W.O.—Red Bulwark."[49]

Weissman was able to extract financial information from Budenz which clearly established that he made very good money from his anti-Communism through lecturing, writing (*Colliers* paid him $20,000 for a series of five articles), and acting as a paid witness in comparison to his modest salary as a teacher. After considerable banter, Budenz admitted that he came into this case with a strong bias against the IWO, having already called for its dissolution in the *American Legion Magazine* article.[50]

A long series of questions about his Catholicism ensued. Budenz had been excommunicated from the Catholic church over thirty years before because he had married a divorced Catholic and because he had been critical of the church. Using Budenz's own autobiography,[51] Weissman challenged his version of when he had made up his mind to reembrace Catholicism in order to demonstrate that for two years, 1943–1945, Budenz had carefully orchestrated his leave-taking from the Party to insure his future; at the point of announcing his break with the Party, he had arranged through the church for a teaching job at Notre Dame. Weissman further elicited that while Budenz and his family were receiving instructions in the Catholic faith, he had remained on the *Daily Worker* payroll, writing articles in support of the Communist Party line. As to this, Weissman questioned:

Q. Did you bear in mind or in your heart any elements of decency when you did that?

A. Well, counselor, that's a peculiar question. I had to consider that I was in a conspiracy which uses gangster methods against those who disagree with it.

Q. You were in a conspiracy in the Communist Party?

A. Yes, sir.

Q. But you were just about to be cleansed after many years of contamination, of any conspiratorial habits?

A. Yes.

Q. And you sat and you fingered the rosary while you corrected proofs for the Communist Party line?

A. That's correct, for a very short time.[52]

Here Weissman was attempting to discredit the pious position of "redeemed sinner" that Budenz was trying to convey. Under intensive questioning, Weissman extracted from Budenz that he had engaged in espionage against the Office of the Strategic Services during the Second World War as late as 1943 or 1944, beyond the point where he had decided to reembrace the Catholic faith.[53]

Any fair reading of Budenz's anti-Communist writing will convey that he was not adverse to mudslinging against anyone whom he attached to the left. Weissman, using transcripts of testimony in prior cases as well as documents he had gathered, portrayed through cross-examination a man who had been divorced by his first wife for desertion, had an affair with another woman he had perhaps gotten pregnant, and had lived with the woman who was to become his second wife prior to their marriage—all facts which he had failed to include in his book, *This Is My Story*. He was also shown to have lied about these matters while testifying in an earlier case. Accused of being in fact a bigamist, Budenz replied, "Before God and morality I have sinned deeply, counselor."[54]

But Weissman wasn't through. He next asked Budenz whether he was charged with immoral conduct relating to his adopted daughter in 1930. This started an uproar, as Budenz responded:

A. That's totally incorrect, counselor. That's a falsehood. . . . It is an utter Communist concocted falsehood.

Mr. Weissman: It comes in ill grace from you, Mr. Witness.[55]

Williams attempted to stop the questioning, reminding Weissman that Budenz had four daughters, but Weissman would not relent. It ended with Budenz admitting that, when earlier asked about this morals charge in another case, he had refused to answer on the grounds of self-incrimination.[56]

Weissman, through cross-examination, attempted to portray Budenz as careless and indifferent about facts and callous in his disregard for the reputation of others. For instance, in Budenz's identification of Kent, he had portrayed him as a Communist speaking to a meeting of Communists. Weissman, however, established that the 1944 meeting had been attended by a wide spectrum of people, including responsible government representatives, showing that Budenz's characterizations were incorrect. At that same meeting held in New York City, a woman who was a professor at Vassar College spoke to the group. While Budenz could not state whether she was a Communist, he had labeled her as a friend of Earl Browder (then General Secretary of the Party) and stated that she had spoken at a meeting where only Communists attended. In the colloquy that followed, insight is gained into Budenz as well as to the times:

Q. Aren't you a little reckless about what you are saying here?

A. No, no.

The Court: I think that last remark was a little reckless, Mr. Witness. You know some people consider it important. The Court of Appeals of the State of New York has held that it is slanderous and libelous per se to call a person a Communist and yet you have glibly here said that Earl Browder told you that this particular professor from Vassar College was a Communist.

The Witness: No, not a Communist.

The Court: A friend of his?

The Witness: Yes, sir. . . .

The Court: In these days of loose talk many people would think if she was a friend of Earl Browder she was a Communist.[57]

Through intense cross-examination, Weissman also established that Budenz was careful to make accusations against certain people only when he was legally protected from libel and slander actions, such as in court cases and before investigating committees, Budenz, he emphasized, had been a practicing attorney for a short time and therefore was sophisticated in these matters.[58]

The balance of the lengthy cross-examination was used by Weissman and then Jones to demonstrate that Budenz was wrong about many aspects of the IWO both during his direct testimony in this case and in his article in the *American Legion Magazine*. In essence, they showed he knew nothing about the internal workings of the Order, its lodge structure, or its insurance programs. But Budenz had the last word when, in response to a question that asked him to admit that he knew nothing about how the IWO functioned, he stated "I know from the top level how it functioned in its link with the Communist Party and was controlled by the Communist Party."[59]

Louis F. Budenz, as one of the leading ex-Communist, anti-Communist crusaders, has received more attention from analysts and critics writing during the Red Scare years, as well as from historians examining those times, than any other single personality. The man, his testimony, his influence, and the accuracy of his accusations have been the subject of intensive review.[60]

Budenz's testimony in the IWO case took place after his career as a professional witness was already well developed. His testimony in 1949 in the *Dennis* case, where he was on the stand for almost two weeks on behalf of the government, had been closely followed by the media. It was during that trial, where he appeared as the government's first witness, that he became the great exponent of the Aesopian-language theory. Under this theory, when any Communist Party literature contradicted the theme of violent overthrow of the government, Budenz claimed that it was deliberately used to provide a security cover and that it was properly to be interpreted as the *opposite* of its literal meaning. Thus, if the Communists stated that capitalism was to be forcefully overthrown, it was to be believed; if they stated that they favored a peaceful transition to Socialism, it was to be understood as meaning the opposite.[61]

White haired, pale faced, and impeccably dressed in expensive dark suits, Budenz presented himself as a sophisticated, mature witness, facile in his ability to handle difficult questions. As a result of some thirty-three appearances before committees, trials, and deportation hearings, and as the author of four books and numerous articles and public speeches, he has been assessed as the ex-Communist with the greatest influence on the public view of the Communist problem. In part, his influence and prestige was by virtue of his association with leading Catholics like Monsignor Fulton J. Sheen, Director of the Pontifical Society for the Propagation of the Faith. Bishop Sheen, a national personality in his own right, had personally handled the reconversion of Budenz to the faith.[62] Archbishop (later Cardinal) Richard Cushing of Boston had also appointed Budenz his advisor on Communism. As glimpsed in his IWO testimony, Budenz made much of his religiosity, blaming the sordid aspects of his personal life on the influence of the Party.

His work, described as "America's No. 1 professional witness in all matters concerning loyalty, patriotism, and political reliability"[63] earned him some $79,000 in fees between 1950 and 1957. Harvey Matusow has recited a conversation he had with Roy Cohn, Senator McCarthy's aide, when the question was discussed of Matusow becoming a witness:

I asked him if I would be used as a witness. His reply was a strange one. 'I think you'll make as good a witness as Budenz,' he said. This really sent me soaring, because in the witness world Louis Budenz was regarded as the witness's witness, and it was quite an honor to be compared and put on a par with the "successful" Mr. Budenz.[64]

Such was the standing of Budenz among professional paid anti-Communists. Matusow, who later labeled Budenz as a perjurer, stated that each professional anti-Communist had a "gimmick." He described Budenz as using a "theological approach" as his particular "gimmick."[65]

In his years as a professional witness, Budenz left "a trail of destruction—people ruined in reputation, people fired from their jobs, people jailed." As the years went on, he became both emboldened and careless, falsely accusing many of being Party members: twenty-three beneficiaries of Guggenheim Foundation grants and four Foundation officials, as well as a number of Rockefeller Foundation beneficiaries. Professor Linus Pauling, one of those he accused, called Budenz a "professional liar"; others proved Budenz dead wrong. But merely being named by Budenz—under his definition of Communist—was a terrible event.[66]

In addition to his role as the leading Government witness in the *Dennis* case, Budenz is noted for his confrontations with Owen Lattimore, an advisor to the State Department on Far Eastern affairs. Before two different Congressional committees, Budenz would assert that Lattimore was a member of the Communist conspiracy, acting under Communist directives to influence American foreign policy. The first confrontation took place prior to the IWO case in March through June 1950; the second ran from July 1951 until June 1952, beginning just a few months after his testimony in the IWO trial. These accusations concerning Lattimore were challenged by other witnesses including famed columnist Joseph Alsop, who attacked Budenz in an article which appeared in the *Atlantic Monthly* entitled "The Strange Case of Louis Budenz."[67]

Alsop was not alone in his criticism. In 1950, prior to the IWO trial, Senator Dennis Chavez of New Mexico, a Catholic and a conservative, spoke from the floor of the U.S. Senate on the subject of Budenz. He attacked him as a man who used the authority of the Catholic church in his anti-Communist activities, noting that while Budenz attempted to blame the corrupting influence of the Communist Party for his sordid past, he had not joined the Party until 1935 "at the tender age of forty-two"—years after his social and legal trespasses. Regarded as an infallible authority on Communism, Chavez said, Budenz "could pass no test of credibility," adding that "many innocent persons are convicted by perjured testimony possibly given by someone like Budenz." He stated:

As a private citizen and a public witness, this man has impeached and exposed himself as a devious, conspiratorial, warped personality who uses words and information as instruments of propaganda and not for their intrinsic truth. Budenz is constitutionally unable to give a straight answer, justifying his foul means by the perverted ends he seeks. I do not think he knows truth from falsehood any more.[68]

In 1957 Budenz suffered a heart attack and retired from testifying; his retirement coincided with the Supreme Court decisions that ended most of the Communist prosecution cases.

Notes

1. Frank J. Donner, *The Un-Americans* (New York: Ballantine Books, 1961), p. 142.
2. David Caute, *The Great Fear: The Anti-Communist Purge Under Truman and Eisenhower* (New York: Simon and Schuster, 1978), p. 216.
3. *Saturday Evening Post*, July 15, 22, 29, 1950.
4. Caute, *The Great Fear*, p. 217.
5. Ibid., pp. 219–20.
6. Jay R. Nash and Stanley R. Ross, eds., *Motion Picture Guide* (Chicago: Cinebooks, Inc., 1986), Vol. IV, p. 1342.
7. Quoted in Donner, *The Un-Americans*, p. 143.
8. *New York Times*, July 12, 1951, p. 9.
9. Donner, *The Un-Americans*, pp. 146–47.
10. Quoted in Hyman Lumer, *The Professional Informer* (New York: New Century Publishers, 1955), p. 20.
11. Trial Record, pp. 2345–55.
12. Trial Record, p. 2356.
13. Trial Record, pp. 2357–69.
14. Trial Record, pp. 2370–79.
15. Trial Record, pp. 2380–84.
16. Trial Record, pp. 2385–87.
17. Trial Record, p. 2388.
18. Trial Record, pp. 2389–91.
19. Trial Record, pp. 2392–2440.
20. *New York Times*, February 24, 1951, p. 9.
21. Trial Record, pp. 2441–50.
22. Trial Record, pp. 2451–57.
23. Trial Record, pp. 2458–75.
24. Trial Record, pp. 2476–88.
25. Trial Record, pp. 2553–2617.
26. Trial Record, pp. 2618–45.
27. Trial Record, pp. 2646–64.
28. Trial Record, p. 2674.
29. Trial Record, pp. 2675–77.
30. Trial Record, pp. 2692–98.
31. Trial Record, pp. 3469; 3503–10.
32. Ibid.
33. Trial Record, pp. 3511–23.
34. Trial Record, p. 3524.
35. Trial Record, pp. 3526–27.
36. Trial Record, p. 4187.
37. Daniel J. Lieb, "Anti-Communism, the FBI and Matt Cvetic: The Ups and Downs of a Professional Informer," *Pennsylvania Magazine of History of Biography* (October 1991), pp. 535–81.

38. Williams Office Files, Correspondence, Letters dated February 12 and 20, 1951.

39. Trial Record, p. 2515.

40. Trial Record, pp. 2516–34.

41. Trial Record, pp. 2534–35.

42. Trial Record, p. 2537.

43. Trial Record, p. 2539.

44. Trial Record, pp. 2540–41.

45. Trial Record, p. 2545.

46. Trial Record, pp. 2549–50.

47. Trial Record, pp. 2551–52.

48. *New York Times,* February 28, 1951, p. 17.

49. Louis F. Budenz, "I.W.O.—Red Bulwark," *American Legion Magazine,* March, 1951, p. 14.

50. Trial Record, pp. 2700–06.

51. Trial Record, p. 2709.

52. Trial Record, pp. 2707–23.

53. Trial Record, pp. 2723–41.

54. Trial Record, pp. 2741–42.

55. Trial Record, pp. 2743–44.

56. Trial Record, pp. 2745–70.

57. Trial Record, pp. 2770–82.

58. Trial Record, pp. 2783–2852.

59. Trial Record, p. 2852.

60. John P. Sisk, "On Hearing Mr. Budenz," *Commonwealth* 50 (July 22, 1949) pp. 360–63; Editorial, "Dementia Unlimited," *The Nation* 170 (April 29, 1950), p. 388; Richard P. Mulcany, "Facing The American Inquisition," *Maryland Historian* 17, 2 (Fall–Winter 1986) (University of Maryland), pp. 1–17; Joseph Alsop, "The Strange Case of Louis Budenz," *Atlantic Monthly* 189 (April 1952), pp. 29–33; Frank J. Donner, "The Informer," *The Nation* 178 (April 10, 1954), pp. 298–307; Herbert L. Packer, *Ex-Communist Witnesses: Four Studies in Fact Finding* (Stanford, CA: Stanford University Press, 1962).

61. Peter L. Steinberg, *The Great "Red Menace": United States Prosecution of American Communists, 1947–1952* (Westport, CT: Greenwood Press, 1984), p. 163; Caute, *The Great Fear* (note 2), p. 190.

62. Richard H. Rovere, "The Kept Witness," in *The American Establishment and Other Reports, Opinions and Speculations* (London: Rupert Hart-Davis, 1963), p. 72; Caute, *The Great Fear,* pp. 108–9.

63. Donner, *The Un-Americans* (note 1), p. 302, quoting Senator Dennis Chavez.

64. Harvey Matusow, *False Witness* (New York: Cameron and Kahn, 1955), p. 62.

65. Ibid., p. 68.

66. Caute, *The Great Fear* (note 2), pp. 124–25.

67. Joseph Alsop, "The Strange Case" (note 60), pp. 29–33.

68. Quoted in Donner, "The Informer" (note 60), p. 198.

Chapter XI
The Defense Begins—Haley as Architect

On March 7, 1951, the cross-examination of Budenz was completed, and with his testimony, Williams announced that "the petitioner [the State] rests." This case had been before the Court since December 14, 1950; now, some three months later, after thirteen witnesses had testified and 171 documents had been introduced into evidence by the State, the IWO defense was to begin.[1]

Williams had made a clever move prior to this point by issuing subpoenas to all the major IWO officers to appear as witnesses for the State. Because they would have appeared under subpoena, Williams would have been able to examine them as "hostile" witnesses, which would have given him wide latitude in terms of his questioning. But more importantly, he would have sent a signal to the Judge: the State's case is strengthened by *my* calling as witnesses the top officers of the Order, because their own testimony will prove the State's contentions concerning their activities and policies. Williams, however, had agreed with Weissman outside the courtroom that Weissman instead would call them as IWO witnesses, giving Williams the right of cross-examination as to each. By following this more orthodox procedure, legal battles over the validity of the subpoenas and the scope of examination of such "hostile" witnesses were avoided.

A parallel difficulty had to be resolved over James B. Haley, the State Insurance Examiner on whose Report on IWO politics the liquidation action was based. Williams had not called Haley as a witness; if Weissman called him, the same issue of scope of questioning would be raised. The two sides agreed that Williams would produce Haley (though Williams stated he did not know what he could testify to) and Judge Greenberg would allow Weissman "the widest latitude in examining him."[2]

That night, March 7, 1951, the IWO held a membership mass meeting in New York City—in effect, an informal National Convention. Similar meetings were taking place in sixteen cities throughout the country, all in protest against the attempted liquidation and the trial. Held at the St. Nicholas Arena, the Order claimed that 5,000 members attended the gathering.

The highlight of the evening was an extensive dramatic presentation, apparently written by IWO officer David Greene, designed to mobilize enthusiasm for the IWO in its fight for survival. The final version must have been written the very day of the mass meeting, because it reviewed events that had taken place in Court that same day. Exhibiting a heavy dose of literary license with the facts, the script read as follows:

In the courtroom adjoining Foley Square, a colossal frame-up attempt is in its final stages. Do you know what the Wall Street attorney [Williams] for the Insurance Department tried to do? He was finishing up with Professor informer Budenz as the last of his parade of stoolies, and things weren't going according to plan.

So he subpoenaed your officers! He wanted your officers to sit in the same witness chair as Budenz and become witnesses for the prosecution. Think of it! He didn't want your officers to testify for the Order and about the Order! He wanted to make your officers unwilling participants to the political inquisition of [Governor] Dewey. He wanted your officers to testify on everything under the sun except the IWO. This he thought would make it easier to add fuel to the war hysteria and under the hysteria liquidate the IWO.

We defeated this dastardly plot. The officers are not going to testify for the prosecution. Yes, we are going to testify. We are going to testify. We are going to give an accounting of our organization and our leadership of the IWO, but as witnesses for the defense—witnesses for the International Workers Order, witnesses for you, against the liquidation of our beloved Order![3]

Using this technique of a dramatic presentation, members played the roles of judge, attorneys, and witnesses who had appeared for the State, interspersed with rebuttal from speakers in the audience as well as on stage. Most of the script dealt with the denial by Judge Greenberg of the authority to hold a National Convention:

Attorney: [Williams] If your Honor assumes, as I must assume, because the Superintendent has so assumed, that this is a subversive organization, that they are organized to defeat the government of the United States and overthrow it by force, while they may not stand up in their convention and do so, I don't think it is a good idea to let them assemble and organize.

Narrator: The voice you heard was that of Superintendent Bohlinger's Wall Street attorney, Special Counsel to the Insurance Department.

Attorney: You know, your Honor, we are at war with Russia . . .

Judge rises and looks heavenward.

Judge: (Cough) This is a court of law: This courtroom is free from the passions and prejudices of war and red baiting! Continue . . .

Attorney: You know, your Honor, we are at war with Russia. 90 percent of the IWO's six million dollars in assets is invested in Government bonds. This can be quickly and easily converted into cash and turned over to the enemy.

Veteran comes up from audience—Baloney!

Attorney: —What? Young man, don't you know that in wartime . . .

Veteran: (Takes place at speakers stand) You can't tell me anything about wartime! I'm a veteran of the last big one! My name is John Alexander and I want to put my two cents worth on the record.[4]

At the meeting, an "Answer to Superintendent Bohlinger" was adopted, which decried his interference with the Order and specifically contested that any other insurance company could offer the benefits of the IWO, challenging him—if he were to succeed in liquidation—to find a commercial insurance company that would "treat us as human beings, not index cards, that will bring presents to the sick, help families in times of hardship [and] promote our welfare in legislative halls and on the job."[5]

Throughout the battles of the IWO for its existence, there was an apparent need to personalize the "enemy"; an attack on merely the State of New York, or its Insurance Department, was too impersonal. Therefore, the focus of its battle became the personages of Governor Dewey and Superintendent Bohlinger—fulfilling the need to attack defined human enemies. Thus the "Answer" accused:

You [Bohlinger] say that our Order is a hazard. We, the members, not you or Mr. Dewey, will decide that. And we *have* decided that the hazard to us and to the people generally are you and Mr. Dewey . . .

We therefore reject your grounds for liquidation and tell you and Mr. Dewey without hesitation or reservation that your offer to turn us over to your big time insurance friends for your mutual profit does not appeal to us.

What is more, we believe that your arms are too short to stick the knife of liquidation in our backs.

We shall stand by our Order in these trying days as we did yesterday. Our Order is our second home and we shall defend our home not only for ourselves, but for the greatest principle of all, the constitutional right of free association and speech for all the people of America.

Signed,
5,000 members of the International
Workers Order[6]

A mass picketing of the Insurance Department Offices in New York City was organized for the next day, at which time the statement addressed to Bohlinger was delivered.

Despite the efforts to rally its membership and to create concern for its survival, the IWO was losing members in significant numbers, a fact that was noted in one of many extensive confidential memoranda to Williams's office from William Karlin, the Insurance Department Examiner stationed at the Order. Karlin, as earlier noted, fed as much information as he could gather by his special telephone hookup with Williams's office and by detailed reports on events within the IWO headquarters. He passed on an astounding amount of paperwork, including letters to and from the officers, so that State's lawyers knew a great deal about the inner workings and events at the IWO. By March 1951, he was reporting on what he believed was an apparent attempt by officers of the Order to sever what he called "fringe activities" in order to preserve these if the liquidation succeeded. Among them were the separate Medical Plan, Cemetery Department, Old Age Home, and schools affiliated with the IWO.[7]

While the Order attempted to build momentum among its members in its struggle for survival, the State did not remain idle. Throughout the month of March, correspondence flowed between Williams's office and state officials in every IWO-licensed state and the District of Columbia apprising them of developments, supplying copies of the Insurance Department's *Petition*, and offering to assist any state that wanted information or materials about the Order and the trial status.

Letters continued to pour into the Insurance Department from members condemning the trial or asking about the status of their insurance, as well as from those commending the Department for its action. Some letters reflected a state of panic, their writers fearful that membership would label them "subversive." Each letter was dutifully noted and some were answered, generally in the format of a neutral tone: this is what has taken place; here is a letter from the Superintendent of Insurance explaining the status of the Order's insurance program.

The result of all of this activity can be clearly sensed: the IWO had its back to the wall in the Foley Square courthouse; internally, it was in disarray. Outside of New York, state after state was, at a minimum, keeping a careful eye on its activities. Some states, including Illinois, Indiana, Washington, and West Virginia, had already put it out of business or were in the process of doing so. Others were content to see what would happen in New York—meanwhile making certain no new members joined the Order. Both Bohlinger's office and the Williams team kept various state insurance department officials apprised of what other states were doing or had already done.

It was clear, however, that the keystone of the entire matter was this trial in the Order's home state. The IWO would never be the same as a result of this ultimate challenge to its existence, but if it could win in court, it could perhaps rebuild—strengthened in fact by this entire ordeal.

Weissman's first move was to introduce into evidence all of the constitutions and by-laws of the IWO since its inception, along with every examination report on the Order by the New York State Department of Insurance since 1932, the year of the first such examination. The point was obvious: the IWO has totally conformed to the insurance laws of the State and consistently expressed its aims and its democratic practices by and through its official documents.[8]

Williams had no objection to the introduction of any of this. He adopted this strategy: by voicing few objections to any testimony or documents presented by the IWO in its defense, he was saying, let them say and produce anything they wish; give them the broadest latitude so that no complaint can be made that the State tried to prevent any avenue of defense. Then, during cross-examination, he would bring the Communist issue into focus and hammer away at it.

James B. Haley, described by an IWO *News Release* as a "mild, elderly man," had worked for the State Insurance Department for twenty-four years by 1951; he had joined as a civil service worker shortly out of college and had always been an Examiner for the Department. For all these years he held basically the same job.[9]

In his examination of Haley, Weissman initially sought to uncover the existence of political influence in the assignment given to him. What he did get in the way of testimony from Haley was undramatic: nothing unusual, no special instructions, no oral "side" instructions— in short, nothing out of the ordinary. Haley, despite his long tenure with the department, had never before examined the IWO. What he did admit, however, was that it was a Department "first" for an examination to be split into two parts—first financial, and then an extensive investigation and report on the politics (the "fraternal activities") of the IWO. That, he agreed, had never been done before.[10]

The crucial question was the origin of the directive for the political investigation of the Order. What Haley recited to a hushed courtroom was this: he was in the midst of the normal financial review of the IWO when he read a newspaper report on the Attorney General's Subversive Organizations list and saw the name of the International Workers Order. This fact, he said, he took to his supervisor, William C. Gould, feeling an obligation to mention what he had read. Gould, a Deputy

Superintendent, told Haley he too had read that news item, and Gould agreed that, in view of this subversive listing, a special investigation was required.

Judge Greenberg jumped in because he sensed how crucial this explanation was, asking Haley in effect to confirm that he alone had suggested the need for a political review and that it did not come from any "higher-ups" in the Department or, for that matter, from the Governor.

Was Haley's examination of the politics of the IWO directed as part of a witch-hunt by politically sensitive State executives? This was the position taken by the Order in its explanation of the entire matter. Haley's responses to the Judge indicated that it all started with him and not with anyone else. He testified that when authorities in Washington refused to explain or supply evidence as to why the IWO had been listed as "subversive," he undertook his own investigation with Gould's approval.[11]

The entire explanation, placing the decision making into this one minor bureaucrat's hands, appeared too simple, too mundane, to be a complete account. Furthermore, although Haley related how, from time to time, Gould might make suggestions as to the research, Haley claimed that he alone made the decision to seek liquidation of the IWO.

Weissman gently but firmly turned the matter over from one angle to another, attempting to climb over, around, or behind such a simplistic explanation. Yes, Haley said, there were policy conferences of the "higher-ups" in the Department, but "No," he did not attend any, nor did he get any instructions from such conferences. No matter how hard Weissman or the Judge pressed for any sign of influence on his work, nothing of substance was forthcoming.

Haley indicated that he personally typed his Report and gave drafts of it to Gould, but averred that neither Gould nor counsel for the Insurance Department nor anyone else substantially influenced, changed, or directed what he wrote, concluded, and ultimately recommended. Judge Greenberg interrupted the questioning to put the matter squarely:

Q. Mr. Haley, let me ask you the very categorical question: Did any one in the Insurance Department directly or indirectly influence you in the decision which you ultimately came to in your report, in draft form or in final form?

A. No, your Honor . . .

Q. No one at all?

A. No.

Q. Not even Mr. Gould?

A. Not even Mr. Gould. In fact, if I can explain a little further on that point—

Q. Yes.

A. As I explained to Mr. Weissman, when I had first gathered part of the material, I hesitated to recommend the conclusion which I finally did. I would hesitate with any insurer. But here I felt—

Mr. Williams: You mean dissolution?

The Witness: Yes, liquidation.

A. (Continuing) I hesitated at that, because it occurred to me we can't countenance these activities in an Order under our supervision and yet, perhaps, they could be corrected. I didn't like to recommend liquidation. And when I spoke to Mr. Gould, along while I was revising the report, it was only after I obtained further material that in my own mind I decided that the situation is not one which could be corrected. I told Mr. Gould, "Mr. Gould, I am afraid I will have to recommend liquidation." And then Mr. Gould, I could see, was disturbed— and so was I, for that matter. Does that answer it?

The Court: That answers my question. I don't know about you, Mr. Weissman.[12]

But Weissman wasn't satisfied. He continued to probe, ultimately extracting from Haley that he had left his conclusions and final remedial recommendations open while he continued his examination of the matter. Thereafter, he stated that one important influence on his decision was his review of the testimony about the IWO given in the 1930s before the House Un-American Activities Committee. He added that the book *Five Years IWO* and the speeches of Max Bedacht also influenced him, reflecting that he initially thought the Order "could be saved by a direction from the Insurance Department" which would end these "activities which I thought were harmful to the public," adding, "I thought at first perhaps that would solve the matter." Weissman jumped at that, injecting, "But you received contrary advice in the office," to which Haley simply said, "No."[13]

When Weissman pressed him to admit that the drastic step of liquidation of a solvent and liquid insurance corporation could not have come solely from Haley as a civil service examiner, Haley retorted that was exactly what had happened—that he alone had made the final decision to recommend liquidation in his report. Weissman was astounded, pressing the point still again:

Q. In other words, Mr. Haley, you want all of us here to understand, that you, the civil service examiner, were picked out in the Insurance Department, to make a decision of that gravity on your own responsibility.

A. Not to make a decision, counselor, a report. I am directed to report to the Superintendent—

Q. That's it.

A. When I have done so the Superintendent does not have to be guided by my report. I knew that, of course.

Q. And you also knew, didn't you, Mr. Haley, from your prior experience in the department, that if the Superintendent is considering a certain conclusion in a matter, it would embarrass him to have his examiner first make a contrary conclusion?

A. I would think so. I don't know the movements of his mind, of course, but I would assume that, yes.

Q. But you want us to understand that in the course of these discussions with Mr. Gould he was greatly disturbed about the possibilities of liquidation, but you firmly came to the conclusion that it had to be liquidated?

A. That's the truth.[14]

Judge Greenberg reentered to elaborate on the significance of the matter:

Q. Are you aware of the fact that up until this recommendation of yours there was no other instance in the Insurance Department where a recommendation had been made to liquidate a company on the grounds indicated in your report?

A. I hadn't known of any others, your Honor. I wouldn't say positively it didn't occur.

Q. But so far as you know there was no other instance of that character.

A. That's right, your Honor.

Q. You also are aware of the fact, according to your own report, that from a financial point of view the company was not only liquid and solvent, but there was no danger of its becoming insolvent?

A. That's right, I would say no practical danger. . . .

Q. In spite of that fact, do I understand it to be your testimony that on your own, without inquiring from any superior, either the legal department of the Insurance Department or any of the responsible officials there, you undertook to make the recommendation that this company be liquidated on the basis of matters which you say you found which did not concern the financial condition of the company?

A. That's right.

Q. There is no question in your mind about that?

A. No question.[15]

Haley the "architect" had initiated the entire matter, moved by nothing other than a newspaper report that had listed as "subversive" the fraternal benefit insurance company he had, by chance, been assigned to review. His drastic conclusions, recommending the ultimate sanction of liquidation, he claimed had been his alone; even his immediate superior had been "greatly disturbed" by this conclusion. If Haley was to be believed—or remained uncontradicted—"David" Haley was bringing down "Goliath" IWO.

Weissman moved further. If Haley was indeed the prime instigator in the matter, then Weissman intended to explore Haley's motivation and, most importantly, to test the empirical bases for his report and conclusions. In effect, the balance of the IWO attorney's long examination of Haley was directed to this point: if indeed this political investigation of the Order was your idea, as well the liquidation recommendation, what exactly moved you to such a conclusion? If they could show that Haley had distorted the political record of the IWO, that his sources were narrow or prejudiced, or that he himself was prejudiced or biased, it might move the Judge to question the entire proceeding.

Thus Weissman probed for answers. Haley stated he would not care "in the slightest" if the Court refused to liquidate the Order, although he admitted he was influenced by the "Government charge" (the subversive list), stating, "My feeling was that I didn't want the State of New York to overlook something that other people knew about."[16]

Haley had difficulty understanding many of Weissman's questions. In one instance, when he finally did grasp the sense of what was being asked, he responded that he did not feel it important to review the entire scope of fraternal activities of the IWO, but rather could depend upon his reading of some speeches by Max Bedacht, concluding that what he had read "was not a good thing and was dangerous to the public." He stated that the Order must have approved of Bedacht's thoughts because it never challenged or repudiated him.

Weissman, an experienced trial lawyer, began to use a technique frequently employed in trials. He would get a response, for instance the statement by Haley regarding Bedacht, and explore the matter in depth, with each question designed to elicit the faultiness of the premise upon which the witness had based his conclusion. Thus Weissman pointed out that Bedacht had been removed from office in the Order some two or three years before Haley had even written his Report;

Haley insisted, however, that "the majority of members must think along the same lines as Mr. Bedacht." It should be noted that Weissman was not arguing with the witness but rather was attempting to expose his faulty reasoning to the Judge.[17]

For hour after hour, Weissman took Haley through the two items he claimed had most influenced him to recommend liquidation of the IWO: Bedacht's speeches and testimony before HUAC, and the testimony of others before that Committee about the Order. What Weissman established was that Haley did not see a need to investigate the link between Bedacht's views and IWO policies.

By reviewing Haley's lack of any special education or training that might have enabled him to understand the significance of what he was relying upon, Weissman was challenging Haley's ability to make "political appraisals." Haley admitted that he had no education or training that would qualify him to make serious judgments about the matter, but "only the training that an ordinary reasonable thinking man has."[18]

Weissman attempted to demonstrate that Haley was using his own untutored, unsophisticated judgment in an area entirely unrelated to the task of examining an insurance company strictly as an insurance company. Thus:

Q. With respect to what even you say was the difficulty you found after reading that testimony, you found that there was an officer in an insurance corporation that was saying certain things that you thought were what, un-American or something?

A. I think un-American, yes.

Q. Dangerous?

A. Yes.

Q. Incidentally, Mr. Haley, had you ever had any instructions from the office or any rules or regulations by which to determine what was American and what was un-American?

A. No.

Q. You just used your own—

A. My own judgment.

Q. Your own judgment?

A. That's right.

Q. Just like you would determine whether or not an investment in a certain corporation would or would not be sound. Is that it?

A. Well, there I would have some corroboration.

Q. That's right. But here you had absolutely no guide whatever.

A. Only, as I say, the intelligence of a thinking, reasonable man, which, without flattery, I thought I was.[19]

To establish that Haley was neither intelligent nor reasonable, Weissman pursued this line of questioning. Unlike all earlier cross-examinations where he frequently baited or directly confronted the witness, Weissman was non-confrontational in his direct examination of Haley; he counted on the intelligence of Judge Greenberg to draw conclusions. For instance, he confirmed with Haley that most of the material he had termed "influential" upon his work was some ten years old, and when Weissman asked him whether "your conscience was satisfied you had enough?" Haley replied, "Absolutely."[20]

Weissman also gained a series of important admissions from Haley: that the IWO was controlled under a form of representative government; that it was not founded by the Communist Party; that he did not state in his Report that the Order advocated the overthrow of the government by force and violence; that the liquidity of the assets of the IWO caused him no problem; and that other fraternal organizations lost membership between 1947 and 1950, as did the IWO. Haley also confirmed that he reported no violations of the Smith Act, state criminal law, or any evidence of "an affirmative subversive act" by the Order.[21]

James B. Haley felt that the IWO taught its members to hate President Harry S. Truman simply because he did not find any praise for the President or his office in the material he had read. Haley admitted that the Order had praised President Roosevelt, insisting however that it had turned against him after the war. Weissman, realizing that Roosevelt had died on April 12, 1945 before the war was over and prior to the advent of the Cold War with Russia, asked Haley to recall the year President Roosevelt died. To the astonishment of everyone in the court, Haley, testifying in 1951, could not remember "the most tremendous political event" in his recent life, the death of Franklin D. Roosevelt only six years before.[22]

Weissman then took Haley to task on the assertion in his Report that the IWO positively supported President Roosevelt for the first time during the Second World War. He reminded Haley that the IWO, at its 1938 Convention, had adopted resolutions praising the President and his program. Asked whether there were differences in the policies of the United States and Russia in 1938, Haley responded that, according to his memory, there were none. Weissman, trying to make sense of this, asked Haley when the Second World War started in Europe, to which Haley responded, "About 1940."[23]

What made this recitation incredible is that the reader must understand that such matters as the date of death of President Roosevelt and the commencement of World War II were common knowledge to schoolchildren in 1951; that to misplace the beginning of the European phase of World War II (September 1, 1939) by one year was unthinkable. But it got worse: Haley thought Truman became President "about 1939 or '40" (the actual date was April 12, 1945). When asked whether he was aware that in his Report he was making "political judgments" about the IWO for the Insurance Department, Haley answered "No."[24]

At this point Judge Greenberg stepped into the questioning, apparently anxious to end the embarrassing scene, to point out that "the question is whether or not the facts have been established, not what was the motivation of this man or even the Superintendent of Insurance." But Weissman retorted that his purpose was "not entirely a delightful *excursus in absurdum*" but rather an attempt to demonstrate why the powers of an administrative agency (the Insurance Department) should not reach into such political matters. By showing what could happen when such power is placed into the hands of "one person who I repeat, is probably very honest, but, no doubt, very simple," he argued, "the evil is demonstrated."[25]

Weissman and Judge Greenberg, joined by Milton Friedman, then argued extensively over the power and role of the Court in this matter. Weissman and Friedman argued that the significance of the Haley testimony was to demonstrate that the office of the Superintendent rightly lacked this very power to conduct a political investigation of the type on which the recommendation for liquidation had been based. Judge Greenberg saw the matter differently, taking the view that only the Court had the power to order liquidation if the evidence warranted that action, agreeing however that if he found there was no initial power even to institute the proceedings or no factual basis in the evidence produced, he would have the authority to throw the case out. Said Weissman:

That's precisely it. That's what we argued with your Honor and we are now demonstrating: the vice of anybody attempting to say that such a matter in the first instance may be lodged with the Superintendent of Insurance, because I knew and everybody knows who knows anything about these things, that in the nature of things, such a tremendously important matter, a political judgment, a judgment on belief, from the nature in which the Superintendent's office functions, will find its way to a desk of a person who is utterly unequipped.[26]

Still, there remained a significant gulf between the IWO view and Judge Greenberg's position: the Judge was *uninterested* in Haley's (and therefore the Superintendent's) interpretation of speeches, documents, and the like. He was focusing on whether there was any *factual basis* for invoking the jurisdiction of the Court regardless of the Haley Report, and based on his—the *Court's*—assessment, any grounds for liquidation. By contrast, the IWO lawyers were arguing that Haley's testimony demonstrated *in and of itself* that the Court had no jurisdiction because an illegal exercise of political judgment was at the core of the Department's action.

Judge Greenberg accepted that position only to the extent that if *his* review of the facts, regardless what the Report had stated, failed to support the State's request for liquidation of the IWO, he would dismiss the suit. He believed he was properly vested with that determinative power; the Order contended that the power to review and assess the politics of the IWO did not lie either with the Department of Insurance or the Court.

Haley's testimony went on for days, interspersed with these legal arguments over the nature of the case. At the end of his testimony, he was asked to identify a large group of exhibits and divide them into those he remembered having reviewed as part of his examination and those he could not remember having read. The exhibits ranged over many areas of IWO activities, from social and labor issues (favoring civil rights and unions) to child rearing advice and patriotic wartime activities. The point of all of this was to balance Judge Greenberg's reading of the State's exhibits with evidence of the broad scope of the Order's involvement with its members and American society, as well as to reveal the highly selective nature of Haley's choices.[27]

After a short recess on March 22, 1951, William C. Gould, Haley's superior, took the stand. All the attorneys as well as the Judge had agreed that Haley's claim to have been the sole architect of the political investigation and liquidation recommendation needed to be verified; therefore Williams agreed to produce Gould.

That same day, two other important pieces of Red Scare history took place. Alger Hiss began serving his five-year sentence for perjury despite his continued protests of innocence and predictions of his ultimate vindication, and in the Federal Courthouse adjacent to where the IWO trial was taking place, the most controversial trial since the *Dennis* case, and still one of the most debated trials in American legal history, reached a dramatic point: Julius Rosenberg took the stand in his own defense in the atom spy case against himself, his wife, and his wife's brother, Morton Sobell.

The chief prosecuting attorney in the *Rosenberg* case was Irving

Saypol, the U.S. District Attorney, whose office had also entered an appearance as an "interested party" in the IWO case. In his cross-examination of Rosenberg, Saypol, who would later become a federal judge, tried to get Rosenberg to admit ties to the Communist Party as well as other Communist-related organizations. Rosenberg, however, using his Fifth Amendment rights, refused to discuss any memberships, affiliations, or political views, and instead professed allegiance to the United States, insisting that he was a loyal citizen who would do battle against any enemy of this country.

Pressed for admissions, Rosenberg stated he had made contributions to the Joint Anti-Fascist Refugee Committee, which Saypol identified as an organization on the same U.S. Attorney General's list of subversive organizations that had named the IWO. Saypol then produced a collection can bearing the Committee's name, and with a loud thump set it down on the jury-box rail, with the announcement that the can had been found in the Rosenbergs' apartment by the FBI when they arrested him. After obtaining an admission from Rosenberg that the can had been in his apartment, Saypol then read the label on the can to the jury: "Save Spanish Republican Child, [sic.] Volveremos, We Will Return," followed by the Committee's address and a statement that the City of New York permits such cans to be used for money solicitation purposes. He then dramatically turned to the witness and asked, "So perhaps you did a little more than contribute?"[28]

Saypol's performance baited Rosenberg to volunteer that he held "insurance in the International Workers Order." "They sent this can to me to ask me to solicit funds," Rosenberg explained. "I just made a contribution to them." Saypol continued:

Q. Do you know that the International Workers Order is now the subject of a lawsuit across the way in the Supreme Court?

Mr. E. H. Bloch [Rosenberg's Defense Lawyer]: I object to the question upon the ground it is incompetent, irrelevant and immaterial and not related to the issue in this case.

By The Court:

Q. What is the International Workers Order?

A. An insurance organization, your Honor.

Q. Is it a public insurance company?

A. Right, sir.

By Mr. Saypol:

Q. Is it not a fact that it is a Communist organization exclusively?

And after objections:

The Witness: I don't believe it is a Communist organization.

Q. Is it not a fact that it is an organization whose members exclusively are members of the Communist Party?

A. I don't believe it is a communist organization.

Q. Is it not a fact that it is an organization whose members exclusively are members of the Communist Party?

The Court: Did you hear the question?

The Witness: I heard the question, your Honor. I don't know if it is a fact or it isn't a fact.

By Mr. Saypol:

Q. How did you join it? What were the circumstances of your joining it?

Mr. E. H. Bloch: I object to this upon the ground that we are going far afield, your Honor.

A. I don't remember.

Mr. E. H. Bloch: Pardon me. I think it is a collateral matter.

The Court: All right, he doesn't remember.

Q. When did you join it?

A. I don't remember when I joined it but I held insurance in it for many years.

Q. Who invited you to join it?

Mr. E. H. Bloch: I object to that.

A. I don't remember.

Q. How did it first come to your knowledge?

A. Somebody solicited my membership.

Q. Who was that somebody?

A. I don't recall.

Q. How many years have been a member?

A. I don't know how many years I have been a member.

Q. What kind of insurance do you have in that order?

A. I hold $5,000 life insurance.[29]

John Wexley commenting on the Rosenberg case has stated:

> With this damning admission, however, Julius [Rosenberg] unwittingly leaped from the tin can into something much worse than fire. . . . And now both Saypol and [Judge] Kaufman pounced on Julius to underscore with special emphasis the damaging name of the International Workers Order.[30]

That Saypol was perverting the truth in his cross-examination of Rosenberg with regard to the IWO should be noted. He knew its membership was not "exclusively" (probably no more than 3 percent) Communist, but apparently was desperately trying to tie Rosenberg to the Communist Party by characterizing the Order as being made up exclusively of Communists.

This key admission of membership in the IWO was recited in the *New York Times* the following day. Judge Greenberg most likely read it, given his specific interest in newspapers and the fact that he read the *Times* regularly, and because the famous *Rosenberg* case was being followed closely by all segments of the bench and bar. The Rosenbergs and Sobell were convicted, and the Rosenbergs were put to death. Judge Greenberg wrote his opinion in the IWO case prior to their electrocution, but after the guilty verdict. Given the times, he could hardly have avoided being influenced by the fact that the only organization on the Attorney General's subversive list in which the Rosenbergs admitted membership was the IWO, which was still on trial before him when the jury convicted them of being atom spies.

Williams's files indicate that he was aware of the connection between Rosenberg and the IWO: to have introduced any evidence or even made reference to the membership connection would have opened up not only a valid challenge to relevance, but might have jeopardized the State's case by wrongfully introducing highly inflammatory, prejudicial material. Williams was too good a trial lawyer to have made such an error.

William C. Gould, Deputy Superintendent of Insurance, was on the stand to test whether indeed the "buck stopped" with Haley, with Gould, or with someone in higher authority (perhaps the Superintendent or the Governor), or whether in fact Gould and the Department merely "rubber-stamped" Haley's work. Over hours of testimony, the answer—if he and Haley were to be believed—was that prime responsibility did rest with Haley and that everything that followed had been in accordance with Department procedures. Every door to the suggestion of "backstairs" influence that the IWO attorneys attempted to open was slammed shut by Gould.

Weissman got Gould to admit the highly unusual, in fact singular, nature of the intensive political investigation of the IWO. This led Judge Greenberg to characterize the case as a "most unusual and extraordinary" proceeding, calling for the liquidation of a financially sound insurance company solely because of its politics. But Gould stuck to his position: that he had no right to change what Examiner Haley had recommended; that his only demand of Haley was that he be certain of his grounds; and that any other remedial path (replacement of officers, rehabilitation of the Order) was not even considered, simply because Haley did not recommend it.

Gould testified that neither he nor any "higher-ups" had influenced Haley, concluding that, although the matter was serious and deeply troubling, he concurred with Haley's recommendation.[31]

There must have been real disappointment in the IWO camp as a result of Gould's testimony that no "red herring" had been uncovered. The Red Scare had obviously provided a fertile field where even a modest minion such as James B. Haley could sow a fecund seed that would, in other times, have lain fallow.

The IWO lawyers declined to call additional Insurance Department people. It was evident that, while so much of what was involved in the IWO case was unique and unprecedented in the history of American insurance companies, State officials were relishing this prosecution as proof of their anti-Communist zeal; the fact that the genesis for the action came from an obscure civil servant using administrative powers provided a realistic "cover" that was apparently impregnable.

The IWO did not publish a news release on the subject of Gould's testimony. The sensationalist-prone *New York Daily News* was the only paper to print an article about Gould's testimony, doing so under the heading, "Denies Surety [Insurance Department] Biggies Prodded Rap on IWO." The article misidentified Gould as Haley giving testimony to the effect that no one ("Biggies") had influenced the Haley Report. The newspaper then quoted a statement attributed to Judge Greenberg in which he was supposed to have described the Order as permeated with a "virus [that] had spread through the entire body of the IWO and that the only cure was the destruction of that body."[32] Judge Greenberg went on record in open court the next day to state, "I think you gentlemen are familiar with what happened yesterday with the witness, and no such statement was made by me." The lawyers agreed, with Weissman adding, "In my opinion the record shows that the clipping is utterly unfounded."

Notes

1. Trial Record, p. 2854.
2. Trial Record, pp. 2855–57.
3. "Presentation at IWO Membership Meeting," March 7, 1951. Script in Williams Office Files, Correspondence.
4. Ibid.
5. "Answer to Superintendent of Insurance Bohlinger Adopted At Membership Meeting of the International Workers Order—St. Nicholas Arena, March 7, 1951"; Williams Office Files, Correspondence.
6. Ibid.
7. A typical report covering these areas in Karlin's eight-page, single-spaced report dated March 9, 1951; Williams Office Files, Documents.
8. Trial Record, pp. 2863–67.
9. IWO New Release, March 9, 1951; Williams Office Files, Documents.
10. Trial Record, pp. 2867–72.
11. Trial Record, pp. 2872–76.
12. Trial Record, pp. 2877–93.
13. Trial Record, pp. 2894–2900.
14. Trial Record, p. 2901.
15. Trial Record, pp. 2903–04.
16. Trial Record, pp. 2905–06.
17. Trial Record, pp. 2906–11.
18. Trial Record, pp. 2926–29.
19. Trial Record, pp. 2930–32.
20. Trial Record, pp. 2933–39.
21. Trial Record, pp. 2940–56.
22. Trial Record, p. 2961.
23. Trial Record, pp. 2966–70.
24. Trial Record, pp. 2971–74.
25. Trial Record, pp. 2976–77.
26. Trial Record, pp. 3073–3106.
27. Transcript of Trial, from the U.S. District Court for the Southern District of New York, as contained in the record in the U.S. Supreme Court, *Julius and Ethel Rosenberg v. U.S.,* Docket III; October Term, 1951, p. 1177; *New York Times,* March 23, 1951, p. 8; John Wexley, *The Judgment of Julius and Ethel Rosenberg* (New York: Cameron and Kahn, 1955), p. 547.
28. Transcript of *Julius and Ethel Rosenberg v. U.S.,* pp. 1178–80.
29. Wexley, *Judgment,* p. 547.
30. Trial Record, pp. 3107–47.
31. *New York Daily News,* March 22, 1951, p. 61.
32. Trial Record, pp. 3146–47.

Chapter XII
A Movie, A Founder, and an Administrator

On Monday, March 26, 1951, the formal defense of the IWO began with an unusual piece of evidence: the last motion picture made by the Order was shown to Judge Greenberg in a darkened court anteroom. The IWO had, over the years, produced a number of films as part of its fraternal activities; aware of this, Haley had commented that many of them focused favorably on Russia.

Made in 1948, the film shown to Judge Greenberg entitled *The IWO Presents Fraternalism in Action* was purely promotional, designed to encourage viewers to join the IWO as well as to educate present members on the nature of the diverse ethnic and racial makeup of the Order. It celebrated nearly twenty years of the Order's existence, depicting scenes which involved the social doings of many of its ethnic divisions as well as battles fought by the parent IWO to improve conditions for working people. In its forty minutes of running time, the movie showed activities ranging from parades (there was an official IWO Day at the New York World's Fair in 1939) to choruses, bands, dramas, dance presentations, and patriotic activities during World War II.

In one scene, a May Day parade that took place in either 1940 or 1941 (but certainly prior to the German attack on Russia in June 1941), IWO members were shown carrying signs where the message had been crudely scratched out by hand on the negative. The signs must have originally carried anti-war sentiments that would have been embarrassing in the light of world developments that followed. Without being forewarned of this alteration, however, no ordinary viewer including Judge Greenberg would have caught it.

At the end of the film were appended membership appeals in some sixteen languages by the leaders of the various ethnic language groups of the Order. Since Judge Greenberg would probably only have understood some Yiddish, only the trailer in that language was shown. The person who delivered the message directed to the largest segment of the Order, the Jewish People's Fraternal Order of the International Workers Order, was Rubin Saltzman, its General Secretary and the first defense witness.

Saltzman, a middle-aged, heavyset man, had been present at the creation of the IWO. While he was an articulate speaker and author, English was not his native language and the trial transcript reflects the syntax of a foreign born person. Identified as the current General Secretary of the Jewish People's Fraternal Order of the IWO and as a vice-president of the parent IWO, Saltzman confirmed that the film was a production of the Order and that its contents were indeed true. His speech from the end of the film had been translated into English and, without objection, was entered into evidence.

The Saltzman testimony was a basic review of the origins of the IWO, its activities, and its operations, delivered by a man who had been there at the creation and had remained a major figure throughout the Order's twenty-year history. But, in addition, the testimony was also an attempt to refute all "sinister" suggestions regarding the Order.

The first line of questioning was directed to the history of the Workmen's Circle, which Saltzman had joined when he had come to the United States in 1911, later rising to a position of power. He portrayed the development of a growing division within the Circle during the 1920s between the "old guard" who wanted to limit the organization to a fraternal benefit insurance company and the "young progressives" who, in line with the Circle's Socialist and pro-union founding, wanted it to be more than an insurance company.

This "young progressives" group, of which Saltzman became a leader, wanted the Workmen's Circle to pursue goals they felt would improve the social and economic life of the Jewish workers who made up its membership. This led to a series of struggles which resulted in intra-organizational clashes followed by expulsions, dramatic battles in conventions, and attempts to reunite the opposing sides. Saltzman portrayed himself as an ignored peacemaker; when efforts failed in 1929, the "progressive wing" broke off. This group then attempted to join an earlier (1906) splintered group. When that failed, the decision was made to form their own fraternal order.

The point to all of this, although never directly stated, was to disprove the idea that Moscow ordered both the split and the formation of the International Workers Order. Saltzman stated that the attorney for the committee of former Workmen's Circle members proposed a number of names for the new corporation, perhaps more than ten, before the State accepted the IWO name. Initially the attorney had tried for the name "Labor Circle," but it had been rejected. A state will not normally allow any name that is the same or "deceptively similar" to any other registered name.[1] Here the aim was to demonstrate that even the choice of name, with its "proletarian" sound, had been the result of chance and conformity with state law—not as ordered from "above."

Saltzman then told how the Workmen's Circle opposed the issuance of a state charter to the IWO and of the subsequent hearing which resulted in a decision favorable to the founders of the IWO and its initial 5,000 members. From that point, Weissman had Saltzman recite the story of the growth of the Order—a quite astounding progression—aided by several smaller fraternals which chose to merge into the IWO.

When the first dip in membership, in 1939 and 1940, was mentioned, Judge Greenberg intervened to ask, "What happened there?" Saltzman was vague in his response. This was probably an error in judgment on Saltzman's part, since the Judge undoubtedly had in mind the IWO support for the Hitler-Stalin Pact which caused members to leave. Saltzman's vague explanation most likely did not impress Judge Greenberg as he tested the credibility and candor of this witness.[2] Perhaps Weissman had not adequately prepared Saltzman in terms of stressing the need for total candor. On the other hand, some witnesses simply cannot be convinced that what they do not say can be as damaging as what they do say.

Saltzman's responses to Weissman's continued interrogation stressed the autonomy of each ethnic section of the IWO and the low cost and accessibility of its insurance plans, which were available to all working people regardless of occupation or race. (It must be kept in mind that any interracial group, especially one involving social and cultural intermingling, was very rare in those times.) When asked by Judge Greenberg how many black members the Order had as of 1949 or 1950, Saltzman indicated "definitely not less than 6,000." Williams, who interrupted to ask a question from time to time, asked the name of the black society of the Order; Saltzman answered, the "Frederick Douglass Society." Saltzman continued by pointing out that black members were treated with absolute equality and were freely welcomed into the Order.[3]

He depicted the IWO as a fraternal organization that never put anyone out who was unable to pay dues and insurance assessments because of unemployment (instead, collections were taken up in lodges to pay them). Saltzman described the Order as an organization that worked earnestly for Social Security and unemployment insurance and organized campaigns among various American fraternal orders to join with them in this effort. He went on to detail for the Court the infrastructure of a typical lodge and how it attempted to aid its members (sickness, education, old age problems). Saltzman explained the IWO's democratic functioning, stressing specifically how power in the IWO started at the lodge level and moved up to the national level, with minimum control from the top downward. In Saltzman's description, autonomy was largely in the individual lodges. When Weissman asked whether "Outside of the assessment of certain dues, were the activities of the lodges at the local level directed or controlled from above?" Saltzman replied rhetorically, "How could we control 1,750 lodges?"[4]

Throughout his testimony, Saltzman exhibited an obvious pride in the IWO, particularly in the Jewish People's Fraternal Order (J.P.F.O.), the Jewish Section of the IWO that was the precursor of the entire Order. With evident ease and pleasure, he told of the cultural events sponsored by the Order, naming some outstanding Jewish cultural figures that were associated with the Section's programs. He also affirmed the celebration of Jewish holidays by lodges, stating that the J.P.F.O. had issued a book on the subject. Once again, each topic Weissman introduced and Saltzman expounded on had a message for the Court. Here is what the IWO is really about: fraternalism with a pro-labor, liberal theme, democratic in organization, and with manifold cultural activities.[5]

Weissman moved Saltzman into a sensitive area when he questioned him about literature distributed and sold at lodges. To counter what State witnesses had said, Saltzman flatly asserted that the IWO did not control the literature and that individual lodges independently chose what literature would be offered. Other than IWO pamphlets and books on subjects such as health insurance and Social Security as well as popular fiction (the last published by the Book League of the J.P.F.O.), Saltzman's explanation of Communist literature was that these publications were all available from local public booksellers and that individual lodges chose what they wanted to offer to their members. He stated that no more than 250 lodges out of 1,750 had actual "literature tables." To further balance what the State through its witnesses had introduced, Weissman used Saltzman to identify and introduce into evidence a number of other pamphlets and books in order to demonstrate the wide variety of non-political publications available to IWO members. Lodge bulletins issued by a variety of individual lodges were also introduced.[6]

This testimony by Saltzman is to be properly understood in the context of accusations made by the State's witnesses; standing alone, it constituted a banal recitation of the operations of a fraternal benefit insurance company. Only in juxtaposition with earlier testimony does it become meaningful. Thus, when Weissman took Saltzman through the convention process, describing how delegates were chosen at the lodge level and how these delegates in turn elected the national committee officers and directors, his purpose was to counter the accusation that the Communist Party controlled the Order and its officers. When the salaries of full-time functionaries were stated, it was to impress the Judge with their modesty in comparison with what the Judge must have known to be the salaries of officers of a major commercial insurance company. When the date was set by Saltzman as to the introduction of the "social" membership classification in the Order, it was to rebut Sylvia Couch's testimony that she was a "social member" at the time she claimed she was.

To challenge the description of the organization as essentially a refuge for leftists, Saltzman testified that "any one who has a good character morally and is physically fit to join the Order could become a member." When asked what classes of people generally belonged to the IWO, Saltzman replied, "Workers, the most, overwhelming, workers from the heavy industry and from the light industry, workers in the factories, and small petty businessmen, shopkeepers. This is the overwhelming membership." Upon further questioning, he added farmers as members, citing farm lodges in New Jersey as an example. Later he made the point that no one had ever been turned down who met the basic physical requirements; he described how admission was "absolutely automatic" at the home office, conveying the point that, in essence, there was no "political" selection of members.[7]

Weissman questioned Saltzman about the official *Manual for Builders,* the publication issued by the Order to its "Builders" (those who most actively solicited members). The *Manual* covered key areas about IWO policy in a simple question-and-answer style. Thus the question "Is the IWO a political organization?" was read into the record with the following response:

No, the International Workers Order is a fraternal benefit society. As American citizens the members of the IWO have the same problems as their fellow citizens and the Order, therefore, considers it a civic duty to encourage its members to take an interest in the political and economic developments in the country.

Organized to seek economic security and well-being for its members and the country as a whole, the IWO, therefore, with the approval of the membership, supports such legislation and action which furthers these aims. The Order does not have, nor is it committed, to any political platform. Its members have the right to belong and be active in any political organization they see fit. No reserve funds are used for the promotion of political parties.[8]

Two more selections were read in an attempt to show that the IWO supported organized labor and that Order membership was compatible with union membership; the answer stated that the IWO "played an important role" in the organization of the steel and auto workers in the CIO and other union efforts of the AFL. To this was added the response to a "question" on whether religious services could be performed at funerals arranged by IWO lodges:

Yes. Believing entirely in the freedom of religious practices, the IWO has no rules as to religious services. It leaves the decision entirely to the individual.[9]

Weissman continued to question Saltzman with regard to a number of areas when Judge Greenberg, obviously moved by what had been read from the *Manual for Builders,* interrupted. Addressing Saltzman, he read a lengthy portion from a pamphlet by M. Olgin which the State had introduced into evidence entitled *The International Workers Order, History—Program—Tactics* dated 1931 and carrying the description: "By order of the national executive committee of the International Workers Order." In the segments the Judge read, the ties of the Order to the Communist Party in terms of endorsing it and its class struggle policy were clearly stated, concluding that members of the IWO "cannot say they have no connection with the Communist Party." Judge Greenberg wanted to know how these statements squared with what had been read from the *Manual.*

Saltzman answered by stating that "This is the point of view of an individual, and the official formulation and ideas of the International Workers Order as a whole is in the *Manual.*" Judge Greenberg was not satisfied. He reacted by pointing out that the pamphlet stated it was "by order of the national executive committee" of the Order; Saltzman responded by pointing out that he had been a member of the committee in 1931 and that the group had asked Olgin to write the pamphlet as an expression of his personal views. Asked by the Judge whether, notwithstanding the question of authority to express official IWO policy, what Olgin said represented in a "general way" the policy of the IWO "from its inception down to the present date," Saltzman responded, "I don't think so."[10]

Weissman then asked the Judge for the pamphlet (which was in English translation), turned to Williams's associate, Henry, and asked for the original in Yiddish. Weissman handed both to Saltzman, asking him to first read the legend attributing the work to the IWO and then asked Saltzman for his translation of the key word (in Yiddish) "OIFTRAG." Saltzman rejected the words "by order," substituting the words "by commission" as the correct translation so that under his version it read, "By commission of . . . ." Saltzman told the Court that the committee had asked a number of people to write their opinions "as to the kind of Order we should have," adding under further questioning that the Olgin position was never adopted as the "exact policy of the Order." By contrast, he affirmed the *Manual for Builders* as officially approved policy.[11]

If the language and views expressed by the Olgin pamphlet had stuck well enough in the mind of Judge Greenberg to have been recalled and used by him, it augured badly for the IWO. What must be remembered is that the Judge had at this point already been exposed to about 200 exhibits from both sides and that he was apparently being very diligent, reading not only the daily record of the proceedings but these exhibits—some of them very lengthy—as well. On the other hand, the Olgin pamphlet was dated 1931, during the first full year of the Order's existence, and a great deal could have changed in twenty years.

Realizing the significance of the Judge's interruption and reference, Weissman pressed Saltzman to elicit that in fact a wide variety of political opinions coexisted in the membership of the IWO. This Saltzman confirmed by adding, "We never ask anybody a question, what is his belief, to what [political] party he belongs. This is not the business of the Order." To demonstrate this, Weissman pointed out to the Court that, in one of the local lodge publications, a member had a letter published supporting Senator Robert A. Taft, a conservative Republican, for President.[12]

Returning to more comfortable grounds, Saltzman's answers were designed to show the "human" side of the IWO. He explained the course of an ordinary lodge meeting, stressing how each lodge cared for its members. He mentioned, for example, the "hospitaler's" report on who was sick, visits that were made, and collections that were taken up to help the sick member's family. Order-wide campaigns in support for public health care centers, public nurseries, the March of Dimes, and the United Nations Children's Relief Fund were described; letters of commendation from the New York Heart Campaign, Red Cross, and the U.S. Treasury Department, among many others, were introduced into evidence.

To counter the earlier allegations that IWO funds had been used for purposes other than insurance, Saltzman explained the dues structure and collection procedures, emphatically denying that any funds had ever been used by the home office for any purposes other than those allowed by state statute. All funds, he assured the court, were properly segregated and regularly audited by the Department of Insurance. Local lodges could carry out fund-raising activities for lodge programs, but in response to direct questioning, Saltzman stated he was "positive" that there was never any home office control over the social activities of the lodges of the Order. When America was at war (1941–45), Saltzman stated, the IWO fully supported wartime activities and received recognition for its efforts.[13]

Judge Greenberg had opened another area that Weissman did not want to leave uncovered: the matter of why IWO membership, after such steady and healthy increases year after year, had fallen in 1940. The Judge's inquiry and the less-than-candid response of Saltzman needed to be addressed, which Weissman did at the commencement of another day's testimony. He offered in evidence a table from a book of *Statistics of Fraternal Societies* for the year 1941 to demonstrate that 92 of the 193 fraternals listed also lost membership that year, in order to establish that the dip in IWO membership was in line with what occurred in about half of all American fraternals. The Judge readily admitted that he had in mind the effect of the Hitler-Stalin Pact when he had raised the matter, reflecting the idea that politics affected the IWO because it was so intimately tied to a political position. Weissman argued that it was a period of national "uncertainty" that explained the drop. While Judge Greenberg averred, it is apparent from his expressed analysis that he remained unconvinced.[14]

To give the Court further indication of the broad base of activities the IWO engaged in throughout its existence, Weissman took Saltzman through the Order's campaigns in such areas as Congressional bills it supported (meeting with elected officials to lobby for them), union activities it endorsed, and civil rights campaigns for blacks. Saltzman specifically detailed how "[the Order] united with all progressive forces in American life to struggle for the freedom of the Scottsboro boys," fought with the Metropolitan Life Insurance Company to allow blacks to live in a housing project it owned, and supported "Negro History Week" as well as anti-lynching and anti-poll tax legislation. The message Weissman wanted to deliver to Judge Greenberg was that the IWO took part in many mainstream liberal activities, including equal rights for blacks, not because of Communist Party directives but because the Order believed in those issues. His questioning also gave Saltzman the opportunity to point out that membership participation in all campaigns was voluntary and all monies used were likewise donations—no insurance funds were ever involved.[15]

Weissman used Saltzman's testimony to "flesh out" the nature of the IWO. Through the question-and-answer method, he brought out that fully one third of the home office staff were "Negroes and Puerto Ricans," serving in all ranks and positions in the Order. The Order's opposition to Fascism and anti-Semitism, termed by Saltzman as "twin brothers," was explained. Saltzman spoke of cooperative efforts with the American Jewish Congress and American Jewish Committee, two mainstream national Jewish organizations.

"Name dropping" of establishment-type organizations as well as nationally known individuals who had some association with the Order was pursued in order to send Judge Greenberg the message that the IWO was not a pariah because of its liberal positions and policies. Thus, while the Order had taken public stances against the Smith and McCarran Acts, the Court knew that other liberal organizations and individuals had taken similar stands. Religious leaders, Congressional, state, and local personalities were identified as having a relationship with the Order on various issues or as having joined with the IWO on specified occasions.[16]

Judge Greenberg interrupted to ask whether it was within the "charter provisions" of the IWO for the organization to engage in these political activities, questioning whether they were indeed "fraternal." Saltzman averred that "every one" of the fraternals engaged in such activities. Challenged by the Judge to name some, Saltzman recited that "our former competition" the Workmen's Circle was so engaged, as was the Knights of Columbus; of the latter, he said that it "went much further than we in a great number of problems," by which he meant that the Knights of Columbus were even more politically active than the IWO.[17]

Returning to the theme of how mainstream the Order was, Saltzman was queried on its policy toward Israel, still a fledgling nation at that time. Questioning on this area was designed to demonstrate to the Judge that, whatever had been the Order's earlier attitude about Zionism, support for Israel and for the Jewish communities devastated by the Second World War was now solid and palpable. Weissman must have assumed that Judge Greenberg had read materials in evidence that went back to a time when, in line with the Communist Party's position, anti-Zionism had been evident in the IWO; therefore the aim was to show how supportive—in accord with all major American-Jewish organizations—the Order now was for the new state. The Judge must also have known, however, that Russia had correspondingly changed its position, having cast a key vote in the United Nations which favored the partition plan that led to the Jewish state.

Beginning with an exposition on how the Jewish branch of the Order had aided Jews in distress in the war's aftermath (for instance, the J.P.F.O. founded orphans' homes in Paris, Brussels, and Poland), Saltzman testified that the Order had also established cooperatives for tailors, bakers, and shoemakers in Europe, giving employment to displaced Jews. Moving to the topic of aid to Israel, the J.P.F.O., Saltzman explained, had paid for the purchase of twelve ambulances and had established a wing of the Jerusalem hospital for tubercular children as well as kingergartens in Tel Aviv. All of this came about through voluntary contributions—not IWO insurance monies. During the testimony, Saltzman noted cooperation with leading Jewish organizations such as the World Jewish Congress and Hadassah. Finally, to emphasize these mainstream associations, the IWO's efforts to raise monies for the broadly based United Jewish Appeal rounded out the presentation.[18]

Weissman closed his examination by asking Saltzman whether the IWO had taken any position "with respect to the question of friendship with the Soviet Union." Having answered affirmatively, Saltzman explained that such friendship was vital in order to avoid a third world war, adding "we believe that all war-mongering is now very dangerous for all of our lives, for the lives of our children and for the future of the world." Williams interrupted to ask when the IWO took this official position; Saltzman responded that formal resolutions to that effect had been passed by the general council of the Order. Thus ended the examination—really a presentation—by the Respondent's lead witness.[19]

It should be noted that Williams had, from time to time, interrupted this witness to ask a question even though direct examination of this witness was not yet finished. Weissman allowed this where the question filled in a factual matter that made better sense of the witness's story. When Weissman felt Williams was stepping out of bounds and should wait for his turn on cross-examination, he said so. Both sides tolerated this informal injection of questioning in order to facilitate clarity. Of course, the Judge interrupted more often, and with wider latitude in his questioning, than did either of the lawyers.

Under the heading of "Saltzman Testifies at IWO Trial," an IWO news release dated March 30, 1951 portrayed the appearance by the witness as follows:

Standing proudly on the solid achievements of the Order to which he contributed so greatly, Rubin Saltzman, General Secretary of the Jewish Peoples Fraternal Order, became the first IWO official to testify in New York Supreme Court.

For four and a half days, a jammed court room heard the Order founder and first IWO General Secretary describe the origin of the organization, its democratic structure and its activities.

Sharp Contrast

After the hate-laden lies of professional stoolpigeons, renegades and moral lepers, Saltzman's testimony brought the very air of sanity and integrity into the court room.

As he described the Order's manifold activities he expressed his deep personal love and respect for Jewish culture and the cultures of all national groups which make up the American amalgam. It was in startling contrast to the sneers of Simon Webber, "Forward" editor, and the slanders of Matthew Cvetic against their own and other nationalities.

The spectators, the overwhelming majority of them Order members, received a vivid understanding of what they are fighting for and against whom they are contending.[20]

No report of Saltzman's testimony appeared in any major New York newspaper.

Not once had Weissman called upon Saltzman to confront directly the specific testimony of any of the State's witnesses; for instance, he did not quote to Saltzman what Cvetic had said about control of lodge activities, split of monies with the Communist Party, or Party control of the Order through Party members who were also IWO officers. Instead, Weissman had Saltzman portray a democratically controlled, worker-oriented, compassionate organization, deeply involved in the bread and butter issues of economic and social concern, interested primarily in the welfare of its members. Only by inference—by the juxtaposition of a totally different portrait of the IWO—did Saltzman rebut the portrait created by the State's witnesses, who had painted the IWO a deep Red; Saltzman's testimony was designed to add the colors white and blue to the canvas.

Paul Williams had barely injected himself during those four and one half days of Saltzman's direct testimony. His basic strategy was to allow Weissman to ask *any* questions (without objecting) he wished and to allow Saltzman full latitude in responding, to send the message to the Court that he was unconcerned with the presentation. In effect he was positioning himself to get at the heart of the State's case by cross-examination—one that would be hard-hitting and confrontational—on sensitive political issues. By not objecting to a single question put to Saltzman on direct examination, he was utilizing a credible trial technique: sending a message that this testimony was not even worth arguing about.

As Williams rose to begin the State's first cross-examination of an IWO witness, behind him were continued news stories of a tense, troubling world and domestic scene for the United States. During March 1951, some 5,000 additional casualties had been reported in the Korean War; by month's end, the casualty count stood at over 57,000.

The battle between General MacArthur and President Truman and his administration was intensifying as the General demanded orders to go north of the 38th Parallel, the dividing line between North and South Korea. The administration and the United Nations were talking of a "victory" if the UN forces stopped at the 38th Parallel. Seoul, the capital of South Korea, had been recaptured, and advances continued with significant casualty costs to that boundary of the country. The dollar cost to the United States escalated as President Truman called for an additional $9 to $10 billion to finance the war. Congress worked on lowering the draft age to eighteen as the war moved toward one year of bitter conflict.

During all these events, the Red Scare continued unabated. By March, HUAC was in the midst of renewed hearings on Hollywood and the Red connection; stars, writers, and other film personalities were being subpoenaed. Larry Parks, an admitted former Party member, named a dozen others and received a commendation from HUAC as a good American citizen for doing so, yet his studio would not release a picture he had starred in because of the revelations.

HUAC also named 624 organizations and 204 publications as "subversive" in a revised, expanded list; the Committee also announced that it had a list of "secret contributors" to the Communist Party. Meanwhile, J. Edgar Hoover stated that the American Communist Party had made a "studied effort" to put Communists into government agencies. The FBI also declared that it was following Reds as the Party went "underground." Spy stories, trials, hearings, and accusations of disloyalty appeared daily, capped by the Rosenberg atom spy trial that ended with three guilty verdicts on March 29, 1951, just as Saltzman was completing his direct testimony and Williams was about to begin cross-examination.[21]

Saltzman got himself in trouble with his response to the very first question Williams asked; wasting no time in getting to the matter of politics, Williams queried whether it had "ever been the policy of the IWO to support the Communist Party in any of its election campaigns?" A simple "No" response brought the Judge immediately into the fray with the warning, "You had better be sure of that, Mr. Saltzman." "You want to think about it a little bit?" he asked. The witness's response was, "Well, I am talking about the policies of the International Workers Order." Uncertain and unclear in this initial exchange, the meaning of this response and the basic strategy of defense would become clear as the hours of cross-examination proceeded: all direct political activity in the Order had been carried on by *individuals* and *committees* of individuals—not by the IWO as an entity—and none of it had involved insurance or other company funds.[22]

Williams refocused his attention on the same subject with the next two questions, when he asked whether the IWO ever supported Party campaigns for contributions within the lodges and whether the Order, through its lodges, ever supported a Communist candidate "as such." To both, Saltzman fumbled with ineffectual and confused answers to the effect that yes, this had happened maybe during the first or around the first year of IWO existence. When asked next whether he personally participated in election campaigns for Communist candidates, Weissman was on his feet to object. Reminding the Court that "We are not trying Saltzman," Weissman was attempting to limit any question to what the witness had done in his role as *officer* of the IWO. But Judge Greenberg rejected such a limitation, adding "Again, like Pooh-Bah [from Gilbert and Sullivan's *The Mikado*] says, it is very difficult to separate the man into various parts." Ordered to answer, Saltzman made a brief speech about his belief in the freedom of the individual and his willingness to answer anything about the IWO, then, in a somewhat garbled manner, refused to answer Williams's inquiry on the grounds of his self-incrimination rights under the Fifth Amendment.[23]

Williams's move to strike the answer was denied; Judge Greenberg accepted Saltzman's plea of the Fifth Amendment as his personal privilege. Williams pressed with, "Are you a present member of the Communist Party? Have you ever been a member of the Communist Party?" To both queries, Saltzman took the constitutional privilege, and the Court sustained his right not to answer the question.[24]

Thus, within no more than ten minutes of cross-examination, Williams was pounding at the theme of Communist Party involvement with the IWO through this officer who was proud to have been there from the beginning. Williams asked no personal background questions, nor did he ease into the sensitive areas; he wasted no time in trying to impress the Judge that politics—Red politics—was what this case was all about.

The IWO news release took quite a different view of what had transpired:

REPELS INQUISITOR [WILLIAMS]
Attempts by the Insurance Department to launch a personal inquisition were resolutely defeated by the IWO vice president. Asked if he were "a member of the Communist Party," Saltzman answered:
"I believe in the freedom of the individual to maintain his own political beliefs without giving an accounting to anyone. I have come here to defend the Order which I have served many years of my life. I am ready to answer all questions about the IWO." In this way, Saltzman upheld the great Order principle of not inquiring into anyone's political beliefs or creed, of not permitting witchhunts among members and officers.[25]

Throughout the State's presentation of its witnesses, the words and deeds of the IWO and its members had been introduced into evidence in the attempt to establish the political connection between the Order and its leaders and the Communist Party. Now Saltzman faced a personal interrogation about his activities in the IWO that bespoke of Party connection. He had already taken his Fifth Amendment privilege on the question of membership in the Party and shaped his responses to differentiate between activities of the Order and those of individuals. Faced with Williams's intensive questioning in which he used copies of the *Daily Worker* and the IWO *New Order* magazine, Saltzman had to explain his role as "manager" (Bedacht was "treasurer") of campaigns to raise money for the election of Communist Party candidates.

Saltzman refused to name other members of the committee (described in the literature as "outstanding national leaders of the Order") stating, "I said before that I wouldn't be like a fingerman here." But Williams kept reading aloud quotations such as "We pledge ourselves to mobilize the members of the International Workers Order in every one of the hundreds of branches [lodges] all over the country to raise $50,000 for the Communist Party election campaign," demanding that Saltzman explain his efforts. Saltzman's responses were vague; he insisted he did not remember details that went back over some fifteen years (1936) and that everything was done by members as individuals or as part of this committee. Williams came back at him by quoting the *Daily Worker:*

Q. This *Daily Worker* article says, "IWO branches"—not individuals, but branches—"should send all funds and make all checks or money orders payable to Max Bedacht, treasurer, 80 Fifth Avenue, New York City." 80 Fifth Avenue, New York City, is the headquarters of the IWO?

A. Yes, sir.[26]

Williams further pointed out that the national executive committee of the IWO knew of the drive for funds and that Saltzman was then, as he would continue to be, on that national executive committee of the Order. It was developed that Earl Browder and William Z. Foster, top Party members, had directly appealed to IWO members in Order publications; Saltzman stated that Foster was also an IWO member.[27]

Saltzman then went on the attack, accusing Williams of carrying on "a personal inquisition, a political inquisition," to which Williams responded, "Don't be rude to me, Mr. Saltzman. This is not a personal political inquisition." Williams, undaunted, pressed the issue of lodges endorsing Communist Party candidates, asking if it was the practice of the branches of the IWO to endorse candidates for public office. Saltzman responded that "in certain times" some may have; it was, he said, "entirely up to the branches for themselves to make [an endorsement] decision." When one of the endorsers turned out to be George Powers, a former IWO vice-president and the first witness for the State in this trial, Saltzman retorted, "That's the famous stool pigeon."[28]

Williams showed Saltzman a letter he had written, published in the *New Order* in 1936, which thanked members for contributing money to the Communist campaign committee. Asked how much money was raised, Saltzman answered that he did not remember, adding that thousands of dollars were raised for "worthy causes, for many things," and with obvious passion stated:

I want to cooperate and as far as the Order is concerned. I want to give every information possible. The Order is dear to me. I love the Order. I have given, as I said, 21 years of my life. I am not here for my own defense. I am here for the defense of the Order and I am willing to give every answer concerning the Order.[29]

Williams was unimpressed. He demanded to know whether such a committee still existed; Saltzman said "No." Pressed as to when the last date such a committee did exist, Saltzman claimed he could not remember. Williams, however, had a 1942 article from the *Daily Worker* indicating that Saltzman was a committee member of IWO supporters who served on "the fraternal" group for a local Communist Party candidate.[30]

The relationship between the IWO and the *Daily Worker* came under close scrutiny as Williams questioned Saltzman. Did the Order support the *Worker* for the good of the paper? Saltzman's response was that the benefit of the IWO was the first and primary concern: to get members and popularize the Order, adding, "and if it benefitted any other institution" there was no objection. Judge Greenberg injected with his version of what Williams was trying to prove by asking, "In other words, is it fair to say that since the *Daily Worker* was in your corner, you wanted to be in the same corner of the *Daily Worker*?" Saltzman's reply was to parry a direct "yes" or "no" by stating that the paper's readers constituted a "reservoir" of potential members, explaining that the IWO also advertised in papers he did not particularly agree with.[31]

The courtroom atmosphere was very tense as Williams dug deeper, knowing he was now in a sensitive area that the Judge, with his particular interest in newspapers, would appreciate. Thus he demanded: "Mr. Saltzman, is the *Daily Worker* the spokesman for the IWO?" "The spokesman for the IWO," he replied, "is the national executive committee of the IWO, and nobody can speak for us." In a follow-up question, Williams asked whether the Order supported the *Worker* by advertising in it. Saltzman retorted that "you can interpret it that it was a support," reminding Williams that the Order's primary reason for advertising was to attract members.[32]

Judge Greenberg helped Williams by reading to Saltzman a comment from the book *5 Years IWO* which said, "From the first day of the

Order's existence, the *Daily Worker* has made itself a spokesman for the IWO. . . . In addition, the columns of the *Daily Worker* have always been open to news of the IWO and its activities." Saltzman's answer was that that was only one person's interpretation—one he was entitled to state. Judge Greenberg was dissatisfied, pointing out that this was in an official publication of the IWO and therefore reflected IWO policy. "Isn't it also the opinion of the national executive [committee]?" he asked; Saltzman equivocated, pointing out that the writing was from some fifteen or more years ago and that the Order had since grown. When asked by Greenberg whether he repudiated the position set forth in the article, Saltzman responded:

I don't repudiate it. As a matter of fact, I personally hold that position, if I may say so, but that isn't the position of the Order as a whole, as I said before.[33]

Loyal Communist that he was, Saltzman had to add his personal endorsement instead of simply holding to the line that the statement did not reflect the official policy of the Order. Weissman must have been exasperated by this response; the problem of the witness who says more than is necessary is a common phenomenon and a genuine concern to all trial lawyers. Weissman attempted to save the situation by interrupting to refocus on the quoted language's reflexive nature, "The *Daily Worker* has *made itself* the spokesman for the IWO."

To strengthen his point, Williams sought information as to whether the IWO had persisted in its ties to the *Daily Worker*. Judge Greenberg interceded with the following line of questioning:

Q. All right. You are a member of the executive, aren't you?

A. Yes, sir.

Q. Do you know what the view of the executive is with respect to the *Daily Worker* in regard to its relation to the IWO?

A. They believe that the *Daily Worker* is supporting the IWO, it is a workers' organization.

Q. The national executive doesn't reject the *Daily Worker*, does it?

A. No, not at all.[34]

In unrelenting fashion, Williams pursued his objective of proving a firm symbiosis between the Party and the Order. Campaigns for the *Worker* and the *Freiheit* were explored. Saltzman spoke of the "love" of members for these papers and their willingness to aid them with money collection efforts. Just as the day's testimony was about to end, Judge Greenberg once again entered the questioning:

Q. Mr. Saltzman, this list which is styled "The Committee of IWO Members to Aid *Daily Worker*" contains the names of men and women who in 1937, and some of them even today, were important officers or members of the general council or leaders of the IWO, is that a fact?

A. Some of them must be.

Q. Well, William Weiner was the president at that time, wasn't he?

A. 1937, yes.

Q. Max Bedacht was the general secretary?

A. Yes, sir.

Q. Dave Greene was the head of the Youth Section at that time?

A. I suppose so, yes, sir.

Q. Rubin Saltzman—yourself—

A. Yes, sir.

Q. Louise Thompson?

A. She was at the time.

Q. Sam Pevzner?

A. He was working for the Order, yes, sir.

Q. Well, they were all important officials in the Order, weren't they, at that time in 1937?

A. Oh, yes.

Q. Wouldn't you say that that committee composed the cream of the top echelon, the top rank, in the Order at that time?

A. I wouldn't call myself the cream—

Q. You don't need to be modest.

A. I don't mean to be modest, but there were important people in the Order.[35]

Immediately following this exchange, the Court recessed until the next morning. Williams then resumed with questions relating to activities and personalities attached to Communist Party causes. Repeatedly, Saltzman exercised his constitutional privilege. Judge Greenberg, exasperated with this exercise, questioned whether "the witness is honestly claiming a Constitutional privilege in the light of the admissions, the written admissions over his own signature and by his own position in the Communist Party." Nevertheless, he sustained every use of the Fifth Amendment, thus avoiding any possible constitutional right of the witness being impaired or limited.[36]

William Weiner had been President of the IWO for many years when he was convicted of passport fraud in 1941 and removed from his office by order of the New York State Department of Insurance; at the time of his removal, he was also treasurer of the Communist Party. Williams had entered into evidence two articles appearing in Order publications while the Weiner passport problems were at hand. From a reluctant Saltzman, Williams and Judge Greenberg elicited that the national executive committee of the IWO supported Weiner's cause—and that of Earl Browder—who had similarly been convicted for passport violations and was in prison. The articles had spoken of "minor infractions" of the passport laws, with prosecution attributed to the fact that the defendants were Communists. One article concluded that "The political acts of the Communists are not only entirely legal, but socially constructive." Williams then asked:

Did the executive committee of the IWO ever take the position that the political acts of the Communists were legal and were socially constructive?

A. To defend persecuted people, surely. We are always for the defense of those that are persecuted for their ideals or for other points. Sure we believe that there shouldn't be these things.

Q. And that was the view of the national executive committee?

A. In general.

Q. Did the national executive committee discuss the conviction of William Weiner at any time?

A. I refuse to answer on that point on the same constitutional ground.

The Court: Sustained.[37]

Through this questioning, Williams wanted to establish that over the years no one in the national leadership of the IWO ever repudiated, challenged, or disapproved of support expressed with respect to Communist Party election fund drives, contribution efforts on behalf of the *Daily Worker,* Communist Party candidates for public office, or its discharged president, William Weiner. Saltzman could not remember any such instance. Williams must have remembered how, from time to time, Judge Greenberg had asked questions in the same vein, to test whether objection, repudiation, or disagreement had been evinced; he had wisely picked up on the Judge's concern.

For hour after hour, Williams continued to probe, using IWO publications, reports of speeches, and the operations of committees of Order members in an attempt to show how they related to Communist Party activities and personalities. With increasing frequency, Saltzman, on his own or with advice of counsel, exercised his constitutional privilege and refused to answer questions. Nevertheless, Williams was able to get into the Judge's hands, as well as read into the record, reports that bespoke of a mutual admiration for and reciprocal support between the Communist Party and the apparent policies of the IWO.

Thus, while Saltzman denied that the Order "as an official body" took a position with regard to the trial in 1948 of the eleven top Communists (the *Dennis* case), between Williams's and the Judge's questions, IWO leadership support for the defendants, in terms of fund raising and articles, was made evident. In a pragmatic but unspoken sense, Saltzman's frequent use of the Fifth Amendment appeared to confirm the relationship between the IWO and the Communist Party.

There were also key instances where Saltzman did not use his self-incrimination rights and instead expressed his principles. When asked about a statement from an October 5, 1949 edition of the *Daily Worker* condemning the trial of the Communists, Saltzman confirmed that he, along with three other IWO leaders, had signed it. He also stated that he believed his denunciation of the prosecution and of the presiding judge, Harold R. Medina, were still correct in 1951 and that he, under his own name, had solicited defense money and had maintained a bank account, turning over the proceeds to the trial defense committee.[38]

Hearing the witness mention Judge Medina's name must have been particularly relevant to Judge Greenberg. The laudatory speech Medina had given him at his installation as a judge was surely memorable to Henry Clay Greenberg. His role as judge in the *Dennis* case had catapulted Medina into national prominence, in good measure because of violent attacks upon him by the left-wing press as well as by the courtroom actions of the battery of defense lawyers. Here was a person who had been close to Judge Greenberg—professionally and personally—being condemned by the leadership of the leftist organization now on trial before him.

Unknown to Judge Greenberg or the defense was a further involvement with Judge Medina; while on the federal bench, Judge Medina, aware of the IWO case, had sent material from his files to Williams's office, apparently in an effort to aid the State. Henry, on behalf of the firm, wrote Medina, thanking him "for keeping us in mind" and returned that which had been lent, adding, "The material was quite helpful and I have made copies of what I needed from it." Judge Medina had evidently forwarded the materials through his former law office, the famous Wall Street firm of Cravath, Swaine and Moore.

Just what a sitting federal judge was doing in seeking to aid the prosecution in a state case may well be questioned. The letter of thanks and return of materials was addressed to "Harold R. Medina, Esq.," and the salutation read "Dear Mr. Medina."[39] The use of appropriate discretion, that is, nothing from the Judge as judge directly and nothing back to him as a judge, indicates the care that was apparently necessary to avoid allegations of impropriety if not outright wrongdoing.

In his continued cross-examination, Williams questioned Saltzman about his activities including a speech he had given at a Communist Party-sponsored mass meeting in 1941 as J.P.F.O.-IWO representative, his work for the Communist Jewish newspaper, the *Freiheit,* and his role as a member of the board of trustees of the Jefferson School, which had been listed as a subversive organization. Williams knew Saltzman would invoke his constitutional rights and refuse to answer any questions relating to these activities, but merely by listing the activities Williams hoped to convey the message of Communist involvement.[40]

An earlier State's witness had testified to the effect that the origin of the IWO was tied to orders "from Moscow" that Communists in the Workmen's Circle should split and form a separate fraternal order. When Williams began a line of questioning in this area, Judge Greenberg intervened:

Is it a fact that that group which broke away from the Workmen's Circle was actually the Communist group, the left wing group?

A. I wouldn't say so. I would say there were members of a great number, progressive members. Some of them had their view in one form or another, but this was a progressive membership in the Workmen's Circle.[41]

Saltzman had testified that he was part of a delegation to eastern Europe and the Soviet Union from the Workmen's Circle in 1929—the same year that the alleged orders had been given. This gave Judge Greenberg an opportunity to probe the matter:

Mr. Saltzman, early in these hearings there was testimony by a witness to the effect that at a conference of the Third International held in Russia in 1929 directives or orders were issued for the formation of a new fraternal order in this country. Did anything like that take place while you were in Russia, so far as you know?

A. No, sir.

Q. Was that the fact?

A. That's a fact.

Q. No, I mean the testimony of this witness.

A. I don't talk about what he said. You are asking me if I participated or if I know about it.

Q. Yes.

A. I would say it is a lie, your Honor.

Q. And you say, so far as you know, there were no such orders from the secretariat or from the executive—

A. Or from anybody.[42]

But even if there was contradictory testimony with respect to the origins of the IWO, there was still plenty of documentary evidence in the form of books and pamphlets from the early years of the Order, some of which had been used in IWO children's schools, which directly endorsed the Communist Party. Saltzman's response was to back into the theme of "it's the opinion of the person writing"; he could not remember if the publications expressed official policy. Williams pressed the point, demanding that Saltzman answer whether the national executive committee currently endorsed the Communist Party. When objections were raised, Judge Greenberg took over, asking whether the national executive committee of the IWO had, in the last five years, endorsed the Communist Party in any political campaigns; Saltzman replied that it had not.[43]

If IWO politics was a vulnerable area, at no time was it more subject to the accusation of following the Communist Party line than in the period from the Hitler-Stalin Pact (August 1939) to the time of Russia's entry into the war (June 1941). Williams moved into this area, obviously making Saltzman very uncomfortable. The isolationist, anti-Roosevelt stand of the Order, demonstrated by published articles and cartoons, was introduced into evidence; thereafter, the "flip-flop" in IWO political policy after Hitler's attack on Russia was amply displayed. The matter was not further elaborated after Judge Greenberg commented that the writings, and thus the stance of the IWO, spoke for themselves. The Order's pro-Soviet, anti-Cold War position after the war was also introduced into evidence; Saltzman responded to a question about the IWO's attitude on the Korean War by stating it took no position on the war then raging.[44]

This entire area of questioning reads in the record like a political discussion between intelligent, interested parties; the Judge freely joined in discussing the Cold War, with Saltzman representing those arguing for a peaceful accommodation with Russia while decrying warmongering elements in the West, while Williams and Greenberg questioned whether Russia did indeed want peace. Though posed as questions, the record comes across more as a current affairs disputation, as topics such as the Marshall Plan, President Truman's policies, and the Korean War were canvassed.[45]

With the cross-examinationn coming to an end, Williams moved in "for the kill" with this question:

Q. From 1936 to date, has it not been the official policy of the IWO secretly but nonetheless faithfully, to follow the Communist Party line?

Objections followed so the Judge tried his hand at it:

By the Court.

Q. If you take into consideration the writings that appeared from time to time in the various publications of the IWO, such as the *New Order* and the *Fraternal Outlook,* together with speeches made from time to time, which have been referred to here, of the leaders, would you say that those speeches and those magazine articles and writings represented precisely the same policies and practices of the Communist Party?

Again Weissman objected on the grounds that there was "no evidence here of the policies and practices of the Communist Party." Judge Greenberg argued with him, but when Weissman persisted in his objection, the Judge this time ruled against himself so that the question did not have to be answered.[46]

Peter Shipka, Secretary-Treasurer of the IWO, was the second witness to take the stand on behalf of the Order. A printer by trade, he had risen to an important post in another fraternal benefit order, the Slovak Workers Society. Weissman sought from him testimony concerning the merger of this and other fraternal orders into the IWO.

In his testimony, Shipka told the story of how the Slovak Workers Society had been in financial trouble as a result of the Great Depression; its assets were in first mortgages on members' homes, and many of these debtors could not make their payments. Shipka related how the democratically voted merger with the IWO literally saved the Society and, at the same time, broadened the insurance benefits available to its members. The IWO, which started in the midst of the Depression, had invested its monies in solid, liquid assets and thus was in a very strong financial position.

Stressing the sickness, death, and other member benefits, Shipka described how the IWO offered specific insurance against tuberculosis, a disease widespread among workers in certain job areas. With evident pride, he told of the medical department which provided doctors at very modest costs; there were eighty-five doctors, surgeons, and specialists who served IWO members in New York alone.[47]

Since Shipka had been a party to the negotiations for the merger of his Society into the Order, and those of other fraternals that similarly merged into the IWO in the 1930s, he was able to summarize "principles and conditions" for such mergers. These included the right of merging members either to retain their prior insurance program or transfer to the Order's, the right to remain autonomous as a group within the Order, and the assurance that the IWO would always remain "a labor organization."[48]

Because Shipka was the financial and administrative head of the IWO, he was in a position to explain its insurance programs, which he did in response to Weissman's questions. Emphasizing the use of mortality tables that were most liberal in terms of rates charged, Shipka explained in detail how each fund for the various insurance programs was maintained and carefully monitored to ensure adequate reserves and prompt payment of claims. Over ninety percent of IWO members, he explained, chose life insurance on what was termed a "step rate" plan, adding that most commercial companies did not offer such insurance, the rates for which were very low, "because there is no money in it." He characterized this insurance program as "suited to the pocketbook of a worker because when he needs the protection most, when he needs the insurance to provide for his dependents, when the children are small, he is able to buy a maximum amount at the lowest possible cost."[49]

Weissman, an insurance expert, was both knowledgeable and comfortable as he queried Shipka with respect to a wide range of insurance matters. The witness, in turn, used every opportunity to extol the democratic nature of the IWO; for instance, he pointed out that a grass roots movement had developed in the mid-1940s which demanded that the Order offer a form of endowment policy. Despite opposition from IWO leadership, the Order did establish such an insurance offering. Shipka also stressed that in the payment of claims, the IWO always gave the benefit of the doubt to the member making a claim. Weissman asked a question which allowed Shipka to confirm that no commissions for insurance issued by the Order were ever paid to anyone.[50]

Shipka added a "human face" to the Order's activities as he described the raising of voluntary monies from its membership to pay the dues and supplemental benefits for those members who needed special help; this included sending "pocket money" to members in tuberculosis sanitariums, and even paying round-trip transportation costs for a needy member who had to spend time in a sanitarium.[51]

Shipka's lengthy testimony, which lasted for days, was designed to focus the Judge's attention on the idea that the organization now being tried before him, fighting for its life, was a carefully run, fiscally conservative insurance company; that the insurance programs were the heart of the IWO, and that all other activities of a fraternal, social—and political—nature were all ancillary to the insurance core. In effect, the message sent was that harm should not come to a sound, socially responsible organization upon which tens of thousands of people depended just because the Insurance Department did not like the politics of its leaders.

Shipka's testimony also attempted to demonstrate how the State had distorted the truth by focusing solely on those activities that bespoke of left-wing politics. The Haley Report had listed eleven organizations as recipients of IWO donations, all of them left-wing, during the years 1944 through 1946, totaling some $3,638.57; Shipka produced a complete list of seventy-three beneficiaries, totaling $13,495.40, which ranged over a broad scope of charitable and educational organizations, as the complete and correct accounting for those years.[52]

Shipka was closely questioned by Judge Greenberg, who interrupted in order to get answers he wanted, most of them relating to money and operational aspects of the Order. On the other hand, Williams remained absolutely silent, never objecting to any question put to the witness or to any document the defense wanted in evidence. Williams's silence was deliberate. Once again, this was part of his strategy directed to the Court: it makes little difference, he implied through his inaction, that the IWO is financially sound and well run as an insurance company—the State does not contest that; all of this is not worth arguing about. Politics is what the IWO is really about—and Communist politics is why the Order is before you.

Weissman turned to Shipka's role as chief administrator of the Order to demonstrate that the IWO's pro-labor and racial ideals were more than mere words. In response to this line of questioning, Shipka testified that the home office staff had a sizeable number of black as well as Puerto Rican employees (16 out of 65) and that all IWO employees belonged to a union, with the exception of six elected officers. Blacks had advanced in employment with the Order under a plan involving "additional and adjusted seniority" to avoid layoff in the event of staff reduction; in effect, it was the deliberate policy of the Order to counter the usual fate of blacks who were so often the last hired and first fired. For a business to place blacks in supervisory positions in 1951 was unusual; to create a form of affirmative action was practically unheard of.[53]

Shipka ended his testimony with a recounting of the "clean bill of health" the IWO had received over many years from the Department of Insurance as a result of its audits; the Order, he emphasized, had met or exceeded all requirements of the Department. Judge Greenberg took up an analysis of the income and costs of the Order and asked Shipka about the per-capita cost of managing the IWO; Shipka testified that the $5.07 per-member cost was considerably lower than many other fraternals.[54]

Quite suddenly, Judge Greenberg issued a highly unusual demand by asking Shipka to tell Saltzman to come back to the courtroom because he wanted to ask him some further questions. Saltzman's testimony, including extensive cross-examination, had lasted almost five days. In all, there were close to 500 pages of record created by his testimony, yet the Judge was now directing that Saltzman return to the stand. But it was not just the extensive time already spent on Saltzman; rather it was the fact that neither attorney had asked for his return, which does sometime occur in civil trials, with the court's permission. This happens when some new evidence or uncovered area requires such a recall. Here, the Judge demanded the recall for his own purposes; he explained that he had, over the past weekend, read all of Saltzman's transcribed testimony and that he was troubled.

He assumed that Saltzman knew the accusations that were the core of the State's case derived from the State's own witnesses' oral testimony and documents. Judge Greenberg said that "the great majority of the officers of the Order are Communists," as were the general council or executive committee of the IWO. Then he cited that the appeal by the Order to help raise funds for the Communists in the *Dennis* case was uncontroverted, implying by this linkage that the Communist leadership in the IWO was manifesting its allegiance by helping fellow Communists.

Judge Greenberg then explained:

In addition to that there was considerable other testimony dealing with your own participation in matters which did not strictly concern IWO affairs. Now, in the light of all of that testimony, which up to now has been uncontradicted, except through the skillful cross-examination by Mr. Weissman, Mr. Friedman and Mr. Jones, there has not been one word from you, as an individual or as an officer, to contradict, at least from the factual point of view, these *damning* charges.[55] [emphasis added]

The Judge then got to the point of his inquiry:

Accordingly, I want to ask you this question: Do you still, in the light of what I have said to you, and in the light of your failure to controvert, during the lengthy direct and cross-examination, any of the matters I have referred to—do you still wish to stand on your constitutional claim of incrimination?

Saltzman replied, "Yes, your Honor."[56]

The key words here are "failure to controvert." For some weeks as the trial unfolded, it had become clear that the Judge wanted the IWO to challenge the Communist connection; he wanted literal refutation of any ties to the Communist Party in terms of support of their candidates, fund-raising on behalf of Party newspapers, or support for the defendants in the *Dennis* case. Realistically, and Judge Greenberg must have understood this, there could be no "controverting" in the sense that most of the officers were Party members who had followed Communist Party policies and, by use of committees, had supported Party candidates as well as raised money for Party members being prosecuted. Therefore, what rebuttal could he expect?

The key question remained, however, whether the State of New York could destroy an otherwise legally conforming insurance company because the politics of its leaders were unacceptable to the State.

Weissman stepped into the fray with these statements:

And may I make this observation in connection with that, your Honor, that after a most soul-searching conference with the officers of this organization and my own humble advice, such as I was able to give them, they do not accept your Honor's formulation that the participations were in any way damning. They take a principled position that the activities, such as they were, whatever they were, were legal, constitutional, open, proper, and not in the least damning.

Those questions [of politics] are utterly incompetent, irrelevant and immaterial; they are illegal; and in my humble judgment, and with the utmost respect, a witch-hunt in an insurance matter; and it was founded upon considerations of policy and such advice as I was able to give them that they accepted what they describe as a principled position, to refuse to participate in what they conceive to be a legal witch-hunt, both in respect to the affairs of the IWO and in respect to such political activities that may or may not be involved.[57]

Judge Greenberg, however, stuck to his point, insisting that his extraordinary act in calling Saltzman back to the stand was an attempt to give him a final chance to controvert "considerable testimony showing that at least, so far as the activities of the individual officers and members of the general council and members of the executive committee are concerned, there was considerable Communistic activity."[58]

The Judge's view as to the legal implications of such unrebutted testimony differed radically from that of Weissman, and had since the beginning of the trial; for if Judge Greenberg's views had been consonant with that of the IWO's counsel, these months of exhausting political explorations would never have come into being.

The next day, just as Court opened, Judge Greenberg said:

Mr. Weissman, unless you have some objection, I would like to strike out the word "damning" which I used in my oration yesterday. On page . . . strike out the word "damning."

Mr. Weissman: No objection.

The Court: And make it, "these charges."[59]

Apparently, he had disclosed more than he wished to with his use of the adjective "damning" and wanted to protect the record from disclosure of obvious prejudice.

When Williams began his cross-examination of Shipka, he began with the matter of literature available in lodges and from an IWO bookstore separately owned and operated by the New York lodges. Using samples of books by Lenin, Stalin, and others, Williams attempted to establish the promotion of this literature to Order members. In the early 1930s, works by Lenin and Stalin had been used as membership premiums; prizes for recruiting for the Youth Section of the IWO in 1934 had been "revolutionary books."

At one point he handed Shipka a magnifying glass to examine a picture of the New York City IWO Bookstore and identify books by Stalin and Lenin that appeared to be for sale. Shipka's basic response during the interrogation was to focus the IWO policy that gave individual lodges complete autonomy as to what kinds of literature they could offer for sale; he contended that, over his many years of involvement with the IWO, he had never seen any literature offered at lodges he had visited that was not official Order publications.

Judge Greenberg entered with two lines of questioning. He first challenged Shipka on the volume and "slant" of articles in the *New Order* and *Fraternal Outlook* as being pro-Russia; Shipka's response was that, in his recollection, the bulk of the articles had been concerned with America and not with Russia. Judge Greenberg, invariably displaying courtesy, then asked Shipka "to do me a favor" and review a 1948 volume overnight to see whether his answer would remain the same. By inadvertence or otherwise, Judge Greenberg failed to bring the subject up the next day, though the matter of article content in these IWO publications did become the subject of extensive cross-examination by Williams, thus giving the Judge every opportunity to raise the matter.[60]

The other issue raised by the Judge was this:

Mr. Shipka, let me ask you this question: From the standpoint of an individual member of a branch lodge of IWO, if they read an article which contained the names of the leading members of the board of officers, or the executive committee, recommending a certain drive, do you think it is unreasonable for such a member to feel that that was a drive conducted officially by the IWO?

A. No, not necessarily.[61]

What the Court was trying to elicit from the witness was an admission that IWO members would assume that anything Order leaders did or advocated would be considered as official IWO acts. Pressed on the point by the Judge, Shipka insisted that lodges and their membership were not compelled to respond, citing the example of a special campaign which was an "official action" of the IWO designed to get contributions for an organization known as the Civil Rights Congress; he reported that only some 300 to 350 lodges out of 1,700 responded at all, though each was individually written to about the matter. Judge Greenberg was attempting to characterize efforts by committees and individuals as, in effect, the acts of the Order; Shipka had countered, using this occasion—one sponsored in the name of the IWO—to illustrate that even "official acts" were subject to democratic choice and evaluation by Order lodges and members. Judge Greenberg then posed this situation:

Suppose there was a decision made at a convention to increase the dues ten cents a month?

To this Shipka responded:

As far as dues, that is a different story. As far as other activities are concerned, outside of dues, sick benefits, and so on, they had a free hand where they could either participate, or not to participate, and to what degree to participate. They had a free hand to do as they chose, and they decided for themselves.[62]

Like Saltzman, Shipka acknowledged that he had participated in committees of IWO people who had attempted to raise money from Order members for the *Daily Worker*. When the question of advertising in foreign language newspapers was raised, Shipka conceded that such ads were placed; Williams characterized these papers as representing "the official language papers of the Communist Party." Weissman objected on the grounds that what kinds of papers they were was irrelevant and immaterial. The Court overruled the objection, to which Weissman asked, "What has it got to do with the issues in this case?" Judge Greenberg responded, "We are back exactly where we began."[63] Weissman clung to the position that the politics of the matter were not at issue; Judge Greenberg was saying that politics were indeed at issue, placed there by the State's case and the times they were living in.

Williams drove home his point by asking Shipka whether he was then a member of the Communist Party. Weissman jumped up to object on the same grounds. Judge Greenberg, overruling Weissman's objection, asked the witness if he claimed his constitutional privilege. Shipka answered:

I would like to say, your Honor, if I may, that as far as my activities in the organization, in the Order, are an open book. I have nothing to hide. But, I refuse to answer this question on the ground that it may tend to incriminate me.

To which the Court responded: Objection sustained on that ground. [He did not have to answer the question.][64]

Williams's last bite at Shipka backfired. He established that the same company that printed the *Fraternal Outlook* for the IWO also printed a publication called *Political Affairs,* a magazine of the Communist Party. Weissman and Friedman objected and Judge Greenberg agreed, adding:

All right. Strike it out. I will sustain the objection. I should hate to feel that if I eat in the same restaurant as Communists, I was a Communist, or if a Fascist restaurant, that I was a Fascist.[65]

Notes

1. Trial Record, pp. 3147–67.
2. Trial Record, pp. 3168–71.
3. Trial Record, pp. 3172–75.
4. Trial Record, pp. 3176–81.
5. Trial Record, pp. 3182–85.
6. Trial Record, pp. 3186–3217.
7. Trial Record, pp. 3218–36.
8. Trial Record, pp. 3231–32.
9. Trial Record, p. 3232.
10. Trial Record, pp. 3238–41.

11. Trial Record, pp. 3241–44.
12. Trial Record, pp. 3244–45.
13. Trial Record, pp. 3246–57.
14. Trial Record, pp. 3257–60.
15. Trial Record, pp. 3261–86.
16. Trial Record, pp. 3286–94.
17. Trial Record, pp. 3294–98.
18. Trial Record, pp. 3298–3307.
19. Trial Record, pp. 3307–08.
20. IWO News Release, March 30, 1951.
21. *New York Times,* March 7, 8, 9, 11, 13, 15, 21, 23, 25, 26, 28, 30, 1951.
22. Trial Record, p. 3309.
23. Trial Record, pp. 3310–11.
24. Trial Record, pp. 3311–12.
25. IWO News Release, March 30, 1951.
26. Trial Record, pp. 3315–22.
27. Trial Record, pp. 3323–30.
28. Trial Record, pp. 3330–32.
29. Trial Record, p. 3335.
30. Trial Record, pp. 3338–41.
31. Trial Record, pp. 3342–45.
32. Trial Record, pp. 3345–46.
33. Trial Record, pp. 3346–48.
34. Trial Record, pp. 3349–50.
35. Trial Record, pp. 3351–61.
36. Trial Record, p. 3364.
37. Trial Record, pp. 3365–74.
38. Trial Record, pp. 3375–94.
39. Williams Office Files, Correspondence, Letter by Henry to Medina dated April 18, 1951.
40. Trial Record, pp. 3399–3410.
41. Trial Record, p. 3411.
42. Trial Record, p. 3412.
43. Trial Record, pp. 3413–28.
44. Trial Record, pp. 3431–44.
45. Trial Record, pp. 3345–3447.
46. Trial Record, pp. 3354–56.
47. Trial Record, pp. 3470–88.
48. Trial Record, pp. 3489–90.
49. Trial Record, pp. 3529–34.
50. Trial Record, pp. 3535–36.
51. Trial Record, pp. 3544–46.
52. Trial Record, pp. 3562–63.
53. Trial Record, pp. 3579–83.
54. Trial Record, pp. 3588–92.
55. Trial Record, pp. 3593–94.
56. Trial Record, p. 3594.
57. Trial Record, pp. 3594–95.
58. Trial Record, pp. 3595–96.
59. Trial Record, p. 3617.

60. Trial Record, p. 3613.
61. Trial Record, p. 3615.
62. Trial Record, pp. 3615–16.
63. Trial Record, pp. 3617–28.
64. Trial Record, pp. 3629–39.
65. Trial Record, pp. 3652–53.

Chapter XIII
An Artist and a Black Activist

The most famous name associated with the IWO was its President and next witness, Rockwell Kent. Kent has been considered one of the leading illustrators in the history of American art. At age sixty-nine, the tall, gaunt figure who called himself "a painter, an artist and a writer" was an impressive piece of Americana.

As art historian Dan B. Jones has observed:

Rockwell Kent was a striking personality, a romantic realist, and a positive force in American art. He was a man of mature will and strong beliefs; he was virile, athletic, adventuresome, prolific, of boundless energy, a rugged individualist, and a dedicated and meticulous creative artist who devoted long hours to his craft.

He thought of himself as a workingman whose trade happened to be the expression of a unique view of life through art. He knew what he believed about life and politics and was in the forefront of battle fighting for those beliefs when they were least popular. Perhaps this is why he was so often referred to as the stormy petrel of American art.[1]

Clearly, no one dealing with Kent could reasonably separate the artist from his politics.

Kent was a fluent, articulate man; Weissman had only to open up an area and out flowed the language of a passionate, sensitive idealist. Asked why he had joined the IWO in 1939, Kent spoke of his belief in close association with "the working classes in America and the world," explaining that he drew strength from his contact with laboring people, an opportunity afforded him through his connection with the IWO. In amplification, he stated:

But beyond that I am as a citizen deeply interested in the enrichment of culture in America . . . because to me, the working of our democracy depends on that. So that was a reason for joining the International Workers Order, and then I heard that it was not only an insurance order interested in paying premiums

Figure 7. Rockwell Kent lithograph done in 1940 to commemorate the tenth anniversary of the IWO. It replaced the earlier logo (Figure 6). Courtesy of the Rockwell Kent Legacies.

after the death of people, but it was possibly the only so-called insurance organization in America that was primarily interested in keeping people alive.

Using the term "insurance," insuring their lives, not indemnifying the survivors for the loss. That appealed to me very much, and the understanding of life as not just a heart keeping on beating, but the enrichment of life, the enjoyment of life. In other words, life, liberty and the pursuit of happiness, and that our Order went into many activities that were directed toward promoting those blessings for all people in America.

I joined it for that and then, last, but not least, I liked the idea that you could get insurance in the International Workers Order, in a highly rated solvent insurance organization for a fraction of the cost that the big commercial companies charge, and for the first time in my life, and I am a man with many children and grandchildren and responsibilities, I insured my life in the International Workers Order. So I joined.[2]

Under Weissman's friendly questioning, which served really as an opening for the witness to make a series of mini-speeches, Kent described how he joined the Order in 1939, attaching himself to the

Figure 8. Rockwell Kent, eminent artist
and illustrator, President of the IWO from
1944 to 1953.

Harlem Lodge of the Frederick Douglass Society of the IWO because,
in his own words, "I want[ed] to join the lodge of the oldest Americans
here and I think that Negroes and we people whose ancestors came
over in the Mayflower are just about equally old as Americans."[3]

Kent described how, one year later, he made a speech during "IWO
Day" at the New York World's Fair and was thereafter asked to accept
nomination as an Order Vice-President. He was elected President in
1944 and reelected in 1947. Asked about his duties and actual participation as an officer, he detailed his attendance at meetings, stressing
the democratic nature of decision making at the highest echelons of the
IWO. These officers were paid no salary; only very modest expenses
were reimbursed. Kent emphasized that, throughout his tenure, his
primary interest was in promoting the cultural affairs of the IWO.[4]

Weissman attempted to demonstrate that this prominent artist and
writer (he had recited lines of his poetry as an acceptance speech at the
1947 National Convention) exemplified what the IWO stood for; he

pointed out that Kent had toured the country for the IWO in 1942 to promote anti-Fascism and the war effort and again in 1950. Kent described his last tour:

I spoke on peace, and I reported a strong yearning for peace that I had observed among the peoples of Europe, and particularly—and I felt this was the best news that I could bring to America—that particularly the people who, we were being told, were our enemies, and who, we were being told, were determined on war, did not want war, but wanted peace. I thought that was great news. It is, isn't it?[5]

In order to bolster the testimony of Saltzman and Shipka that matters of opinion as well as official policy were expressed in IWO publications, Weissman asked Kent about a series of articles he had written for the *Fraternal Outlook* magazine, entitled "We Hold These Truths." Queried about censorship or approval of his sentiments, Kent confirmed that no one had censored, supervised, or controlled his writing and that they were merely expressions of his personal opinions.[6]

What Weissman wanted to establish with Kent's testimony was the legitimacy of fraternal activities as carried out by the component ethnic groups of the IWO. Thus, in an unabashed, unapologetic manner, Kent praised the cultural and political exertions of the Order as thoroughly American. Specifically, he stressed that the Order rejected the idea of the "melting pot" as a national goal, instead preferring to foster ethnic diversity which, he explained, "would make the culture of America more like a tapestry, woven of brilliant colored threads, every one of which can be distinguished, and [which] keep its own characteristics." "I feel strongly," he told the court, "that it would be a richer and more beautiful America if these cultures were kept alive."[7]

Kent defended the legitimacy of IWO policies in such political areas as civil rights, opposition to the Smith Act ("unconstitutional threat to our basic civil rights") and the McCarran Act ("an aggravation of the objectional features of the Smith Act"), and support of black Americans "in their efforts to secure equality and equal justice."[8]

Weissman, knowing that it was important for Kent to contest what Louis Budenz had said about him ("Comrade Kent"), offered Judge Greenberg a direct rebuttal. Kent said he had heard Budenz's testimony about him, but when asked whether he had any recollection of the man, Kent said that he had recalled Budenz only when Weissman had pointed him out in the hall prior to his taking the stand. Citing his "good visual memory," implicitly because he was an artist, Kent was able to say exactly where he and Budenz had sat at the meeting to which Budenz had referred. Kent went on to describe the meeting as one where public concerns abut postwar problems were aired; he noted that the letter inviting his sponsorship contained the names of a number of persons he knew and respected, including clergymen, whom he felt represented "good liberal causes."

While admitting that one of the announced purposes of the meeting was to raise money for the *Daily Worker,* Kent asserted that it was an open meeting—not at all limited to Communists. Weissman used correspondence with which he had cross-examined Budenz to establish Kent's version of the meeting and contact with Budenz, which contradicted the State's witness.[9]

Weissman concluded Kent's direct testimony by questioning him about the attitude of the IWO toward Russia. Kent stressed that the desire for world peace was the Order's first priority and that only through "friendly relations" with that country could peace be maintained. In essence, Kent was proposing that the IWO stood in opposition to the basic Cold War doctrine of containment and confrontation with the Soviet Union, and had consistently demonstrated this from the time Russia was recognized by the Roosevelt administration (1933), down through World War II to 1951. He concluded:

Great hope for the future had been built on the continued friendship with the Soviet Union. I do not recall that we [the IWO] ever had reason to start over again and assert a new position. We continued our adherence to that policy which had been established by him [President Roosevelt], believing it to be basic to peace on earth, and we still believe so.[10]

After Budenz called Kent a Communist during his testimony for the State, Kent had told a reporter that he had never been and was not now a Communist. Williams opened the cross-examination by asking Kent if his statement to the reporter was indeed correct. Thus Judge Greenberg heard the first witness for the IWO who, under oath, said he was not a Communist.

Satisfied that Kent was not a Communist, Williams moved to a line of questioning that threw the Court into a session of verbal bombastics: He asked Kent if Max Bedacht was a member of the Communist Party, a question Weissman strenuously objected to as being irrelevant to the issues of the case, asserting that it was in effect a demand that Kent "finger" others. Williams reminded Weissman and the Court that the same question had been asked of every prior witness. Judge Greenberg entered the fray to remind Weissman that if that question had nothing to do with the issues of the case, "we have wasted nine weeks."

Instructed to answer, Kent responded that he could only relate that which he had read, but that he had no personal proof or knowledge with respect to anyone; with an undertone of sarcasm, he noted that he had read that President Roosevelt and Shirley Temple were Communists. Nevertheless, he stated that based on what he had read and that which was public knowledge—and because it was undenied—he believed Bedacht and Weiner were Communists. As to Brodsky, Saltzman, and Shipka, Kent responded that "I have no reason for believing that he was or was not a Communist." Judge Greenberg asked about a number of others, to which Kent responded with the same answer, adding:

I want the Court, I want your Honor, to realize that this is the truth, that I am not acting evasively. These answers are consistent with a principle of mine that I have always pursued, of never asking any man anywhere his political faith or his religious faith. I don't give a damn about it. I judge people by how they act.[11]

In an attempt to lessen the impact of this moving and forthright testimony, Williams next asked Kent whether it would be accurate to characterize him as a "dignified front for the IWO," adding that he was not using the label in an offensive or disparaging way. Kent agreed that the real work of the Order was done by its paid officers and employees, but added that he demanded to be consulted about every decision and each important document, that he did voice his views, and that he was always listened to respectfully.[12]

Because he was facing a witness of the highest standing in the IWO who stated he was not a Communist, it became Williams's objective to characterize Kent as pro-Communist. To that end, he inquired about his writings that appeared to be sympathetic to Communism. Kent parried by pointing out that the information he received from Communists about events and conditions often turned out to be truthful and, because of this, he had almost came to believe "in Communists," but not Communism. Williams had rough going as Weissman, and Friedman objected to and argued over every question. Finally, Judge Greenberg stepped in to ask, "Is it your view that the only way to remedy all social ills is through Communism?" The Judge overruled objections to his own question.[13]

Weissman pressed his objections, pointing out that the essence of the Court's question was "Do you believe," where there was no such issue in the trial, adding that the United States and New York State Constitutions made political beliefs private. Judge Greenberg responded by leaving the matter of answering to "a most intelligent witness himself." Friedman insisted that was still wrong because the question allows "it to degenerate into a trial of ideas," which the Judge had promised would not happen. But Judge Greenberg insisted, "The question I asked of

Mr. Kent is no further removed from that [issue of Communism] than the remainder of the testimony we have had throughout this trial."[14]

The Judge would not let the matter die. Apparently, he had prepared for this testimony by reading material that Kent had written, including an article in the Communist publication, the *New Masses,* published in 1936 and containing the following statement which he proceeded to read to Kent:

"To be a true American, a man must have the will to right our social wrongs. How, is his own concern. For me, the way is Communism."[15]

Instead of Kent answering questions about his views, the lawyers and the Judge renewed their arguments. Weissman asserted that the article was written three years before Kent joined the IWO and, in any event, was not an expression of IWO views or policy. That brought the Judge to expound on his view of Kent's corporate responsibility—a key legal issue, expressed with an evident level of exasperation:

The Court: It is not a question of being binding on the corporation. Here we have a case—and we might as well get it clear on the record once and for all— where certain leading officers, responsible officers, over and over again, are charged with certain activities, many of them being Communist activities, the support of certain Communistic programs. Even though it could be said that the Order did not by official resolution approve it, in the eyes of the law, if the Order knew or ought to have known over an extended period of time what these officers did, I don't think the Order can be heard to say that it is not responsible for these things, whatever the consequences may be, which took place over a period of twenty years. That is one elemental principle in our law, that their approval may be by express authority or by ratification.[16]

Friedman responded by pointing out that Kent had been an IWO officer for over a decade, and that during that time he had written and spoken on behalf of the Order many times, adding:

If, in all of those speeches and those articles he cannot be attacked upon the grounds set forth in the petition, how does it add to anything in this case to show that three years before he even became a member of the Order, he may have said to some other people, not IWO members, but to someone else, that he has certain beliefs?

How can that be binding on the 162,000 policyholders, and how can their rights be prejudiced by such a document. That is entirely different from attacking him on the basis of what he said to them, on the basis of what ideas he is asking them to adopt.[17]

Finally, Kent got to answer the Judge's question. No, he told the Court, he did not believe that Communism was the way to right the social wrongs of this country; he then offered a long explanation about how he had rejected Soviet Communism for America, but endorsed Socialism, providing participants to the discussion agreed-on definitions and terminology.[18]

The next day Kent was back on the stand; Williams moved in on him from a number of angles, essentially designed to discredit Kent as a dupe of the Communists who ran the IWO. Every question aimed at eliciting this idea was blocked by objections which the Judge sustained. At one point, in apparent frustration, Williams asked Kent, "Do you believe in the American Constitution?" Though the Court suggested that the witness would like to answer that question, he had to sustain Weissman's objection.[19]

A few minutes later, Judge Greenberg took over the questioning. He wanted to get at what he felt was the essence of the matter, so he bluntly put what he termed "a very serious question" to Kent. The Judge said that most of the national officers and that at least two thirds of the IWO executive committee were also members of the national committee of the Communist Party; he pointed out that, similarly, at least two members of the five-member IWO board of trustees were Party members, as well as Saltzman, whom he said was the head of the Communist International in the United States. After these statements, the Judge rather lamely asked, "Do these things surprise you that I am telling you?" Kent replied to the effect that he had not concerned himself with such facts. Judge Greenberg then took him to task, stating that since he was the Order's President for years, he "should have known what was going on." He lectured Kent to the effect that

a tremendous institution like the IWO with over 160,000 members at one time, I think reaching 183,000 members, carried a tremendous responsibility in so far as the President is concerned, and I think you will agree that the President ought to familiarize himself, ought to know about what is going on.

Kent responded:

The president certainly should know what is going on in the conduct of the affairs of the Order, but membership in a political party, the Order not being a political organization, seems to me entirely extraneous to the activities of the Order, and I have always considered it so. . . .
    I can add this, too. I have thought this over. From the best of my recollection, I have never heard the Communist party mentioned in any of the meetings of the executive committee or the general council or in any of the private conversations I have had with officers of the Order.[20]

Judge Greenberg allowed Williams to continue his questioning, as they grappled with Kent's response. As if there were no intervening questions, the Judge returned to his interrogation:

According to you, Mr. Kent, even if you knew that all of these people were Communists, that would be no concern of yours, because you say that is a man's own personal political beliefs?

This gave Kent an opening to expand on his beliefs:

Yes, and we are not a political organization and I judge of my associates in an Order like ours by how they carry out their duties in the Order, by nothing else. I would like to make my position in this clear. . . .

His Honor has asked me about how I would feel if I knew that fellow members, fellow officers of the Order, were members of the Communist party, and I have stated that their political affiliations to me are quite irrelevant. I feel the same way that I would feel if I were a young man and in the war and going over the top in a battle and I knew that my buddy next to me was a member of the Communist party. What has that got to do with it? . . . If they are doing the job they are out to do, that's all that counts to me.[21]

Another discussion of world politics, far removed from the subject of the IWO, was initiated by Judge Greenberg. Using Kent's writings as a starting point, the Judge would read aloud a short excerpt and then ask Kent for an explanation, or whether what he had written reflected his "current sentiments." For example, Kent had written in one of his books prior to 1941 that he was distrustful of English and French leaders and believed therefore that the United States should stay out of the war. What the Court wanted to know was whether the attack on Russia that year changed his views. In effect, by resisting any joint effort prior to Hitler's June 1941 attack on Russia, Kent had expressed the Party line, as well as the IWO position, in that time between September 1939 and June 1941—after which the position was reversed.

Kent explained that, with good reason, he had been distrustful of the war aims of the combatants, stating, "I feared that if we got into the war in Europe it would be a big gangup with Hitler, Germany, with England, with France, to wipe out the Soviet Union," which he considered the "most important social experiment in the world." He added that, if for no other reason, he wanted all countries to keep their hands off Russia to "let us see how it works; maybe we can learn something."[22]

The Judge retorted by suggesting that it "might work in both directions," with the nations of the world telling Russia to keep its hands off of other nations. Kent agreed with the idea, but added that "as far as I can see they haven't done much to the nations of the world." Judge Greenberg fired back at him:

Latvia, Lithuania, Finland, Estonia, Bulgaria, Hungary, Czecho-Slovakia mean nothing to you, big countries with human beings in them?

Kent addressed only the question of the Baltic states, by telling the Court he felt that their peoples "felt themselves as one with the Russian people." Judge Greenberg retorted, "It is hard for me to believe that you really mean that." Kent replied that he did. Kent continued to defend his position by delving into the history of the Russian Empire under the Czars, concluding that the workers of the Baltic countries "welcomed the virtual annexation by the Soviet Union." The Judge countered by asking whether there had been any elections on the issue; Kent said he was uncertain, but believed there had been no armed seizure.[23]

Weissman, silent through this political debate, finally tried to intervene and "object to this excursion into politics," but Judge Greenberg and Williams continued to throw political belief questions at Kent and debate Cold War issues with him. Williams, however, never lost sight of his ultimate goal, which was to tie Kent to as many left-wing causes, organizations, and positions as possible so as to discredit him in the mind of the Judge as just another "fellow traveler."

The climax to this testimony came in the form of a summary question put to Kent by the Court:

Mr. Kent, do you concede it to be part of the function of a fraternal benefit society to engage in all of the activities that the IWO was engaged in?

A. I consider it to be to the special honor of the International Workers Order that they filled their obligation to exercise their rights as citizens to make this a better country, to make democracy work.

Q. That is not exactly the answer to my question. What I am trying to find out is, do you concede it to be part of the functions, within the framework of the constitution and by-laws, to engage in these activities which have been described during the course of this hearing and with some of which you are familiar?

A. I always have considered it so, yes.[24]

Williams's message must have gotten across, because the Judge interrupted once again to place this query:

Mr. Kent, let me ask you this question. In the light of your writings and your books and your art work and your testimony here in court, what else would you have to do within your own definition to become a Communist?

Kent responded that he would have to be a Party member, pay dues, and be accepted by them—all of which he was not. Before further questioning as to beliefs, he insisted that there be agreement on what the terms Communism or Socialism meant. Weissman interrupted

Kent's elaboration on the point by objecting to the entire line of questioning, commenting that from "what I have heard Mr. Kent testify [about] and what I know about American History . . . he is as close a Jeffersonian democrat as he is any other category of politician," to which he added:

there are no criteria in law, that I have never been taught nor can find in the books by which I can help my client in the trial of a case where people are asked questions of the kind that is asked of this witness here now. What is one to do about being a Communist, not a card-carrying Communist? I don't know what we are doing here. . . .

Judge Greenberg countered with a reference to Judge Learned Hand's opinion in the *Dennis* case; Weissman pointed out that the opinion was about a party, not "something so amorphous [political beliefs] that in the law it is very vicious." When Weissman objected that "I don't think they have any place here even within the frame of reference that your Honor has been trying this case," the Judge sustained it.[25]

Kent's testimony ended on a lighter note: Williams stated that he wanted to ask Kent one more question. Weissman suggested sarcastically that Williams take Kent out to lunch so that the two could "have a nice private conversation," which would "be to your mutual understanding." Williams caught the dig to the effect that his questioning was irrelevant to legal issues and rejoined with, "and enjoyment, too, because I enjoy talking to Mr. Kent, both on the stand and off the stand." The latter reference seems to confirm that indeed Kent had spoken with Williams outside of his sworn testimony, (see Chapter III) supporting at least the fact of their conversing, though leaving at issue the matter of what was said.[26]

The domestic fight against the "Reds" continued in high gear in April 1951. More indictments, more firings, and more accusations filled the newspapers. On the world scene, this was a month of continued warfare along the 38th parallel in Korea. United Nations (mainly U.S.) casualties continued to mount, while a real threat of a third world war loomed; Sam Rayburn, Speaker of the House of Representatives, intimated to the House that reports of Russia massing troops in Manchuria pointed to the fact that a third world war "may be near." This was also the month when President Truman fired General MacArthur.[27]

The House Committee on Un-American Activities issued a long report which attacked the worldwide "peace offensive" as "the most dangerous hoax ever devised by the international Communist conspiracy." Listing 550 names of individuals associated with alleged Communist Front organizations, including actors Jose Ferrer and Judy Holliday, the report aimed to expose as "subversive" those persons and organizations that, under various guises, were attempting to promote "world peace." To HUAC, any person or group favoring "peace" in 1951 was Communist or duped by the Party. Among those mentioned was Rockwell Kent, who, according to the report, "has been affiliated with at least eighty-five Communist front organizations." Two days after this report made headlines, the Rosenbergs were sentenced to die.[28]

On April 6, 1951, Louise T. Patterson took the stand as the next IWO witness. Whatever problems were presented by her testimony at this trial must have been overshadowed by another legal proceeding going on at the same time: her husband, William L. Patterson, was on trial in Washington, D.C., having been indicted by an Act of Congress for contempt. He had been called before the House Lobby Investigating Committee in August 1950, as executive secretary of an organization known as the Civil Rights Congress, a group also on the Attorney General's Subversive list. Patterson had refused to name the backers of and contributors to the organization. At the Committee hearing, a bitter exchange had taken place between Patterson and a Congressman from Georgia, Henderson Lanham, when Patterson had spoken about treatment of blacks in Georgia. Lanham called Patterson a "black S.O.B." According to reports he had actually said, "God damn black S.O.B.," but Lanham denied that expanded version at Patterson's contempt trial, claiming he never "used God's name in vain," adding "I should have used the word Communist instead of black."[29]

An all-out attack by government agencies had been mounted against the Civil Rights Congress, which had been founded in 1946 and had attracted people such as Paul Robeson, Representative (and IWO Vice-President) Vito Marcantonio, and novelist Dashiell Hammett; the latter (among others) served a jail sentence for refusing to name contributors to the Bail Fund segment of the Civil Rights Congress. This group was exclusively involved with defending the civil liberties of the pro-Communist left. It had attracted many non-Communists concerned for the civil liberties of leftists and had condemned the Smith Act. Its most important function was raising money to provide bail and defense lawyers to those prosecuted as Communists. The day-to-day activities of the organization were in the hands of two Communists, one of whom was William L. Patterson.

Shipka, during his earlier testimony, had given an example of the autonomy of IWO lodges by telling of the official Order policy to support this Civil Rights Congress and its Bail Fund, and how only a fraction (some 300 out of over 1,700) of the lodges had responded. As David Caute has noted with respect to the link between the two organizations, "Like the International Workers Order, the CRC [Civil Rights

Congress] Bail Fund had been marked down for administrative destruction." Within one year of the IWO trial, the New York Attorney General, using powers delegated to him under state banking laws, had moved to freeze the assets of the Fund and had enjoined it from activity. This action in New York, followed by similar suits in other states, succeeded in effectively destroying the organization.[30]

An IWO news release reported the opening of Louise Patterson's testimony with these words:

A jammed and hushed courtroom on Wednesday heard the attractive, dignified witness tell of her 18 years with the IWO and of her experiences as student, teacher and organizer in many states of the Union, including the deep South.[31]

The news release noted the fact that she was testifying before Judge Greenberg, "a native of Durham, North Carolina." The implication, common at that time, was that since the Judge came from the South, an axiomatic prejudice against blacks was to be expected.

Unlike prior IWO witnesses, with whom he had explored little personal background, Weissman wanted to use Patterson's life story to demonstrate the idealism of racial equality championed by the Order. Fifty years old at the time of her testimony, Patterson told a story, common for Southern blacks of her generation, of poverty, degradation, and deprivation, and of her struggle to reach a level of dignity in her life. The story was more impressive because, as a black woman, she carried the double disadvantage of sex as well as race. Her story was even more moving because she was apparently light-skinned enough to "pass" as a white person (which she did, posing as Mexican for a time), which enabled her to obtain education and employment.

Raised and educated in segregated communities in the South where, she told the Court, "all schools are segregated," Patterson gained entrance to the University of California, graduating cum laude with a B.S. in commerce; her family had pawned the family silver to pay her tuition. Despite her academic accomplishments, she was not allowed into the Honor Society of the School of Commerce because it was a "lily white group."

After a succession of low-level jobs, she returned to the South to teach in an all-black school in Arkansas. Evoking terrible scenes of poverty and racism (she recalled that a lynching had taken place in her community), Patterson eventually moved north for more education and opportunity, and traveled abroad in 1932. This trip was organized by a film company to make a movie in the Soviet Union; the film was never made, and Patterson returned early because of her mother's illness. In her work on behalf of the defense of the Scottsboro boys, she attended a 1933 IWO convention in Chicago as a delegate of a group called the National Committee for the Defense of Political Prisoners, which was headed by William L. Patterson, whom she later married.

Under Weissman's questioning, Patterson told the Court why she joined the IWO:

I was interested for a number of reasons: first, when I found that it was an organization, a fraternal insurance society, and found that it was a non-discriminatory fraternal insurance society. This was very important to me, because I had as a principle not joined insurance companies such as the Metropolitan, which every Negro knows about, because I protested against being a part of an organization which made me pay more and get less, and due to the fact that my family had no insurance, and my mother who had died that year—I had checked the last penny out of the bank in order to pay for her funeral.

So therefore I became interested, and when I learned about what the IWO was, I joined.[32]

Asked to explain further about the Metropolitan Life Insurance Company, she stated:

Well, I meant that we knew that there were only limited types of insurance that the Metropolitan offered to us, primarily industrial insurance, the most expensive kind, and the least for your money; that other forms of insurance were not available to Negroes. Further, that the Metropolitan did not even have agents in the Negro area, and at that time here was quite a tremendous campaign against the Jim Crow offices that were established by the Metropolitan, where Negroes had to come and even pay for the insurance that they got.[33]

Apparently finding a comfortable "home" in the IWO, Patterson helped organize a multiracial lodge and then, in 1933, became the first black employee of the Order. With vivid detail, she described her intense feelings of devotion to the IWO as a fraternal organization where fraternalism incorporated brotherhood and sisterhood; promoted from office worker, she took this message to the South as an organizer. As a result of her work among striking miners in Birmingham, Alabama, she was arrested for vagrancy. She contrasted that earlier court setting where "the judge was not sitting, by himself, in dignity" but rather "was surrounded by members of the White Camellia, which was the local name in Birmingham for the Ku Klux Klan." Nonetheless, she was acquitted.[34]

She continued to detail her work for the Order, to the point of her election in 1935 as National Recording Secretary. Challenged by Judge Greenberg as to how she rose so quickly in the Order, she responded that, for persons of talent, the IWO practiced what it preached, affording opportunity for advancement to all regardless of race.[35]

Over hours of questioning that continued into a second day, Louise

Patterson described her full life in the Order as an organizer and executive, which had culminated in her election at the 1940 National Convention as a Vice-President, "the first woman and the first Negro to have this honor." She was deeply involved in organizing black members in Chicago, where, in 1940, she helped recruit 2,000 new members, initiated in a mass ceremony at DuSable High School. Thereafter, in coordination with labor and civic organizations, a community center was established with fund-raising assistance from Paul Robeson and Lena Horne. By the time of her testimony, she had resigned her salaried position as an organizer to care for her child, retaining only her unpaid office as a vice-president.[36]

A current biographical sketch of Louise T. Patterson (who, as of 1990, was still alive) gives a different view on many aspects of her life. In this account, she is portrayed as a prominent figure in black cultural circles; her apartment was a gathering place for black artists and intellectuals well into the 1930s. Her work with the National Committee for the Defense of Political Prisoners led to an invitation in 1933 to join the Communist Party, the same year she joined the IWO as a full-time employee. She has been assessed as "a critical liaison linking black popular culture and Harlem's literati with Communist Popular Front politics." That she was also an important Party figure throughout her IWO years cannot be disputed.[37]

Williams designated Henry to cross-examine Patterson. All of the questions Henry put to her went to one purpose: to bring into evidence that she had been a prominent member of the Communist Party during all her years of service as an IWO officer.

Henry asked about articles she had written in IWO publications, schools and conferences she had attended and sometimes appeared at as a lecturer, and a New York City voting registration record dated 1936 where apparently she had registered in a primary as a Communist. In addition, she was asked directly about her Party membership. To all these questions, under advice of counsel, Patterson exercised her constitutional rights against self-incrimination and refused to answer; in each case the Court sustained her right. Judge Greenberg entered the fray once, asking whether, as earlier testimony by several State's witnesses had stated, she had attended "an extraordinary conference of the Communist Party" in New York in 1933. Upon advise of counsel, she "took the Fifth" and Judge Greenberg sustained her right not to answer his own question. So ended Louise Patterson's testimony.[38]

Insight as to the progress of the trial at this point can be gained from correspondence between Paul Crouch and Williams's office. Crouch, whose wife but not he had testified for the State, wrote on March 31, 1951 to inquire how the case was going and to offer his services in any rebuttal the State would make to the IWO defense. Though he was traveling around the country in his role as professional anti-Communist (he was speaking that day at an American Legion conference in Fairmont, West Virginia), Crouch apparently had kept track of the case and knew the Order was in the midst of its defense. He added a detailed itinerary so that he could be contacted.

Besides the offer of testimony, Crouch sent some Communist Party election campaign literature from 1932, with the explanation that Sylvia Crouch had been the head of the Campaign Committee and that the return address on the literature was "that of the IWO hall in Norfolk (Virginia)." He also passed along his wife's regrets that she had not been a more effective witness.[39]

Henry answered on behalf of the Williams team four days later, during the cross-examination of Kent. Henry opined that "I think the case is coming along very well." He noted that Saltzman and Shipka had claimed their constitutional privilege against self-incrimination "when asked about their connection with the Communist Party." He went on to say that because of the length of the trial, and the "position that the IWO officers were taking," it was very doubtful that "we will call any witnesses in rebuttal," and asked Crouch to return a travel voucher he had been sent some time before which he had never used.

Henry's letter went on to assure Sylvia Crouch that "we all thought she was extremely alert and that all of us felt that her testimony was very valuable and made a particularly good impression on the Court." A fair reading of the record would indicate that, to say the least, Henry was being liberal with the truth. As an indication as to how well things were going, Henry reported that West Virginia, Indiana, and Pennsylvania had all taken action to deny the crucial annual license renewal to the IWO—this prior to any verdict in New York.[40]

The key idea in this letter is contained in the reference to the "position" taken by the Order's officers. By these witnesses "taking the Fifth," the State was satisfied that the message had gotten to the Judge that they were Communists—regardless of their constitutional right not to answer such questions. As individuals, there was no threat to them implicit in the State's case, but by the group denial (except as to Kent) they were confirming the State's accusation of Communist domination, something the Judge could implicitly accept. Since the witnesses were Party members, to lie about their affiliation would have opened them up to perjury charges. Regardless of their "principled" position on their Constitutional rights, the State was content that it had delivered the desired link between the IWO leadership and the Party.

In legal theory, nothing was to be properly adduced from a refusal to answer on the grounds of self-incrimination. The reality of 1951, after the convictions in the *Dennis* case and McCarthy's use of "Fifth Amendment Communist" accusations, was that Judge Greenberg—if he was so inclined—could in this civil case, where no threat of jail was involved for anyone, conclude that the IWO leadership was almost entirely made up of Party members. With that as a given, the question would then become: should this make a difference in determining the fate of this insurance company?

Notes

1. Dan Burne Jones, *The Prints of Rockwell Kent: A Catologue Raisonné* (Chicago: University of Chicago Press, 1975), p. xi.
2. Trial Record, pp. 3655–57.
3. Trial Record, pp. 3657–58.
4. Trial Record, pp. 3659–66.
5. Trial Record, pp. 3667–70.
6. Trial Record, pp. 3673.
7. Trial Record, pp. 3675–76.
8. Trial Record, pp. 3677–78.
9. Trial Record, pp. 3678–82.
10. Trial Record, pp. 3683–84.
11. Trial Record, pp. 3686–87.
12. Trial Record, pp. 3687–91.
13. Trial Record, pp. 3692–96.
14. Trial Record, pp. 3696–97.
15. Trial Record, pp. 3697–98.
16. Trial Record, pp. 3699–3701.
17. Trial Record, p. 3702.
18. Trial Record, pp. 3702–06.
19. Trial Record, pp. 3707–12.
20. Trial Record, p. 3715.
21. Trial Record, pp. 3717–18.
22. Trial Record, pp. 3719–21.
23. Trial Record, pp. 3721–22.
24. Trial Record, pp. 3723–33.
25. Trial Record, pp. 3740–42.
26. Trial Record, p. 3743.
27. *New York Times*, April 5, 1951.
28. *New York Times*, April 4, 6, 1951.
29. *New York Times*, April 10, 11, 1951.
30. David Caute, *The Great Fear: The Anti-Communist Purge Under Truman and Eisenhower* (New York: Simon and Schuster, 1978), pp. 178–79.
31. IWO News Release, April 6, 1951.
32. Trial Record, pp. 3749–73.
33. Trial Record, p. 3773.
34. Trial Record, pp. 3774–87.
35. Trial Record, pp. 3788–95.
36. Trial Record, pp. 3796–3813.
37. "Louise Thompson Patterson" in *Encyclopedia of the American Left*, ed.

Mari Jo Buhle, Paul Buhle, and Dan Georgakas (New York: Garland, 1990), p. 564.

38. Trial Record, pp. 3815–30.

39. Williams Office Files, Correspondence, Letter by Paul Crouch to J. B. Henry, March 31, 1951.

40. Williams Office Files, Correspondence, Letter by J. B. Henry to Paul Crouch, April 3, 1951.

Chapter XIV
With the End in Sight

In Henry's letter to Crouch in early April 1951, he stated, "The psychological thing at this point would seem to be to finish [the trial] as quickly as possible." He said this in turning down Paul Crouch's offer to be a rebuttal witness for the State.[1]

With the trial now in its fourth month, both sides were getting worn down. Henry's "psychological" point was a confirmation of the Williams team's basic strategy in handling the IWO's defense: challenge no question put to these witnesses as they give their testimony, and nail everyone as a Communist doing Party work using the "front" of an insurance company. The IWO strategy, by contrast, was to try to draw attention away from politics and refocus on the insurance and fraternal work of the Order. The problem here was that so many of the fraternal activities had an implicit if not overt political implication, for example, promoting health care legislation and offering its insurance programs to blacks at the same rates as to whites.

The political climate in 1951, with the Korean war in progress and the potential of the Cold War turning into World War III, made relevant the otherwise irrelevant politics of the officers of the company. In any "normal" insurance company litigation, the officers would be questioned or tested in terms of their business and financial actions vis-à-vis the corporate health of the organization. These times, however, were abnormal, and this generated the easy slide from questions of business policies to questions of politics. The dynamics of the trial were similar to a game of paddle ball: the board (the Order) would keep hitting the ball in different directions (fraternal, cultural, social, educational, and recreational activities), but the long rubber attached to the ball (the then current political scene) kept pulling it back to the board. The IWO defense team of lawyers kept trying to move that ball beyond the pull of the rubber. With this strategy in mind, the IWO brought seven of its current members to the stand to testify about the insurance benefits they received as Order members and to demonstrate how vitally important those benefits were to their survival, in that they had enabled them to maintain a level of dignity in their lives.

The first of these witnesses told how initially he had belonged to the Workmen's Circle, but was expelled for nonpayment of dues when he lost his job during the Depression. (The Judge had already heard testimony that people were not expelled from the IWO if they could not pay their dues because they lost their job.) He joined the Order in 1934 and became ill with tuberculosis a year later. The balance of his testimony told how the IWO paid him sickness benefits and got him into a hospital, how members visited him, and how, when his benefits ran out, Order charitable funds were forthcoming. While he was in a sanitarium, the IWO furnished entertainment, movies, and concerts for himself and others, as well as supplying money to keep him and his family functioning. This went on for the many years he experienced recurrent bouts with the disease.

Williams, seeing where the testimony was going, tried to head it off with the following remark:

Mr. Weissman, it occurs to me that we can save a lot of time. I do not think that I will dispute or even cross-examine this witness, if his testimony is with reference to the benefits which he received from the IWO. I am perfectly willing to have you put your statement on the record of what you will prove through this witness.[2]

Weissman would not have it. From the IWO standpoint, it was vital for the Judge to see the human aspect of this litigation—the role the Order played in the lives of ordinary people, disassociated completely from any political question. And if there would be a time and redundancy "price" to pay, the defense team felt it was well worth it. They were playing the same game in this regard as the State had played. Williams, adhering to his strategy, almost kept his promise and cross-examined only a few of the witnesses, none of them in depth.

Beyond insurance benefits, others testified about the cultural, educational, health, and recreational activities in their lodges as well as the absence of any political activities either by the leadership of the local lodge or as directed by the Order. The democratic process in choosing local officers and delegates to National Conventions was described.

The parade of witnesses reflected a cross section of the IWO: young and old, American and foreign-born, white and black, plain working people and small businessmen. All talked about every activity of the Order, from commemorative memorials for those members who died in the service of their country to the formation of drum and bugle corps. In response to Williams's questions, these members all denied the presence of any leftist political activities in their lodges. At times Weissman himself put the question of politics to a witness; a typical exchange follows:

Q. Do you have any political discussions at your lodge meetings?

A. No, I don't think nobody have any time for this. We were all too busy to take care of our interests. Just insurance and help one another, that's about all. We never ask no questions of the other fellow's opinion.

Q. Did you ever see any literature sold at lodge meetings, any books, pamphlets?

A. Not where we meet, the room was bare, there was nothing there, was just a few chairs, so—

Q. There was no literature sold?

A. There was nothing in that room.[3]

In addition to the seven member witnesses who testified for the IWO, the Intervenors' Committee, made up of Order members, put eight more witnesses on the stand, so a total of fifteen active members of the IWO testified in the case. Furthermore, an agreement was reached between counsel for both sides allowing the IWO to file affidavits from members all over the country which would be deemed to "be of the same force and effect as evidence as though the testimony were given by the witness in open court from the witness stand."

In this rather unusual arrangement, the State had the right to raise an objection to any affidavit that they found problematic; a total of 106 affidavits were filed, and none was objected to by Williams. Again, they presented a colorful cross section of people from different places, describing the activities of the IWO at their lodge level and stressing the importance of the Order in their lives. It should be noted that, to the dismay of the Williams team, not one then-current member of the IWO testified for the State. Although the State followed up leads, nothing came of them in terms of viable and available witnesses who were still Order members.

When forty-five-year-old John Middleton, a Vice-President of the IWO, took the stand, he, like Rockwell Kent, came across as a political radical whose family roots ran deep in American history. In 1988, some two years before he died on his farm in Frenchtown, New Jersey, Middleton wrote and published the first of a projected multivolume autobiography called *Nebraska Maverick.*[4]

This volume, which covers his early years on a Nebraska farm, unfortunately stops with 1920, but a reading of the book delivers a picture of a man proud of his American farm-family heritage and equally proud of his "maverick" politics. In a thinly veiled reference to his former membership in the Communist Party, Middleton wrote:

No longer do I make party-line (any party) Pavlovian knee-jerk responses to current events. Most of my age peers who were associated with me in the "old left" (the few who are still alive) consider my present lack of any party loyalty as outlandishly eccentric and rather perverse. For their part, nearly all of these old timers, my fellow fighters in the heroic struggles of the 1930s, have drifted willy-nilly into the democratic party.[5]

It was, he told the Court in response to Weissman's questioning, during those "heroic struggles of the 1930s" that he had joined the IWO. He had gone broke in his own small business, had cashed in his commercially issued insurance policies, and needed the low-cost coverage afforded by the IWO; he said he was "equally attracted by the program and activities of the Order."[6] Soon Middleton was elected to various local offices within the organization, moving on to become a paid organizer for the Philadelphia area. In 1938, he was elected an Order vice-president and was paid as a general organizational director.

At a relaxed pace, Weissman took Middleton through his IWO duties, such as conducting annual youth pilgrimages to Valley Forge and organizing various other cultural and social activities for lodges. Since he spoke only English, Middleton's work was primarily directed toward building up the English-speaking enrollment and lodges. The high point of his recital was when he told of his speaking appearance as a representative of the IWO before a National Health Conference called by President Roosevelt. There, his message had been that fraternal benefit societies could not single-handedly solve the health and social security problems of the American people and that, while voluntary membership organizations like the IWO could help, only the federal government, through mandatory universal coverage, could adequately solve these problems. Weissman then had Middleton elaborate on how the IWO vigorously supported the idea of a "National Health Act" by promoting the bills in Congress that would have established a national health care system.[7]

Williams then rose to cross-examine Middleton. His aim, as before, was quickly to label Middleton as a Party functionary working in the IWO and downplay all other employment activities as irrelevant. Within the first two minutes of this questioning, before Middleton was able to respond to the question of whether he had even been in contact with Matthew Cvetic (Middleton had worked extensively in Pennsylvania, where Cvetic claimed to have operated), Weissman was on his feet reminding the witness of his constitutional privilege. With the Court's permission, Middleton exercised this privilege, emphasizing however that he did not think he had "ever done anything dishonorable or anything to harm my country, the United States of America," and did not wish to be perceived as in the same company as the "gangsters and racketeers and corrupt political people associated with the Kefauver organized crime investigation," who had exercised the same privilege.[8]

Unmoved by Middleton's response, Williams put the routine questions to him: whether he currently was, or had ever in the past been, a member of the Communist Party; in response to both, Middleton exercised his Fifth Amendment rights.[9]

Judge Greenberg then redirected the proceeding to his particular interest. He asked Middleton whether he regarded the IWO as a revolutionary mass organization; Middleton said he did not. The Judge proceeded to read to him passages from Olgin's 1931 pamphlet, which expressed the view that, while Order members were not Communists or under Party discipline, they were indeed part of the broader class struggle and would support the Party and should under no circumstance oppose it. Judge Greenberg wanted to know what Middleton thought about those views. Stating that he had been actively involved in the IWO for fifteen years and therefore knew "something" about the organization, he declared that "anyone who knows anything at all about building a fraternal organization knows you couldn't build a fraternal organization with that kind of program." "We wouldn't have gotten to first base," he explained, "with a super-radical, leftist, sectarian policy."[10]

The Judge liked this witness and candidly said so, telling Middleton, "I am happy to notice you have been much more helpful to us than all the other witnesses combined called by the respondent [IWO]." Feeling he finally might be able to get some direct answers to what apparently troubled him, Judge Greenberg recounted that previous witnesses had testified that most of the executive leadership of the Order, including Middleton himself, were Party members. In what was a very tense moment, the Judge asked Middleton to disregard his inclusion and state what significance this fact had so far as the Order was concerned; Weissman tried to interrupt, but Middleton insisted on answering the Judge, explaining that he did not understand the question. "I will be very frank," Judge Greenberg responded; he wanted to know "whether or not the Order was dominated by Communists or controlled by Communists." To the Court's obvious disappointment, Middleton refused to answer, electing once again to exercise his constitutional privilege.[11]

Williams, content to let this drama play out without interruption, then began his cross-examination. In responding to Williams, Middleton maintained the position that fund raising for the trial defense of the eleven top Communists had been conducted by voluntary groups of individuals, of which he was one. His motivation, he explained, was to support "right-thinking Americans in civil rights and justice for minority opinions in this country."

Williams returned to familiar territory in an effort to advance the State's cause, questioning Middleton about IWO support for Communist Party candidates and the witness's own relationship to known Communists; Middleton's response to the former inquiry echoed that of the other IWO witnesses: all Party support came from individuals and groups, not from the Order; as to the latter, he took the Fifth.

Williams continued to press these matters, and Middleton made the following response:

Well, I guess I must be pretty stupid or naive, or both—and I am not trying to be smart and impertinent—but I just can't, for the life of me, figure out what such a question as Mr. Williams is asking has to do with the operation of the insurance business in the state of New York or with the duties—

Judge Greenberg interrupted Middleton here, to explain:

That is just it. He is trying to show that the IWO was only operating an insurance business incidental to its political activities. That is its purpose. I do not say that is what he is doing. That is one of the things he is trying to prove in support of the application of the department.[12]

Relentlessly, Williams pursued Middleton on the subject of IWO support for the *Daily Worker,* and the converse—*Daily Worker* support of the Order. Middleton firmly denied any official connection or policy, insisting that it was instead essentially an advertising medium for the IWO. When Williams, over Weissman's objection (which the Court overruled), asked whether "top leaders of the IWO . . . ever, by word or deed, make any appeal for support of the *Daily Worker* to the general membership of the IWO," Middleton exercised his Fifth Amendment rights and refused to answer. This response touched off a most revealing colloquy:

Q. You claim the privilege of self-incrimination on that question?

A. That is true.

The Court: I am sorry. I had begun to have a great affection for you as a witness. However, that is your privilege.

Mr. Weissman: I hope your Honor, as a judicial officer, will not lose his affection for the witness, by reason of his assertion of a constitutional privilege.

The Court: I can't see for the life of me how a claim of constitutional privilege in this instance can be urged with any sincerity. However, that is entirely up to you.[13]

Had this been a jury trial, such comments by the judge would have been reversible error; however, without a jury the latitude afforded the judge is much greater.

Judge Greenberg raised the level of questioning to the area of international affairs, asking Middleton whether "it was fair to say that whenever there was a clash of policy between Russia and this country, the IWO always took a stand with Russia." Middleton, after engaging with the Judge in a lengthy discussion, concluded:

I firmly believe that unless some sort of a modus vivendi can be arrived at, to straighten out this constant tension between the two major countries of the world, that we are sure headed for disaster. And I take whatever position I have taken, with regard to the Soviet Union, not from the point of view of whether or not it was decisive and important to the Soviet Union, but whether or not it was decisive and important for the benefit of America.

That has always been my position and is today.

Middleton, when asked, added that "I felt that that [this position] is true of the IWO."[14]

But Williams was not willing to let this stand as an answer on behalf of the Order; he wanted to prove the contrary—that the IWO had followed the lead and interests of Russia. Thus he moved to the one salient and apparently vulnerable point: the great "flip-flop" where, after Russia was invaded in June 1941, the IWO (like the Communist Party) switched from attacking President Roosevelt as a "warmonger" and demanding that this country stay out of the Second World War to total support of the Allied effort, urging the President and the country to join the war. Williams raised this matter in order to put Middleton on the spot with regard to his assertion that, according to the IWO, the best interests of this country took precedence over those of Russia.

Middleton fought back valiantly with a general review of the shifting international scene during the 1930s down to Hitler's attack on Russia, in an attempt to show that the IWO position was both tenable and independent of Russia's position. But from the questioning and comments of both Williams and Judge Greenberg, it became clear that neither, especially the Court, was convinced. In truth, it was difficult to refute the assertion that a policy switch had occurred only because Russia had been attacked. Aware of this, Weissman attempted to avoid further damage by refocusing the attention of the Court:

If your Honor please, we have the facts on the record and I think we have had enough of this political discussion. I do not think that the judicial process is geared to it. It would be better on the political level, and I am sure that lots of people in the courtroom would like to participate.[15]

After further questioning by Williams about whether the IWO had any "official position" on the war raging in Korea, Middleton said there had been no discussion and therefore no policy; he gave the same response with respect to the rearmament program of the United States. With that, Middleton was excused from further questioning.

Earlier in the trial, a few witnesses had brought up the name David Greene, some having identified him in a group picture; Greene was the person who had authored the satirical review of this court proceeding for the huge IWO protest meeting which had substituted for the denied National Convention. Greene was the last witness for the Order and the last person to testify in the trial.

At the time his testimony commenced, on April 11, 1951, Greene was forty-six years old and had been in the IWO almost since its inception, having joined the Order in April 1931, exactly twenty years before. Weissman's questioning enabled Greene to draw an outline of his long association with the IWO, most prominently in terms of his experience organizing and directing youth and younger members' sections of the Order. Along with his organizational abilities, Greene had brought to the IWO an enthusiasm for the concerns of sons and daughters of Order members as well as young people generally. Greene knew that the future of any organization ultimately depended on its ability to attract and hold successive generations of members; the IWO had recognized this, and Greene had risen rapidly in the Order hierarchy.

Having successfully organized the first youth lodge of the IWO, Greene was rewarded for his efforts by being given full-time employment with the Order at a salary of fifteen dollars per week. His testimony detailed his work in responding to the social and athletic needs of young people; Greene did make it plain, however, that the IWO agenda included political action as well. Thus, along with a variety of social and cultural activities such as dances, drama groups, bands, and ball teams, issues like racism, anti-Semitism, and the needs of the unemployed were addressed.

Weissman had some difficulty containing his witness; Greene tended to make speeches rather than answer questions. His obvious enthusiasm for what the IWO had done to bring together ethnic and racial groups of young people became clear when he responded to a question about training schools for youth organizers:

I think even though it wasn't taught, the thing that impressed most of the young people and perhaps out of which they got even more than the actual discussions that took place was the fact that here were young people of different nationality, Jewish young people, Slovak young people, Hungarian young people, Negro young people living together, eating together and playing together. To me and to the students that was the best lesson in democracy that could be learned.

As to the actual subjects that were taught, we had, of course, the question of insurance, the question of the history of the fraternal movement and of the IWO.

There was a sports director who conducted a sports program, how to organize various teams and promote tournaments and gymnastics. There were discussions on programming, of functions of officers in a youth lodge, there were discussions on economics. There were lectures and discussions on the Negro problem and anti-Semitism.[16]

With the passing of some years, Greene had gravitated to other areas of work within the Order. He became an expert on the subject of IWO insurance and traveled throughout the country, giving "hundreds upon hundreds of lectures upon the question of insurance." This gave Weissman the opening to allow Greene to describe his experiences in bringing the IWO insurance message to mine workers. Using a personal anecdotal style, Greene told of the problems of miners who were prone to so many terrible diseases and their inability to obtain any sick benefit insurance since "there [was] no insurance company that would touch it, offer sick benefits to miners." Describing the initial reluctance of miners to believe that the IWO would actually pay benefits, Greene told how an organizer took an actual benefit check around to miners' homes as proof that the IWO would pay, thereafter signing up everyone in sight.[17]

Because Greene was an expert on insurance matters, Weissman had him compare IWO insurance programs with those of commercial companies. Pointedly, he alleged that mortality tables used by commercial companies were "unscientific and unfair"; he explained about large commissions paid to agents and the high administrative costs and salaries of executives, adding with respect to the latter, "I once figured out that the president of one of the largest insurance companies got more in one week in salary than the highest paid officer in the IWO got in a whole year." Judge Greenberg injected himself into the questioning by challenging Greene to the effect that comparing the IWO with commercial companies was "utterly unfair"; comparisons, the Judge felt, should be made between fraternals only. Greene countered by defending his comparisons as valid.

Weissman then turned his questioning to emphasize the willingness of the Order to insure working people who were otherwise uninsurable, or insurable only at high rates, because of the high risk of their jobs or because they were black.[18] Hours of testimony by Greene on the IWO insurance programs followed, all pointing to the idea that the insurance operation was the heart and foundation of the IWO—not its politics.[19]

After this extensive review of its insurance programs, Weissman moved to other areas of the Order's fraternal activities such as its extensive—and pioneering—medical plans, where doctors and specialized medical and health services had been organized with low-cost member participation. Extensive services were available in major cities across the nation at negligible cost to IWO members. Greene told that he himself had contracted tuberculosis; as a participant in the plan, he declared that he owed his life to the early detection of his ailment.[20]

Cultural activities were also covered; an IWO concert and lecture bureau supplied entertainment. Paul Robeson had recorded "Ballad for Americans" for the Order. Greene reported that by 1940, on some 1,700 occasions in New York City alone, the IWO had supplied lodges with cultural and musical programs.[21]

Weissman was willing to risk repetition and redundancy in order to demonstrate the broad and diverse scope of IWO activities that bespoke of very "palatable" mainstream activities and associations. Thus, Greene testified about cooperation with the Red Cross, the Tuberculosis Association, and the Cancer Association, as well as in organizing FDR memorials, conducting programs on black and Jewish contributions to American life, and sponsoring national basketball and softball tournaments.

Weissman wanted to deliver one more specific point to Judge Greenberg, and he used Greene to do it: he wanted the Judge to know that if he ordered the liquidation of the IWO, the promise given to policyholders by Superintendent of Insurance Bohlinger contained in a letter to Order members could not be kept. Bohlinger had written:

> I have stated to the Court that if liquidation is granted I will try to reinsure the present policyholders on as nearly the same terms as possible with some other insurance company or companies. In that event substantially the same insurance will continue for the present policyholders. During this litigation, policyholders who continue paying their premiums will receive exactly the same insurance protection they have previously received.[22]

Weissman then asked whether, based on Greene's insurance expertise and research, the Department of Insurance could keep its promise. Greene said no. There followed an exhaustive review of the classifications and types of coverage under the IWO insurance plans; at each major point, Greene asserted that such coverage, terms, or conditions either were not otherwise available or would not be economically feasible for a commercial insurance company to offer. This testimony completed the direct examination of David Greene.[23]

In 1980, twenty-nine years after he had testified at the trial, Greene was interviewed about his involvement with the IWO by students from an industrial and labor relations course at Empire State College in New York; Greene was then seventy-five years old. He told the students that when he was a young man, already a member of the Young Communist League, he had taken part in picketing at a Coney Island restaurant to help in a unionization effort, which landed him in jail. When he was released, he was told by the League's leadership that a new organization, the IWO, was looking for a youth director; they told him they were recommending him for the job. Greene, who had been working part-time as an accountant, took the opportunity offered. He traced his involvement with the Young Communist League beginning in 1924, when he was only nineteen years old, to his life with the IWO which had begun when he was twenty-six and had continued down to the trial.

"Of course," Greene explained about the break with the Workmen's Circle, "insurance was the last thing in the world that anyone was interested in. . . . Purely by accident we later found that the insurance plan we had adopted was probably the best one available at the time." What they primarily wanted was a vehicle to pull together these left-wing Workmen's Circle elements, as well as enlarge their membership.

What they learned, however, was that offering liberal, low-cost insurance was an attraction in and of itself, and it became the major focal point of further organizational efforts. In turn, as expressed in his trial testimony, Greene became deeply involved in the insurance program. He portrayed the insurance business conducted by commercial insurance companies of the day as a "racket," but noted that "the one organization that never got into financial difficulty was the life insurance company"; all other enterprises, he felt, were much more vulnerable. Therefore, from a necessity of organization, the Order's insurance programs evolved into its chief offering, eventually yielding the financial stability that had allowed the organization to prosper.[24]

Williams was on his feet to conduct this final cross-examination. In this work, he pursued such areas as Greene's own writings and his teaching at IWO schools; he phrased the questions to prove that both were designed to further the importance of arousing "class consciousness" in Order members and leaders. Rejecting Williams's suggestion that all of this, and specifically with respect to blacks, was to "move these people toward revolutionary ideas," Greene explained that the

IWO's objective was to get people to recognize the need to solve economic, social, and racial problems beyond the immediate relief that IWO insurance benefits and fraternal activities could provide. "That is the kind of class-consciousness we want to develop," he told the Court.[25]

Greene responded to the inevitable questions as to whether he was then or had ever been a member of the Communist Party by declining to answer on the grounds of constitutional privilege. Yet Williams pressed Greene further about his ties to the Communist Party and its press. Much of this questioning resulted in Greene exercising his Fifth Amendment rights. At one point, Williams asked whether Greene remembered a publication called the *Young Worker,* a Party paper directed to young people. After consultation with Weissman, Greene took the Fifth Amendment, which resulted in an immediate outcry from Judge Greenberg: "How can there possibly be a claim of [constitutional] privilege, Mr. Weissman, on that? Isn't it stretching it pretty far? Suppose he asked him about the *Atlantic Monthly?*"[26] Weissman realized the error and promptly backed off, advising Greene to "just answer the precise question" put to him. With this opening, Greene admitted to Williams that he had urged members of the youth section of the IWO to support the *Young Worker* in an article he had written in 1935—sixteen years before the trial.

Sound professional that he was, Williams would not relent from his goal of painting Greene a deep Red hue in terms of his personal politics, a prejudice, Williams stressed, which he brought to the IWO as an officer, teacher, and writer. Williams questioned Greene about raising money for the legal defense of the top Communists, making the point that Greene had been a member of IWO committees which endorsed Communist candidates. Despite Greene's exercise of his Fifth Amendment privilege, Williams was able to get across to the Judge the fact that Greene had run for Congress in 1938 as a Communist Party candidate. There was also evidence (an article in the *Daily Worker* in 1946) naming Greene as a member of the New York County executive committee of the Communist Party.

With no realistic doubt left that Greene was indeed an active Party member for many—perhaps all—of the years since 1931 while he was working for the IWO, Williams then made his move to tie the witness, the Party, and the IWO together. He asked whether the IWO had sent a representative to the Tenth Convention of the New York State Communist Party (1938); Greene said no. Williams then read from a speech by Greene from the report of that Convention, which opened with the declaration:

Comrades: I bring to our party at its tenth convention greetings and best wishes from the 40,000 members of our International Workers Order.[27]

Greene, on advice of counsel, stood on his constitutional rights, refusing to answer whether he had delivered the speech or whether the IWO had authorized that particular statement.[28]

Williams expected Greene to use the Fifth Amendment in refusing to answer these questions and, to be sure, to some extent *wanted* him to give this response. In this way, Williams accomplished two goals: he established that Greene was a Communist Party member, and he got into the trial record and before the Judge what had been said or written about the issue of IWO leadership involvement with the Party.

The work of the State's staff of attorneys, under the direction of Williams, was prodigious in this regard. They had, as earlier noted, the benefit of all of those documents and testimony in the Dmytryshyn hearing (the "rehearsal" for the IWO case), the files from the Immigration and Naturalization Service, police surveillance materials, total access to IWO files (because the Department of Insurance was on the IWO premises with their "mole" supplying Order materials), and whatever Judge Medina had provided. Beyond this, they scoured libraries and newspaper morgues for additional materials.

The staff then had to read, organize, index, and prepare all the materials. In turn, Williams had to review it and decide what was to be used. The payoff came in that the State was able to produce materials that related to all of the IWO witnesses—their words, their writings, and their deeds, all of a political nature. As was clear from the cross-examination of the State's witnesses, the IWO lawyers had been just as diligent and comprehensive in the work they did under Weissman's supervision.

Judge Greenberg had also been doing his homework. He had taken home and read through portions of bound volumes of the IWO's magazine, *Fraternal Order,* and its predecessor, the *New Order,* and posed the following question to Greene:

Let me ask you, Mr. Greene: During the entire period that you were editor or assistant editor, or connected in any way with the *New Order,* was there ever one article in there that was somewhat favorable to America?

As I read through these articles of 1946, 1947, 1948, 1949 and 1950, and other exhibits that are in evidence, they are all along the Russian Communist theme and painted the high spots of achievement in Russia and Russian-bound territories and so on. I was interested to know whether or not any of these magazine articles carried something—and there must have been something in this country that was worth while speaking of—some article that was favorable to his country, to America. Can you think of any?

The Witness: I can think of every item in there, your Honor, that is favorable to America. I can think of the articles on the American Youth Congress, to go back to the days of the youth movement.

I can think of articles on unemployment insurance and social security, very favorable to America. I can think in terms of articles on peace which are very favorable to America.

The Court: . . . I am not talking about these general problems which arise from time to time, which appeal to everyone. I mean specific instances, for example, like the Moscow trial. Did you ever carry an article commenting on a trial in this country, or is it your view that there is no trial in this country that can equal the dignity and integrity and purpose of the Moscow trial . . . I do not see any such articles. I went through these very carefully in the last several nights, and I got the distinct flavor and impression that they are all slanted in the direction of Russia, of Communism, and of Russian-dominated countries.

The Witness: Well, your Honor—

The Court: Maybe I am wrong.

The Witness: Your Honor, all I can say is that they are definitely slanted, but they are slanted in the interest of the working men and women in America. That is the kind of slanting I see in the magazine, and I am sure that if I look through it very carefully, I will find that we endorsed actions by individuals, no matter where they came from, if their actions were in the interests of the American people.[29]

Immediately Weissman, always ready with a response or rejoinder, rose to point out to the Judge a specific article that favorably reported on American trials. It was clear, however, that Judge Greenberg was extremely displeased with the pro-Soviet contents of what he had been reading; apparently the entire leftist political slant of the Order was problematic for him.

Williams used Greene to develop material on another paid official of the IWO, its Executive Secretary Samson Milgrom. Milgrom was too ill to testify, but Williams was determined to get information about him before the Court. After developing that Milgrom had been a U.S. resident for twenty-six years and had never become a citizen, Williams dropped his "bomb":

Q. Do you know that he is ordered to be deported as an alien Communist?

Mr. Weissman: I object to that.

The Court: Yes, sustained. Is that a fact, Mr. Williams?

Mr. Williams: Yes, your Honor; it is a fact.

The Court: Then it is important to establish that. Do you say that there is an order out for his deportation?[30]

Williams went on to explain that in 1935 an order had been issued for Milgrom's deportation, but he had been ordered to a country which would not take him. Williams told the Court, "he is subject to deportation and the order is out for the deportation hearing." Note that the Judge sustained the objection as valid, yet he then asked Williams "Is that a fact," allowing Williams in effect to give the evidence about Milgrom without any testimony or documentary proof. Williams followed this opening by getting Greene, over Weissman's further objection, to state that he voted for Milgrom to get his IWO post. He attempted to characterize Milgrom as a powerful, influential IWO officer—this non-citizen, ordered-to-be-deported, alien Communist—through questions placed to Greene.[31]

In the closing hours of the trial on April 13, 1951, with the testimony and cross-examination of the last witness completed and the final documents placed in evidence as part of the record, the attorneys and the Judge turned their attention to the matter of tying up that had been left undone. This is when Judge Greenberg ruled on the issue of whether to strike all of Matthew Cvetic's testimony because the Attorney General of the United States had refused to turn over any written reports Cvetic may have given to the FBI. The Judge ruled to keep Cvetic's testimony in as part of the record of the case; while he felt he had the power to order the Department of Justice to turn over the reports, he chose not to do so.

Predictably, Weissman then moved to renew his *Motion to Dismiss* the entire matter, based on his prior argument about the legality of the petition (complaint) by the State. Had the Judge ruled on the IWO motions at the beginning of the trial, a basis for appeal by the losing party would have been possible; instead the Judge had simply, but most significantly, chosen not to rule one way or the other. In turn, that had led to the taking of evidence—witnesses and documents—over the intervening months.

Judge Greenberg again refused to rule. Instead, he told the attorneys to submit briefs to him, that is, to argue in writing the legal issues involved. He emphasized that since the oral and written testimony was very fresh in his mind, he wanted to read the legal arguments of both sides, adding that he thought "the outcome of this case will depend largely upon the legal implications or the legal significance of the various [issues] that are presented here."[32]

Judge Greenberg then went on to express his thanks to the lawyers:

I also wish to say at this time, at the close of the case, that I am deeply grateful to counsel representing all of the parties for the extreme courtesy and high order of respect shown the Court at all times. Being the type of a case it was, where emotions could have been unfortunately engendered, where feelings could have become bitter, the expression of those feelings might have manifested themselves in a disrespectful attitude toward the Court.[33]

It is not unusual for a judge to thank the attorneys for their courtesy and to acknowledge the proficiency with which they have handled an especially lengthy and complex matter; coming from this respected judge who exuded Southern courtesy, such an acknowledgment was to be expected. Here, however, Judge Greenberg knew that all the participants were well aware of courtroom scenes of the most acrimonious nature in other trials where Red Scare matters were involved, wherein shouting, demonstrations, and accusations against the fairness, if not the judicial abilities of the presiding jurist, had commonly taken place. The recent trial before Judge Greenberg's mentor, Judge Medina, of the top Communist leadership exemplified this tendency; the lawyers had been held in contempt of court, with all of them going to jail and some losing their licenses to practice law. So it was with a great deal of relief that the attorneys and the Judge in the IWO trial could end on a note of compliment by Judge Greenberg which was then returned by Weissman:

Before we close, let me on my own behalf, and I think I speak here on behalf of all attorneys, say here that we are deeply grateful to the Presiding Judge—to you, sir—for the uniform courtesy and consideration that you have shown us over these many weeks.

This kind of a trial, as your Honor has stated, very easily lends itself to the kind of a situation that your Honor described, where counsel are necessarily under tension. . . .

If this trial has been conducted with due dignity and decorum, the greatest credit is due to your Honor. I say this with the greatest of pleasure. These remarks indicate in but a small measure the feelings I have on this occasion, and I am grateful to be able to make this statement, inadequate as I am sure it must be.[34]

Williams, in turn, concurred with Weissman's assessment.

With these words of admiration, this four-month trial, recorded in over 4,000 pages of testimony and involving hundreds of documents, affidavits, pleadings, books, articles, and reports, came to a quiet end. The issues, however, were far from quiescent ones, breathing, as they did, fire from the place where politics meets the law—all at a most provocative time.

Notes

1. Williams Office Files, Correspondence, Letter by J. B. Henry to Paul Crouch, April 3, 1951.

2. Trial Record, pp. 3831–38.

3. Trial Record, pp. 3839–89.

4. John E. Middleton, *Nebraska Maverick* (Frenchtown, NJ: Guild Press and Publishers, 1988).

5. Ibid., p. 194.

6. Trial Record, p. 3902.

7. Trial Record, pp. 3903–27.

8. Trial Record, pp. 3929–31.

9. Trial Record, p. 3932.

10. Trial Record, pp. 3933–36.

11. Trial Record, pp. 3937–38.

12. Trial Record, pp. 3944–45.

13. Trial Record, pp. 3950–51.

14. Trial Record, pp. 3959–60.

15. Trial Record, pp. 3961–68.

16. Trial Record, pp. 4018–35.

17. Trial Record, pp. 4036–45.

18. Trial Record, pp. 4046–56.

19. Trial Record, pp. 4057–76.

20. Trial Record, pp. 4081–88.

21. Trial Record, p. 4089.

22. Trial Record, p. 4111.

23. Trial Record, pp. 4111–19.

24. David Greene interview, March 17, 1980, by Lisa Pearlstein and Kathie Noonan.

25. Trial Record, pp. 4121–26.

26. Trial Record, pp. 4148–49.

27. Trial Record, pp. 4146–56.

28. Trial Record, p. 4145.

29. Trial Record, pp. 4168–70.

30. Trial Record, pp. 4178–79.

31. Ibid.

32. Trial Record, pp. 4187–88.

33. Trial Record, p. 4189.

34. Trial Record, pp. 4190–91.

Chapter XV
Judge Greenberg Decides

> A political trial often clarifies basic questions. Within some trials
> there are, in effect, two trials. The trial of the legal issues is neces-
> sary, of course, for us to recognize the trial itself as authoritative.
> Otherwise, lacking a legal agenda, the trial would be a sham, at best
> a debate, at worst a partisan trial. But when in one trial the legal
> and the political agendas are in tension, fundamental questions
> can be better confronted.
>
> *Political Trials in History*, Ron Christenson, ed.

The IWO attorneys had good reason to be hopeful after Judge Greenberg gave his closing comments and directions to the lawyers. The
Judge had indicated that he wanted the legal issues argued in the briefs
of the parties, not the facts or testimony. That was advantageous to the
IWO because it was precisely on the legal issues that the Order lawyers
had, from the first day in court, attempted to focus the Judge's attention. The area of law applicable to insurance companies and the powers of the Superintendent of Insurance to regulate insurance carriers,
they knew, appeared to favor the IWO. The IWO attorneys wanted to
avoid the political questions of alleged relationship to the Communist
Party, the core of the State's case. It appeared from the Judge's instructions that he was at last ready to deal with the legal "meat" of the
controversy and not the Red Scare-political aspects.

The only major daily newspaper that noted the end of the trial was
the *New York Times,* which reported the close under the headline "Decision Is Reserved in IWO 'Red' Case." In a short article, the *Times*
recounted that the record was so voluminous that Judge Greenberg
had stated he might ask his superiors to relieve him of all court duties
while he studied the record, exhibits, and briefs.[1]

Meanwhile, as the lawyers worked to prepare their briefs, activities

Figure 9. Rockwell Kent lithograph, "The Smith Act," completed in 1951 during the IWO trial. Courtesy of the Rockwell Kent Legacies.

IWO News Bulletin

INTERNATIONAL WORKERS ORDER—80 Fifth Avenue, New York 11, N. Y.   MAY, 1951

Fight For Our Order!

DEAR BROTHERS AND SISTERS:

In these pages you will read about the trial of the IWO which ended April 13.

It was a *mass* trial. Though the Insurance Department does not name any of our 162,000 members, it is acting to seize the insurance of every one of us!

We shall fight liquidation to the highest court, if necessary! Nor shall we liquidate our interests in the Order through non-payment of dues!

There is no question that each and every one of us will lose insurance and fraternal benefits if our Order is liquidated. But more than life insurance is at stake. Some of life's most precious values are threatened: 'the right to practice interracial fraternalism, to belong to a multi-national pro-

FLASH!

IWO Off Subversive List

As we go to press, the U. S. Supreme Court, on April 30, took the IWO off the Attorney General's "subversive" list! The Attorney General, without hearings or charges, questioned the loyalty of our organization. We challenged this scandalous libel before the U. S. Supreme Court as an arbitrary and illegal action. The Supreme Court upheld us! This will undoubtedly have profound bearing on the illegal liquidation proceedings!

labor society, to speak one's mind

without fear of censorship or property confiscation, to teach our children to understand their parents' struggles and the meaning of brotherhood.

YOU CAN HELP SAVE YOUR INSURANCE AND YOUR ORDER

It goes without saying that dues MUST be kept up. You can also fill out a TESTIMONIAL to the Order. Testimonial forms are in your lodge. They ask you to "give your own experience of how the IWO has served you and your family through its fraternal insurance and sick benefits and how your lodge reflects the democratic character of the IWO as a whole." You can fill these forms out *in any language you desire.* They are to be mailed to IWO, 80 Fifth Ave., N. Y. 11, N. Y.

────── STICK WITH YOUR ORDER ──────── DEFEND YOUR ORDER ──────

THIS WAS THE TRIAL . . .

From March 26 when Rubin Saltzman took the stand as the first IWO witness, until April 13 when the liquidation trial ended, our leaders and members gave chapter by chapter the matchless history of our 21-year-old organization.

Six Order officials and 15 rank and file members proudly testified to what the Order is, what it accomplishes for its members, the community, the nation.

Judge Henry C. Greenberg, who presided over the proceeding in New York Supreme Court, indicated that a decision on the N. Y. Insurance Department's petition to liquidate the Order may be expected in July.

We said in court and in law briefs that the entire proceeding against our Order is illegal.

In the first place, the Insurance Superintendent has absolutely no legal

power to liquidate a sound and solvent organization, which he concedes our Order to be. Our attorneys pointed to the insurance laws and numerous court decisions to prove this.

OUR LEGAL ARGUMENTS

In view of our organization's outstanding financial soundness and contributions to the general welfare, the Insurance Superintendent's charge that our Order is a "hazard" to its members and the people is fantastically false.

Our answer to the Insurance Superintendent's outrageous statement that the Order is "subversive" was on two grounds: the facts and the law. The facts show that our organization, as every member knows, consistently acted in the best interests of our country. Even Insurance

Examiner Haley, whose report is the basis for the court action, admits that he found no evidence to support the charge that the Order is "subversive."

On the law, we said this. The Insurance Superintendent was never given thought control powers by the state legislature and in trying to usurp such powers he was acting illegally and in violation of Federal and state constitutions.

The "public hazard," we charged, comes from the Dewey-directed attempt of the Insurance Department to liquidate our Order and destroy the insurance protection of 162,000 members and their families.

We termed the whole proceeding a witchhunt without precedent which depends on red-baiting and appeals to war hysteria to cover up its brutal and dictatorial nature.

"The possibility is not to be ignored," Paul W. Williams, attorney for the Insurance Department hysterically argued, 'that in the event

(Continued on page 2)

Figure 10. IWO News Bulletin issued in May 1951. The trial was over and the judge's decision awaited. Note the box announcing the Supreme Court decision in the subversive listing case.

continued at a lively pace on both sides. The IWO issued news releases, letters, and bulletins to its members reviewing the trial and encouraged members and lodges to send letters and sign petitions directed to Governor Dewey and Superintendent Bohlinger urging them to "withdraw the liquidation proceedings"; the State had, of course, no intention of doing so nor, given the legal process and the current political climate, was there any reason to do so. Each petition and each letter was duly noted and forwarded to Williams's office for recording. The IWO, though significantly hamstrung by the presence of and controls by State officials from the Insurance Department, retained a public relations agent and tried to keep up the pressure on State politicians, as well as bolster the morale of its members.

Every internal move by the Order was carefully monitored by Insurance Department representatives. For instance, about a week after the trial ended, the IWO placed advertisements in New York papers urging the public, unions, fraternal groups, and others to write Dewey and Bohlinger. William Karlin, the lead agent for the State on the IWO premises, took umbrage at the ad and, while admitting to Williams that it probably came under the title of "Defense of the Order," sought to stall payment for it.[2]

Although the lights on the courtroom scene had darkened, the larger background of this battle was ablaze; the war continued to rage in Korea, while Cold War conflicts between Russia and the United States furthered the Red Scare. The war in Korea had been going poorly, and casualties mounted daily. President Truman, in a highly controversial decision, stripped General MacArthur of command on April 11, 1951; this was followed by MacArthur's triumphal return to the United States, where he addressed a joint session of Congress and was welcomed to New York City by a massive ticker tape parade. Calling U.S. Asian policy "blind to reality," MacArthur's attacks on the Administration had led to Congressional demands for a wide policy investigation on the conduct of the war. President Truman, meanwhile, was booed as he threw out the first pitch of the new baseball season.[3]

Red Scare developments continued to fill the news media with reports of loyalty hearings, firings, confessions, and more accusations. Representative Harold H. Velde of Illinois, HUAC member, reported that "certain" Hollywood writers had slipped Red propaganda into films. Larry Adler, world-famous harmonica artist, left the country to reside in England when he was denied engagements to perform in America after being called "Pro-Red."[4]

The May 1951 edition (in different languages) of the *IWO News Bulletin*, (see Figure 10) which went out to the Order's membership with the headline "Fight For Our Order," contained an appeal for members to pay their dues and to fill out a testimonial to the IWO; forms could be obtained from the local lodges. Members were asked to "give your own experience of how the IWO has served you and your family through its fraternal insurance and sick benefits and how your lodge reflects the democratic character of the IWO as a whole." The forms could be filled out in "any language you desire." The *Bulletin* also reviewed the just-completed trial, featuring pictures and brief summaries of the Order's officer witnesses and voicing thanks to those rank-and-file members who had made brief trial appearances. As could be expected, there was no attempt at balance in the recitation of praises for the Order, its lawyers, and its witnesses and no restraints in its damnation of the State's witnesses, each of whose evil nature was reviewed under the heading, "To Say For Pay." Throughout the *Bulletin* were admonitions to "Stick With Your Order—Defend Your Order."[5]

But the big news, coming too late for anything but a box on the *Bulletin*'s front page, proclaimed:

FLASH!
IWO OFF SUBVERSIVE LIST

As we go to press, the U.S. Supreme Court, on April 30, took the IWO off the Attorney General's "subversive" list! The Attorney General, without hearings or charges, questioned the loyalty of our organization. We challenged this scandalous libel before the U.S. Supreme Court as an arbitrary and illegal action. The Supreme Court upheld us! This will undoubtedly have profound bearing on the illegal liquidation proceedings!

This stunning decision was the result of an intense legal battle which had been fought over some years by three of the organizations listed as subversive in 1947 by the Attorney General of the United States. Under President Truman's Loyalty Program, these names had been given to the Loyalty Review Board of the United States Civil Service Commission. Besides the IWO, the listing and its legality had been challenged by the Joint Anti-Fascist Refugee Committee and the National Council of American-Soviet Friendship, Inc. Attorney General Tom C. Clark, who had first compiled and promulgated the subversive listing, was, ironically, now a Justice of the U.S. Supreme Court and therefore could take no part in the decision.[6]

On a few occasions during the trial, the fact had been raised that the Order had challenged its listing as "subversive." Most relevant was that Haley had testified that his motivation for investigating the IWO beyond its financial status had come from its inclusion on the list. Once again, irony enters the picture; the removal of the IWO from the list had come too late to stop Haley, or for that matter even to have influenced the trial proceedings. Despite this, the *IWO News Bulletin* declared that the decision would "undoubtedly have profound bearing on the liquidation proceeding."

With more hope than substance, the IWO had issued a statement under Kent's signature lauding the decision as a vindication of "our two-year fight against the arbitrary and unconstitutional listing by the Attorney General," adding the belief that the decision would "nullify the liquidation proceedings . . . since the Attorney General's listing was the motivating factor in [initiating] the proceedings."[7] What the IWO failed to acknowledge was that the rationale behind majority opinion in the subversive listing case was the unlawful absence of an opportunity to be heard and present evidence before being listed; in the Insurance Department-IWO case, on the other hand, full opportunity for a complete hearing had been afforded.

Judge Greenberg had indicated during the trial that he found fault with the entire concept of listing organizations as "subversive" without allowing a hearing, response, or rebuttal from those listed; in fact, he had predicted that the Supreme Court would rule against the government in the matter.

The vote in the listing case (the three organizations had filed separate suits, but were decided together) was five to three, with Justices Douglas, Frankfurter, Jackson, Black, and Burton favoring the IWO and Chief Justice Vinson, along with Justices Minton and Reed, dissenting. Justice Burton, in his opinion, characterized the Attorney General's conduct as "patently arbitrary."[8] Justice Hugo L. Black was willing to go even further:

in my judgment the executive has no constitutional authority, with or without a hearing, officially to prepare and publish the lists challenged by petitioners. In the first place, the system adopted effectively punishes many organizations and their members merely because of their political beliefs and utterances, and to this extent smacks of a most evil type of censorship. This cannot be reconciled with the First Amendment.[9]

Clearly, he viewed the issue of freedom of political belief as germane.

The IWO made the most of the decision, notifying not only the members through their bulletins and news releases, but also taking out ads in four major daily newspapers under the title "The Supreme Court Speaks" at a cost of almost $3,000. Karlin called Williams to see whether there was a way to prevent these ads, but Williams advised him that, since the IWO claimed the expenditure was in "defense of the Order," he had to approve it. Karlin did, however, enforce changes in the ads, including the exclusion of language which characterized the ads as being "Presented as a Public Service."[10]

In the May 1951 *IWO News Bulletin,* the featured article was entitled "IWO Lawyers on Decision of the Supreme Court." Frank Donner and Arthur Kinoy had a statement above their names, which read:

As a result of the Supreme Court decision it is illegal to discriminate against the International Workers Order or its members because of this improper designation by the Attorney-General.

A refusal to permit the International Workers Order or any of its lodges to use a meeting place, to purchase radio time, or place advertisements in the public press because of this former listing would be a clear violation of law.

Any attempt to boycott or blacklist the International Workers Order or its members in any manner in this respect would be inconsistent with the decision of the highest court of the land.[11]

The delisting of the IWO was a true Pyrrhic victory; it changed nothing. The day after the Supreme Court announced its decision, it was reported that U.S. government attorneys declared that membership in the three organizations "would continue to carry weight in Federal employees' loyalty investigations," despite the listing case. This was echoed by Loyalty Review Board lawyers. The attorneys said the high court's decision "would not eliminate the groups from consideration even temporarily." So much for the "bombshell" tossed into the entire loyalty program, the underlying legality of which had not, in any event, been decided in the listing case.[12]

States other than New York continued to prosecute the IWO as an organization, and loyalty boards—on the federal and state levels— continued to use membership in the Order as grounds for dismissal from public jobs. Similarly, there is no indication that the Immigration and Naturalization Service stopped prosecuting aliens for membership. As David Caute noted, "The executive [President and executive branch agencies] took no notice whatsoever of the decision and the Attorney General continued his declamatory riot."[13] The Court's decision, in effect, changed nothing. In ignoring the IWO listing case it may well have been another instance, similar to the famous remark attributed to President Andrew Jackson in 1832, that "John Marshall [then Chief Justice of the Supreme Court] has made his decision—now let him enforce it." Jackson may not have said it, but he acted on that principle. This same "principle" seems to have been acceptable and operational in 1951 in relation to the listing case.

In a similar vein, in another case involving an employee facing loyalty charges, the chairman of a loyalty board remarked, "Of course the fact that a person believes in racial equality doesn't prove that he's a Communist, but it certainly makes you look twice, doesn't it."[14] A further case involved seventy FBI interviews, found necessary before clearing a bootblack working in the Pentagon of charges that he had contributed ten dollars to the Scottsboro defense fund; the allegation was shown to be false since it was supposed to have been contributed ten years before he was born. With this proof, he was cleared as safe to shine shoes.[15] Such were the times.

Judge Greenberg had called for briefs from the lawyers by May 15, 1951, knowing full well that delays in their preparation and printing were almost inevitable. As noted earlier, formal briefs are usually associated with appeals after a trial; they constitute, along with the trial record (or an agreed condensation of it), the basic documents that present the case on appeal. On the other hand, as was already the case in the IWO trial, a judge can require the parties to prepare briefs on important issues that have arisen during the course of a trial; extensive *Briefs* had been filed on the matter of the IWO *Motions To Strike and Dismiss*. Now, after the actual trial had concluded, Judge Greenberg had once more exercised his power to elicit briefs from the parties.

The word "briefs" as used in American law is a derivative of the English term, where it was and still is the basic document prepared by the solicitor to enable the barrister to become informed about the case as he prepares for its trial. The American variation reflects the absence of the solicitor-barrister bifurcation in the practice of law and emphasizes the concept of creating a "brief of argument" before an appellate court, or, as in this case, to present to the trial court the essential legal position of the parties at the conclusion of the trial.

Both sides knew they must put forth their very best efforts in their respective *Briefs*; they were aware that after a long trial appellate level courts are loath to overturn a trial court's decision and command a retrial. They also knew that Judge Greenberg, regardless of which side he came down on, would render a carefully crafted opinion, and therefore his decision would more likely be affirmed than reversed. Unlike briefs submitted to an appellate court where oral argument is generally allowed as a supplement to the written briefs, the lawyers knew that there would be no further oral argument; all argument must be contained in the briefs. Because the deadline was the same for both, and therefore there was no assurance that one side would see the work of the other prior to filling their briefs with the Court, each, when drafting their arguments, was forced to anticipate what the other side would say.

Following the standard for a brief to an appellate court, these *Briefs* each contained a table of contents, a table of decided cases cited or used in the *Brief*, and statutes (federal and state) cited or used, followed by the heart of work: legal arguments divided under major headings. Behind this formal structure and ordered appearance may breathe the fire of passionate arguments involving life and death—of persons and groups as well as ideas. In most legal briefs, such dramatic issues are clearly not at stake. But in the IWO case, they certainly were.

Good brief writing is an ages-old art. It requires such special skills and tastes that in the large compartmentalized law firms of today, attorneys can be found whose entire work is dedicated to this task alone. Forty years ago, brief writing was already considered enough of a specialty that many, if not most, attorneys retained a separate lawyer devoted exclusively to this task. In the IWO case, however, both sides had the talent and resources to do their own brief writing—and do it well.

The State's *Brief* ran a lengthy 202 pages, printed and paperback bound. Traditionally, the plaintiff's—here "Petitioner's" *Brief* carried a white cover; the defendant's—here "Respondent's" *Brief* carried a blue cover, so the work of each side could be easily identified. The Intervenors also filed a separate *Brief*; since it was on the responding side, it too carried a blue cover.[16]

Paul Williams has acknowledged that the State's *Brief* was essentially the work of James B. Henry, Jr., his chief assistant in the case. Brief writing was Henry's forte, just as trial work was the speciality of Williams. Another subtle factor is reflected in the *Brief*: Henry was something of an anti-Communist zealot, which Williams was not.[17]

If the IWO attorneys thought that the Williams team would limit itself to any strict interpretation of what Judge Greenberg had said about legal issues to be argued, they were deluding themselves. The cry of "Communism" came forth from almost every page of the State's *Brief*. It is not until well over one half of the 202-page *Brief* that what truly can be called legal arguments even appear; until that point, there is a general review of the thousands of pages of testimony, succinctly compressed to extrapolate the Communist Party-IWO nexus. The first three Points (then subdivided into headings that support the contention) indicate the direction of the work:

POINT I.—The International Workers Order, Inc., from its foundation to the present has been dominated by the Communist Party, and its primary purpose is the support of the Communist Party and dissemination of Communist doctrines. . . .

POINT II.—The Communist Party and the International Workers Order advocate the overthrow of organized government in the United States by force and violence. . . .

POINT III.—The Communist Party and the International Workers Order teach loyalty to the Union of Soviet Socialist Republics and disloyalty to the United States of America. . . .

Page after page exhorted the Court to recognize the dangers and threat of Communism and, in turn, the role of the IWO as an adjunct of the Party. The evidence presented by the State's witnesses and the documents introduced (speeches, pamphlets, books) were interpreted to present the most damning, forceful argument. The gloves were off: all testimony of the paid professional witnesses was taken as gospel. The officers and leading members of the IWO were each subjected to a listing of all evidence: oral testimony, written documents, and pictures—which linked them to the Party. The history of the Order was reviewed and described as commanded and approved by the Communist International. All policies of the IWO were described as dictated by Communist Party fractions operating within the Order. The insurance and social reform activities were characterized solely as "lures to bring members within the sphere of the Communist Party."

The IWO was reported as a source of financial support for the Party, a medium for dissemination of Party propaganda, and as a recruiting ground for the Party. All of this led to the conclusion that "the foregoing facts make the further transaction of business by the International Workers Order hazardous to its policy holders, its creditors, and the public," within the meaning of "hazard" under New York insurance law.

Here the State's *Brief* had to tackle the nature of the word "hazardous" in the applicable statute and urge that a refusal to enlarge the concept from financial to political would leave the State unable to deal with the "Frankenstein monster" it had created. The State argued it was "not committed to any such self-destroying proposition," just because "this monster remains solvent, as long as it observes the technical requirements of the Insurance Law."[18]

Acknowledging that it was entering new legal territory, the State maintained:

It is difficult to imagine how an insurance organization could constitute a public hazard, aside from its financial operations, except by being an organization dedicated to revolution or to a foreign power. The IWO, especially at this juncture of history, presents such a hazard.[19]

The "take the money and run" proposition received a thorough treatment:

If the Communist Party instructed these life-long Communists—Milgrom, Greene, Shipka and Polak—or the many other convinced Communists in responsible positions in the IWO, to take what assets they could lay hands upon and disappear, can it be doubted that they would obey? Can it be doubted that the Communist Party of the United States would issue these instructions if Moscow required them to be issued, or if it considered them expedient?

The danger that such instructions will be issued is no more fanciful than the threat of war.[20]

For good measure, the State argued that the IWO violated the Smith Act, the federal statute under which the leading Communist Party members had been convicted in the *Dennis* case, as well as state criminal statutes. Perhaps more convincing was the claim that the IWO violated and abused its corporate charter by exceeding and perverting the purposes for which it was founded as an insurance company.[21]

The State maintained that since the Order did not fulfill—and never intended to fulfill—"the general fraternal, altruistic, educational, patriotic, recreational and other purposes" which it had stated in its corporate charter purpose clause, "the entire existence of the IWO had been fraudulent and therefore invalid."[22]

The IWO's *Brief,* by contrast, reads as if it dealt with an entirely different case. With few exceptions, the words "Communist" or "Communist Party" occur on every page of the State's *Brief*; in some 200 pages of the IWO *Brief,* the words barely appear. This difference goes to the heart of the entire case. To the State, the Order's political activities and ties through its leadership with the Communist Party required a legal remedy—the destruction of the Order. To the IWO, however, the State had no right to go beyond the letter of the law in regulating its affairs; here the law clearly involved the interest of the policyholders, as well as the public, in the financial soundness of the organization. To tread beyond that limit was to trample on the political rights of the Order, in violation of recognized legal guarantees, and invoke such fundamentals as freedom of belief and expression, the separation of powers within government, and due process of law.

The IWO *Brief* contains a carefully assembled case for a narrow construction of New York insurance law. Point I of the *Brief* states: "The Insurance Law of New York does not authorize the liquidation of the respondent." The legal argument in support of this Point runs over 140 pages, wherein the IWO cites over 100 cases, statutes, and legal authorities to buttress its contention. The thrust of the argument was that the statute used by the State did not expressly authorize the relief sought (liquidation) and that to expand the statute by conferring such power would violate the concept of separation of governmental powers by giving the Superintendent of Insurance the power, in effect, to legislate in insurance regulation, an area outside the limits of his authority. If the Superintendent were allowed to expand his power to the degree that he could revoke permission to do business for political reasons, such an expansion would violate state and federal constitutional guarantees of due process of law, as well as free speech, press, and assembly rights.

The IWO lawyers also attended to the crucial matter of the word "hazard" by delving into a history of the legislation containing that word, seeking the legislative intent and its administrative and judicial interpretation, concluding in effect that "hazardous" had always referred solely to the risk of financial loss—never politics. Thus, they argued, since the statute conferred "no authority to seek liquidation on political grounds, the proceedings must fall, for no other valid grounds for liquidation supports the Superintendent's case."[23]

The IWO attorneys urged the Judge, in effect, to rise above the hysteria of the times and confirm the rule of law over current political exigencies:

When we examine in calmness the simple, unequivocal words of the statute and the context of these words, we can immediately measure the enormous gap which separates what the Legislature called on the Superintendent to do, and what he is seeking to do in this case.[24]

It is utterly fantastic to read into the New York State Insurance Law a political provenance. Only a boldness born of hysteria could lead an administrative official to such defiance of the legislative mandate, to such abandonment of his own responsibilities.[25]

It was only toward the end of the *Brief* that any mention was made of testimony given in the case; all comments were addressed to the State's witnesses, none to those testifying for the Order. Throughout the IWO *Brief*, an attempt was made to appeal directly to the Judge to maintain the highest level of dispassion, to see all that was at stake and to evaluate what had been presented in the cold light of reason. The Judge was reminded that "every State's witness was either a professional, paid 'anti-Communist' witness or an ex-Communist or both" and that the State could not find a current member of the Order to testify in support of its contentions.[26] With respect to the State's witnesses, the IWO lawyers added:

It is important to bear in mind that when either revenge or money becomes an inducement to testify, the truth must inevitably suffer, and it suffers not merely because such witnesses find it convenient or profitable to distort what occurred, but also because distortions pass over almost imperceptibly into fabrications or inventions.[27]

"Liquidation of an insurance company," the *Brief* concluded, "should not be sanctioned upon testimony which is bought and paid for."[28]

Arthur Kinoy has described a last-minute panic that hit just as the

IWO lawyers were completing the writing on their *Brief*. On June 4, 1951, the U.S. Supreme Court, over the powerful dissents of Justices Black and Douglas, upheld the constitutionality of the Smith Act, affirming the convictions of the top Communist Party officers in the *Dennis* case. Kinoy has written that, "when the word reached us, we were jamming out the last pages of a brief to Judge Greenberg. . . . We frantically tried to rewrite our brief, arguing that the news out of Washington did not affect the IWO case because not even the Superintendent of Insurance had ever charged that the IWO officers or the society itself had violated the Smith Act."[29] In fact, and apparently unknown to the IWO lawyers at that moment, the State's *Brief* did allege that the IWO violated the Smith Act, as well as sections of the New York Penal Law.[30]

The Intervenors' Committee also produced a brief. Apparently unable to afford the luxury of a formal printed brief, they settled for a mimeographed format of 46 pages. Most of their *Brief* consisted of a compilation of testimony of IWO members given at the trial and by affidavit, stressing the cultural, educational, and patriotic activities of the Order, with special emphasis on the cruciality of the insurance programs to the lives of those giving witness. In terms of legal arguments, the Intervenors' *Brief* mirrored all of the points and positions taken by the Order's *Brief*.

Claiming to represent 23,000 members "and still growing," the Intervenors' *Brief* sought to convince the Court that the IWO "has been clearly and without substantial dispute demonstrated to be a true Fraternal Benefit Society devoting its every effort to the welfare of its members" and that liquidation would result in the "total loss of insurance protection," since it would be impossible to get a commercial insurance company to reinsure on the same terms and costs.[31]

No reference to Communism or the Party appears in the *Brief*. Instead, it asserts:

> The International Workers Order, Inc. is perhaps the greatest exponent of true fraternalism left in the United States. It is one of the few large fraternal societies which still maintains their fraternal activities on a high level, and have not degenerated into simple insurance companies. It is a tragic commentary on the direction being taken by the current hysteria, "the hue and cry," that so sharp a blow against the people's freedom of association is being directed against this shining example of fraternalism in action.[32]

The palpable attempt of this *Brief* was to present and focus on the "human" face of the IWO, as opposed merely to advancing legal arguments.

The *Briefs* for both sides were dated June 7, 1951. That means the writing was completed and sent to the printers on the same day, though to separate legal brief printing specialists. The IWO used a union printer; the State did not.

Some time between that day and June 20, 1951, the IWO lawyers got their first look at the State's *Brief,* and were outraged by what they read. Galvanized into action, they immediately prepared a 32-page *Reply Memorandum for Respondents,* but did not have time to have it printed because they wanted to get it into Judge Greenberg's hands before he wrote his decision, which was expected at any time.[33]

The IWO lawyers, offended by the State's *Brief,* made their reasons known explicitly in their *Reply Memorandum.* Judge Greenberg had instructed counsel to limit themselves to the legal aspects rather than the factual setup; the IWO had complied willingly with this direction. "The State, however," argued the IWO in its *Reply Memorandum,* "saw fit to discuss almost exclusively the evidence adduced during the hearing"; the first 119 pages of the State's *Brief* "develop in the greatest detail the Superintendent's version of the 'factual set-up' which the Court quite specifically requested counsel to omit from the briefs."[34]

Where the IWO *Brief* had been a model of cogent arguments, pleading with the Court for the calm application a conservative rule of law approach, restrained in tone and language, the *Reply Memorandum* was just the opposite. It lashed out against the State with sarcasm, irony, and anger, with as strong a use of language and sentiments as one is likely to find in any civil case:

Realizing perhaps that the record simply will not support any such distorted picture of the IWO, the Superintendent once again has attempted to camouflage the weakness of a position by legal sleight-of-hand.[35]

. . . we cannot refrain from one final observation in respect to the Superintendent's studied attempt to avoid the consequences of decided law. Perhaps the most vivid illustration of the Superintendent's determination to destroy this organization, regardless of the confines of the law, is his somewhat amazing effort to turn every conceded virtue of the organization into an "evil." His plaintive argument that the insurance activities of the Order are too attractive (petitioner's brief, p. 55), or that its assets are too liquid (petitioner's brief, p. 129), or that its fraternal activities are too appealing (petitioner's brief, p. 55), is a little hard to comprehend. Would he prefer that the organization did not offer a sound insurance program, that its assets were frozen, or that its fraternal activities were nonexistent? In that event, he would most certainly argue that the organization should be liquidated. . . .

The simple and sobering realization which stems from the position the Superintendent has taken before the Court is that, for whatever partisan motives are involved, the Superintendent is determined that come what may, this organization must be destroyed. This determination not only leads the Superintendent to absurd and contradictory positions. It more fundamentally exposes the constitutional and statutory barriers to his petition.[36]

Aside from biting back at the State's *Brief* for violating the Judge's directions as to the scope of contents, the IWO lawyers were obviously concerned enough about one particular legal argument contained in the State's *Brief* to devote the major portion of their *Reply* to the issue. As legal justification for liquidation of the Order, the State had charged that the IWO willfully violated its corporate charter. Under fundamental corporate law, a corporation (including a fraternal benefit insurance corporation such as the IWO) could be compelled to forfeit its charter of incorporation—a most dramatic penalty—if it was found to have committed serious, substantial, and continued acts beyond and abusive of authority contained in its state charter. Such acts are known under the Latin phrase *ultra vires*. The State's position was that by engaging in political activities—by being an arm of the Communist Party—and by not conforming truthfully to the purposes recited in their charter, the IWO had acted in *ultra vires* fashion.

The *Reply* argued that "the Superintendent cannot seriously urge that he has shown that the alleged *ultra vires* activities have 'continued to exist'"; that, in fact, was precisely what the State was in all seriousness saying. The length of the IWO response, which for the first time in the *Reply* went deeply into the legal arguments on the issue, indicated that they recognized the gravity of the matter.[37]

The Intervenors' attorneys, too, were unwilling to remain silent after reading the State's *Brief*; they also filed a *Reply Brief*.[38] Among other arguments, the *Reply* reminded the Judge that he had the power to "deal with any corporate problems of the IWO which have been mentioned in this proceeding" (a very cautious, almost comical way of expressing the matter) by ordering rehabilitation of the IWO in lieu of liquidation. While not admitting rehabilitation was necessary, this lesser of evils, the *Brief* argued, was certainly desirable.[39]

The State did not make any response to the *Reply Memorandum* of the IWO or the *Reply Brief* of the Intervenors; the matter was now in Judge Greenberg's hand. There was, however, yet another brief filed: an *Amicus Curiae Brief* signed by some 200 individuals. *Amicus curiae* comes from the Latin phrase meaning "friend of the court"; the proposition is that with the help of an intervening, ostensibly independent view, the court will perceive the matter at issue in a clearer light and thus reach the soundest determination. Here, as in many instances, the views expressed were partisan, essentially informing the Court that there were persons or organizations, external to the parties before the Court, that had an interest in its outcome.

Although Judge Greenberg acknowledged that the *Amicus Brief* had been received, he incorrectly stated that those signing the *Brief* were "said to be members of the IWO." While some may have been, the range of names was far broader, including clergymen from many faiths, people from the arts, and notable public figures and academics. Subscribers included actor Howard daSilva, black leader W. E. B. Du-Bois, labor leader Henry Bridges, authors Howard Fast and Dashiell Hammett, singer and activist Paul Robeson, and entertainer Earl Robinson. All introduced themselves as follows:

We, the undersigned, including persons from all walks of life—lawyers, doctors, teachers, trade union officials, business men, and workers—are deeply concerned with the basic issues in this case, involving as they do the assertion of power by a state official to liquidate a large and solvent fraternal insurance organization only because he does not approve of the political views or associations of its officers. . . . We believe that such efforts are an increasing menace to the democratic structure of American life.[40]

More was involved, the *Amicus Brief* argued, than the field of insurance or, in terms of the right of free association, merely association in fraternal groups; what was truly at stake was "the right to prescribe what shall be orthodox in politics . . . with whom Americans may insure themselves . . . or carry on other business affairs."[41]

The *Amicus Brief* itself was short. It did not attempt an in-depth issue analysis. Rather, it addressed the implications of the entire proceeding, arguing that fundamental civil rights and liberties were at stake.

The *Brief* pointed out that the IWO was "the only fraternal organization which invite[s] and accepts membership without regard for race, color, or creed"; how ironic, it observed, that "under the guise of protecting democracy, the Superintendent seeks to destroy this most democratic of all fraternal organizations."[42] Calling for the Court to resist the "hysteria" of the times exemplified in the take-the-money-and-run argument, the *Brief* concludes with the statement, "We believe that the success of this prosecution will go far towards destroying democracy . . . [and] we ask the Court not to sanction such a tragic step."[43]

Though not stated, this *Amicus Brief* constituted an effort apparently organized by the IWO to garner a broader base of support and to remind the Court that a large number of people were watching the case. In the copy of the *Amicus Brief* in the Williams office files, someone had gone through the names, checking some of the more famous signatures. Once again, the State made no response to this *Amicus Brief*.

On June 21, 1951, Judge Henry Clay Greenberg issued his long-awaited *Opinion*. Judge Greenberg took pride in writing his own opinions and in doing the essential research involved, though he had the aid of his secretary (law clerk) and other resources, including the notes he had taken during the trial, the *Briefs* of the parties citing the cases they felt were relevant to the legal issues, and certain court personnel whom he could call upon for research and writing assistance. Because of the length of the trial and the importance of the case, Greenberg took his time to spell out his views, findings, and decision; his printed *Opinion* ran 31 pages. The length alone immediately meant that he was not ruling in favor of the IWO *Motions to Strike and Dismiss* which had been held in abeyance since the matter first came before him; had he ruled that as a matter of law the State had no authority to seek liquidation, or that the Court lacked the power to rule in the case, the *Opinion* would have been a great deal shorter.[44]

The *Opinion* begins with a brief review of the charges brought by the State, with emphasis on the "hazard" issue and the alleged willful violation of its state charter—the *ultra vires* and the fraud arguments. He then recounted all which had, in the formal sense, come before him: 46 witnesses, 113 IWO members' affidavits, 350 documentary exhibits, and the enormous trial record that tied everything together, along with all of the *Briefs* that were submitted. He stated his recognition of the influence of the Red Scare times:

In the light of contemporary political conditions, the existence of any element relating to communism or the Communist Party tends to fill the atmosphere with emotionally charged feelings engendered by the controversy which now rages around this subject. It therefore places a special burden on the court to remove itself from the prejudice of the venue, to scorn the infection from the ill temper and to abjure the passion and political currents of the general controversy and to confine itself to an objective analysis of the factual and legal issues in the case before it.[45]

Judge Greenberg declared that he must and would remain neutral in this atmosphere, adding "this does not mean that the court should be so removed [as] to be unrealistic, nor so close [as] to be intimidated."

To demonstrate his dedication to the "widest margin of protection to the respondent [IWO] by the most scrupulous observance of due process," Greenberg stated that any effort by the State to impress the Court with the importance of the IWO listing as subversive "fell upon deaf ears." Finding that the listing process involved "the *ex parte* judgment of the [U.S.] attorney general," a method unthinkable and shocking to his conscience, the Judge declared that he refused to consider the subversive listing as having any bearing on the matter before him. He noted with approval the U.S. Supreme Court's listing case as reflecting principles which were at "the very concept of our democracy."[46] On the other hand, it was apparent that he was ready to make his own "subversive" evaluation—and that such an evaluation would be important in deciding the case—a position rejected by the IWO, who had argued throughout the trial the irrelevance of the organization's politics.

Judge Greenberg gave a brief history of the Order and a review of its membership and financial standing, concluding that "it is concededly solvent and in a sound financial condition at this time." By adding the phrase "at this time," Greenberg hinted at his final determination. He then undertook a brief recital of the State's accusations made in support of the demand for liquidation, concluding that "the evidence presented by the Superintendent [at the trial] overwhelmingly establishes the basic political nature, purposes and activities of the IWO." For page after page of his *Opinion,* Judge Greenberg evinced having accepted every major accusation concerning politics of the Order put forth by the State, including its origin: "The IWO was therefore founded, as is stated and restated proudly, as a revolutionary proletarian fraternal organization to serve as an instrument to further the class struggle and the Communist Party here and abroad."[47]

His *Opinion* fully accepted the "evil plot" charge: everything the Order did, including its insurance offerings, seemed to support the Communist Party in its political aims. Though recognizing that most of the damning material he cited came from its early years, he concluded that while the language was "more guarded" after 1935, the "program and the nature of activities appear to be the same," including "serving as a spawning and recruiting ground for members of the Communist Party."

The Judge made special note of the "flip-flop" made by the IWO once the U.S.S.R. entered the Second World War in 1941. At the very least, Greenberg concluded, the Order was "ideologically attuned" to Russia. Here he expressed disgust with the IWO "peace" position of 1940, noting that "at the time this article [in an IWO magazine] was written, what was left of England was standing with its back to the wall and single-handedly it was mustering its strength to thwart the devastating purpose of the Nazis." Using very graphic, caustic language, he asserted that once Russia had been attacked by Hitler, "The blood-soaked European battlefields no longer held any horror for the officials of the IWO."[48] With an air of evident patriotism, Judge Greenberg excoriated the Order for fostering

an uncritical admiration of the U.S.S.R. as the epitome of all that is good and true and as the Utopia to be striven for by the United States. In marked contrast is the attitude adopted toward the government officials and policies of this country. Any action, comment, or person deemed to be unfriendly to the U.S.S.R. is the subject of devastating criticism.[49]

Even those political activities he found commendable, such as the Scottsboro defense, campaigns for better working conditions, and social legislation, he considered to be "adopted and exploited by the Communist Party." Even the "good" was therefore "bad."[50]

He wrote that he believed that none of the ties between the Party and the IWO were "a result of coincidence," of both happening to have walked down the same ideological path. Rather, he pointed to the fact that from the time of incorporation (1930) onward, the leadership of the Order was dominated by members of the Party. Thus he found that "from 1935 to 1938, every national officer was identified as a member of the Communist Party," that "nine out of ten of the present [1951] national officers had been similarly identified, as well as sixteen of twenty-two members of the Order's executive committee." Greenberg failed to mention that the masses of membership were overwhelmingly non-Party members.[51]

With one sweeping paragraph, Judge Greenberg uncritically accepted the testimony of all the State's witnesses. All of this testimony he felt helped to fill in "the details of the operating ties between the IWO officers and executive committee on the one hand and the organization of the Communist Party on the other hand." No mention, and thus no evaluation, was made regarding the fact that all but one of the State's witnesses were paid professional informers; evidently he concluded this was irrelevant.[52]

Judge Greenberg found, with comparative ease, that the Communist Party exercised control over the IWO. Once more he summarily dismissed all of the evidence presented by the Order which demonstrated its involvement in what he characterized as "many worthy undertakings, undertakings which are harmless in concept and for the general welfare of the community," ranging from public services including its excellent record of fraternal benefits and aid to its policyholders to its work against racial discrimination and on behalf of civil liberties:

However, as to the main issues raised by the petitioner, namely, the basic political objectives and activities in line with Communist purposes and program and its ties to the Communist Party, the answers [of IWO officers] were evasive and unconvincing.[53]

He chastised the IWO officers for the use by all but Rockwell Kent of their Fifth Amendment rights, for refusing to "answer pertinent questions which would have assisted" him in determining the validity of the Superintendent's charges. Judge Greenberg charged that their use of constitutional privilege "was not made in good faith." He found them damned anyway, adding:

However, their own writings and speeches and activities in the past have so completely incriminated them that it is doubtful whether any of their testimony at this hearing would have added to such jeopardy as they might find themselves in at the present time.[54]

Here was a thinly veiled threat that, in these Red Scare times, these people might find themselves facing Smith Act charges because of what they had said and written. Furthermore, Judge Greenberg found untenable the position that, when officers had formed committees or acted as individuals in promoting political activities, these acts were severable from that of the Order as a whole.

Summing up a factual review of what he had seen, heard, and read, the Judge stated that the "testimony of the respondent, as a whole, failed to meet and refute the charges made by the Superintendent of Insurance." While acknowledging its insurance function, "much" of its fraternal, social, and charitable activities, as well as its support of civil rights and labor organizations, of which the latter, "while political in nature," were "commendable" and "proper," he nevertheless concluded:

this evidence does not overcome or even equal the evidence of the Superintendent of Insurance establishing the fact that the leadership and direction of the I.W.O. was Communist, and that the immediate objectives of the insurance and fraternalism were means toward developing a wide organization of workers which, under Communist guidance, could be developed from their political views into adherents of the Communist program.[55]

Judge Greenberg apparently had no difficulty making personal judgments as to what was politically "commendable" or "proper" and what was not.

He granted that while "many" of the IWO members "may not have been aware" of the objectives of the Order's leadership, that leadership still was what determined the issue for him. The political activities of these officers, he reasoned, were no "individual frolic" but a consistent, essential part of the corporate activities of the IWO.[56]

Judge Greenberg ended his factual review with this conclusion:

The facts which have been presented above make inescapable the conclusion that the I.W.O. has functioned as a political organization, attracting workers by providing insurance benefits and thereafter subjecting them to a process of political education along Communist lines, involving them in the militant political activity of the I.W.O. and of other kindred groups, including the Communist Party itself.[57]

Having completely accepted the State's evidence and thus reaching the same political conclusion, Judge Greenberg turned to the legal issues presented: Was the continuation of the IWO "hazardous" to policyholders, its creditors, and the public, and had the IWO violated state insurance and penal laws as well as the federal Smith Act?

As to the crucial "hazard" issue, the Court found favor with the State's position that "hazard" could be construed beyond that of financial to include "political hazard." He expressed the idea in this way:

Where the competitive or superseding objective is a political faith linked with a party whose leaders have been convicted [the *Dennis* case] of advocating the overthrow of the government by force and violence and is 'ideologically attuned' to a foreign power now engaged in controversy with this nation, the fortunes of insurance functions are indeed hazardous.[58]

The Judge supported this interpretation by noting that "the inclusion on the list, whether or not justified, is a direct result of the respondent's involvement in political activities and illustrates the inherent hazard of mixing politics and insurance."[59] The listing case victory for the IWO was apparently as Pyrrhic in this Court as elsewhere.

In further support for enlarging the "hazard" definition, Judge Greenberg embraced the take-the-money-and-run argument, noting the liquidity of the Order's assets (97 percent in cash and government bonds) and determining that:

If the time arrives when there is a conflict between the interests of this country and the world of Communism, it is not beyond the realm of reasonable probability that the funds of this Order will be expropriated.[60]

His position, he believed, was bolstered by the *Dennis* case convictions, just then affirmed by the U.S. Supreme Court. "An even greater danger now faces the IWO," he stated, "[because] its active participation in the program of the Communist Party" may result in a Smith Act prosecution, with a "calamitous" result to the policyholders, threatening a decline in membership and a "serious threat to its financial structure."[61] Thus, the earlier reference to the financial soundness of the Order was modified in his opinion by "at this time," by the dire events he foresaw.

Judge Greenberg concluded:

The question here involved is whether under the laws of the State of New York a political group may organize in the guise of a fraternal benefit society and carry on its political activities using the facade of its insurance functions. Subjecting an insurance function to a competing political objective, whether Republican, Democratic or Communistic in nature, creates a hazard to the insurance functions.[62]

Of course, the case was before him not because of just any politics, but politics that reflected Red Scare times.

Moving to a consideration of the question of State insurance law, Judge Greenberg's judgment was that the IWO willfully violated its state charter by exceeding or abusing its powers, through its abdication of control "in favor of the Communist Party." The IWO had, he stated, "in its very genesis . . . perpetrated a fraud upon the State," because while "ostensibly" a fraternal benefit society, actually "it was intended as and did in reality become a political front for a revolutionary group which was to follow a clearly prescribed political program." Thus he found a "fraud of unconscionable magnitude," which compelled him to come to the aid of the Superintendent of Insurance in dissolving the corporate existence of the IWO.[63] Although he found "clear evidence" that the IWO violated the federal Smith Act and penal statutes of the State of New York, in effect he left that for others to deal with.[64] He did not have to rule on these issues, since he had decided the matter on the basis of New York insurance and corporate law.

Toward the end of his *Opinion*, Judge Greenberg addressed the matter of his power to order rehabilitation of the IWO, a matter to which he had given "considerable thought." His determination was that:

After much consideration it [the Court] is forced to conclude that its [the IWO's] affiliation with the Communist Party . . . cannot be eradicated by the removal of some or all of the leaders who are Communist Party members nor by rehabilitation. The virus has spread too far and has polluted the entire corporate body. Mere excision of parts of that body would now be ineffectual. The only remedy lies in complete dissolution of that body.[65]

Anticipating a claim on appeal that the entire proceeding was an abridgement of freedom of speech, press, or assembly, he denied that these issues were involved. The Judge declared that, while the officers may express their minds, write as they please, and assemble as they wish:

They may not, however, by a claim of constitutional guaranty, commit the I.W.O. officially as they have done by their writings and speeches to a perversion of the charter privileges and to a political program dominated by foreign ideologies which have by the highest court in the land been declared to be inimical to the interests of the people of this country and to present a "clear and present danger." [A reference to the *Dennis* case.] The constitutional guaranty of freedom of speech, press and assembly was never intended as a license for illegality nor an invitation for fraud.[66]

Promising that the interests of the policyholders would be safe-guarded, Greenberg concluded that the Superintendent of Insurance was entitled to "an order of dissolution and liquidation of the IWO," but agreed to stay his order provided the IWO promptly appealed his decision. Notwithstanding any appeal, he ordered the IWO to turn over its "books, papers and documents which concern the affairs of the Order" to the Superintendent.[67]

Notes

1. *New York Times,* April 14, 1951.
2. Williams Office Files, Correspondence, Inter-Office Correspondence, April 19, 1951.
3. *New York Times,* April 11, 1951–April 23, 1951.
4. *New York Times,* April 11, 1951–April 23, 1951.
5. *IWO News Bulletin,* early May, 1951.
6. *IWO v. McGrath,* 341 U.S. 123, 71 S. Ct. 624, 95 L. Ed. 817 (1951).
7. Quoted in *New York Herald Tribune,* May 1, 1951.
8. *IWO v. McGrath.*
9. Ibid.
10. Williams Office Files, Clippings, Vol. I; also, Correspondence files, Williams to Karlin, May 2, 1951.
11. *IWO News Bulletin,* later in May 1951.
12. *New York Times,* dateline May 1, published May 2, 1951.
13. David Caute, *The Great Fear: The Anti-Communist Purge Under Truman and Eisenhower* (New York: Simon and Schuster, 1978), p. 170.
14. Quoted in Caute, *The Great Fear,* p. 168.
15. Quoted in Caute, *The Great Fear,* p. 280.
16. Supreme Court of the State of New York, County of New York, *Brief for the Petitioner,* June 7, 1951; Supreme Court of the State of New York, County of New York, *Brief for Respondent,* June 7, 1951; Supreme Court of the State of New York, County of New York, *Intervenors' Brief.* All references are to these Briefs.
17. Williams interview, July 25, 1988.
18. *Brief for the Petitioner,* p. 120.
19. Ibid., p. 127.
20. Ibid., p. 134.
21. Ibid., pp. 161–62.
22. Ibid., pp. 169–71.
23. *Brief for the Respondent,* p. 98.
24. Ibid., pp. 132–33.
25. Ibid., p. 134.
26. Ibid., p. 159.
27. Ibid., p. 160.
28. Ibid., pp. 161–65.
29. Arthur Kinoy, *Rights on Trial: The Odyssey of a People's Lawyer* (Cambridge, MA: Harvard University Press, 1983), p. 95.
30. *Brief for the Petitioner,* pp. 140–55.
31. *Intervenors' Brief.*

32. Ibid., p. 3.

33. *Reply Memorandum for Respondents,* June 20, 1951.

34. Ibid., p. 1.

35. Ibid., p. 7.

36. Ibid., p. 9.

37. Ibid., pp. 10–27.

38. *Intervenors' Brief,* p. 2.

39. Ibid., pp. 8–14.

40. Supreme Court of the State of New York, County of New York, *Petition for Leave to File Brief Amicus Curiae, and Brief Amicus Curiae,* p. 1.

41. Ibid., p. 2.

42. Ibid., pp. 3–6.

43. Ibid., p. 6.

44. *Opinion,* Justice Greenberg in *Application of Bohlinger,* 199 Misc. 941, 106 N.Y.S.2d 953 (N.Y. Sup. June 25, 1951).

45. Ibid., p. 958.

46. Ibid., p. 959.

47. Ibid., p. 961.

48. Ibid., p. 968.

49. Ibid., p. 967.

50. Ibid., p. 968.

51. Ibid., pp. 969–72.

52. Ibid., p. 972.

53. Ibid., p. 973.

54. Ibid., pp. 973–74.

55. Ibid., p. 974.

56. Ibid., p. 975.

57. Ibid., p. 976.

58. Ibid., p. 979.

59. Ibid., p. 979.

60. Ibid., p. 979.

61. Ibid., p. 981.

62. Ibid., p. 981.

63. Ibid., pp. 982–84.

64. Ibid., p. 984.

65. Ibid., p. 986.

66. Ibid., p. 987.

67. Ibid., p. 987.

Chapter XVI
On Appeal

Given what was at stake and the prodigious labors involved, it takes little imagination to appreciate the impact of Judge Greenberg's decision on both sides. The State had completely triumphed: the Judge had accepted and adopted every major factual conclusion it had put forth; similarly, the Court had favored the State on every major legal issue generated by the facts of the case.

It was a devastating blow to the IWO. The lawyers for the Order had been encouraged by Judge Greenberg's reputation for being a "good law" judge—that is, one who was bright, unemotional, and unprejudiced, able to rule with fairness on legal issues where considerable partisanship was involved, knowledgeable on the applicable law, capable of responding to the larger implications of the issues raised, and unintimidated by the fact that government was on one side of the case. Despite all their efforts to get Judge Greenberg to focus on the legal issues, and in that focus to take a narrow view of the powers of the State which reflected the plain intent of the insurance and corporate laws of New York, they failed. Judge Greenberg's *Opinion* bounded over every legal obstacle to the State's power to destroy the Order, placed there by the *Briefs* of the IWO.

Removed from the passions of the times, the interpretations Judge Greenberg made of relevant statutes and case law appear unfounded, and reflect a willingness—if not eagerness—to use existing law for the "higher" purpose of liquidating the perceived political threat posed by the continued operation of the IWO.

The Judge refused to use the Court's power to change the leadership, and presumably the nature, of the Order by a process of "rehabilitation." A death sentence and nothing less was his judgment, unprecedented in American legal history for a financially solvent fraternal benefit insurance company.

The general consensus of opinions reached by attorneys on both

THE PEOPLE'S CASE

The Story of the IWO

by Albert E. Kahn

Figure 11. Pamphlet issued by the Policyholders Protective Committee in 1951 (22 pages). Albert Kahn was president of a section of the IWO.

sides reflects the belief that Judge Greenberg's decision was a product of the times. The IWO lawyers had hoped he could rise above the intense Red Scare pressures; this was not to be. How Judge Greenberg came to feel about his decision in the years that followed cannot be clearly ascertained, but that the case remained prominently in his mind is clear—he would characterize it, in retrospect, as his "toughest decision" and his "most difficult case." In 1961, ten years after his decision and four years before his death, he asked Williams's office to send him a copy of the record in the case. Henry responded by sending him materials and commenting, "Looking at this old record reminds me of many interesting and instructive years in your Court."[1]

Judge Greenberg's decision set many wheels in motion. The IWO lawyers had to prepare their appeal papers and briefs; the State, knowing there would be an appeal to the Appellate Division, the intermediate court between the trial level and the highest State court, began its preparations. Williams's office circulated the *Opinion* to all the states where the IWO operated as well as to other interested governmental and private parties. Although a stay in the liquidation proceedings pending appeal was part of Judge Greenberg's decision, control of the Order by the State's Department of Insurance was in fact tightened. Preliminary work began on seeking a company to take over the insurance business of the IWO.

Meanwhile, within the leadership of the Order, the Greenberg decision led to a number of moves. One was to seek the involvement and advice of Vito Marcantonio, U.S. Congressman and IWO Vice-President. Marcantonio's name had come up on a number of occasions at the trial, but neither side had called him as a witness; his IWO involvement consisted essentially of holding an honorary post and appearing and speaking from time to time at National Conventions. A meeting was arranged at his office, attended by all of the officers, Jerry Trauber as secretary of the Policyholders' Committee, and at least one of the IWO lawyers. Prior to the meeting, materials had been sent to Marcantonio so that he would be informed about what had taken place at the trial; apparently he also was shown the trial record and the Greenberg *Opinion*.

According to Trauber's description of the meeting, Marcantonio was furious with what he had read, and told the group in the plainest language that "If we manage to save this organization, what Judge Greenberg is trying to do is nothing compared to what I am going to do to you." Marcantonio, Trauber explained, was amazed by what he had read and he attacked the Order's leadership for having allowed itself to mix the IWO with the Communist Party. Marcantonio's criticism was in a sense Machiavellian—criticizing the leadership of the IWO for not being smarter and more skillful in concealing their relationship. "And," Trauber added, "he was just the kind of a guy who would do that— appear at a convention of the IWO and wipe the floor with everybody." Marcantonio also attacked the Party for having laid itself open to what had transpired. Thereafter, Trauber reported, Marcantonio and the others calmed down enough to talk about strategy for the appeal.[2]

Another IWO officer who was astounded and reacted strongly to the Greenberg opinion was the Order's president, Rockwell Kent. Kent had worked diligently with the other officers in promoting the IWO cause in the face of the attack upon it, using to the limit his name recognition and personal and professional contacts. In addition to his testimony as a witness, he was kept abreast of the case developments, but a reading of his correspondence with IWO officers suggests that he was only shown the briefs of the defense—nothing that the Williams team had produced. Whether this was deliberate cannot be stated, but his reaction to reading the Greenberg opinion reveals his feeling of betrayal.[3]

Writing to Samson Milgrom on July 18, 1951, Kent stated that he had carefully studied the Greenberg opinion, noted that he had never read Williams's work, and went on to excoriate the Order's leadership for their deep involvement with the Communist Party, concluding that

With the aims and character so established in the mind of the judge, and with the Supreme Court's support of the judgment against the Communist leaders and of the Smith Act [the *Dennis* case], I am forced to conclude that Greenberg's verdict was correct. . . . the omission of the clearly expressed political purpose of the Order from the constitution on which its license was obtained seems to me to have been an act of such deliberate omission, aimed virtually at fraud, that good ground was furnished for the court to sustain the Insurance Department in its action. Consequently, and regardless of the legal aspects of the case, I cannot condemn the judgment.

He went on to say that Greenberg's decision was "inevitable" given the times, concluding:

Deeply as I believe in the Order as, to my knowledge, it has [in later years] functioned, I am yet resentful of the now apparent fact that it has had—and for all I know still has—political ties of which I had not been aware and of which, certainly, a large number of our members have been kept in ignorance. These members deserve to have been full informed. Now that I am informed and—perhaps more to the point—that I have the Judge's opinion before me, I would be unwilling to make any attempt to enlist liberal support for us. . . .
In recapitulation, I would say that however important a role the Order's revolutionary principles and affiliations played in the establishment of the Order and throughout the earlier Thirties, it had come to have a life of its own and to truly belong to its one-time 180,000 members. I think it was a tragic

mistake that the facts were not at that time fully aired and discussed and a genuine political severance determined upon.[4]

Notwithstanding this threat to cease his efforts on behalf of the IWO, over the months and years that followed, Kent fully and openly supported the IWO in its continued court efforts. He did, however, confidentially advise "that we ought at this time [December, 1951] repudiate those statements [of relationship and support for the Communist Party] as being not only unacceptable to the Order today but as having been completely out of order at the time that they were made."[5]

No refutation or disavowal took place. From a legal standpoint, it would have had no positive impact; quite the contrary, it could have been used as an admission of guilt, or at least muddied the legal waters for the IWO.

To Milgrom, Kent avowed, "I would not have joined an organization that was controlled by another organization, [the Communist Party] of which I was not a member," adding:

If I believed that this control existed today, I would resign from the Order. That control does not exist, for the very simple reason that, all past assertions to the contrary, it may not exist. But, as I have said, those past unhappy claims are of record. I hold that the sooner we disavow them—not because we have had a change of heart or because they should never have been tolerated—the better it will be for us, both internally and in the eyes of our friends and enemies.[6]

Kent never went public with his views, nor did he reveal his feelings in his autobiography, *It's Me, O Lord*, published in 1955. Was Kent simply a figurehead who had naively looked the other way as to who his fellow officers were and how the Party line had dominated IWO politics and programs? Part of this puzzle may be explained by his deep personal belief in the programs and policies fostered by the IWO, and a consequent unwillingness to associate the close connection of its leadership and programs with the Communist Party.

A series of unusual involvements and events also took place. Apparently independent of IWO efforts, the prestigious American Jewish Committee organization and the Anti-Defamation League of B'nai B'rith took an interest in the case. They obtained copies of the *Briefs*, and of Judge Greenberg's *Opinion*; two of their attorneys were authorized to review this material. As a result of their review, a Joint Memorandum was written, addressed to all major officers and divisions of these two organizations. This six-page document included a careful review summarizing the allegations of the Superintendent of Insurance and his attorneys, the factual and legal issues the State had relied on, and the responses of the IWO. In the memorandum, issued exactly one month after Judge Greenberg's decision and after examination of the entire matter, the attorneys came to the following, cautiously expressed conclusion:

On the law: Critics point out that the I.W.O. is being dissolved because it is deemed to be a political "hazard" to its policyholders, creditors, and to the general public. Yet, the dissolution is being ordered under a statute which, it is recognized on both sides, was never intended to be used in this manner.

Neither administrative agencies nor the courts have ever before sanctioned such a use, and Justice Greenberg's decision runs counter to all previously decided insurance law. [The conclusion is] that although there may be reasonable objection to the policies of the I.W.O., nevertheless, to dissolve it is also to destroy America's most cherished doctrines of due process of law, for the very essence of law is that it be applied equally to all.[7]

A meeting followed with a Vice-President of the American Jewish Committee, Benjamin Hertzberg, IWO lawyers, and some IWO officers, including Peter Shipka and Rubin Saltzman, in attendance. The meeting was most likely arranged by Nathan Witt, a prominent left-wing lawyer whom the IWO and its lawyers had apparently consulted from time to time on strategy matters.

At this meeting Hertzberg, who was also an attorney, offered to take on representation of the IWO in the appeal process, on the condition that the Order would throw itself on the mercy of the Court, with all officers tendering their resignations. An IWO National Convention, under Court or Insurance Department supervision, would take place. At the Convention, an all-new slate of leaders would be chosen, all of whom would execute a non-Communist affidavit. The objective was to remove or substantially reduce Communist influence in the IWO. The Order would continue to operate under this new leadership and under continued state supervision until the following National Convention. This entire procedure was advanced as a method of resolving the litigation and keeping the IWO alive.

Trauber described the proposal as a "complete surprise" to "those of us on the other side of the desk." Reflecting on the meeting, Trauber recalls that both he and Shipka came away with the impression that what Hertzberg was putting forth was not "something he had pulled out of thin air, but [sometime] he had discussed . . . with some other people." By "other people" Trauber probably meant State Insurance Department officials; Hertzberg apparently had reason to believe it could be accomplished. "I'm convinced," explained Trauber, "that it was a well thought out plan of his which might have been acceptable, [to the Insurance officials] or at least that he wasn't told 'keep out of this—there is no chance whatsoever.'" Trauber stated that Hertzberg was not just meeting to give advice, and that he would not have met at all if there was not a deal in the making. Hertzberg repeated that acceptance of his plan was the only basis upon which he would take on representation of the IWO.

There is a ring of plausibility to the scene as related by Trauber. While the State had won on all counts with Greenberg's *Opinion*, there was always the chance of reversal by an appellate court. These appeals would cost both sides a great deal of time and money; the IWO had the money, and no choice but to invest the time. Furthermore, there was the political factor: letters and protests continued to pour into the Governor's and Superintendent's offices. Destroying the organization's insurance program—even with reinsurance through another company—would cause a great deal of hardship to many thousands of innocent people. The State would also attain its political objective of destroying the Communist affiliation. Asked about reaction to the Hertzberg plan, Trauber stated that while "everyone was stunned . . . Saltzman began to bluster. He didn't have any arguments. He couldn't express himself, even."

While the IWO leaders said they would take the matter under advisement, they bristled at the idea. Trauber explained that Saltzman was "the domineering character in the leadership group," and that he could not "conceive of the organization without him. . . . It was his baby." Furthermore, in Communist Party circles, anyone who signed this kind of non-Communist affidavit was considered to have committed "an act of treason against the working class." The CIO had, by use of these affidavits, been cleaned out of Communists in positions of union power; here the IWO would be cleaned out of most of its chiefs.

The Order's leadership refused to accept the proposal. Led by Rubin Saltzman, they could not imagine an IWO without them. They preferred to rely on and risk the appeal process.[8]

Four days before Judge Greenberg's decision, the newspapers were filled with news of the indictment of and issuance of arrest warrants for twenty-one members of the Communist Party; this was the beginning of the so-called "second string" prosecutions throughout the country of Party members under the Smith Act, which followed on the heels of the U.S. Supreme Court decision in the *Dennis* case earlier that month. Headlines on the IWO articles convey the essence of the reporting:

COURT DISSOLVED IWO AS RED-LED HAZARD.
—*World Telegraph and Sun*, June 25, 1951

IWO ORDERED CLOSED BY COURT AS RED FRONT.
Ruling Declares Fraternal Insurance Organization Serves Communist Party.
—*Herald Tribune*, June 26, 1951

IWO DISSOLUTION ORDERED BY COURT.
Justice Greenberg Rules Group with $6,000,000 Assets is Communist Dominated.

—*New York Times,* June 26, 1951

The only newspaper that printed an IWO reaction to the decision was the liberal, left-wing *Daily Compass,* which quoted an unidentified IWO spokesman who compared this battle to the one successfully waged in the listing case. According to the spokesman, the Order was "confident of similar indication in the present fight, for never before in the history of the Insurance Law of this state . . . has an attempt been made to liquidate a fraternal insurance organization which is in no financial jeopardy whatever—and soley upon the basis of political considerations."[9] The Executive Committee of the IWO met two days after Judge Greenberg's decision was announced. Attorneys Donner and Kinoy were present to report on the Court's decision. The lawyers had already been back before Judge Greenberg and obtained a ruling from him extending the stay of execution of the liquidation order through all appeals, including, possibly, to the U.S. Supreme Court. Donner reportedly stated that the Judge took the position of giving the IWO every possible opportunity to continue to litigate in court, and not to change the status quo.

In the weeks following Greenberg's decision, chaotic activities took place on both sides. The lawyers had to work out means to run the IWO during the appeal process, and prepare an agreed-to record of the trial proceeding. Because Judge Greenberg had conditioned his stay of an order of liquidation on promptness in perfecting the appeal process, both sets of attorneys went quickly to work.

The Department of Insurance sent letters to all lodge officers, containing orders on handling dues collection and remittance. It also sent letters to each individual policyholder, in addition to those sent by the Order. Mail poured into the State Insurance Department from members, some protesting the decision, some pathetically asking what was going to happen to their insurance benefits on which they were so dependent. All the latter were answered by the Insurance Department, assuring those to whom benefits were owed that they would be paid. To those who had written asking whether they should remain members, the Department responded that the decision was up to the member. The Department did not recommend permitting insurance to lapse "while any appeal is in progress," and cautioned that "The foregoing advises are not to be construed as a recommendation that you remain active or that you cease to be active in the fraternal affairs of the Order."[10]

Just before midnight on July 19, 1951, someone attempted to break in to the IWO headquarters at 80 Fifth Avenue in New York. A night watchman apparently frightened off the intruder. Just who had tried to gain entry was never discovered; the doors where the break-in had been attempted were repaired and overall security increased. While the issue remains a matter of speculation, it is known that the FBI did perform unauthorized break-ins at the IWO headquarters on at least three other occasions: July 1944, March 1945, and August 1953. These have been documented by biographers of J. Edgar Hoover.[11] Additionally, beginning in 1945, the FBI (with the U.S. Attorney General's approval) wiretapped the IWO headquarters' phones.[12]

On July 27, 1951, proper notice of appeal was filed by the IWO and by the Intervenors' Committee. The attorneys had already been diligently going over the trial transcript, making corrections and working out stipulations about agreed changes. By August, 1951, the IWO had spent in excess of $100,000 in legal fees and trial-associated costs. Additionally, the Order had to pay for all expenses connected with the Department of Insurance's involvement, including the salaries of state employees working on the IWO premises. In all, over $175,000 had been spent by the Order in fighting the liquidation attempt, a significant sum by 1951 standards. The amount spent by the State was probably less, but not by much.[13]

Overall, the Order was facing increasingly hard times: unable to recruit new members, having to explain the complexities of the legal action it had thus far lost in court (and to place the best face on it), tightly controlled by the State and now under attack by a number of state departments of insurance throughout the country. Members were leaving or failing to pay dues. Without new members to replace those dying or quitting, lodges were closing down from attrition. Time was on the side of the state, and the legal appeal process takes time.

On any appeal of this nature, only *legal* issues are in question. Factual matters, which have been heard and determined at the trial, are not retried on appeal. The distinction between a factual matter and a legal one can best be understood through an example. For instance, whether A killed B is a question of fact to be determined at the trial level. By contrast, the determination of whether A's act amounts to murder as defined by the laws of that particular state, or whether evidence was properly or improperly admitted, are questions of law which may be appealed, testing, in effect, whether the trial judge properly applied the law in instructing the jury and in ruling on evidentiary questions. Thus, the argument on appeal would consist solely of whether the *law* had been correctly applied by the judge based upon the factual evidence generated at the trial.

Each side has two opportunities to convince the appellate level court: written briefs tied to a transcript of the trial record and oral argument before the appeals judges. The latter step is not mandatory, and no new evidence or testimony of witnesses is allowed; lawyers from both sides present arguments on the legal issues and the judges (always more than one and usually three to five on the intermediate appeals level) have an opportunity to question counsel concerning the case and the specific legal issues. On appeal, the court can reverse the trial court's decision and dismiss the action, reverse the decision and remand the matter back to the trial court for retrial, affirm the decision entirely, or affirm but modify it. These are basic powers; there are variations on each that bespeak of a broad spectrum of choices.

The process of composing an appellate brief for such a complex trial is a daunting task. The writer must give the reviewing court a real sense of what was involved in a complicated trial that went on for months and cogently identify and argue the relevant legal issues. This task, of course, was compounded for the IWO by the added burden of arguing from the losing side and addressing the political implications of the case against the background of a war in progress. In many ways, the task appeared not only difficult but monumental. Weissman, Donner, and Kinoy, however, succeeded in producing a 205-page *Brief* that attempted to meet all of those challenges. They cited in the "Table of Cases" over 150 cases to support their position on the legal issues, and included three pages of relevant "Statutes and Authorities." Raphael H. Weissman was designated to argue the case orally before the five Judge Appellate Division panel.[14]

While all the major issues covered previously by the IWO in the *Briefs* that had been submitted to Judge Greenberg were dealt with in the new *Brief*, it was no "rehash" or "cut and paste" job. Each issue was freshly and thoroughly examined, with emphasis on where Judge Greenberg had incorrectly applied governing law, and where he had erred with respect to admission of the State's evidence.

In reviewing the factual matters, the IWO lawyers had to deal with the charges of Communist influence and control developed by the State's witnesses. Unlike the instance when they had submitted their initial *Brief* to Judge Greenberg, they now knew that the State would certainly come down hard on the evidence they had used and which the Judge had accepted. Thus they stated, "We will demonstrate that much of the evidence of paid informers and professional witnesses was admitted [into evidence] in violation of the most elementary rules prohibiting hearsay evidence." On the matter of facts relating to "hazard," they stated:

Over 95 percent of the oral testimony of the Superintendent's witnesses related to alleged occurrence in [the period] 1930 to 1934. Thus the Superintendent did not attempt to prove that the IWO is presently engaged in any allegedly "hazardous" activity . . . but reveals the complete failure of the Superintendent to prove any *present* hazard sufficient to justify liquidation, dissolution and confiscation of millions of dollars of insurance property.[15] [Emphasis in original]

If the *Brief* submitted to Judge Greenberg at the end of the trial by the IWO attorneys could be characterized as rather aloof in that it dealt with the legal issues in a formal manner (probably led to this approach by the Judge's directions at the close of the trial), the language of this *Brief* was, by contrast, hard-hitting. For instance, the *Brief* attacked Judge Greenberg's political evaluation of the IWO:

The lower court did not consider that it was "patriotic" to oppose entry into the last war in its early stages and support our government in its latter stages. The lower court may not have believed that it is "patriotic" to support individuals indicted under a peace-time sedition statute, the Smith Act . . .

When any official, appointed or elected, seeks to arrogate to himself the responsibility of deciding for Americans and their organizations just what constitutes "educational" activity and what is "patriotic", then we have indeed passed over into the shadow of dictatorship.[16]

The IWO, the *Brief* continued, "cannot be liquidated without overturning the most settled principles of the statutory and constitutional law." The *Brief* ended with this plea:

. . . to all of these [IWO member] families liquidation means the destruction of a fraternal life rich with the warmth of cultural and social values. The most elementary precepts of justice and decency cry out against this imposition of indiscriminate mass punishment. 160,000 families await the judgment of this Court, confident that the solid foundation of our statutory and constitutional law will stand unshaken by the passions of the moment.[17]

Because the Williams team was defending against the appeal by the IWO, they had the advantage of having the IWO *Brief* in hand while they composed their final draft for the appeals court. The style and thrust of the State's 222-page *Brief* differed significantly from that of the IWO.[18] While the Order's attorneys had faced an uphill battle, pleading as it had for a conservative approach in the application of the law in the midst of a Red Scare storm, the State needed only to defend its total trial victory. The Red Scare was precisely the atmosphere it sought to exploit.

The State's *Brief* cited fewer cases and statutes than had the IWO *Brief,* instead emphasizing the Communist issue, including an entire table of "Exhibits" consisting almost exclusively of Communist Party documents, articles from Party publications, and books on Communist Party doctrine by Lenin and Stalin. (No such table appeared in the IWO *Brief*.) A four-page "Index of Individuals" enabled the reader to track the appearance in the text of the *Brief* of everyone from Earl Browder to Adolph Hitler and Joseph Stalin to Thadeus Zygmont. Naturally, most of the references were to witnesses for the State, and those whom the State's witnesses had identified as Communists.

The *Brief* gave an in depth review of the factual basis of the Order's Communist involvement on both theoretical and practical (control) levels. Every ounce of juice was squeezed from the Party writings, the early 1930s IWO publications, and the testimony of the State's witnesses in order to support the proposition that the IWO was dominated by the Communist Party. Over one-half of the *Brief* was dedicated to this thesis; less than half dealt with the legal issues raised by the case. Most of the latter was given over to answering or contesting what the IWO *Brief* had argued.

The Intervenors also filed a 44-page *Brief* in an attempt to put a "human face" on the proceeding. The *Brief* reviewed, in some detail, the wide variety of fraternal activities promoted by the Order. It stressed the importance of the IWO insurance benefits to the financial security of its members, and pointed out that even the Superintendent of Insurance, prior to the liquidation attempt, had admitted that the Order "in all its functions and operations, has met every test of law. It is fully solvent, has discharged and can discharge all its obligations, although many of its risks would not be accepted by any other insurance company."[19]

Using examples drawn from English and American history, the Intervenors' *Brief* argued that administrative tyranny must be prevented from destroying the IWO. These high-flown sentiments, often tinged with sarcasm, were balanced by an astute political move. The Intervenors' Committee retained the services of a former New York Supreme Court judge, Philip J. McCook, to argue the case for them before the Appellate Division; he is identified in the *Brief* as "of Counsel," and the statement is made, "To be [orally] argued by Philip J. McCook." Just as the Order had sought the services of John W. Davis when the matter had first arisen, once again the reach was for an "establishment" lawyer whose credentials were known and respected. Judge McCook had retired from the bench in 1943 at age 70, and returned to the practice of law; he was 79 years old when he undertook this representation.

One week after the State's *Brief* was filed, a *Reply Brief* was composed, printed, and delivered by the IWO lawyers. The *Reply Brief* was only eight pages long and presented two essential points: that, lacking a sound legal basis for seeking liquidation of the IWO, the State had depended on Red Scare tactics, and that even the recently decided *Dennis* case (which found top Communists guilty of violating the Smith Act) would not have encompassed the activities of the IWO.[20]

Yet another voice was heard. The New York City Chapter of the National Lawyers Guild, itself under the pall of "subversive," with the permission of the Court, filed a nine-page *Amicus Curiae* brief.[21] The organization characterized itself, in relation to the IWO trial, as a bar association, "devoted to the maintaining and securing of basic constitutional rights." It charged that the Superintendent's position "is without precedent in statutory or case law in both this and other states" and, while "nominally one involving the Insurance Law [of the State], it encroaches upon territory covered by the Bill of Rights, [because] the corporate existence of the International Workers Order is at stake as a result of the exercise of the rights of freedom of speech and free press by itself, its members and officers."[22]

Just what impact, positive or negative, the National Lawyers Guild *Amicus Brief* had on the appeal is subject to speculation; given the temper of the times and the "subversive" label already attached to the organization, the fact that it filed the only *Amicus* brief may not have been a politically astute move. The intervention, in theory, did not require permission or consent by the IWO, but the question remains: was it a wise move, which would truly promote the Order's cause? *Amicus* briefs from unions and other organizations such as the American Jewish Congress or the American Civil Liberties Union would probably have had a more positive impact.

Paul Williams described the scene on June 4, 1952 when the Appellate Division heard oral arguments on the case. The courtroom "was crowded. . . . All the galleries and the side seats were packed with IWO people." It is highly unusual for spectators to attend appellate proceedings in any significant number; the IWO attempted to deliver a message about the importance of the case by this display.

Williams felt that retaining Philip McCook, a former Supreme Court Judge and a highly respected member of the New York bar, gave the IWO side the "best chance they had," though he felt that McCook ultimately did not argue the case well.[23]

Paul Novick, Editor of the *Freiheit,* reported on the proceeding. In an article entitled "How Crazy Can They Get? Thoughts and Reflections About the Trial Against the Order," Novick described his attendance at the oral arguments before the appeals court. Novick believed that Williams, an otherwise quite decent man, had been, like many others, infected with the Red Scare hysteria which caused him to make "crazy" statements about the IWO, the "take the money and run" argument, and the Communist Party. Describing Williams as "a victim" of the times, Novick asked, "Did not Mr. Williams hear the walls laughing at his words?" Novick himself, however, was engaged in self-delusion about Williams, what the "walls" might be doing, and whether Williams indeed had "exposed himself to public ridicule" by these arguments. The five Judges of the Court were to point their ridicule elsewhere.[24]

Each of the attorneys—Williams, Weissman (for the IWO), and McCook (for the Intervenors)—made his oral presentation before the five Justices of this appeals court; Judge John Van Voorhis wrote the opinion dated July 1, 1952, in which the other four concurred; there were no dissents.

If Cold War-Red Scare themes were evident in Judge Greenberg's decision, the opinion by the Appellate Division even more blatantly pursued these themes, from first to last. Finding no reason to discuss the evidence in depth, the decision simply stated:

The record amply sustains the finding that IWO is operated as an arm of the Communist Party and the USSR. . . . The Superintendent of Insurance has been upheld by Special Term, (Judge Greenberg) and is upheld in this court by reason of the primary loyalty of the officers and directors of IWO to the USSR, with the consequence that at any crisis which may occur wherein the interests of the USSR, as its government conceives them, conflict with those of the policyholders of IWO or of the United States of America or of the State of New York, the interests of the USSR will be first served.[25]

It fully endorsed the expansion of the "hazard" argument, stating that "moral risk enters into what constitutes financial hazard." To this Court, "the conduct of the organization demonstrates that its management is so deeply involved in Soviet Russian Communism that it makes little difference who are the particular officers or directors at any given moment; . . . to be an officer or director, one must be a Communist." While admitting "There is nothing which indicates, to be sure, that the officials would steal funds of the organization for their personal advantage . . . they would not hesitate to do so for the Party under orders."[26] Given the international and domestic scene, the Court apparently believed the risk was there.

The Court went on to assert that the IWO had exceeded its corporate powers (the *ultra vires* argument) by acting "primarily for the Soviet Communist state."[27] If Judge Greenberg's decision saw too much "pink," these Justices saw nothing but "deep Red."

Paul Williams has taken credit for the "take the money and run" argument. While Judge Greenberg had, to the astonishment and chagrin of the IWO attorneys, accepted and recited the idea, the appeals court not only heavily relied on it, but even elaborated by expounding on the "moral risk" aspect. The Court expressed concern that IWO officers would not be bound by "bourgeois morality," stating:

If a domestic insurance society is operated by men who act under the philosophy that their identity is subordinated to and merged in a foreign state, the risk must be appraised in the light of the morality of the state in which they consider themselves to be merged.[28]

This Court, operating from the perspective of a preconceived notion about the "immorality" of the Soviet State and what Communists in general believed in and behaved like, was prepared to find the existence of a "hazard" as palpable as financial distress, irregularity, or plain dishonesty in the bare fact that Communists were involved in running the IWO.

The decision, confirming Judge Greenberg, concluded by stating that while there may not have been sufficient evidence of Smith Act violations by "particular individuals," the State had succeeded in showing that the Order's primary purpose was to further "the overthrow of our Government by violence." The Order not only lost on this appeal, but had to pay the State's out-of-pocket costs, mostly printing fees, totaling over $1,400.

In its news release of July 3, 1952, in reaction to its second defeat in court, the Executive Committee of the Order expressed its shock over the decision and indicated that immediate steps were being taken to appeal the case to the highest court in the state, the New York State Court of Appeals. A plea was issued for members of lodges "to stand by their organization in this critical period," promising "vindication of our Order and a reversal of what we consider an outrageous and unjust decision."[29] Another round of regional meetings, trips by officers, and other activities to bolster support were undertaken.

In a confidential memorandum to IWO officers dated July 8, 1952, IWO attorney Arthur Kinoy delivered his thoughts and analysis of the decision. The Court, he began, "in a conscious manner brushed aside all previous existing law in its efforts to uphold a political result." Characterizing this as a "civil liberties case," Kinoy accused the Court of making "no effort to reconcile its political conclusion with existing theories of law." Pointing out that even in the *Dennis* case such reconciliation had been attempted, here the Court had not even made the effort. "The Appellate Division" Kinoy wrote, "merely disregards and brushes aside the established law in order to sustain the end sought." To Kinoy, this technique came "perilously close to the boundary between democratic forms of law and government and the abandonment of democratic forms which characterizes fascism." "This," he added, "is

why this decision is so deeply significant to the American people."[30]
The question remained whether the IWO lawyers could convince any
further appeals court that such issues were indeed involved.

In his memorandum, Kinoy also pointed out two new aspects of the
Appellate Division's opinion. The first was that the insurance offered
by the IWO was "no good in any event," making liquidation not so
harsh a remedy. He noted that Justice Van Voohis admitted that the
type of insurance offered by the Order was not available through "the
great majority of insurance companies." This view, Kinoy felt, "should
be one of the central handles for attacking the opinion," since it invaded property and business rights and reflected the views of commercial insurance companies.

The other new aspect Kinoy raised was that the decision characterized the IWO as a "foreign" or "alien" insurance company because of its
ties to Russia through its Communist leadership. If this was true, then
the ability to liquidate the Order under insurance laws pertaining to
such "foreign" or "alien" as opposed to "domestic" insurers, would be
more easily justified. Kinoy characterized this approach as a "novel and
dangerous distortion of the insurance law," which threatened the many
fraternal benefit insurance companies with ethnic ties or sympathies
with various foreign countries. Such an approach by the Court, he felt,
reflected an "anti-foreign-born animus reflective of the most anti-
liberal thinking in the country." The existence of a strong anti-foreseen
movement was apparent in news stories of the day, reporting that
aliens were being deported from the United States on a substantial
scale.

Under both English and American law, the losing party in a trial has
the right to one initial appeal; any further appeal is a matter of privilege, not of right. Since the IWO lost in its appeal to the Appellate
Division, its only recourse under New York law was the possibility that
the Court, at its own discretion, would reopen its decision on a motion
for rehearing (which is rarely granted) or allow an appeal to the highest
court in the state, the New York Court of Appeals.

The attorney who had shouldered the burden of the IWO case
throughout the trial and in the first appeal, Raphael H. Weissman,
stepped down. The IWO brought in a new lawyer, prominent New
York attorney Osmond K. Fraenkel, to handle the petition for rehearing or, in the alternative, for permission to appeal their case further.
Fraenkel, aged sixty-four, specialized in civil rights cases and was a
partner in the well-known firm of Hays, St. John, Abramson and
Heilbron. Donner and Kinoy remained as backup for Fraenkel.

The reason for this shift in representation by the IWO remains
unclear. It is certain, from interviews with others involved in the case,

that there was no sense of dissatisfaction with Weissman's work; IWO personnel were in fact pleased with the work of all their lawyers. A plausible speculation on the matter appears to be that the Order wanted a fresh look and new approach, which Fraenkel offered along with his personal talents and the name of a prestigious firm. It also seemed to signal that the next appeal would focus more directly on constitutional issues. With Fraenkel in the lead, proper *Notice of Request* and *Motion to Reargue* the case before the Appellate Division or in the alternative to grant leave to appeal to the Court of Appeals were filed on September 8, 1952.[31]

Arguing that the legal theories underlying the Appellate Division's decision raised problems of importance and were "novel and of first impression" (meaning they had never been ruled on before), the *Motion* did indeed raise constitutional and First Amendment issues related to property interests (the insurance policies) and civil rights under the United States Constitution and the Constitution of New York State.

Fraenkel further pointed out that there were ten different state proceedings pending against the IWO, all of which looked to the New York determination on the issues. He also emphasized the importance of the new propositions raised by the Appellate Division in its decision: the "moral hazard" concept, and the claim that the IWO was "a domestic society in form but in reality a foreign society." The Order had not had the opportunity to respond to the latter since these ideas were first raised in the Court's decision itself. On these bases, the request was for re-argument of the appeal before the Appellate Division, or for grant of leave to appeal to the Court of Appeals. The *Motion For Leave to Appeal* was followed two days later by a lengthy *Memorandum of Law* in which Fraenkel treated each issue in depth.[32]

The Intervenors filed a *Memorandum in Support of Motion* six days later, joining in the IWO *Motion* and arguing that the Appellate Division's decision was contrary to legal precedent.[33] The Policyholders' Protective Committee (Intervenors) had also hired a new lawyer, Samuel Nirenstein, to assist them in their cause. Williams responded for the State, taking issue with each of the Order's contentions and disputing any re-argument or leave to appeal.

On October 8, 1952, the Appellate Division issued its decision: the *Motion to Reargue* was denied but the *Motion for Leave to Appeal* was granted, in accordance with both sides' expectations. The Court, although unwilling to re-open the matter before them, believed the issues were too important to deny an appeal to the higher court.[34] With the filing by the IWO of a surety bond in the nominal amount of $500 to cover costs in the event it lost this second appeal, the lawyers were off again, this time aiming for the highest state Court, the New York Court of Appeals sitting at the capital in Albany.

The attorneys for the Department of Insurance, knowing that the appeal process could completely reverse their accomplishments, were working equally hard. Their work also included other responsibilities ancillary to the case, such as maintaining contact with the states involved in parallel liquidation efforts, and guiding the Insurance Department in its control over the IWO. Furthermore, serious questions about what exactly constituted assets of the Order (e.g., a retirement home, a summer camp) had to be investigated and worked out.

A new year, 1953, was at hand. The work of brief writing for the Court of Appeals moved into its final stages. With Weissman gone, the responsibility for research and writing fell to Fraenkel and Arthur Kinoy; the Kinoy firm had expanded, adding Marshall Perlin as a partner, thus allowing Kinoy to devote greater time to the case.

The IWO *Brief,* which ran 81 pages in printed form, was sent to the Court of Appeals and to Williams's office on January 13, 1953. The task of composing this *Brief* had proven a difficult one for the IWO lawyers, who had to distill the many issues generated by the voluminous pleadings and a trial that had lasted for months. Moreover, they had to argue that Judge Greenberg and subsequently the Appellate Division had, in their respective decisions, made erroneous interpretation of both the facts and applicable law. In essence, they were before the highest court of the state, the end of the legal "line" unless they lost again and the U.S. Supreme Court was willing to hear the case. The IWO lawyers had to convince the Court that the facts did not conform to the conclusion of Communist Party domination drawn by the lower courts; that State insurance law had been distorted and mis-applied; and that the case involved significant Constitutional issues mandating a reversal of the lower courts' decisions.

The *Brief* began with a concise review of the proceeding to the point of this latest appeal, summarizing two years of a complex legal proceeding in only two pages. The lawyers recited the four grounds developed by the State as the basis for liquidation: Communist Party domination; the "take the money and run" argument; violation of the Smith Act and Penal Law of New York; and the claim that Communist Party domination violated the IWO Charter. In one paragraph, a summary rebuttal was made against all four bases, with an emphasis on constitutional due process protections. The emphasis on due process opened the constitutional arguments, in an attempt to focus the Court of Appeals on the ramifications on those issues involved in the case.

This *Brief* also took a new approach to the case by focusing on civil liberties aspects, and, in turn on violations of constitutional guarantees. The lawyers urged the Court of Appeals to view the Greenberg and Appellate Division opinions as violative of freedoms of speech, assembly, property rights, and the right encompassed by these constitutional protections to political beliefs, expressions, and activities. The Department of Insurance, they argued, was engaging in "administrative censorship"; by interpreting the State's insurance laws in the manner called for by the State, Constitutional protection of property rights was being violated. Some of these contentions had certainly been raised before, but now they were the central focus of the writing and arguments.

Using extensive references to cases, statutes, and trial testimony, the *Brief* decried the State's attempt to use the "morals" and politics of the IWO as grounds for destruction of the Order. The *Brief* argued that "the Statute [Insurance Law "hazard" concept] if susceptible of the interpretation placed upon it by the lower courts, violates the rights of freedom of speech, press and assembly as guaranteed by the Fourteenth Amendment to the Federal Constitution, as well as the Constitution of this State." Specifically it was argued that "the statute if susceptible of the interpretation placed on it by the lower courts, would be invalid as an unconstitutional delegation of legislative power [the Department of Insurance in effect legislating]."[35]

The *Brief* left no argument, case, statute, or aspect of constitutional guaranty unexplored. It concluded:

> This imposition of indiscriminate mass punishment upon 160,000 Americans and their families offend against the most elementary principles of justice and fair play which we have come to associate with the fundamental guarantee of due process of law.[36]

The Intervenors' Committee attorneys filed their *Brief* of 55 pages the same day as did the IWO. Once again, the thrust of the Committee's argument was how "fraternal" and "beneficial" the IWO had been throughout its existence. Pages were filled with personal accounts of what the insurance benefits meant to IWO members and how there could be no commercial substitute for the Order's insurance programs, and the compassion with which the IWO treated its members.

The State had significant advantages in responding to this appeal: it had won at the trial and intermediate appellate levels, and by virtue of Court rules, since it was *responding* to the appeal by the IWO, its lawyers had the Order's and Intervenors' *Briefs* prior to submission of its own, which allowed the State to shape its response with its opponents' work at hand.

Though having the clear advantage, the attorneys for the State did not slacken their efforts; their *Brief,* at 194 pages, exceeded the combined length of the IWO and Intervenors' *Briefs.*[37] It was, however, almost entirely a word-for-word repetition of the State's *Brief* filed in the Appellate Division. It was, of course, "updated" in the sense that the State tailored its response to the *Briefs* of the IWO and Intervenors. In essence, however, the State's *Brief* was a refitting—a stitch here, a seam there—rather than a new garment. It did not, interestingly, attempt to endorse or expand on the two new issues raised by the Appellate Division's opinion: that a "*moral* hazard" was involved, and that the IWO was really a "foreign" and "alien" corporation (because of Soviet control) and therefore could be treated differently from a domestic corporation.

The State did respond to the constitutional issues raised by the IWO's *Brief.* Recognizing that by raising these issues the IWO had laid potential groundwork for an appeal to the Supreme Court of the United States, the State devoted a section of its *Brief* to denying that any U.S. or New York State constitutional questions including civil rights issues were involved.[38]

The IWO, the State argued, could not say that the New York Legislature improperly delegated to the Department of Insurance its power to proceed for liquidation in the case of a *financially* hazardous insurer, concluding that "If [!] a problem exists as to whether Section 511(e) [of the Insurance Law] authorizes the Superintendent [of Insurance] to proceed against a *seditious* insurer, that is one thing; but improper delegation has nothing to do with it. The question is one of statutory interpretation [the "hazard" issue]."[39]

Although the IWO lawyers filed no reply to the State's *Brief,* the Intervenors did.[40] In a short ten page *Reply Brief,* they argued with great vigor and considerable anger that the State, in pressing for liquidation, was ignoring the devastating impact it would have on individual policyholders, that "the present welfare of the thousands of human beings who are members of the IWO" was "utterly disregarded." The interests of thousands of otherwise uninsurable members, they maintained, were being casually and callously disregarded. No commercial insurance company, they reminded the Court, would insure blacks and "those members who work in coal mines and other hazardous industries," concluding that "reinsurance by a commercial company on the same terms is impossible." The Intervenors concluded by calling on the Court to resist the State's plea for liquidation, and instead use the powers of the insurance laws and the courts to preserve the Order by making changes (which the law did encompass) that would accomplish the ends of both the State and IWO policyholders.[41]

In the oral arguments made before the Court of Appeals in Albany,

New York, Fraenkel spoke first, followed by Friedman for the Intervenors; the arguments concluded with an hour-long presentation by Williams. There is no record extant of exactly what oral arguments were made by the attorneys. A record of Paul Williams's presentation before the Appellate Division still exists; it would appear that what he said before that Court was repeated in substance before the Court of Appeals.

From beginning to end, Williams, in his presentation, sought to paint the IWO as thoroughly committed to and controlled by the Communist Party. It was as unbalanced a treatment as those by Fraenkel and Friedman, in their *Briefs*. Made under an advocacy system of law, these arguments reflected American legal practice, which, even more than its English progenitor, champions the art of advocacy.

Under the advocacy process, the attorney argues the facts and presents other cases as precedent, in a manner which favors the cause of the client. No responsible lawyer will deliberately misrepresent the law or, for that matter, the facts. A good lawyer will, however, interpret and argue the strongest implications in support of his or her client's cause.

Lawyers for both sides used this method throughout the IWO case; its effectiveness was, of course, heightened dramatically by the political setting and the emotions of the times. The Red Scare was present in that court in Albany, and Williams succeeded in making the most of it. The seven Justices were left to sort out what they felt was at issue, and what law was applicable—in effect to judge impartially between the advocates; yet despite this theoretical objectivity it must be kept in mind that they were not functioning in a vacuum.

In addition to the hundreds of pages of *Briefs*, the Court of Appeals had a trial transcript of over 4,000 printed pages, over 500 exhibits, numerous affidavits, and hours of oral arguments. Two months later, six Justices (the seventh had died in the interim) issued a unanimous opinion in favor of the State. Even for the State, which won the Appeal, the opinion must have been disappointing in the sense that it failed to reflect the hard work they had put into the case. On a total of only two double-spaced typewritten pages, one paragraph of New York insurance law was quoted and one case cited.[42]

The opinion was a curious one. It began by declaring that the State had incorrectly interpreted the term "hazardous"; the Court held that it "encompasses only dangers financial in nature." It went on to say that "In our view, however, the record before us supports the conclusion that further operation of the IWO would prove 'hazardous' in a financial sense." The Court set forth its conclusion with no explanation of any kind. What it apparently meant was that the State, in its attempt to expand the definition of "hazard" to "political hazard" or to "moral risk" (as in the Appellate Division's opinion) was *incorrect,* and the IWO's position correct, but that this Court believed "further operation" of the Order would *nevertheless* prove hazardous in the financial sense. The Court may have been making a veiled reference to the "take the money and run" argument; another possibility was that in the Court's view, the Order was under such a cloud that its continued operation would be financially risky.

The conclusions, followed by other, similar findings meant that the thrust of the opinion was to sustain liquidation on the narrow grounds of *ultra vires* activities—in this case, political in nature. In the Court's view, by engaging in politics, the IWO had made itself susceptible to liquidation as punishment for acts beyond its proper corporate functions.

What is remarkable, if not astounding, is the Court's failure to address any other arguments, contentions, or issues raised by both sides in the case, not the least of which were the constitutional issues. There is, however, a basic rule in American jurisprudence to the effect that, if a case can be decided on *other* than constitutional grounds, it will be. The Court of Appeals, in deciding the IWO appeal, evidently adhered to this rule. In doing so, however, it seems to have utterly disregarded the significance of the constitutional issues that underlay the compelling reason for the appeal in the first place—and might ultimately have served as a defense against liquidation.

Three decisions on the issue of liquidation had been written; each had framed the issues in a distinct way, and each announced its own legal basis for its determination. Judge Greenberg had agreed with the State that "hazard" could mean "political hazard," that Communists dominated the history of the IWO, and that such domination was a political "hazard" sufficient to justify the destruction of the organization. The Appellate Division focused on this same issue, but went further: it expanded "hazard" to include "moral risk" and evinced a dramatic fear of Communism and its alleged "moral" control over its adherents, thus accepting the "take the money and run" argument as central to its decision. To bolster that idea, the Court labeled the IWO a "foreign" or "alien" company. Finally, to the Court of Appeals, it was the *ultra vires* political activities that mandated liquidation.

In view of all three court decisions, it seems evident, in retrospect, that Judge Greenberg's opinion contained the grounds for the two appellate level decisions that followed: he had it "all" in his decision— at least the foundation upon which the higher courts' decisions would be based. Thus the Appellate Division chose to emphasize, elaborate, and extend beyond the point Judge Greenberg was willing to go with respect to the "risk" that IWO leaders would steal the money and run to

Russia. The Court of Appeals latched onto Judge Greenberg's reference to the Order exceeding its corporate charter limitations and
defrauding the state by not honestly stating all its purposes. By basing
its determination on this theory, the Court apparently cast aside, or at
least clouded, the "hazard" issue.

The single factor at the heart of all these decisions was, inescapably,
politics. Just as slavery was at the heart of the causes of the Civil War, so
the Red Scare, the fear of Communists and Communism as an alleged
political threat, served as the overriding factor not only in all three
decisions but in the very attempt to destroy the IWO. Red Scare times
were "in court" and at the core of each court's variation on the grounds
for liquidation.

None of the courts, and none of the twelve judges who heard or reviewed the case, were willing to "swim against the tide" of the political
seas, either by dissenting or by bringing to the level of open discussion
in any opinion some of the more obvious factors. Was this a political
prosecution? Were the State's witnesses tainted by their paid, professional informer status? Were constitutional guarantees of speech,
press, political rights being violated? In order to save the insurance
benefits of its members, should the court direct some form of "rehabilitation" in lieu of liquidation? The unwillingness of any of these
judges even to enter the arena of these troublesome but obvious questions exemplifies the sheer power of the Red Scare in these courts.

Since 1953, the IWO case stands as the only instance of liquidation or
destruction of an insurance company for reasons of its politics. The
case itself, in terms of legal precedential value in insurance law, has
been negligible. Up until 1991, it has been cited in only four New York
cases, all for the purpose of showing that the state does have the power
to regulate the insurance industry (in effect stating, if you do not
believe it, see the IWO case).[43] In these four cases, no political issue was
at stake, nor was the IWO case ever central to or dispositive of the case
then before the court. It has never been cited with respect to any other
case involving a fraternal benefit insurance company, and no other
state court has ever cited the IWO case for any reason.

Notes

1. Williams Office Files, Correspondence.
2. Trauber Interview, March 8–10, 1988.
3. Rockwell Kent papers, Smithsonian Institution Archives of American Art,
Washington, D.C. All referenced correspondence is contained in this collection.
4. Letter by Kent to Milgrom, July 18, 1981, Rockwell Kent papers.
5. Letter by Kent to Milgrom, December 23, 1951, Rockwell Kent papers.

6. Ibid.

7. *Joint Memorandum,* American Jewish Committee and the Anti-Defamation Legal of B'nai B'rith, dated July 25, 1951.

8. Trauber interviews, March 8 and 10, 1988 and July 23, 1988.

9. *Daily Compass,* June 26, 1951.

10. Williams Office Files, Correspondence.

11. Athan G. Theoharis and John Stuart Cox, *The Boss: J. Edgar Hoover and the Great American Inquisition* (Philadelphia: Temple University Press, 1988), p. 13, p. 441 n.55.

12. FBI Files, Memorandum, November 6, 1945, Reference: IWO, 61-7341-1012.

13. Williams Office Files, Correspondence.

14. *Brief for Respondent–Appellant–Respondent International Workers Order, Inc.,* before the Supreme Court of the State of New York, Appellate Division–First Department, dated March 31, 1952.

15. Ibid., pp. 13–15 (emphasis in original).

16. Ibid., p. 175.

17. Ibid., p. 204.

18. *Brief for Respondent,* before the Supreme Court of the State of New York, Appellate Division–First Department, dated May 12, 1951.

19. *Brief for Intervenors–Appellants–Respondents* before the Supreme Court of the State of New York, Appellate Division–First Department.

20. *Supplementary Memorandum for Respondent–Appellant–Respondent, International Workers Order, Inc.* before the Supreme Court of the State of New York, Appellate Division–First Department, dated June 4, 1952.

21. *Brief for the National Lawyers Guild, New York City Chapter, as Amicus Curiae,* before the Supreme Court of the State of New York, Appellate Division–First Department, dated May 2, 1952.

22. Ibid., p. 2.

23. Williams interview, July 25, 1988.

24. *Morning Freiheit,* June 17, 1952; translation in Williams Office Files.

25. Appellate Division *Decision: Matter of International Workers Order, Inc.,* 280 App. Div. 517, 113 N.Y.S.2d 755 (N.Y.A.D. 1 Dept., July 1, 1952) July 17, 1952, pp. 755–58.

26. Ibid., p. 758.

27. Ibid., p. 761.

28. Ibid., p. 761.

29. IWO News Release, July 3, 1952.

30. "Preliminary Notes" Memorandum by Arthur Kinoy to named IWO officers, July 8, 1952. Donner and Kinoy Office Files.

31. *Motion,* Supreme Court of the State of New York, Appellate Division–First Department; *In the Matter of the IWO,* etc., dated September 8, 1952.

32. *Memorandum of Law For . . . the International Workers Order, Inc., in Support of Motion for Re-Argument or in the Alternative, for Leave to Appeal to the Court of Appeals,* dated September 10, 1952.

33. *Intervenors' Memorandum in Support of Motion,* dated September 16, 1952.

34. Appeal Granted, Reargument Denied by: In re International Workers Order, 280 A.D. 915, 115 N.Y.S.2d 824 (N.Y.A.D. 1 Dept., Oct. 7, 1952).

35. *Brief of Intervenors–Appellants–Respondents,* Court of Appeals of the State of New York, January 13, 1953.

36. Ibid., pp. 9–10.

37. *Brief for Respondent,* Court of Appeals of the State of New York, January 31, 1953.

38. Ibid., p. 171.

39. Ibid., p. 173 (emphasis added).

40. *Intervenors' Reply Brief,* Court of Appeals of the State of New York, February 24, 1953.

41. Ibid., pp. 1–5; p. 10.

42. *In re People by Bohlinger, Superintendent of Insurance. Appeal of International Workers Order, Inc.,* Court of Appeals of New York, 305 N.Y. 258, 112 N.E. 2d 280 (N.Y., April 23, 1983).

43. *Massachusetts Mutual Life Insurance Company v. Thatcher,* 15 A.D.2d 242; 222 N.Y.S. 339, 1961; *Nassau Insurance Company v. Ebin,* 82 Misc. 2d 513; 369 N.Y.S. 994, 1975; *Health Insurance Association of America v. Hartnett,* 44 N.Y.2d 302; 405 N.Y. S.2d 634, 1978; People ex rel. *Lewis v. Safeco Insurance Company of America,* 98 Misc. 2d 856; 414 N.Y.S.2d 823, 1978.

Chapter XVII
To the Supreme Court and Beyond

> The Power of the [Supreme] Court is awesome, and it is the end of
> the line.
>
> Justice Harry A. Blackmun, Speech, March 6, 1991.

The loss by the IWO in the Court of Appeals devastated the organization, its leadership, and its lawyers. It was now the spring of 1953, two
years after the Greenberg decision; two appeals courts had refused to
reverse that decision. For the IWO, there remained only two hopes:
that the Supreme Court of the United States would hear its cause, or
that New York Governor Dewey would order an end to the litigation,
involving an administrative compromise that would save the Order.

Letters and petitions continued to pour into the Governor's office.
While theoretically he might have used his executive powers to intervene with the Department of Insurance, the reality of such a move was
unlikely.

The IWO Policyholders' Protective Committee, the Intervenors,
tried a political tack: they prepared a circular with a "Petition to the
Supreme Court of the United States" attached, to be signed by Order
members and forwarded to the Committee for use in its appeal to the
Court. It read:

A PETITION TO THE SUPREME COURT OF THE UNITED STATES

I, the undersigned policyholder of the International Workers Order, Inc.,
respectfully petition the Supreme Court of the United States to accept for
review the case of the I.W.O.

This is the first time in American history that a financially sound fraternal
insurance society has been ordered liquidated. Can such an injustice pass
without review by the highest court of the land?

Liquidation of the Order would mean destruction of my lifelong insurance

A Fraternal

Organization

Sentenced to Death!

The Strange Case

of

the International Workers Order

Now Before the U. S. Supreme Court

The International Workers Order, a fraternal insurance society of some 160,000 Americans, has been sentenced to *death by liquidation* by the courts of New York State.

In the appeal of the International Workers Order from this unprecedented act of injustice, the United States Supreme Court is now faced with a decision which will be momentous to the maintenance or destruction of American liberty and the right of free association.

What are the facts in the strange case of the IWO? How does this case affect the lives, not only of the organization's members, but of all Americans in every walk of life?

Figure 12. Pamphlet issued by the IWO to explain its position as its case was on appeal before the U.S. Supreme Court.

Figure 13. Supreme Court justices, October 1953. Front, left to right: Justice Frankfurter, Justice Black, Chief Justice Warren, Justice Reed, Justice Douglas. Rear, left to right: Justice Clark, Justice Jackson, Justice Minton, Justice Burton. Courtesy of the Office of the Curator, Supreme Court of the United States.

protection—sick benefits, burial rights, welfare funds, life insurance, medical care and other valuable services which I now enjoy on a cooperative basis.

Liquidation would deprive me and my family of the fraternal, social, and cultural values which I have long shared with my lodge brothers in this inter-racial organization.

My rights of free speech, free assembly, and the right to organize for mutual welfare would be irreparably damaged by liquidation of the I.W.O.

For the protection of my personal benefits and rights, for those of my family and friends, and for the preservation of America with liberty and justice for all, I sign this appeal for justice.

Signature _____

Lodge No. _____

On July 18, 1953, the IWO attorneys gave notice that they had filed for a Writ of Certiorari in the Supreme Court of the United States.

At that time, there were two methods by which cases were appealed to the Supreme Court. The first was by way of "Appeal"; in this method, the appealing party grounded its entry to the Court on the basis of a direct constitutional question. This route required the party to make a straightforward challenge to the constitutionality of a federal or state statute; it was a narrow one which generally ensured that the Court would hear the appeal. The IWO was precluded from using this approach because it was not challenging as unconstitutional any portion of the New York State insurance law but rather the interpretation and application of that law by the Insurance Department.

Therefore, the only avenue open to the IWO involved the procedure of asking the Supreme Court to issue a "Writ of Certiorari." "Writ" in modern law means order. "Certiorari" means "to be informed of"; in current usage, for a higher court to be "informed" of an alleged error by a lower court. The term "Writ of Certiorari" means an order by a higher court (the Supreme Court) directed to a lower court (the New York Court of Appeals) to send the record to the higher court for review of the lower court's decision. When the Supreme Court of the United States is asked to issue its Writ of Certiorari, this involves a *request:* the petition is designed to convince the Court that it should exercise its discretion and issue the Writ. (It takes the form of a "request" because there is no inherent right to have the case heard.)

The IWO filed its petition for the October 1953 term of the Court. That meant that in October 1953, when the Court's term commenced, the Justices would make the determination as to what Writs of Certiorari they would issue. Few petitions are found acceptable. For the October 1953 term, 591 petitions for Writs of Certiorari were filed; 88

petitions were granted—just under 15 percent.[2] It is immediately evident how slim the chances were for any petition for the Writ.

The Supreme Court's determination as to what Petitions for the Writ will be granted is by confidential vote of the Justices: four must vote in the affirmative. If four vote for the Writ to issue, the Court will hear the case. If not, barring a rehearing and revote of four in favor, the petitioner will indeed have reached the end of the judicial line.

The IWO leadership knew what was at stake in this last court appeal. They called on their membership to stick with them and to sign petitions to the Supreme Court. The Policyholders' Protective Committee remained active, not only in circulating petitions but also in the attempt to involve other organizations in their efforts by encouraging them to pass resolutions addressed to the Court and to write to Governor Dewey and Superintendent Bohlinger. The Committee circulated a four-page pamphlet whose face read:

A FRATERNAL ORGANIZATION SENTENCED TO DEATH!
THE STRANGE CASE OF THE INTERNATIONAL WORKERS ORDER NOW BEFORE THE U.S. SUPREME COURT

The International Workers Order, a fraternal insurance society of some 160,000 Americans, has been sentenced to death by liquidation by the courts of New York State.

The rhetoric was very strong, reflecting a sense of desperation as the pamphlet alleged that the "IWO is a victim of a McCarthy-like attempt to make cheap political capital out of destruction of a law-abiding people's organization, regardless of the injury this would inflict upon the members involved."[3]

A comparison was drawn to Hitler Germany, "where liquidation of organizations and confiscation of their property for political or religious reasons was a common occurrence." The call was directed to all fraternal organizations with the appeal, "If these [political reasons] can be the basis for liquidation, who can feel safe?" Black organizations and unions were also asked to act. The Committee closed with these thoughts:

A FATEFUL DECISION CONFRONTS THE COURT.

Will the Supreme Court permit Censorship—Suppression—Confiscation?
The IWO may pass from the American scene by an unjust political liquidation, but will Justice and Liberty still call themselves American?

The woes of the IWO were manifold. Since early 1951, it had been unable to add new members, the lifeblood to any functioning organization, particularly an insurance company. What is remarkable, however, is that the overwhelming majority of Order members did retain their membership through these years. Perhaps they simply wanted to keep their insurance; the Superintendent had promised the membership as well as the courts that comparable insurance would be obtained if the liquidation became final. But the pressures to drop out were real as well, particularly if a member's job was susceptible to Red Scare tensions or the member was an alien.

To make matters worse, in May 1953 Herbert Brownell, Jr., the Attorney General of the United States, petitioned the Subversive Activities Control Board, asking it to order the IWO to register as a "Communist Front" organization under the Internal Security Act of 1950, commonly called the McCarran Act.[4] The IWO was one of twelve organizations Brownell asked the Board to act against.

With this development began a new battle for the besieged IWO. The potential for the Order was dramatic: the obligation to register as a Communist organization was not just a public admission at a time when even the implication of Communist activity involvement would be damning; it also involved significant restrictions in the operation of the organization. For example, every letter or publication addressed to two or more people had to carry the statement, "Disseminated by ———— [e.g., the IWO], a Communist organization."[5] The threat was even graver for members of such an organization because each would then have to publicly register as a member of a "Communist Front." So began another lengthy and complex legal battle (with attendant newspaper publicity) as the IWO sought to challenge the demand by the Subversive Activities Control Board (SACB) that the IWO register as a "Communist Front" organization. This struggle before the SACB and in the federal courts would last some two years.

In yet another arena, the IWO was involved in the commencement of hearings with respect to the matter of reinsurance; the State was not waiting until the Supreme Court ruled on the Writ of Certiorari application. Judge Greenberg appointed a referee to take testimony on offers from insurance companies to assume the assets and policy obligations of the Order.

The IWO continued to struggle in many courts and administrative bodies to forestall its doom. In the midst of these battles, the Order remained hopeful that the United States Supreme Court would take its case, hear its cause, and stop its destruction.

The IWO was not unknown to the Supreme Court. It had been one of three organizations that had challenged the Attorney General of the United States listing of each as a "subversive" or Communist organization. Having lost in the District of Columbia trial level and the D.C.

Court of Appeals, these three organizations had petitioned for Writs of Certiorari, which had been granted. For review purposes, the three cases were combined. On April 30, 1951, just two months before the Greenberg decision, the Supreme Court had decided the listing case in favor of the three organizations.[6]

Of the Justices that decided the listing case, seven were still on the bench when the IWO petitioned for another Writ of Certiorari—this time from the liquidation proceeding. Of those seven, five had favored the IWO in their decision on the listing case (Justices Burton, Douglas, Black, Frankfurter, and Jackson) and two (Reed and Minton) had dissented. Chief Justice Vinson, who had also dissented, died prior to the 1953 Petition for the Writ; Justice Clark, who had been the Attorney General promulgating the list, took no part in either case.

In early 1952, almost one year after the listing case was decided, the Supreme Court decided another New York case where, parenthetically, the IWO became the subject of attention during the oral arguments. The circumstances as they involve the IWO were quite unusual and would have been lost but for a combination of incidents. In this case, the plaintiffs, teachers in the New York City school system, directly challenged the constitutionality of a New York statute that allowed the discharge of any teacher who taught or advocated the overthrow of the government by force or belonged to an organization listed by the Board of Regents as subversive.[7]

Osmond K. Fraenkel, the attorney brought into the IWO case before its last state appeal, had also served as the plaintiffs' (teachers') attorney in this earlier case. He presented the oral arguments for his clients on January 3, 1952. In the 1950s, when oral arguments were heard before the Supreme Court of the United States no recording (stenographic or otherwise) was made as to what was said; in fact, it was at that time against court rules for any type of recording to take place.

James Henry, Williams's associate, wrote to the Washington, D.C. office of their firm asking for a report on the oral argument in the teachers' case. His reason for requesting the report remains a mystery, as he would not have known in advance that the IWO would come up as a subject of oral argument. He received a response from an attorney in the Washington office who attended the oral arguments and then sent a report back to Henry. The attorney, "according to my best recollection," recalled an exchange between Justice Black and Wendell Brown, attorney for the State of New York, concerning the standards the Board of Regents applied in "determining what organizations to list [as 'subversive']." Court attendants, he recalled, forbade him taking notes. He did attempt, nevertheless to reconstruct the colloquy:

[Justice] Black: Would it be possible for the Regents to find a corporation to be "subversive"?

[Attorney] Brown: I don't think so.

Black: Let us take the case of a mutual insurance company. Do you think it would be possible to find such a mutual insurance company, engaged in the business of mutual benefit insurance, in competition with old line insurance companies, to be "subversive".

Brown: That couldn't be.

Black: Well it was done. An Attorney General of the United States designated such an organization as subversive.

Brown: What organization was that?

Black: Some workers order.

[Justice] Frankfurter: It was the International Workers Order, and not only did the Attorney General do it but I understand that a State Supreme Court Justice in New York has also done it.

Black: Will you tell me how that could be done?

Brown: I don't believe it could be done.

Black: Suppose their constitution and by-laws do not say anything about the overthrow of the government, how would you go about proving it?

Brown: I have confidence in our people up in New York doing the right thing.

Black: Well tell me how they do it if the constitution and by-laws say nothing about the overthrow of the government by force and violence. And suppose their minute books say nothing about it.

Brown: You would need more than that.

Black: Suppose their resolutions do not show anything about the overthrow of the government by force and violence. What else would you need?

Brown: You would need more than that.

Black: Suppose the president of the organization made a subversive speech, how would you, on the basis of that, find the whole organization to be subversive?

(Brown made an inaudible answer.)

Black: How could you destroy the rights of all the policyholders because of anything that the officers did.

Brown: You would need more than that.

Black: Would you tell me exactly what proof you would need if terms of minutes, actions, publications, to find the whole organization to be subversive because of actions of its officers?

Brown: I have confidence in the action of our people in New York.

The lawyer continued:

At this point the Justice gave up because of his inability to obtain any answer from Brown's floundering and made some comment about how wrong it was to destroy rights of a whole organization even if the president made a subversive speech.

Earlier in the argument, Mr. Justice Frankfurter had made a similar comment about the "terrorizing" extent to which listings were being made, referring to the action of Judge Greenberg in revoking the charter of the IWO as an example, and there were other frequent references to the impropriety of the Attorney General's action in preparing the list.

At the end of the argument, Mr. Justice Jackson asked Mr. Fraenkel (who was arguing for the unconstitutionality of the statute) whether the Regents intended to use the Attorney General's list and Mr. Fraenkel said that he did not know.[8]

This recollection reveals that both Justices Black and Frankfurter remembered the IWO from the listing case and that, remarkably, Frankfurter and perhaps Black knew about Judge Greenberg's decision. Given the burden of the Court's work, that one or more Supreme Court Justices would have noted a state trial court decision and remembered it many months later is remarkable. That Justices Black and Frankfurter, it appears, would have been sympathetic to some of the IWO's legal arguments, particularly the kind of evidence that the State would have to produce to sustain its charge of "subversiveness," and that both Justices showed apparent regard for the property rights of policyholders, is also notable.

In addition, in this teachers' case these Justices were unable to extract from the attorney representing the State of New York any viable grounds for the State's attack on the IWO as a corporation offering fraternal benefit insurance. If these very strong comments given during oral argument, at least as recalled by the witnessing attorney, could be translated into votes to favor issuance of a Writ of Certiorari, the Order would have two (Black and Frankfurter) of the four it needed. Fraenkel, most likely, recalled this colloquy and structured his *Petition* in support of the issuance of the Writ in view of what he had heard and remembered.

It is no exaggeration to say that everything depended on what the

Supreme Court would do with the IWO case for a Writ of Certiorari in 1953. If the Court refused to hear the case, or if it took the case and then affirmed the constitutionality of the State's action, the organization was through. There were no further appeals or legal avenues available. The State would liquidate the IWO and some commercial insurance company would take over its assets and issue policies to those remaining members who sought to retain their insurance. The IWO, as a twenty-three year old organization, would be destroyed.

The lawyers for the IWO and the Intervenors worked through the summer preparing their *Petitions* and, in the case of the State, their *Brief for Respondent in Opposition*.[9] These printed works were bound in six-inch by nine-inch format, each with a different colored cover. Because Supreme Court rules and tradition mandated a certain style and format, all that each party wanted to say had to be in reasonable conformity. The IWO's *Petition* was 51 pages long, the Intervenors' 21 pages, and the State's 39 pages. In addition, parts of the trial record and additional documents such as the Affidavits of IWO members were included. Under Supreme Court rules, no oral argument at the petition stage was allowed.

In these *Petitions* and *Opposition Brief,* the work took on a different focus; until this point, all the issues and arguments had related essentially to State of New York insurance law. Thus, the question of "hazard," the powers of the Superintendent, and the *ultra vires* matter essentially revolved around interpretations of state law. While the State had attempted to bring New York Penal Statutes and the federal Smith Act into the case, these matters were not seriously at issue. Similarly, the IWO's attempt to raise the sights of the New York courts to consideration of the constitutional (U.S. and state) and civil rights ramifications of the case had been unavailing. Now, however, if the *Petitions* were to succeed, they had to demonstrate directly that significant U.S. constitutional issues were involved in the State's liquidation efforts— important enough for four Supreme Court Justices to want to vote to hear the case. In turn, the State's aim in its *Opposition Brief* was to convince the Court that such constitutional questions were not involved. The State had to argue that this case involved only issues of New York law, where the interpretations of New York courts, under our federal system, had the final word.

There was, however, a larger canvas upon which all of these arguments were being made: politics in the Red Scare era. In reality, an organization accused of ties to—even control by—the Communist Party was seeking to define its right to exist by virtue of Constitutional and civil liberties protections before the highest court of the land in the midst of the Red Scare. This political aspect was palpable and translated into a question of the political bias or leaning of those Supreme Court Justices. The Justices, like the State of New York, were not operating in a vacuum.

In its *Petition*, the IWO posed nine "Questions" which it stated were involved in its cause, each fashioned in terms of constitutional issues. The *Petition* then listed "Reasons for Granting the Writ [of Certiorari]." Each "Question" was elaborated into reasons—really arguments—as to why the Supreme Court should take the case, supported by case law and statutes.

While the *Petition* made no reference to the teachers' case, its tone, the choice of language, and the overall argument did reflect the concerns Justices Black and Frankfurter had raised. This can be sensed from a portion of the concluding section:

> No legislature in this country, neither the Federal Congress nor any state legislature, has until now sanctioned a policy permitting the liquidation and dissolution of otherwise lawful associations and organizations of the American people because of the expression of political opinions, ideas and beliefs. The very enactment of such a policy would lead to serious and profound constitutional issues.[10]

The State's *Opposition Brief* filed on September 17, 1953 was a carefully crafted document designed to convince the Justices of the Supreme Court that there were no valid grounds for review of the case. It argued that the government's proceedings against the IWO were fully justified by the Order's close ties to the Communist Party, a connection which it exhaustively detailed. Hardly a paragraph is found in the entire document that does not contain the words "Communist" or "Communist Party."[11]

The efforts of the IWO and the Policyholders' Committee continued. Mass meetings were being held and petitions signed by members were being gathered, assembled, and sent to the Supreme Court. The Committee organized a demonstration for October 4, the day before the Supreme Court's October 1953 term was scheduled to begin. Walter Winchell, famed news commentator of that time, reported in his weekly Sunday broadcast over the American Broadcasting Company's radio network on September 15, 1953:

> The International Worker's [sic] Order [who] are grieved about an appeal which may put them out of business . . . will stage a march on Washington October 4th. . . . The demonstration will be directed at the United States Supreme Court . . . which reconvenes October 5th.[12]

The lineup of the nine Justices of the Supreme Court for the October 1953 term of the Court was as shown in the table. Fred M. Vinson,

Name	Appointed by	Year	Age in 1953	Prior political affiliation
Hugo L. Black	Roosevelt	1937	67	Democrat
Stanley F. Reed	Roosevelt	1937	69	Democrat
Felix Frankfurter	Roosevelt	1938	71	Democrat
William O. Douglas	Roosevelt	1939	55	Democrat
Robert H. Jackson	Roosevelt	1941	61	Democrat
Harold H. Burton	Truman	1945	65	Republican
Sherman Minton	Truman	1949	63	Democrat
Earl Warren	Eisenhower	1953	62	Republican
Tom C. Clark	Truman	1949	53	Democrat[13]

who had been Chief Justice, died prior to the opening of the Court in 1953, and his place on the Court as Chief Justice was taken by Earl Warren, President Dwight D. Eisenhower's first appointee. Because Justice Clark had been U.S. Attorney General under President Truman when the "subversive" organizations list which included the IWO was promulgated, he took no part in the proceeding. That left eight Justices to read the work of the attorneys and vote as to whether to grant the Writ. When the Court convened on October 5, 1953, the matter of reviewing all the submitted Petitions would be on the early agenda.

The normal method by which such Petitions are traditionally handled is for one or more of each Justice's clerks to read the case materials relating to each Petition and then confer with the Justice about the issues and merits of the case. These clerks are young law school graduates chosen by each Justice; it is a highly prestigious appointment to serve as clerk for a Supreme Court Justice. This is not to say that the Justice himself does not read each Petition case; practices varied.

When the Supreme Court convened, the first order of business was the swearing in of the new member, Earl Warren, as Chief Justice. The Court at that time had been analyzed as embodying a division between conservatives and liberals with respect to the positions of the Justices on the subject of civil liberties. In the dramatic period of Red Scare legislation and prosecutions, this division was crucial. The conservatives who would decide the IWO case included Justices Burton, Minton, and Reed; the liberals were Justices Black and Douglas. Justices Frankfurter and Jackson were not clearly identified with either bloc. The Chief Justice's position on civil liberties was, at the time, unknown. Given their access to each Justice's voting record in prior cases, the attorneys on both sides of the IWO case undoubtedly engaged in predicting how each Justice might vote. Four positive votes were needed for a Writ of Certiorari to issue.

Black and Douglas seemed reasonably certain to favor the IWO. The three conservatives could most probably be placed in the "no" column. That left three swing votes; of these, two were needed for the Petition to be granted. Frankfurter looked likely, given his remarks during the oral arguments for the teachers' case the year before. The votes of Justices Jackson and the newly appointed Chief Justice seemed the most unpredictable.

With the passage of time, some of the internal work of the Justices has become available to researchers. What can now be ascertained is the actual voting (which has been considered confidential, and is so as to current matters) along with some insight into the reasoning, as well as the voting technique.

Each case has an assigned number. A sheet was prepared for the IWO and a separate one for the Intervenors' *Petition*. Each sheet has the name of the case and the date when the *Petition* was filed. Then there appears a "box score" that lists each Justice's name and a place to check off how each voted: "G" if the Justice voted to grant the *Petition* and "D" if the vote was to deny.

The discussion (of which there is no record) and the voting took place on October 19, 1953. Justices Douglas and Black voted for granting the Writ; all of the others voted to deny the *Petition*. The same voting results took place with respect to the Intervenors' *Petition*.[14] Neither the 15,500 Petitions from individual members of the IWO that were filed with the Court nor the mass demonstration at the Supreme Court building had any apparent impact on those voting to deny the *Petitions*.

Some insight as to the thinking behind the votes of two of the Justices can be gleaned from memoranda prepared by the clerks for Justices Burton and Reed. Whether these clerks conferred with each other is not known, but that their thinking was quite similar is evident. Both saw the case as essentially one of the state's inherent power to regulate corporations it had chartered and recommended denial of the Writ.[15]

It is clear that these clerks, in view of the political and economic philosophies of their mentors, were feeding the predilections of these Justices. In a ranking by academics who have studied the first one hundred Supreme Court Justices, Burton and Minton, (two of the Justices who voted against the *Petition*) notably have been ranked as among the "Eight Failures." Reed was rated "Average." Jackson was rated "Near Great," and the two others, Frankfurter and Warren, were ranked among the "Twelve Greats." Black, who voted to grant the Petition, was ranked among the "Twelve Greats," and Douglas, whose vote also favored the IWO, received a "Near Great" listing.[16]

The basis for Justice Frankfurter's decision remains unclear. There are no revealing memoranda available, but his wont to relegate First Amendment safeguards as of minor importance against his respect for the police power of the states, his preference for enforcing the legislative will, and his unwillingness to reach constitutional issues where the case could be decided on other grounds are all well documented and likely played a significant role here. Thus, Frankfurter did not join Black and Douglas in their dissent in the *Dennis* case.

On differing grounds, Frankfurter had frequently joined with them, particularly Black, as historian James F. Simon has noted, "in the area of constitutional rights directly affected by the terrorism of the McCarthy era."[17] The year before, for example, Frankfurter had joined Black and Douglas in one of the votes relating to hearing the Rosenberg atom spy case, but there again, only three votes were garnered, thus confirming their death sentence.

In a letter to Black from Frankfurter, written at the end of the October 1953 term, Frankfurter noted their agreement, among others, on two Red Scare cases, even though they did not see the issues "through the same lenses."[18] But Frankfurter did not agree with Black on the IWO case. The IWO case apparently presented the kinds of issues where Frankfurter's concept of the proper limitations of the Supreme Court's functioning militated against the *Petitions*.

The new Chief Justice, Earl Warren, pursued a cautious position during his first year on the Court. An analysis of his voting record on Petitions for Writ of Certiorari suggests that the two liberals, Black and Douglas, had been unable immediately to obtain his support; during the first term of the Warren Court, liberal gains were minimal.[19]

Justice Jackson's voting record during this time placed him between Frankfurter and the conservatives, particularly with respect to economic affairs and civil liberties; as late as 1950, he had taken a position against labor and human liberties emphasizing his view of the Court as a "tribunal of limited jurisdiction."[20]

The political content of the IWO cases can scarcely be overlooked. Few Justices were willing or perhaps able to abide by the admonition of Justice Douglas when he said:

The judge that quavers or retreats before an impending crisis of the day and finds haven in dialectics or weasel words or surrenders his own conviction for a passing expediency is likewise not born for the woolsack[21] [an allusion to the English practice of high court judges sitting on a sack of wool].

When on October 19, 1953 it received word of the denial of the Writ, the State lost not a moment; Williams's office immediately moved before Judge Greenberg to assume sole control of the IWO despite the intent of the IWO and Intervenors to petition the Supreme Court for a rehearing on its Petition. The Judge granted the State's motion, and the IWO appealed the matter to the Appellate Division, which stayed Judge Greenberg's decision until the matter of control of the Order and the issue of IWO officers' participation in the reinsurance plan could be heard by that Court.

Meanwhile, the loss in the Supreme Court was obviously indicative of the fact that, for the IWO, the end was near. Nevertheless, mass meetings of the membership were called and were well attended. At one meeting, Saltzman stated that "the Order will continue to exist in one way or another."[22] On November 13, 1953, the IWO lawyers filed their *Petition for Rehearing* before the Supreme Court; six days later, the Intervenors filed theirs.[23]

If the percentage of Petitions for the Writ of Certiorari that were granted was (and still is) small, then the odds of succeeding on a *Petition for Rehearing* were close to zero; it is a rare though not unheard of event for the Court, in effect, to change its mind and implicitly state, we were wrong; we should have granted your Petition. But being the only avenue left, it was taken. These final efforts failed by the same vote of the Supreme Court Justices.[24]

The legal battle over the liquidation of the IWO, then some three years in its unfolding, was finally ended. The joint control by the Department of Insurance and the IWO ceased on December 15, 1953; now the State "owned" the IWO and its assets. Notice was sent to all lodges of the Order to stop operating and turn over all IWO property to the State of New York. After a life of twenty-three years, the International Workers Order was destroyed.

Battles ensued over what assets belong to the Order. For example, the two summer camps affiliated with the Order were found not to belong to the IWO; similarly, children's schools maintained by the Jewish Section (J.P.F.O.) were not taken over, although the old age home was.

Another fight continued over the nature of the reinsurance program. Here the Policyholders' Protective Committee continued to function, along with a committee of former IWO officers, eventually succeeding in obtaining favorable terms and conditions for the members who wanted to maintain certain of the basic insurance programs of the IWO; the Continental Assurance Company in Chicago, Illinois, became the carrier. To this day, a separate IWO department is maintained by that Company.

A different battle with unusual twists had been ongoing: the demand that the Order register under the Internal Security (McCarran) Act of

1950. Despite the liquidation of the Order, this conflict continued to pose significant dangers to the members of the IWO.

While attempting to fend off the liquidation effort by the State of New York, the IWO was also struggling to avoid compliance with the demand that it register as a "Communist-front" organization, challenging the constitutionality of the law and the work of the Subversive Activities Control Board (SACB). Once the State took over sole control of the Order, the SACB, to the astonishment of the IWO lawyers *and* the State, continued to demand that it register. This put the State and the IWO on the same side: the IWO because it contested the law, and the State because it ran and in effect owned the IWO. The inevitable implication was that the State was running a "Communist-front" organization![25]

This time the State authorized money for the Donner, Kinoy, and Perlin firm to fight the matter in court and before the SACB. In November 1954, the U.S. Court of Appeals canceled the registration order by SACB against the IWO. At that time, Jerry Trauber, executive secretary of the IWO Policyholders' Protective Committee, stated:

> The decision of the United States Court of Appeals is a vindication and victory for the policyholders of the former IWO. . . . The court has thus prevented the mass conviction of over a half-million people in all walks of life, of all ages and all political and social beliefs, on charges of subversion and disloyalty. It is a matter of public record that the history of the liquidation proceedings by the New York Insurance Department against the IWO does not contain any charge or proof that the policyholders of the Order were subversive or had violated any law whatsoever.[26]

The national organization was gone; the New York State liquidators fired most of the Order's employees; other states where the IWO had existed closed down all operations.

Members of the Order frequently continued to associate, forming "clubs" and carrying on social, political, and educational functions. The more vibrant segment of the IWO, the Jewish People's Fraternal Order (J.P.F.O.), was reconstituted as Jewish Cultural Clubs and Societies into a national organization that continued to function, including the remnant of a school system, through the 1980s. The camps were saved; one of them, Camp Kinderland, still exists.

But the heart of the organization, the basis for its national, multiethnic and multiracial appeal—its insurance program—was gone, another casualty of the Red Scare.

In an angry editorial entitled "The Crime of IWO 'Liquidation'" appearing in *Jewish Life* in December 1953, a poignant analogy was made:

Conform or be "liquidated," said Hitler to the people's organizations of Germany.

Conform or be "liquidated," say New York's Governor Thomas E. Dewey and his Insurance Department to the great multi-national people's fraternal organization, the International Workers Order.[27]

But for all these brave words, the IWO was, nevertheless, destroyed—not by Governor Dewey or Senator McCarthy, but because the Red Scare, rightly or wrongly, won a signal victory in the American court system.

Notes

1. *An Important Message to All Policyholders of the IWO; A Petition to the Supreme Court of the United States,* IWO Policyholders' Protective Committee, dated June 15, 1953, IWO Archives.

2. Statistics obtained from the office of the Clerk of the Supreme Court of the United States.

3. *A Fraternal Organization Sentenced to Death!* pamphlet, Williams Office Files, Clippings, Vol. 2.

4. Internal Security Act of 1950, 64 Stat. 987 (1950).

5. Ibid., Section 10.

6. *IWO v. McGrath,* 341 U.S. 123, 71 S. Ct. 699, 95 L. Ed. 1352 (1951).

7. *Adler v. Board of Education,* 342 U.S. 485, 72 S. Ct. 380, 96 L. Ed. 517 (1952).

8. Williams Office Files, Correspondence, December, 1951–September, 1952.

9. *Petition for Writ of Certiorari to the Court of Appeals of the State of New York,* IWO v. People of the State of New York, by Alfred J. Bohlinger, Superintendent of Insurance of the State of New York; *Petition* by the IWO dated July 22, 1953; *Petition* (same title) by the Intervenors, dated August 20, 1953; *Brief for Respondent in Opposition* (the State's response to the *Petitions*), dated September 17, 1953.

10. Ibid., *Petition* by the IWO, pp. 36–37.

11. *State Brief For Respondent in Opposition.*

12. Letter of the American Broadcasting Company to the IWO dated September 18, 1953 reciting the Walter Winchell statement during his broadcast; IWO Archives.

13. Albert P. Blaustein and Roy M. Mersky, *The First One Hundred Justices: Statistical Studies on the Supreme Court of the United States* (Hamden, CT: Archon Books, 1978), Appendix.

14. International Workers Order, Inc. v. People of State of N.Y., 346 U.S. 857, 74 S. Ct. 68, 98 L.Ed. 371 (U.S.N.Y., Oct. 19, 1953). (NO. 190); The Intervenors: Seligson v. People of State of N.Y., 346 U.S. 857, 74 S. Ct. 73, 98 L.Ed. 371 (U.S.N.Y., Oct. 19, 1953) (NO. 283).

15. Harold H. Burton Papers, Library of Congress, Case Number 190, 1953 Term; Stanley F. Reed Papers, University of Kentucky Library, Lexington, KY, Box 41 (certiorari memos).

16. Blaustein and Merksy, *First One Hundred Justices,* pp. 37–40.

17. James F. Simon, *The Antagonists: Hugo Black, Felix Frankfurter and Civil Liberties in Modern America* (New York: Simon and Schuster, 1989), pp. 200–201.

18. Letter quoted in ibid., pp. 201–2.

19. Clyde E. Jacobs, "The Warren Court—After Three Terms," *Western Political Quarterly* 10 (1956) pp. 938–39.

20. Quoted in Sidney H. Asch, *The Supreme Court and Its Great Justices* (New York: ARCO, 1977), p. 181; Alan F. Westin, ed., *The Supreme Court: Views from Inside* (Westport, CT: Greenwood Press, 1984), p. 1.

21. Quoted in Westin, p. 2.

22. Quoted in news report appearing in *The Jewish Day,* November 18, 1953.

23. *Petition for Rehearing of Petition for Writ of Certiorari to the Court of Appeals of the State of New York,* IWO v. People of the State of New York by Alfred J. Bohlinger, Superintendent of Insurance of the State of New York; *Petition* dated November 13, 1953, *Petition* (same title) by the Intervenors dated November 19, 1953.

24. Rehearing Denied by International Workers Order v. People of the State of New York, 346 U.S. 913, 74 S. Ct. 237, 98 L.Ed. 409 (U.S., Dec. 7, 1953) (NO. 190.); The Intervenors: Seligson v. People of the State of New York, 346 U.S. 913, 74 S. Ct. 238, 98 L.Ed. 409 (U.S., Dec. 7, 1953) (NO. 283).

25. Donner, Kinoy, and Perlin office files; Williams office files, Insurance File #6.

26. Quoted in *Jewish Life,* January 1955, p. 19.

27. Editorial, "The Crime of IWO 'Liquidation,'" *Jewish Life,* December 1953, p. 3.

Chapter XVIII
Retrospectives

> . . . political trials present a tantalizing prospect for study. They are those key moments in the life of a society when conflicts over basic issues rise and converge, are held in tension at a point, and, while not resolved, are confronted and clarified for public dialogue. Admittedly, that dialogue may continue for decades, even centuries, but . . . certain trials are reinterpreted every generation. Such trials provide us with an insight into the most vital aspect of our public life, the civilizing capacity of politics.
>
> *Political Trials in History,* Ron Christenson, ed.

With the exception of certain labor unions, the International Workers Order was the largest, most successful left-wing organization in modern American history. It was also the strongest, most enduring, and most sizable Communist-affiliated group since the Communist Party first appeared in the United States.

The IWO's birth and phenomenal growth took place during the Great Depression of the 1930s, when its insurance programs, combined with a broad range of social, political, and fraternal activities, appealed to a multiethnic, mainly recent immigrant group of working people. Not until the breakdown of the wartime alliance between the Soviet Union and the United States which brought with it the Cold War and its domestic component, the Red Scare, did the IWO face significant jeopardy and begin its subsequent decline.

The danger to this otherwise financially healthy organization came from its source of legal authority to exist, the State of New York, which had licensed the IWO as an insurance carrier. Without the Cold War and Red Scare, the IWO would have continued to exist, subject only to the vicissitudes that any fraternal benefit insurance organization would have encountered over the passage of time. The chief prosecuting attorney confirmed that there would have been no case made against the IWO but for the Cold War-Red Scare times.

That it was the "times" and no other factor which motivated the prosecution leading to the Order's destruction is without question. The Order was financially sound and successfully run. It complied with all applicable insurance regulatory laws in its home state and all other states in which it operated. But if its operation, in this instance its "fraternal activities," was successfully challenged as a basis for liquidation in New York, then the entire organization would fold, since all other states followed the lead of the state where it was chartered.

Believing its political orientation safely ensconced in and protected by compliance with the insurance laws of the State of New York, IWO leadership failed to react to the coming of the Cold War-Red Scare era. Thus, while it did tone down the leftist political rhetoric of the early years, the Order failed to recognize its own vulnerability because of its history of intimate ties to the Communist Party, including the Party's domestic and foreign leadership positions. Even though Communists did hold most of the key leadership positions in the IWO, the vast majority of members were not Party members.

These Communist leaders failed to act in response to what was plainly evident: that all organizations, committees, or unions which could rightly or wrongly be labeled "Communist," "leftist," "fronts," or "progressive" were going to be attacked, smeared, or prosecuted in the face of a national paranoia over "Reds under the beds" and as an alleged threat to the domestic peace of the country.

With the prosecution of individuals and of the Communist Party leadership, enough evidence was on hand to warrant a realistic examination of the vulnerability of the IWO by the Order's leadership or by the Communist Party; that assessment never took place. To the extent that the leadership of the IWO failed to take ameliorative steps in the post-World War II years, it opened itself up to being "hung" by the words and deeds of its own leadership during the earlier years of its existence. While this is "wisdom born of the event," it is just as evident that IWO leadership exhibited both an absence of foresight and a stubborn resolve not to accommodate or change in response to the handwriting on the wall.

A reading and analysis of the voluminous trial record makes clear that Judge Greenberg would have accepted a line of defense to the effect that what was done, said, and followed as IWO policy were mainly things of the past, that its current leadership and programs had been modified by the late 1940s. But what he saw and heard was essentially the same leaders, programs, and policies. Having lived through the terrible Great Depression, it seems evident that Greenberg was amenable to the defense that the 1930s in and of themselves generated the Order's extreme language and political policies, but that these had changed and were not representative of the IWO of 1951. He did not hear such a defense and therefore became caught up in a Red Scare reaction. Rightly or wrongly, Greenberg was unwilling to go against the times; the Red Scare had arrived in his Court.

Was there a conspiracy to destroy the IWO? The trial record demonstrated, and the Order's attorneys were shown, that there was no conspiracy. Haley, the Insurance Examiner, was the chief architect of the downfall of the Order. As abysmal as Haley's understanding of politics, economics, and society was, his recommendation to liquidate this "unpatriotic" insurance company did reach receptive ears: the Insurance Department would not stand in his way and indeed endorsed his views. The IWO and its sympathizers blamed Governor Dewey, Superintendent Bohlinger, and Senator McCarthy, each of whom had been willing participants in the national crusade against the "Reds," but there had been in fact no "orders from the top" to destroy the IWO. That neither they, nor ultimately the legal system, would act to stop the process was clear and predictable. As one IWO officer put it, how would it look for a state Republican administration to be the home of, and thus implicitly sanction in their state, the largest Communist-affiliated organization in the country?

Was an administrative resolution, short of a trial, a viable alternative? In other, more sanguine times, the answer would have been yes. William Weiner's earlier removal as President of the IWO, under pressure from the Department of Insurance, proves the point. Saul Rogers was hired to try such an administrative remedy, but the Red Scare made the matter too politically hot, thus closing that avenue. The statutory authority for rehabilitation was there, but the times militated otherwise; the Dewey Administration did not want to be labeled "soft on Communism," the accusation that had been made against President Truman and other New Deal Democrats. Judge Greenberg probably could have pressured the parties into a rehabilitation plan, but chose not to do so.

Did Judge Greenberg conduct a fair and impartial trial? There are many ways to assess fairness and impartiality; in this instance, the matter was complicated by the length of the trial, the openly political nature of the issues and people involved, and the passions of the times. The range of evidence allowed was much broader than would have been the case had this been a jury trial. Judge Greenberg was not, however, openly prejudiced, as can be said about judges in some of the other political trials during that time.

On the other hand, he was willing to allow the State to build a case on the testimony of paid "professional informer" witnesses. Furthermore, by refusing to rule on the initial IWO motions that went to the heart of the case by questioning whether the Superintendent of Insurance had the power to liquidate the Order on other than financial grounds, Greenberg denied the IWO the opportunity to focus attention on that primary legal issue.

Judge Greenberg wanted a full-blown trial concerning the politics of the IWO, knowing the volatility of those politics in Cold War-Red Scare times. The Korean War, a battle against Communist expansion that was going very badly for the United States during the trial months, and the hysteria over alleged Communists or Reds of many hues in government, schools, the motion picture industry, and all areas of American life were in the news and thus on his mind and in his courtroom. During the trial, he also read that the accused atom bomb spies were admitted members of the very organization before him.

Judge Greenberg's decision at the end of the trial was not fairly grounded in then existing legal precedent. Furthermore, he accepted all of the testimony of the State's paid witnesses and rejected out of hand the position of the IWO leaders that their personal politics and the political and economic stances of the Order were protected by constitutional guarantees of free speech, assembly, and press. The Judge's decision reflected a Cold War-Red Scare mentality.

Judge Greenberg's obituaries spoke of how he characterized the IWO case as "his toughest decision" and his "most difficult case." These reflections, combined with other evidence, might well yield the following interpretation: that more was involved than simply a long trial, and that he regretted his handling of the case and perhaps ultimately his decision in it.

Greenberg had the reputation of being able to withstand the instant emotions or pressures of a controversy without succumbing to the intimidation imposed by popular clamor. Despite this, however, he did yield to Red Scare times, not just in his decision, but in his handling of issues during the trial. His refusal to rule on the motions of the IWO attorneys which clearly had addressed the legal issues and his decision to opt instead for hearing the political controversy, his refusal to let the Order hold a convention, his total reliance on the paid "professional informer" witnesses, and his backing away from making the government produce the Cvetic reports are all indicative of the overly deferential attitude Greenberg exhibited toward the State. Furthermore, his decision was so thoroughly one-sided, so accepting of every State argument, and so couched in Cold War-Red Scare terms that it confirms his unwillingness to stand against the pressures of the times.

There can be little doubt that the Communist Party was a dominant force in the IWO throughout its existence. Most of the leaders were Party members, and the IWO, in terms of political and economic policies, followed the Party line. But this was not against state or federal law; the Communist Party was not illegal and it was never, as a political party, directly put on trial in American history. Yet while Judge Greenberg vehemently denied that the U.S. Attorney General's listing of the IWO as a subversive organization influenced his decision in the case, he effectively convicted the Order not only of being "subversive" but also its leadership, because most were Communists, of furthering the cause of Communism through the IWO.

In an interview with one of the State's attorneys, this tack was defended by drawing comparisons to current efforts to reach behind a legal facade, such as a business which in reality is a "front" for drug traffickers, to seize the assets of an illegal business. The analogy fails, however, when one considers that drug trafficking is obviously illegal, and the policies, politics, and programs of the IWO were not.

The weakest argument developed by the State was the "take the money and run" contention; the strongest was the *ultra vires* (acting beyond its corporate powers) accusation. Yet the Appellate Division's opinion relied and even expanded upon the first, twisting the "financial hazard" concept into a "moral hazard," thus again reflecting Cold War-Red Scare attitudes. The Court of Appeals muddied the entire "hazard" argument and relied chiefly on the *ultra vires* contention; in doing so, it ignored constitutional guarantees of political expression. There was no evidence that any policyholder money was used for political purposes, because none in fact was. The IWO as an organization did not endorse Communist candidates, but it did come close. The question was, did it come close enough to warrant destruction of the entire organization, in lieu of remedial measures available to the State to stop these activities without liquidating the IWO? If not, the State was engaged in an effective encroachment on the property rights as well as constitutional guarantees of Order members.

The United States Supreme Court Justices of the time reflected the division between those who demonstrated a willingness to hear cases involving the constitutional rights of accused "subversives" and those who were not. Given the decisions commencing in the 1957 Court term, the IWO case perhaps came to the Supreme Court too early; the fateful element of timing is evident in court cases as well as in other aspects of life. The Court, under Chief Justice Warren's maturing leadership, would become more liberal and thus more willing to hear such cases over the next few years. Appertaining to other issues, but decided by unanimous vote of the same Justices, the *Brown v. Board of Education* case exemplifies this trend; it was decided less than one year after the same Court rejected the IWO case. It is interesting to note that the attorney who argued against desegregation of schools in the case was John W. Davis, one of the lawyers who refused to represent the IWO.

Was the IWO case ultimately a miscarriage of justice? A dictionary defines miscarriage as "the failure to bring about a proper conclusion." If constitutional rights and civil liberties are to be held above the apparent exigencies of the moment, the destruction of the IWO without doubt was a miscarriage of justice, reflecting and driven by Red Scare times.

One way the law grows is by interpreting statutes and constitutions through case law. The stretching of financial "hazard" into "political or moral hazard" in the IWO case involved an act of judicial activism. This is an accepted way in which the law grows. The question underlying this process is, what motivates a court to engage in an enlarged or new interpretation, as opposed to retaining a narrow scope, sometimes defended on the basis of "original intent?" The New Deal Supreme Court, after 1936, responded to the dire circumstances of the American economic crisis with new and broadened interpretations of the Commerce Clause of the Constitution. The motivation for the extension of financial "hazard" into "political or moral hazard" in the IWO case was the Cold War and Red Scare. Neither Judge Greenberg nor the New York appellate level courts, nor for that matter the U.S. Supreme Court, were constrained by the plain intent of the New York legislature or prior case law to limit the meaning of "hazard."

A review of American legal history yields this relevant interpretation: *inter arma silent leges*; during war, courts remain silent. In effect, the legal system will not interfere when the government is at war. Our legal history is replete with examples; during every major war, almost all attempts to impede the conduct of that war as directed by the President and/or Congress, through use of the courts, have been unsuccessful. This has been true from the War of Independence to the Persian Gulf war. A prime example took place during the Civil War when President Lincoln suspended the "Great Writ," the habeas corpus privilege; another was the internment of Japanese Americans during the Second World War.

The Cold War and its domestic component, the Red Scare, were apparently sufficient motivation for the courts to remain silent while the government of the State of New York sought to liquidate the IWO as part of a war against Communism—"silent" in the sense of developing and applying interpretations of the law that would accomplish, not impede, the government's objective.

There should be no mistake about it: state government and state and federal bureaucratic agencies were at "war" with what they perceived to be the "enemy"—domestic Communism and "subversion." That constitutionally protected property rights and civil liberties of individuals and organizations would be trampled upon was merely a fallout—they were "casualties" in a very real sense, from this "war." The IWO was one such casualty.

This IWO case also demonstrates the power of government and bureaucracies to punish and persecute. On the federal level, the FBI, the Immigration and Naturalization Service, the Internal Revenue Service, the House Committee on Un-American Activities, the Subversive Activities Control Board, the Department of Justice, and the federal loyalty program administration, among others, all went after the IWO and its members. On the state level, the attack came not only from departments of insurance, but also from local school boards, loyalty boards, and public housing administrations. Though the Order was "officially" off the U.S. Attorney General's Subversive Organizations List, membership in the IWO was used extensively as a basis for denying everything from jobs to housing, passports, or, in the case of aliens, the right to remain in the country.

What were the politics of the IWO that led to its downfall? They were the politics derived from the platforms and positions of the Communist Party during the 1930s, 1940s, and early 1950s. Judge Greenberg was clearly concerned by the parallel paths taken by the Party and the Order. He wanted to see deviation, but the IWO would offer none because there was none. The right of any organization to take positions on political and economic issues was acceptable; many of the ethnic and religious fraternal benefit insurance organizations did just that. It was not that the IWO took a path per se that led to its downfall, but rather that the path they chose was that of the Communist Party at a time when the Party was considered a threat to the nation.

Specifically, the participation of the IWO in the "peace" movement of the immediate post-war years was suspect. The movement included those who believed that the Cold War and its threat to world peace was the result of American and not Russian actions and attitudes, or at least a combination of the policies and acts of both. Bucking the tide of the nation, its President, and Congress, many Order members saw the Marshall Plan, the Truman Doctrine, and the American foreign policy concept of "containment of Communism" as fostering a wrongful Cold War. In 1950, particularly after the Korean conflict began, this view was a distinctly minority position.

By 1950, the IWO's domestic program for the most part ceased to be considered radical. This was the result of the New Deal-Fair Deal programs and policies which had over the years co-opted many of the programs of the left, such as Social Security, unemployment and work-ers' compensation, public housing programs, a Fair Employment Prac-tices Commission (dealing with discrimination in the job market), and the beginnings of a program of general medical care for the poor and elderly which would come to fruition in the Medicare and Medicaid programs of the 1960s. Labor unions had won the right to exist and to develop collective bargaining agreements through the National Labor Relations Act (the Wagner Act). But, as seen at the trial, it was the historical record, involving radical rhetoric of the 1930s along with its following the Communist Party line on foreign affairs—including its position on the Cold War—that made the IWO vulnerable during the Cold War-Red Scare era.

At its foundation, the battle over the IWO was a war between "believ-ers"—those who believed that Socialism or Communism was the an-swer to the world's and this nation's problems, and those who believed that these were evil people, out to destroy the nation, who were being promoted, abetted, and controlled by a foreign power. Those who were fearful of the IWO, its leadership, and its programs were driven by a national paranoia of imminent subversion if not revolution; they had essentially lost faith in America as an open society where ideas would and should clash. Manipulated and exploited by the J. Edgar Hoovers and McCarthys of the time, these self-styled patriots saw an enemy and sought to destroy it. The powers of the federal and state governments were aligned with them.

What was the significance of the IWO case? It was the first and only time in American legal history that an insurance company was put out of business for its politics. The absence of any significant citation of the IWO case to any further insurance company litigation, over a period of over forty years anywhere in any court, is indicative not only of its idiosyncratic nature but also that its principle of political persecution was not repeated. It should be noted in this regard that a number of other fraternal benefit insurance organizations maintained an impor-tant political element in their operations, not the least of which was the IWO's parent and chief rival, the Workmen's Circle, with its strong Socialist bent. But Socialists, especially those like the Workmen's Circle who were critical of Communists, were relatively safe from the nets of the Red Scare.

The IWO case did not at the time receive the attention of the public or media because it did not send anyone to the electric chair or to jail, even though a number of the Order's leaders were prosecuted as Communists or deported. Nonetheless, its importance is confirmed by the result: a death sentence for the most successful Communist-affiliated organization in the nation's history. Thus, it clearly merits study as a major Red Scare case, demonstrative of what can happen when a nation succumbs to a level of national political paranoia where it loses trust in itself and its political freedoms.

There is reason to believe that the IWO, had it not been destroyed, would have significantly diminished and perhaps even died by the 1990s. The Order's vitality was in its ethnic base and ethnic identification, which has changed considerably in the last four decades. As the immigrant generations of the 1920s through the 1940s were replaced by new generations that placed a smaller value on their ethnic heritage and foreign language use, a major binding force of the Order would have disappeared. Furthermore, where the insurance programs of the Order were truly vital to the working class IWO members during those decades, the evolution of health and medical benefits guaranteed merely through employment, together with the creation and expansion of government programs and the broader availability of private health care and life insurance plans, would in many ways make the IWO's services redundant or obsolete. This is particularly true in terms of appeal to the post-immigrant generation of potential IWO members who would have matured in these different and generally prosperous economic times.

On the other hand, recognizing that the Order may have been flexible enough to offer new and different membership benefits, it might have survived, responsive to what one writer has stated on this theme:

Today the evils of 20th century capitalism in the USA, even though we enjoy extensive but far from complete democracy here, afflict us at every turn. Let the homelessness of millions in a highly productive society that multiplies luxury dwellings and luxuries galore serve as a symbol of what oppresses my senses every day, of what afflicts me continually with the need both for present struggles against glaring social evils—and for an inspiring vision that would generate the energy to devote oneself to the current struggles as the Old Left devoted itself to old left struggles at home. Are there new words for the old socialist ideals? I do not know them. Hence my recommitment to my old concept of socialism, democratic socialism, democratic-socialism—perhaps to be spelled as democraticsocialism, one word to symbolize the unbreakable, never-to-be-broken, fusion between the two parts.[1]

Supreme Court Justice Harry A. Blackmun stated in a recent speech that man's inhumanity to man still prevails in this country, adding, "we are still a racist, intolerable, intolerant and bigoted society."[2] Perhaps a continued IWO would still be striving to improve upon these conditions.

Notes

1. Morris U. Schappes, *Jewish Currents*, january 1991, p. 15.

2. Speech of Justice Harry A. Blackmun, reported in the *Chicago Daily Law Bulletin*, March 3, 1991.

Afterword

Over forty years have elapsed since the IWO was on trial in New York. Curious how the passage of time may have altered the attitudes of lawyer-participants in the trial, I asked Paul W. Williams, the chief prosecuting attorney for the State, and Arthur Kinoy, one of the lead IWO attorneys, to provide brief statements of their respective views. As will be evident, time has not dulled their disparate convictions about the case.

PAUL W. WILLIAMS:

As far as I was concerned the case was not in any way related to the other Communist cases pending or the later McCarthy Hearings, of which I thoroughly disapproved. Nor did I have any contact with the lawyers involved.

The State of New York retained me to present a case, based on the available evidence, and like all those of lawyers representing clients my own personal opinion was irrelevant.

The case was important, and I represented the State to the best of my ability, but I was not asked to pass judgment. I did not know the individuals involved personally, nor did I have any animus toward them.

The legal issue, I still think, was correctly decided by the various courts involved, and those who were insured by the IWO were protected, and did not lose any money.

I do not believe insurance companies should be involved in politics—especially when they support a foreign government dedicated to the destruction of our own.

ARTHUR KINOY:

Professor Sabin's powerful portrayal of the destruction of the International Workers Order by the governmental power structure during the height of the Cold War-Red Scare of the early 1950s is an invaluable exposure of one of the most frightening moments of our history, until now, buried from the knowledge of most Americans. It forcefully presents critically important lessons for the future, if the American heritage of a constitutional system of written law designed to preserve fundamental rights of all people is to survive.

For me as a young lawyer just four years out of law school, and having lived through three years of intense combat experiences in World War II, the lessons learned from being deeply involved in the legal proceedings brought by the State of New York to dissolve the IWO, were incredibly valuable. The case bespoke an outrageous attempt to undermine, if not abandon, the most elementary guaranties of our written Constitution. The harassment and intimidation of any opposition to Cold War-Red Scare foreign and domestic policies on the part of any group—including the IWO—was made evident.

At first, it was unbelievable to us as young lawyers that the government would dare to move to dissolve a fraternal benefit insurance company so financially successful as the IWO and so important to thousands of working people, including Afro-Americans and newly arrived immigrants. To allow the word "hazardous" to be read as totally unrelated to finances, and to be enlarged to mean "politically" hazardous, was perhaps naively beyond belief to us. More than this: to distort the obvious meaning of the written law in order to destroy a functioning, successful organization of thousands of people was utterly to disregard and abandon the elementary mandates of the Constitutions of the United States and New York State, which were, after all, designed to safeguard the rights of the people to gather together, to organize, to express their views, though they might be in opposition to the then existing power structure of society.

As Professor Sabin discusses in his book, this utter disregard for established law led me to write to the officers of the IWO in 1952, concluding that this was "perilously close to the boundary between democratic forms of law and government and the abandonment of democratic forms which characterizes fascism." And this insight led me to state in my memorandum "this is why this decision is so deeply significant to the American people."

Professor Sabin's detailed account of this disastrous attack on the IWO forty years ago leads me to agree strongly with Howard Fast in his Foreword to the book, that today this story "must be told and understood, so that nothing like it will ever happen again."

Index

This book was set in Baskerville and Eras typefaces. Baskerville was designed by John Baskerville at his private press in Birmingham, England, in the eighteenth century. The first typeface to depart from oldstyle typeface design, Baskerville has more variation between thick and thin strokes. In an effort to insure that the thick and thin strokes of his typeface reproduced well on paper, John Baskerville developed the first wove paper, the surface of which was much smoother than the laid paper of the time. The development of wove paper was partly responsible for the introduction of typefaces classified as modern, which have even more contrast between thick and thin strokes.

Eras was designed in 1969 by Studio Hollenstein in Paris for the Wagner Typefoundry. A contemporary script-like version of a sans-serif typeface, the letters of Eras have a monotone stroke and are slightly inclined.

Printed on acid-free paper.